FORGOTTEN TRIALS OF THE HOLOCAUST

PRAISE FOR *FORGOTTEN TRIALS OF THE HOLOCAUST*

"Takes the reader on a journey across nearly six decades, seven countries, and ten different judicial settings to examine a wide variety of ways in which attempts were made to bring Holocaust perpetrators to justice. The authors do not shy from assessing the strengths, weaknesses, and difficulties of each trial and the degree to which justice was served. An important contribution to the history of the judicial aftermath of the Holocaust."
—Christopher R. Browning, author of *Remembering Survival: Inside a Nazi Slave Labor Camp*

"Provides lucid summaries of ten lesser-known trials of participants in Nazi war crimes, along with acute and balanced conclusions about the legal legitimacy and legacy of each proceeding. The authors bring fresh and illuminating perspectives to a matter of urgent concern: understanding how the claims of law and justice should interact in the aftermath of atrocity."
—Peter Hayes, Theodore Zev Weiss Holocaust Educational Foundation Professor of History, Northwestern University

"Brings to the reader important trials that have fallen beneath the general public's radar. The authors, as both academics and practicing lawyers, bring a fresh and incisive approach to these trials, dissecting the strategies of the trial lawyers as well as the decision making by the presiding judges. They manage, in each of these trials, to focus on the defendants, the victims, and the players in the courtroom scene. They present a vivid picture of the Holocaust in operation, which is an essential undertaking as the survivor generation decreases in number. This book is worth reading for anyone interested in trials and for anyone interested in the Holocaust, and it is compulsory reading for anyone interested in both."
—Robert M. Morgenthau, Former District Attorney, New York County

"For too long, lawyers and legal academics have relegated the Shoah to the margins and shadows of legal discourse. The killing of six million European Jews has been treated either as an extraordinary and unique circumstance beyond law or, more recently, as little more than a precursor event to the development of international criminal law. Michael J. Bazyler and Frank M. Tuerkheimer have rendered an invaluable service to legal practice and scholarship by bringing the Holocaust to the center of the legal profession and discipline. This extraordinary book, by examining the intersections and encounters between law and the Shoah in a number of jurisdictions, across a significant time period, makes it impossible for us to ignore or forget the intimate and complex relationship between law and the Holocaust."
—David Fraser, author of *Law after Auschwitz: Towards a Jurisprudence of the Holocaust*

"An invaluable book about significant trials conducted by the United States, certain European countries, and Israel against German government officials, military officers, and non-German collaborators with the Holocaust. It will educate, expand, and enlighten every reader's knowledge about one of the most tragic events in human history, perpetrated by one of the most culturally, medically, scientifically, artistically, and politically advanced civilizations the world has ever known. Bazyler and Tuerkheimer have made a most significant contribution to the study of the Holocaust, and the world's response."
—Stan Levy, Founding National Director of the Bet Tzedek Holocaust Survivors Justice Network

Forgotten Trials of the Holocaust

Michael J. Bazyler and Frank M. Tuerkheimer

NEW YORK UNIVERSITY
New York and London

NEW YORK UNIVERSITY PRESS
New York and London
www.nyupress.org

LIBRARY OF CONGRESS CATALOGING-IN-PUBLICATION DATA
Bazyler, Michael J., author.
Forgotten trials of the Holocaust / Michael J. Bazyler and Frank M. Tuerkheimer.
pages ; cm
Includes bibliographical references and index.
ISBN 978-1-4798-8606-7 (hardback)
1. War crime trials—History—20th century. 2. War crime trials—Europe—History—20th century. 3. Holocaust, Jewish (1939-1945) 4. War criminals—Europe—Trials, litigation, etc..
I. Tuerkheimer, Frank M., author. II. Title.
KZ1174.5.B39 2014
341.6'90268—dc23
2014017283

New York University Press books are printed on acid-free paper, and their binding materials are chosen for strength and durability. We strive to use environmentally responsible suppliers and materials to the greatest extent possible in publishing our books.

Manufactured in the United States of America

Also available as an ebook

publication of trial histories
made possible by a grant:
Jewish Federation of Greater Hartford

CONTENTS

ACKNOWLEDGMENTS

The impetus for this book came from our many years of offering Holocaust-focused courses at our respective law schools and as visiting professors at other law schools around the world. It occurred to us that while several books have been written about individual trials concerning the mass murder of Jews during the Second World War, none has attempted to provide an overview of these prosecutions by actually focusing on the trials themselves. Further, it struck us that since most books on Holocaust trials have been written by academics, our backgrounds both as academicians and trial practitioners could provide a different perspective on these trials. Knowing that much has been written about the Nuremberg trial of major Nazi defendants and the Eichmann trial, we quickly decided that there was no need for yet another book on these trials. Rather, we aimed to focus on trials that remain largely unknown, not only to the general public, but even to many scholars. The ten trials we selected aim to reveal to the reader not just an intimate description of the Holocaust in operation, but an illustration of how different legal systems, over almost six decades, confronted the German plan to exterminate European Jewry.

We are indebted to many persons who have provided invaluable assistance to us as we have written this book. Both of us are indebted to Jennifer Hammer, our editor at New York University Press, and her assistant, Constance Grady. Their comments and advice, and their selection of extremely knowledgeable reviewers who have provided us with numerous helpful suggestions, vastly improved the end product which follows in these pages. Thanks also to Dan Geist and Professor Peter Hayes for their many helpful editorial suggestions.

With respect to the chapters written by Michael Bazyler, he is grateful to his faculty assistant Mary DeVlugt and law library assistant Deborah Lipton of the Dale E. Fowler School of Law at Chapman University. Professor Marilyn Harran at the Rodgers Center for Holocaust Education at Chapman University is a superb colleague, educator, and scholar, who took time out of her busy schedule to review the manuscript and provide very useful comments. A large number of Chapman law students provided invaluable research and cite-checking assistance. They include Tamara Rider, Malka Barhodari, Alison Bollbach, Nicole Hughes, Blair Russell, and Kellyanne Gold. William Elperin, president of The "1939" Society and his wife Rosemary also provided inspiration and guidance. Last, Michael is especially thankful to his independent editor, Bonny V. Fetterman.

With respect to the chapters written by Frank Tuerkheimer, he has been enormously assisted by Cheryl O'Connor of the University of Wisconsin Law Library and Michael Roffer of the New York Law School Library. Each has provided invaluable help in obtaining the background literature, not all of which is in English, but essential to the end product. Assistant Dean Kevin Kelly of the University of Wisconsin Law School was extraordinarily helpful in sharing his knowledge of U.S. military law. He is also indebted to Eileen Dorfman and Melissa Young, law students whose assistance has been essential in finalizing his chapters. Finally, his wife, Barbara Wolfson Tuerkheimer, has been a steady and constant source of encouragement over the years it has taken to bring this book to fruition. She has shared his sense that these trials should not be forgotten because the facts they reveal cannot be consigned to oblivion.

We dedicate this book to the many prosecutors who have labored tirelessly, sometimes with emotionally wrought and shaky witnesses, sometimes with ancient documents in a foreign language, sometimes with hostile tribunals, and always with engaged and effective opponents, in an effort to bring the perpetrators of mass murder to justice. Our admiration for them is unbounded. We single out two: Murray Bernays, who died in 1970, and Benjamin Ferencz, who at age ninety-four in 2014 is still pursuing the fight against genocide. Bernays was a lawyer with the United States Army who envisaged and helped implement a comprehensive postwar effort at Nuremberg to bring to justice those responsible for the carnage of the Second Word War in Europe. Ferencz was a young lawyer on the prosecution staff at Nuremberg who carried out the Bernays idea, prosecuted the *Einsatzgruppen* trial covered in Chapter 6, and who, in the almost seventy years since Nuremberg, has steadfastly continued his effort to expand and apply the principles of international criminal law developed at Nuremberg to the contemporary world.

Introduction

The Holocaust: a conspiracy to murder eleven million people that succeeded in killing six million of them.[1] Unlike most conspiracies, which operate in secret to avoid detection and subsequent prosecution by the state, this one operated above ground, and not just with the state's awareness, but with the state as the driving force. There is no clearer evidence of this conspiracy to murder the Jews of Europe than Reich Marshal Hermann Göring's directive to Reinhard Heydrich, head of the Reich Main Security Office (RSHA), dated July 31, 1941:

> I hereby charge you with making all necessary preparations in regard to organizational and financial matters for bringing about a complete solution to the Jewish question in the German sphere of influence in Europe. Wherever other governmental agencies are involved, these are to cooperate with you. I charge you furthermore to send me, before long, an overall plan concerning the organizational, factual and material measures necessary for the accomplishment of the desired solution of the Jewish question.[2]

This directive came with the rapid advance of the German military into the Soviet Union after its June 1941 invasion, bringing the vast majority of European Jewry under German control.

The conspirators wasted no time. In short order, the four separate groups of the Nazi security organization—the SS—known as the *Einsatzgruppen* followed the German Army eastward and proceeded to annihilate close to one million Soviet Jews in less than one year.[3] The

Germans reported these murders with chilling accuracy in regular reports from the field. From killing by shooting, to asphyxiation in mobile vans where the carbon monoxide exhaust was pumped into the trucks loaded with Jewish victims, to the more elaborate killing process in the death camps, the conspiracy continued unhindered. Even as the tide of the war turned against the Germans—when the Soviets pushed the German military westward after the Battle of Stalingrad in early 1943 and American and British troops landed at Normandy in June 1944—the killings continued. The German invasion of Hungary on March 9, 1944, then subjected Hungarian Jewry, the last large Jewish community standing in Europe, to the "desired solution"—annihilation. In the ensuing ten months, more than four hundred thousand Hungarian Jews were sent to their deaths at Auschwitz, where 80 percent were gassed upon arrival. The brutality and sheer inhumanity of German excesses could not be swept under the rug of the peace that ended the war in Europe in May 1945.

At the war's end, how were the Allies to respond to this enormous crime? Even in an ideal world, it would have been impossible to bring all the perpetrators to trial. There were too many; as the massive task of rebuilding began, they blended into the background of a Europe devastated by war. In too many cases, the witnesses had been killed. Nevertheless, an attempt was made to prosecute some of the perpetrators.

The first major trial after the war took place at Nuremberg before the International Military Tribunal (IMT) between November 1945 and October 1946. Judges from the United States, the United Kingdom, France, and the Soviet Union presided. The prosecutors had organized their evidence under difficult circumstances in postwar Germany, with its wrecked transportation and communications systems. They reviewed hundreds of thousands of documents. They synthesized different legal systems and the differing approaches of the four Allied powers, and the end product was made available in four languages: English, French, Russian, and German. While the prosecutors made mistakes,[4] these are minor when one considers the amazing amount of organization that went into preparing for the trial with such limited time, and in incredibly taxing conditions. Under the circumstances, their ability to put together such a massive case as effectively as they did must rate as one of the great accomplishments in the history of criminal trials.

The focus of the IMT trial, however, was *not* the Jewish genocide—the crime that later came to be known as the Holocaust—for several reasons.[5] First, the principal concern of the prosecutors at Nuremberg was the charge of crimes against the peace, defined in the Nuremberg Charter as "the planning, preparation, initiation, or waging of wars of aggression, or a war in violation of international treaties, agreements or assurances, or participation in a common plan or conspiracy for the accomplishment of any of the foregoing."[6] After the carnage of the Second World War, initiated by Germany's invasion of Poland in September 1939, the drafters of the Nuremberg Charter felt that all steps should be taken to unambiguously affirm that the waging of aggressive war was an international crime, for which political and military leaders were not immune from prosecution. In his opening address, Justice Robert H. Jackson would refer to crimes against peace as the "supreme crime."[7]

Second, at the time that the prosecutors were putting together their evidence for the IMT trial they were only beginning to appreciate the extent of the conspiracy to exterminate European Jewry. For example, it is instructive that Justice Jackson made no reference to Auschwitz in his opening address. In his memoir of the Nuremberg trials, Jackson's assistant and successor, Telford Taylor, recalls that he knew nothing of the mass extermination of the Jews when he arrived at Nuremberg.[8] While it was the legal actors who first unearthed the conspiracy, as they were combing through the vast depository of undestroyed Nazi documents to find legally admissible evidence of criminality, even they did not fully comprehend at the time what they had discovered. The term "genocide" had not yet entered the criminal vocabulary and the "Holocaust" would not take hold as the term referring specifically to the extermination of six million Jews by the Germans until two decades later.

Finally, none of the defendants at the first Nuremberg trial had hands-on responsibility for the Holocaust. Hitler and Himmler were dead; Eichmann was still at large; Reinhard Heydrich, the person directed by Hermann Göring to implement the Final Solution, had been assassinated; and his successor, Ernst Kaltenbrunner, while an IMT defendant, left the job of administering the plan to murder Europe's Jews to his subordinates, Heinrich Mueller, Adolf Eichmann, and others. While Göring may have formally initiated the plan for the Final Solution with his directive of July 31, 1941, the bulk of Göring's responsibilities fell under the other Nuremberg charges—crimes against the peace and war crimes—and those were understandably the focus of the case against him. When it finally came time to cross-examine Göring about the conspiracy to exterminate the Jews, he simply denied knowledge of its full scope.

To be sure, the prosecutors were quick learners, and so the conspiracy to exterminate the Jews did comprise part of the case that the prosecutors put on at Nuremberg. Count One of the indictment (titled "The Common Plan or Conspiracy") speaks of the conspirators' "program of relentless persecution of the Jews, designed to exterminate them" and concludes: "[I]t is conservatively estimated that 5,700,000 have disappeared, most of them deliberately put to death by the Nazi conspirators. Only remnants of the Jewish population of Europe remain."[9]

At trial, the prosecutors presented considerable evidence about the mass murder of the Jews. SS General Otto Ohlendorf testified that, as a commander of an *Einsatzgruppen* unit, his instructions to his men were to "liquidate" all Jews they encountered, and he acknowledged responsibility for the murder of ninety thousand Jews in Ukraine. (His trial is discussed in chapter 6.) Rudolf Höss, commandant of Auschwitz, testified as to the killing of two million Jews at Auschwitz, a number since reduced to about one million Jews.

And in their summations, both the French and British prosecutors spoke about the mass murder of the Jews. Chief British prosecutor Hartley Shawcross personalized the killing process by reading from the affidavit of German engineer Hermann Graebe, who witnessed the mass execution of the Jews of Dubno, Ukraine by an *Einsatz* commando killing squad. Shawcross read Graebe's account, which focused on the mass extermination of the Jews, in open court:

> On October 5, 1942, when I visited the building office at Dubno, my foreman told me that in the vicinity of the site Jews from Dubno had been shot in three large pits, each about 30 meters long and 3 meters deep. About 1,500 persons had been killed daily. All the 5,000 Jews who had still been living in Dubno before the pogrom were to be liquidated. As the shooting had taken place in his presence, he was still much upset. Thereupon, I drove to the site accompanied by my foreman and saw near it great mounds of earth, about 30 meters long and 2 meters high.

Several trucks stood in front of the mounds. Armed Ukrainian militia drove the people off the trucks under the supervision of an SS man. The militiamen acted as guards on the trucks and drove them to and from the pit. All these people had the regulation yellow patches on the front and back of their clothes, and thus could be recognized as Jews. My foreman and I went directly to the pits. Nobody bothered us. Now I heard rifle shots in quick succession from behind one of the earth mounds. The people who had got off the trucks—men, women, and children of all ages—had to undress upon the orders of an SS man, who carried a riding or dog whip. They had to put down their clothes in fixed places, sorted according to shoes, top clothing, and underclothing. I saw a heap of shoes of about 800 to 1,000 pairs, great piles of underlinen and clothing. Without screaming or weeping, these people undressed, stood around in family groups, kissed each other, said farewells, and waited for a sign from another SS man, who stood near the pit, also with a whip in his hand. During the fifteen minutes that I stood near I heard no complaint or plea for mercy. I watched a family of about eight persons, a man and a woman both about fifty with their children of about one, eight and ten, and two grown-up daughters of about twenty to twenty-nine. An old woman with snow-white hair was holding the one-year-old child in her arms and singing to it and tickling it. The child was cooing with delight. The couple were looking on with tears in their eyes. The father was holding the hand of a boy about ten years old and speaking to him softly; the boy was fighting his tears. The father pointed to the sky, stroked his head, and seemed to explain something to him. At that moment the SS man at the pit shouted something to his comrade. The latter counted off about twenty persons and instructed them to go behind the earth mound. Among them was the family, which I have mentioned. I well remember a girl, slim and with black hair, who, as she passed close to me pointed to herself and said "Twenty-three [years old]." I walked around the mound and found myself confronted by a tremendous grave. People were closely wedged together and lying on top of each other so that only their heads were visible. Nearly all had blood running over their shoulders from their heads. Some of the people shot were still moving. Some were lifting their arms and turning their heads to show that they were still alive. The pit was already two-thirds full. I estimated that it already contained about 1,000 people.[10]

It was not until fifteen years later at the Eichmann trial that the same scenario was testified to, but this time from the victim's perspective.

The Eichmann trial in 1961–62 in Jerusalem is generally seen as the "other" Holocaust trial, if not the major Holocaust trial. Although grounded on the same legal principles that came out of Nuremberg, the formal charge against Eichmann was not the commission of "crimes against humanity" but, specifically, "crimes against the Jewish people." Since Gideon Hausner, the Israeli attorney general, aimed to show the full scope of mass murder of the Jews, he called a Holocaust survivor from each country where Jews were murdered. Eichmann, of course, was not personally present or even directly involved in the acts that the witnesses testified to, and so much of the live testimony dealt with events with which Eichmann had little or no connection. Because the charge alleged that Eichmann, together with others, agreed to the murder of Europe's Jews, under basic principles of conspiracy law, the conduct of others in furtherance of the underlying criminal agreement became admissible against Eichmann.

These two trials—at Nuremberg in 1945–46 and Jerusalem in 1961–62—though by far the best known, were not the only trials in which the major focus, or even a significant portion of the trial, was the mass murder of the Jews. Over the last seventy years, tens of thousands of individuals who were part of the German regime and their local collaborators in the occupied countries have been prosecuted for crimes committed during the years of German rule of occupied Europe. In somewhat sporadic and unorganized fashion, many of these trials dealt either directly or indirectly with the genocide of the Jews. A close look at some of these other Holocaust trials tells us a great deal about the implementation of the conspiracy to murder European Jewry and how various justice systems have tried to address it. While some of these trials are well known to scholars, they have been overshadowed by the Nuremberg and Eichmann trials. Because they have faded from public memory, we call them "forgotten trials of the Holocaust."

The ten trials discussed in this book have taken place over the last seventy years in a range of countries. While separate books have been written on some of these trials, this book is the first to provide an overarching, global picture of the various efforts to prosecute those responsible for the murder of Jews under Hitler's plan, both high-ranking statesmen and minor foot soldiers involved in one of the momentous crimes in human history. The ten specific snapshots provided here illustrate how both international law and various domestic legal systems have dealt with Nazi-era perpetrators. Legal historian David Fraser speaks of the "shadow and gloom of legal and historical forgetfulness"[11] that has been cast over the judicial processes used to handle Nazi war crimes. This volume is meant to undo some of that forgetfulness.

The ten trials covered, albeit a small fraction of the multitude of the prosecutions of Nazi-era perpetrators, were chosen for this book because they are representative of the various types of prosecutions of war criminals and collaborators. In reviewing these trials, we look at the prosecution's case, defenses, the ultimate verdicts, and the legitimacy of the verdicts and sentences.

Can one ever hope for justice in these cases? For the murderer of hundreds or thousands of individuals—and many of the defendants discussed in this volume fit that description—even the ultimate punishment of death may seem unsatisfactory, both to the immediate survivors and to society at large. To use the terms "Holocaust" and "justice" in the same phrase itself appears incongruous.[12] As Holocaust historian Michael Berenbaum has commented: "In one sense, the entire quest for justice in the aftermath of genocide is futile, because you cannot punish all the killers, and the punishment itself is incommensurate with the nature of the crime."[13]

In choosing the trials analyzed here, we have tried to present a vertical picture of the detailed operation of the conspiracy to murder that (1) Hitler, Himmler, and Göring initiated, (2) Eichmann coordinated, and (3) many hundreds of thousands of Germans, Austrians, and others implemented. We have thus selected trials involving concentration camp commandants, guards, and prisoner-functionaries (known in concentration camp slang as *kapos*) that assisted in the murder process. Also, we have selected cases prosecuted under different legal systems so that, by virtue of comparison, something can be learned about the varied legal responses to the enormity of crimes committed during the Nazi era in Europe.

Chapter 1: The Kharkov Trial of 1943: The First Trial of the Holocaust? The very first trial held of Germans for Nazi-era crimes took place in December 1943, before the war was over, in the newly Soviet-liberated

Ukrainian city of Kharkov. The three-day trial took place as the war was still raging and the Red Army was pushing westward. The defendants consisted of three Nazi personnel and a Russian collaborator. Almost all of their victims were Jews but the word "Jew" was never uttered during the trial. This chapter examines why.

Chapter 2: The Trial of Pierre Laval: Criminal Collaborator or Patriot? The Laval trial in Paris in October 1945 involved the collaborationist prime minister of Vichy France responsible for the deportation of seventy-five thousand Jews from France to the death camps in Poland. Laval's defense rested entirely on his claim that he ended up saving the lives of most of French Jewry, albeit at the expense of some French Jews and almost all non-French Jews who were in France at the time. Did that justify the collaboration he openly acknowledged?

Chapter 3: The Dachau Trial under U.S. Army Jurisdiction. Dachau, located in Germany, was the first of Hitler's concentration camps and among the last to be liberated. Soon after its liberation on April 29, 1945, American military authorities began prosecuting Dachau camp personnel on the very grounds of the former camp. The U.S. Army conducted trials of 1,672 alleged war criminals. These trials, brought under the U.S. military justice system, continued from 1945 to 1948.

Among the diversity of inmates at Dachau, Jewish inmates were singled out for the harshest treatment, pursuant to the euphemistic German term "special handling." Jews lived under the worst conditions, received the least food, and constituted a clear plurality of the many thousands murdered at Dachau through starvation and disease. Their death rate was the highest of any of Dachau's sizable population groups. This chapter focuses on the trial of forty Dachau administrators that took place in November–December 1945, concurrently with the major trial in Nuremberg.

Chapter 4: The Trial of Amon Göth in Postwar Poland: Poland's "Nuremberg." We then turn to the trial of Amon Göth, the brutal commandant of the Płaszów concentration camp on the outskirts of Kraków, whose deeds would have been forgotten were it not for Steven Spielberg's film *Schindler's List.* Göth's trial spanned a two-week period in August–September 1946 before the Supreme National Tribunal of Poland. It was one of seven trials conducted by this special Polish court for German war criminals, which applied both local Polish law and international law principles. In the Göth trial, and the other six trials conducted by this court, the Poles modeled their proceedings on the Nuremberg trial in session at the same time.

A notable feature of the trial was the use of the term "genocide" (in Polish, *ludobójstwo*) to describe the crimes Göth committed. This was one of the first uses of the term "genocide," coined just a few years earlier in 1944 by Raphael Lemkin, a Jewish refugee from German-occupied Poland living in the United States.

Chapter 5: The Hamburg Ravensbrück Trials in British-Occupied Germany: Women as Perpetrators, Women as Victims. Having covered trials under Soviet, French, Polish, and U.S. military law, we turn to British military law and a series of trials conducted between December 1946 and July 1948 in the British-occupied zone of Germany. The seven trials, known as the Hamburg Ravensbrück trials, involved personnel from the Ravensbrück concentration camp, the largest penal complex ever constructed for women.

Because of the unique status of Ravensbrück in the multitude of camps the Nazis established, the trials at Ravensbrück also demonstrate another element of the Holocaust: the roles of women not only as victims, but also as perpetrators. Generally speaking, the perpetration of the Holocaust was an all-male affair. The macho mentality and ideology of the Third Reich placed German men as the planners and implementers of the glorious future that would create the Thousand Year Reich for all German people. Nevertheless, some German women were part of the SS, and provided the necessary female staff at the concentration and labor camps where female victims were held.

Other trials featured women as defendants. The female brutes put on the dock at these trials had a celebrity quality to them, typical of other female defendants throughout time who have been charged with ghastly murders. Hence, the female perpetrators at the other trials went by such colorful monikers as the "Bitch of Belsen" or the "Stomping Mare." None of the women on trial at Hamburg enjoyed such notorious celebrity status, though the depravities of some of the female Ravensbrück staff equaled those of the better-known German female war criminals.

Chapter 6: The Einsatzgruppen Trial at Nuremberg: Did Anyone Have to Follow Orders to Kill? The *Einsatzgruppen* trial is one of the twelve subsequent Nuremberg trials conducted just by the Americans. This trial was a latecomer to the post-IMT trials with the discovery in 1947 in war-ravaged Berlin of "smoking gun" evidence that implicated *Einsatzgruppen* commanders in the murders of more than one million Jews and others in German-occupied Soviet territory. The Graebe affidavit describes these mass murders in detail. By such means, the *Einsatzgruppen* squads murdered men, women, and children one by one, bullet by bullet, town by town, and city by city. These massive killings elevated the scale of German atrocities to totally new levels. To present the fullest picture, we have included a victim's perspective on one such horrific instance of mass murder.

Because the *Einsatzgruppen* commanders claimed to have followed orders from Berlin, this trial also illuminated the defense of "following orders" in far more depth than the IMT proceeding. More information was available to the *Einsatzgruppen* prosecutors in 1947 than was available in the cramped period in 1945 and the inception of the IMT trial. In addition, the chief trial judge, Michael Musmanno, was firmly committed to getting all facts, and a considerable portion of the trial was devoted to determining whether there was any factual basis to the claim that SS men had to kill in order to save their own lives.

Chapter 7: The Jewish Kapo Trials in Israel: Is There a Place for the Law in the Gray Zone? The next chapter examines one of the most morally and legally difficult set of trials arising out of the Second World War in general and the Holocaust in particular: those in which the defendants were Jewish *kapos* charged with committing crimes against other Jews. The primary focus here is on the various trials of such former *kapos* held between 1951 and 1964 in the new State of Israel. These individuals were tried under the same Israeli law as applied to Eichmann in 1961. However, the first Israeli Knesset (parliament) enacted the so-called Nazi and Nazi Collaborators Law not to bring to account Germans who might find themselves within the borders of Israel after the war—seen as a ridiculous impossibility at the time of the law's enactment in 1950—but Jews who became part of the machinery of death in the camps (*Lagers*), and then survived the *Lagers* and became citizens of the new State of Israel. This chapter explores the legal and moral issues unique to this hybrid class of prisoner-functionary who occupied the "gray zone" between master and slave in the camps.

Chapter 8: The Frankfurt Auschwitz Trial: The Germans Trying Germans under German Law. The next trial deals with how Germans themselves prosecuted their own nationals for German criminality, specifically those Germans who were part of the most profound symbol of the Holocaust: Auschwitz. The Frankfurt Auschwitz trial, which took place over twenty months between December 1963 and August 1965, was a highly dedicated effort by West German prosecutors to charge Germans operating the Auschwitz death camp under German criminal law. Defendants at Nuremberg, Eichmann in Jerusalem, and others often raised arguments that they were being tried under *ex post facto* laws. This claim could not be raised here. Nevertheless, the use of the German Penal Code of 1871 to deal with Nazi criminality, before a postwar German judiciary, whose origins were largely in the Nazi era, had its own set of problems.

Chapter 9: The Trial of Feodor Fedorenko: Treblinka Relived in a Florida Courtroom. None of the trials discussed up to this point was brought in the United States. Any U.S. prosecution of Holocaust-era crimes would run afoul of the *ex post facto* clause of the U.S. Constitution, which precludes any such proceeding. However, criminal trials are not the only vehicle by which persons in the U.S. can be charged for their participation in the Holocaust. After the war, the United States, as well as other countries, became a haven not only for Holocaust victims, but also for perpetrators who became citizens. In such a case, the legal route taken with such persons is first to denaturalize and then to expel them from the U.S. The usual basis for denaturalization is that the person made a false statement in an entry application to the United States. Concealing one's role as a guard at a concentration camp by misstating one's activities during the war is such a false statement. Since the mid-1970s over one hundred naturalized Americans have been stripped of their citizenship for participating in the murder of Jews in German-occupied Europe and then hiding their role when immigrating to the United States.

A Ukrainian in the Red Army captured by the Germans in 1941, Feodor Fedorenko was trained as a concentration camp guard and then posted as a guard to the Treblinka extermination camp in 1942. Between July 1942 and October 1943, approximately 900,000 men, women, and children were murdered there—almost all Jews. In *United*

States v. Feodor Fedorenko, brought in 1978 in Fort Lauderdale, the U.S. Justice Department sought to denaturalize Fedorenko on the basis of his role at Treblinka. Ultimately, the case was heard by the U.S. Supreme Court. In 1984, Fedorenko became the first and only war criminal to be deported from the United States to the Soviet Union, where he stood trial for his crimes.

Chapter 10: The Trial of Anthony Sawoniuk at the Old Bailey: The Holocaust in the British Courtroom. The trial of Anthony Sawoniuk took place in the Central Criminal Court (the "Old Bailey") in London between February and April 1999. Like Fedorenko, Sawoniuk was a collaborator from Eastern Europe who began a new life after the war in a new country, in this case England. In the 1980s, the British rejected the Americans' choice to simply denaturalize and then deport Nazi-era perpetrators and instead decided to prosecute them for their crimes directly. To do so, Parliament enacted the War Crimes Act 1991, a novel law that established criminal jurisdiction in England for conduct committed by a naturalized British citizen who committed crimes in German-occupied Europe. Sawoniuk's hidden past was exposed after the passage of the law, and he was arrested and subsequently tried at the Old Bailey for multiple murders of Jews he allegedly committed in 1942 while a policeman in German-occupied Belarussia. As a result, Sawoniuk attained the dubious distinction of being the only person to be tried for Nazi-era crimes on English soil.

* * *

As this overview makes clear, the trials discussed in this book are each distinctive—in the issues with which they contended, in the legal contexts in which they were prosecuted, and in the way in which the genocide was presented. Yet taken together we can see the progressive formation of public memory of the Holocaust in courtrooms throughout the world. In the 1943 Kharkov trial, Jews were not an explicit focal point, though almost all of the victims were Jewish. By the 1999 Sawoniuk trial in London, the entire focus was on the murder of Jews. Each trial explored here presents a landmark in apprehending the dimensions of the Jewish genocide. Indeed, these trials reveal the significant role the legal process has played in the formation of an understanding of the Holocaust even as they illuminate how understanding of the Holocaust shifted over time.

It is difficult to contemplate the murder of six million people. Thus it should not be surprising that efforts to prosecute the perpetrators of so many murders are also far from perfect. Nevertheless, each such effort represents part of the human endeavor to reach for justice. This book is dedicated to the many who labored at not forgetting and attempted to bring some measure of justice to those bearing responsibility for genocide and other mass atrocities.

The four defendants at the Kharkov Trial: (l to r) Wilhelm Langheld, Reinhard Retzlaff, Hanz Ritz, and Mikhail Bulanov. Photo Archive, Yad Vashem.

1

The Kharkov Trial of 1943

The First Trial of the Holocaust?

In the brutal history of humanity, no other tragedy compares to the scale of death and destruction brought by Germany in the years between 1941 and 1945 to the territories of present-day Russia, Belarus and the Ukraine. During the forty-seven months of what is known in the region as the Great Patriotic War, approximately 30 million Soviet civilians and soldiers lost their lives. Twenty million of these were civilians. Over sixty years later, more than 2.4 million are still officially considered missing in action, while 6 million of the 9.5 million buried in mass graves remain unidentified.

When describing what befell them, the people of the region often reference the brutal hordes of Mongol invaders in Europe during the twelfth and thirteenth centuries. Such an analogy is a fair one. In a throwback to the Mongol style of warfare, and on direct orders from Hitler, the German military on its Eastern Front did not follow the rules of warfare that had been developed by Europeans over the centuries to minimize civilian casualties as well as special status recognition of captured enemy soldiers.

Prior to the start of military operations in June 1941, Hitler announced to his generals: "The war against Russia will be such that it cannot be conducted in a knightly fashion. This struggle is one of ideologies and racial differences and will have to be conducted with unprecedented, unmerciful and unrelenting harshness."[1] Pursuant to Hitler's instructions, the German generals issued specific orders to their regiments regarding how the upcoming invasion of the Soviet Union was to be conducted. This included the so-called "commissar order," instructing the troops to take severe and decisive measures against "Bolshevik agitators" (the Soviet political commissars), partisans, saboteurs, and Jews. These orders provided the purported legal basis under German law for the mass executions of suspected political opponents and, eventually, Soviet Jews. It also permitted the German military to conduct a policy whereby approximately three million Soviet soldiers would die of starvation or cold in German POW camps.

In Ukraine, some of the fiercest battles between the German forces and the Red Army took place around Kharkov, Ukraine's second-largest city. As a result of these battles, Kharkov became the only Soviet territory that changed hands four times during the war. The Germans captured Kharkov and the rest of eastern Ukraine in October 1941. In May 1942, the Red Army led a disastrous counterattack in an attempt to recapture the city. Hundreds of thousands of Red Army soldiers lost their lives in what David Glantz calls "one of the most catastrophic offensives in Russian military history."[2] In February 1943, the Red Army launched another offensive, this time successfully liberating the city. Soon thereafter, German forces countered with another attack, recapturing Kharkov in March 1943. This turned out to be the last major German victory on the Eastern Front. On August 23, 1943, the Red Army carried out what is known as Operation Rumiantsev and liberated Kharkov once and for all from German occupation.

Four months later, in December 1943, the Soviet Union conducted a trial in Kharkov of three captured Germans and one Ukrainian collaborator, charging them with the murder of Kharkov civilians, almost all Jews. The highly publicized Kharkov trial was the first trial of Germans held by any of the Allied powers. Earlier that year the Soviets held a public trial at Krasnodar, but the defendants were all Soviet citizens tried for treason stemming from their collaboration with the German invaders. The Soviets had also been conducting summary military trials of captured Germans, followed by quick executions. These, however, were not public trials and so were virtually unknown to the outside world. In contrast, the Kharkov trial was a highly publicized affair, and an attempt (partly successful, as we shall see) by the Soviets to conduct a Western-style legal proceeding.

It would take another two years, after Germany's unconditional surrender in May 1945, for the Allies to organize and begin the trial of the so-called major war criminals at Nuremberg. As we noted earlier, the trial before the International Military Tribunal at Nuremberg was not, in a strict sense, a trial of the Holocaust since the murder of the Jews was not the central focus at Nuremberg. In Kharkov, in contrast, much of the focus of the trial was on the murder of the Jewish population of Kharkov, although not identified as such. Instead, the victims were referred to in the generic as "Soviet citizens"—for reasons discussed below.

The Holocaust in Kharkov

The Jews of the Soviet Union were the first group to be targeted for mass murder. Following the invasion of the Soviet Union in June 1941, special action murder squads known as the *Einsatzgruppen* followed the regular German army into newly conquered territory. Operating just behind the advancing German troops, these mobile killing squads would round up and murder all the Jews and other "undesirables" such as the Roma and the Sinti (commonly known as Gypsies), perceived communist political leaders, professionals, and "criminals," often with assistance from the local populace. The regular German armed forces, the *Wehrmacht,* also were heavily involved in the killings.

Later on, police battalions—initially organized to keep order in the occupied territories—joined in the killing process. They were supplemented by troops of the *Waffen-SS* (the military wing of the SS), the German Order Police, and non-German-staffed auxiliary police units comprised of Ukrainians, Estonians, Latvians, Lithuanians, Crimean Tartars, Belorussians, and Russians—all of whom participated in mass killings of civilians. As Israeli historian Yitzhak Arad notes: "A substantial number of people, particularly in the Baltic countries and Ukraine, collaborated with Hitler's troops, and many participated in the murder of the Jews. Without the active support of the local inhabitants, tens of thousands of whom served in police units, the Germans would not have been able to identify and exterminate as many Jews in the occupied territories of the Soviet Union."[3]

The murder operations in Ukraine were conducted by *Einsatzgruppe C*, organized with the other three *Einsatzgruppen* in a police academy in Pretzsch, a town about fifty miles southwest of Berlin. *Einsatzgruppe*

C troops were transported to Ukraine, where they joined the Army Group South, composed of *Wehrmacht* and *Waffen-SS* troops, which spread itself across the western Ukraine, including Kiev and Kharkov. On September 19, 1941, German forces captured Kiev, the capital of Ukraine. Ten days later, detachment 4a of *Einsatzgruppe C* led by *SS-Standartenführer* (colonel) Paul Blobel massacred, over a period of two days, 33,771 Kiev Jews in the ravine at Babi Yar.

The German forces first entered Kharkov a month later, on October 23–24, 1941. In November 1941, they ordered that a census of the city be taken, in order to identify Jews among the population. In December 1941, the Jews of Kharkov were forced into a ghetto and then taken, in a similar fashion to Kiev, to the countryside to be shot. During this killing operation, at a ravine outside Kharkov known as Drobitsky Yar, approximately 15,000 Jews were murdered by the same detachment 4a troops and their collaborators. In total, Unit 4a—according to field reports sent to Berlin—executed 59,018 Jews in the Ukraine. The Drobitsky Yar mass grave is exceeded numerically only by the mass grave at Babi Yar, but remains largely unknown today to the outside world.

The Unknown Black Book, a compilation of testimonies from Jews who survived open-air massacres and other atrocities carried out by the Germans and their collaborators in Soviet territories, contains the testimony of one survivor of the Drobitsky Yar massacre, engineer S. S. Krivoruchko:

> I, a resident of Kharkov, by nationality a Jew, by training an engineer, could not be evacuated from the city in October 1941, due to illness. . . . On the morning of December 14, a decree was posted throughout the city from the German commandant of Kharkov ordering all Jews to move to barracks on the grounds of a tractor factory within two days; persons found in the city after December 16 would be shot on the spot.
>
> Starting on the morning of December 15, whole columns of Jews headed out of the city. . . . For many of the elderly and the handicapped, the journey from the city to the barracks of the tractor factory was the last of their lives. The corpses of no fewer than thirty old people lay on the ground. The pogrom began at about twelve o'clock, along with the robbing of the Jews who were on the move. As a result, many Jews arrived at the barracks without anything to their name and, more importantly, with barely any food. . . .

The barracks . . . were one-story, ramshackle structures, with smashed windows, torn away floors, and holes in the rooftops. . . . In the room which I had found myself more than seventy people had arrived by evening, whereas no more than six to eight people would have been able to live in it under normal circumstances. People stood compressed against each other. . . . From the dreadful overcrowding, hunger and lack of water, an epidemic of gastro-intestinal diseases broke out. . . . Robbery and murder were daily occurrences. Usually, the Germans would burst into the room on the pretext of searching for weapons and would steal anything that came to mind. In the event of any resistance, they dragged people out into the yard and shot them. . . .

On January 2, 1942, at 7:00 am . . . [a] German sentry shouted out an order for everyone to gather their things and be outside in ten minutes. . . . I went outside . . . then German sentries and policemen formed a tight ring around us and announced that we were being evacuated to Poltava. We marched out onto the Chuguyev-Kharkov highway but then were directed away from the city, although the road to Poltava ran through town. It was obvious that they were not taking us to Poltava. But where exactly we were going, nobody knew. . . . Two kilometers past the last houses of the tractor factory workers' quarters, they turned us in the direction of a ravine. The ravine was strewn with bits of rags and the remains of torn clothing. It became clear why they had brought us here. The ravine was sealed off by a double row of sentries. On the edge of the ravine stood a truck with machine guns. Terrible scenes erupted when people understood that they had been brought here to be slaughtered. . . . Many said goodbye to each other, embracing, kissing, exchanging the last supplies they had. . . .

From the standing column, the Germans began using clubs to drive groups of fifty to seventy people one hundred paces or so forward, then forcing them to strip down to their underwear. It was -20 or -25 degrees C. Those undressed were driven down to the bottom of the ravine from which were heard occasional shots and the chattering of machine guns.

I was in a daze and did not notice the screaming behind me. The Germans began driving forward the group that I was part of. I moved off, ready to die within a few minutes. Just then, something happened: the Germans brought up the aged and handicapped to be executed. The belongings of those who had been killed had been loaded onto these

> trucks and brought back to the city. I moved along behind one of these vehicles. Two young Jews were in the truck; the Germans had assigned them to do the loading. In a flash, I jumped into the truck and asked the youngsters to cover me. Then they hid themselves as well. When the truck was full, the German drivers took off with it and in this way took me and the two boys away from the awful ravine. . . .
>
> I went to find my wife (she is not a Jew and had stayed behind in the city with our adopted daughter) who hid me with a girlfriend of hers. I stayed with her for six and a half months. For four months later after that I wandered from village to village with a false passport and, in this way, held on until February 16, 1943, when Kharkov was liberated for the first time from the German occupiers.[4]

The German account of the roundup—Operational Situation Report U.S.S.R. No. 164, transmitted from the field to Berlin and dated February 4, 1942—summarizes the actions taken regarding the Jews of Kharkov:[5]

> *Einsatzgruppe C*—Arrest of the Jews in Kharkov
>
> The extensive preparations that became necessary in the matter of the arrest of the Kharkov Jews were sped up within the framework of SK 4a responsibilities. First of all, it was necessary to find a suitable area for the evacuation of the Jews. This was accomplished with the closest understanding of the municipality's housing department. An area was chosen where the Jews could be housed in the barracks of a factory district [in Rogan on the edge of town]. . . . The evacuation of the Jews went on without a hitch except for some robberies during the march of the Jews in the direction of their new quarters. Almost without exception, only Ukrainians participated in the robberies. So far, no report is available on the number of Jews that were arrested during the evacuation. At the same time, preparation for the shooting of the Jews is underway. 305 Jews who have spread rumors against the German Army were shot immediately.[6]

An alternative method of killing used in the Kharkov region was through the use of carbon monoxide gas pumped though the exhaust of mobile death vans. The Nazis first tested carbon monoxide gas on Soviet prisoners of war in September 1941 at the Sachsenhausen concentration camp, located north of Berlin. By the following year, approximately fifteen gas vans had fanned out throughout German-occupied Soviet territory to exterminate Jews and other "undesirables." The victims were packed into the back of closed vans, specially sealed, while carbon monoxide was piped through a hose attached to the van's tailpipe. The bodies were then unloaded, and either buried in mass graves or incinerated in open flames.

When the Red Army liberated Kharkov for the last time in August 1943, almost no Jews remained. That the Nazis had managed to make Ukraine (including Kharkov) *judenrein* is confirmed by the account of great Soviet Jewish writer and journalist Vassily Grossman, reporting from the field: "There are no Jews in Ukraine. Nowhere—Poltava, Kharkov, Kremenchug, Borispol, Yagotin. . . . All is silence. Everything is still. A whole people have been brutally murdered."[7]

Grossman's description is applicable for the rest of Soviet territory occupied by the Germans. Of the approximately 2.5 million Jews who had been trapped in German-occupied Soviet Union, only 100,000 to 120,000 survived. Most did so by joining the Jewish partisans or going into hiding. Yitzhak Arad sums up the aftermath: "All told, of the five million Jews who lived in the Soviet Union on the eve of the German attack on June 22, 1941, about half lost their lives as a result."[8]

The Trial

As the Red Army liberated Soviet territory, it repeatedly found mass graves containing remains of Jews who had been systematically slaughtered. In the Kharkov region some of these sites were discovered after the first liberation in February 1943, but before the German troops recaptured the region a month later. Most of the Jews of Kharkov had already been murdered by that time. The Red Army liberated Kharkov for the second and last time in August 1943. The defendants on trial were part of the German troops captured during this last liberation.

Earlier in the year, in July 1943, the Soviets put eleven local Soviet citizens who collaborated with the Nazis on trial in the northern Caucasus city of Krasnodar. After a three-day trial, the eleven Krasnodar defendants were found guilty of treason. Eight were executed and three were given sentences of twenty years of hard labor.

On November 1, 1943, the foreign ministers of the U.S., U.K., and U.S.S.R. issued the so-called Moscow Declaration, putting on notice Germans participating in "atrocities, massacres and executions" that they would be tried for their "abominable deeds" in the countries where they committed these deeds. The Kharkov trial of December 1943, the first public trial of German nationals by any Allied power, was the Soviet signal to the Allies that they were now putting into practice the Moscow Declaration. Greg Dawson, in his *Judgment before Nuremberg*, rightly labels the Kharkov trial as "the first Nazi war crimes trial."[9]

Three Germans and one Ukrainian were tried in Kharkov before a military tribunal constituted by the 4th Ukrainian Front of the Red Army, composed of three military judges. The prosecution of the case was led by a military colonel with a legal background, State Prosecutor of Justice Colonel N. K. Dunaev. Three Soviet defense counsel were appointed to represent the defendants. A six-member forensic team of medico-legal experts also took part in the trial, serving as expert witnesses and providing a report.

The four-day trial began on December 15, 1943, exactly two years after the German massacre of the Kharkov Jews at Drobitsky Yar. To accommodate the large attendance, and to provide the necessary gravitas to the proceedings, the trial was held in the auditorium of the Kharkov Dramatic Theater. The theatrical atmosphere was accentuated by the illumination of the auditorium with klieg lights, used to film the proceedings by a slew of cameras. The audience was rotated each day to ensure maximum attendance. Foreign correspondents were specifically invited to attend but, due to a glitch, only arrived on the last day of the trial.

The most knowledgeable of the foreign observers was American journalist Edmund Stevens. Stevens was a seasoned Soviet "old hand" who first went to the Soviet Union in 1934 to study the "Russian experiment" and married a Russian woman who returned with him and their son to the United States before the war. In 1945, he published *Russia Is No Riddle*,[10] describing his journeys through the Soviet Union before and during the Second World War. The book included a chapter about his visit to the Kharkov trial. Unlike some Westerners that became enamored with the Bolshevik revolution, and so viewed all things Soviet in a positive light, Stevens aimed to be objective about what he observed. His descriptions of the court proceedings in the Kharkov Dramatic Theater reflected this critical outlook:

> The Russians are past masters at *mise en scène*,[11] and the atmosphere of that Kharkov trial room was distinctly reminiscent of the famous Treason Trials of 1936–38. In fact, two of the defense lawyers, Kommodov and Kaznacheyev, had defended some of the figures in the treason trials. Their presence provided an element of direct continuity. This, too, was a military tribunal: judges, prosecutor, and attendants were all in uniform. . . .
>
> During the recesses, I discovered that many of the people in the audience had personal knowledge or experience of the events and atrocities described, and had seen or known the defendants during the German occupation. Several times during more gruesome bits of evidence there were stifled sobs from some woman—not out of pity for the defendants. For the most part the proceedings took place against a background of concentrated silence.[12]

The defendants were correctly characterized by Stevens as "small fry" and "non-entities"[13]—chosen to embody various ranks of the German military command that occupied the Kharkov region. He describes the three Germans on trial at Kharkov as follows:

- Wilhelm Langheld, a fifty-two-year-old captain of the German Military Counter-Espionage Service (*Abwehr*) and a commander of a POW camp for Soviet prisoners. Stevens describes Langheld as "stocky, red-headed [and] beefy-faced . . . whose carriage, heel-clicking, and rows of ribbons proclaimed a German soldier of the old school."[14]
- Hans Ritz, an *SS-Untersturmführer* (second lieutenant) in the *Sicherheitsdienst* (SD), one of the security organizations of the SS, and an assistant SS Company Commander of a *Sonderkommando* unit. Stevens describes Ritz as a "Nazi horse of a different color from the hard-bitten Langheld[,]. . . . a baby-faced youth of twenty-four, with a tender little mustache."[15] Ritz, trained in music and law, worked as a lawyer before fighting with the SS on the Eastern Front.
- Reinhard Retzlaff, a thirty-six-year-old corporal and member of the 560th Group of German Secret Field Police. Unlike the other two German defendants, Retzlaff was not a Nazi Party member.

All three Germans were charged with playing a "direct part in [the] mass and brutal extermination of civilian Soviet people by the use of specially equipped automobiles known as 'murder vans,' and also with having taken a personal part in mass shootings, hangings, burnings, plunder and outrages on Soviet people."[16]

Along with the three Germans on trial, the Soviets added a Soviet citizen: Mikhail Bulanov, a twenty-six-year-old Ukrainian collaborator who worked with the Germans from October 1941 to February 1943. The indictment characterized Bulanov as a *shafior* (chauffeur) with the Kharkov *Sicherheitsdienst.* Bulanov was charged with "betrayal of the motherland . . . [and] with having taken a direct part in the mass extermination of the Soviet people by means of asphyxiation in 'murder vans,' [and] with having personally shot civilian Soviet citizens, among whom were old people, women and children."

The four defendants were charged under both international law and Soviet law. The legal basis under international law was the Moscow Declaration issued by the Allies a month earlier announcing that Germans participating in atrocities would be tried by the countries where the atrocities took place. In the sphere of the Soviet legislation, on April 19, 1943, the Presidium of the Supreme Soviet (parliament) of the U.S.S.R. issued a decree entitled *On measures of punishment for German-Fascist villains guilty of killing and torturing the Soviet population and captive Red Army soldiers, for spies and traitors to the Motherland from among Soviet citizens and their accomplices.*[17] The April decree became the prime legal tool for prosecution of German Nazis and their Soviet collaborators. Alexander Prusin notes that "[t]he [April] decree became a binding tool with which to handle all accused war criminals, and its very language signifies its designation as an instrument of deterrence against collaboration with the Germans."[18] The decree used the terms "atrocities" and "evil deeds" to broadly encompass the war crimes committed by the German (foreign) and Soviet (domestic) war criminals while stipulating punishment by public execution or long-term prison time.[19]

The German defendants appeared in court dressed in full military attire, which was not common in Soviet trials. After public reading of the indictment,[20] the defendants all entered guilty pleas. However, under continental civil law legal systems, emulated by Soviet socialist law, a plea of guilty is not automatically accepted by the court. The court must still satisfy itself that the evidence proves the guilt. Additionally, evidence is presented to help determine what sentence should be rendered. The trial, therefore, continued despite guilty pleas.

Undoubtedly, the Soviets did not constitute this public trial for the defendants merely to plead guilty and subsequently sentence them without going into specifics of the atrocities committed. Almost all public trials held of Nazi war criminals and collaborators over the last seventy years have had a didactic component, and this first trial of the Nazis was no exception. Detailed evidence of the brutal atrocities committed by the "Fascist-Hitlerite" invaders in the Kharkov region was going to be introduced during the trial and subsequently disseminated to the outside world. As confirmation of this intent, the Soviets translated excerpts of the proceedings into English shortly after the trial's conclusion and published them in a book, *The People's Verdict*. The book included commentary and also excerpts from the Krasnodar trial. The Soviets also produced a documentary, which was widely shown in Soviet theaters, though never screened in the West.

Stevens, the American correspondent, noted that "all legal niceties were observed to a fault. The defendants and their counsel had full latitude to speak or interpolate, and every comma of what was said was translated into German for their benefit."[21] Each defendant took the stand and was questioned by the prosecutor, members of the tribunal, and defense counsel. George Ginsburgs comments that "[t]here [was] no indication that the German defendants had either been rehearsed or coerced."[22]

The trial began with the most senior of the three German defendants to take the stand: Captain Wilhelm Langheld. He explained that the German high command encouraged atrocities against civilians and decorated soldiers for fulfilling orders to exterminate Soviet citizens.[23] Langheld described the use of gas vans by the German military for mass slaughter:

> I saw the "gas van" in Kharkov . . . [s]ome time in May, 1942, when I was on a service visit to Kharkov. . . . As far as I remember the "gas van" is a vehicle dark grey in colour, completely covered in, having hermetically sealed doors at the back. . . . [It holds] [a]pproximately 60 to 70 persons. . . . I was at 76, Cherniskevsky Street at the H.Q. of the S.D. and heard a terrific noise and screaming outside. . . . A gas van at that moment had driven up to the main entrance of the building, and one

> could see how many people were being forcibly driven into it, while German soldiers were standing at the doors of the van. . . . I was a few paces away from the gas van and saw it being done. . . . Among the people being loaded into the gas van were old men, children, old and young women. These people would not go into the machine of their own accord and had therefore to be driven into the gas van by SS men with kicks and blows of the butt ends of automatic rifles. . . . I presume that these people guessed the sort of fate that awaited them.[24]

Describing the child of a woman who was killed, Langheld explained: "He clung to his dead mother, crying aloud. The lance-corporal who came to take away the woman's body got tired of this so he shot the child. . . . Such things happened everywhere. It was a system."[25]

Stevens described his observation of Langheld's testimony:

> When the prosecutor asked Langheld whether the German High Command ever punished its soldiers or officers for ill treatment of civilians, he pondered a moment, rocking slightly back and forth on his toes and heels, and then answered, in the same quiet, measured voice in which his entire testimony had been delivered, that on the contrary such treatment was deliberately encouraged and rewarded. At each conclusion of his testimony, Langheld saluted smartly, turned on his heels, and strode back to his seat in the prisoners' box.[26]

The next defendant to take the stand was Second Lieutenant Hans Ritz, who testified that the functions fulfilled by SS troops included "shooting, forcible evacuations of villages, [as well as] the transportation and guarding of arrested persons."[27] Like Langheld, Ritz also indicated his awareness of "the extermination of civilian citizens in Kharkov"[28] and his involvement in such killings. Prosecutor Dunayev sought out Ritz's mindset for his murderous acts:

> PROSECUTOR: You, Ritz, are a person of higher legal education and apparently consider yourself a man of culture. How could you not only watch people being beaten, but even take an active part in it, and shoot perfectly innocent people, not only under compulsion but of your own free will?

RITZ: I had to obey orders, otherwise I would have been court-martialed and certainly sentenced to death.

PROSECUTOR: This is not quite so, because you yourself expressed a desire to be present when people were loaded on to the gas vans and nobody specially invited you to be there.

RITZ: Yes, that is true. I myself expressed a desire to be present, but I beg you to take into consideration that I was then still a newcomer on the Eastern Front and wanted to convince myself as to whether it was true that these lorries of which I had heard were used on the Eastern Front. Therefore, I expressed my desire to be present when people were loaded on them.

PROSECUTOR: But you took a direct part in the shooting of innocent Soviet citizens?

RITZ: As I have testified earlier, during the shooting at Podvorki, Major Hanebitter said to me: "Show us what you are made of," and, not wanting to get into trouble, I took an automatic rifle from one of the SS men and started firing.

PROSECUTOR: Consequently, of your own free will you entered upon this vile course of shooting completely innocent people, as nobody had forced you to do it.

RITZ: Yes, I must admit that.

Ritz also acknowledged that German policy was not to recognize the laws of warfare on the Eastern Front:

PROSECUTOR: Now, Ritz, you are a man with some knowledge of law. Tell us, were the standards of international law observed to any extent by the German Army on the Eastern Front?

RITZ: I must say that on the Eastern Front there was no question of international or any other law.

PROSECUTOR: Tell us, Ritz, on whose orders did all this take place? Why was this system of complete lawlessness and monstrous slaughter of perfectly innocent people instituted?

RITZ: This lawlessness had its deep seated reasons. It was instituted on the instructions of Hitler and his collaborators, instructions which are capable of detailed analysis.[29]

The third defendant to take the stand was Corporal Reinhard Retzlaff. His testimony included a description of how he participated in the murder of Soviet civilians.[30]

PROSECUTOR: Tell the Court how you exterminated Soviet citizens.

RETZLAFF: Every person detained by the military authorities and sent to the Secret Field Police for examination, was first of all beaten up. If a prisoner gave the evidence we needed, the beatings were discontinued, while those who refused to give evidence were further beaten, and this frequently resulted in their death.

PROSECUTOR: This means that if a person did not confess, he was murdered. And if he did—he was shot. Is that correct?

RETZLAFF: Yes, that was so on most occasions.

PROSECUTOR: Was there any occasion when cases were trumped up and evidence was faked?

RETZLAFF: Yes, all this happened and rather frequently. One may say that this was quite normal procedure.

The final defendant to take the stand was Bulanov, who described the transport of medical patients from a hospital to shooting sites. Bulanov acknowledged that on four occasions he drove a three-ton truck with a total of about 150 patients from the Kharkov hospital to a shooting site:

BULANOV: When I arrived at the hospital I was told to drive up to one of the hospital blocks. At this moment Gestapo men began to lead out patients dressed only in their underwear, and load them into the trucks. After loading, I drove the truck to the shooting site under German escort. This place was approximately four kilometers from the city. When we arrived at the shooting site, screams and sobs of patients who were already being shot filled the air. The Germans shot them in front of the other patients. Some begged for mercy and fell down naked in the cold mud, but the Germans pushed them into the pits and then shot them.[31]

Bulanov also discussed a similar trip from a children's hospital to transport children aged six through twelve for extermination.[32]

Once examination of the defendants was concluded, the court and counsel proceeded to interrogate percipient witnesses. These included both Kharkov residents (including hospital personnel) who witnessed the atrocities as well as captured German soldiers. None testified directly about the defendants on the dock. Rather, their testimony served as background, adding to the overall picture of the horror that had taken place in the Kharkov region: mass shootings, gas van descriptions, discussions of the plunder of agricultural products, instructions from superiors in command (to implicate those higher-ranked officials), the disgraceful prison camp conditions, and murder of hospital patients.[33]

As part of the prosecution case, forensic experts from the Commission of Medico-Legal Experts also testified and presented a report based upon their examination of the various mass graves found at the Drobitsky Yar gully and other places in the Kharkov region. The expert report confirmed by forensic evidence that the methods of murder by the German forces of local civilians and POWs consisted of shooting the victims and gassing them through the use of carbon monoxide.

> The medico-legal experts examined in Kharkov and neighbouring localities the scenes of the crimes of the German fascist invaders—the places where they carried out the extermination of the Soviet citizens. These included the burned-out block of the army hospital, where they shot and burned war prisoners—severely wounded personnel of the Red Army; the place of the mass shooting of the healthy and sick, of small children, juveniles, young people, old men and women in the forest park of Sokolniki, near the village of Podvorki, in the Drobitsky gully, and in the therapeutic colony of Strelechye. At these sites the medico-legal experts examined the grave-pits and exhumed bodies of Soviet citizens shot, poisoned, burned or otherwise brutally exterminated.
>
> The medico-legal experts examined the places where the German fascist invaders burnt bodies to destroy evidence of their crimes—the poisoning with carbon monoxide. This is the site of the conflagration on the territory of the barracks of the Kharkov tractor plant. Examination of territories on which bodies were burnt or buried, examination of the grave-pits and positions of bodies in them and comparison of material thus obtained with data of the Court proceedings, provide grounds for considering that the number of bodies of murdered Soviet citizens in Kharkov and its environs reaches several tens of thousands, whereas the

figure of 33,000 exterminated Soviet citizens given by accused and some witnesses is only approximate and undoubtedly too low.

In the 13 grave-pits opened in Kharkov and its immediate vicinity were found a huge number of corpses. In most graves they lay in extreme disorder, fantastically intertwined, forming tangles of human bodies defying description. The corpses lay in such a manner that they can be said to have been dumped or heaped but not buried in common graves. In two pits in the Sokolniki forest park bodies were found lying in straight rows, face downward, arms bent at the elbow and hands pressed to faces or necks. All the bodies had bullet wounds through the heads. Such a position of the bodies was not accidental. It proves that the victims were forced to lie down face downward and were shot in that position. . . . The fact revealed by the investigation—namely, that before being murdered Soviet citizens were stripped of their footwear—is fully confirmed by the medico-legal examinations: during exhumation the experts in most cases discovered naked or half-naked bodies.

In order to ascertain which Soviet citizens were exterminated and in what manner, the experts exhumed and examined 1,047 bodies in Kharkov and its environs. These included the bodies of 19 children and adolescents, 429 women and 599 men. The dead ranged in age from two to seventy years. The fact that the bodies of children, adolescents, women and old men as well as invalids were discovered in grave-pits with civilian clothes and articles of domestic use and personal effects on the bodies or near them proves that the German fascist authorities exterminated Soviet citizens regardless of sex or age. On the other hand, the fact that [among] the bodies of young and middle-age men were found clothes of military cut worn in the Red Army, also articles of military equipment (pots, mugs, belts, etc.) is evidence of Soviet war prisoners. [. . .] On the basis of all the combined data of their proceedings—the medico-legal experts have established the presence of: (a) A vast number of burial sites in the city of Kharkov and its immediate environs. (b) A huge number of bodies in the grave-pits. (c) Varying times of burial in various graves. (d) Varying degrees of preservation of the bodies in the same graves. (e) Distinction of bodies in regard to sex and age. (f) Uniformity of methods of extermination of human beings.

We regard the above as proofs of systematic, methodically organized, mass extermination of Soviet civilians and war prisoners.[34]

The defense strategy was to argue that ultimate guilt for the defendants' crimes lay with the Nazi regime and immediate higher-ups. Langheld explained: "I fulfilled the orders of my superiors. Had I not done so I would have been court-martialed."[35] Retzlaff stated: "I plead guilty to all the crimes I have committed upon the orders of my immediate command."[36] The reliance on following superior orders and the defense of duress were, of course, the most-repeated defenses in subsequent trials of Germans and local accomplices by the Allies, both at Nuremberg and thereafter.

On the morning of December 18, 1943, after three days of testimony, prosecutor Dunayev gave his closing argument. While seeking to confirm that the defendants all acted on the superior orders of others, he argued that this should not exculpate defendants from their personal guilt. In so doing, Dunayev utilized an argument that was later to be used in the Nuremberg trials: German law itself rejected the defense of superior orders. The precedent specifically relied on by Dunayev was a result of the trials held in Weimar Germany after the First World War before the German Supreme National Tribunal at Leipzig, where German judges found German military defendants guilty of war crimes.[37]

One of the classic decisions from the Leipzig tribunal is the *Llandovery Castle* case in 1921, in which two German naval submarine officers were convicted of war crimes for shooting survivors in lifeboats after torpedoing the Canadian hospital ship *Llandovery Castle*, despite the fact that their acts of shooting upon the lifeboats was carried out on orders of their submarine captain. Dunayev specifically referred to the case in his closing argument.[38]

Dunayev concluded on an emotional note. After an obligatory nod to "[t]he heroic Red Army, led by the great Stalin," he ended:

> Concluding my speech for the prosecution, I appeal to you, citizen judges, to inflict severe punishment on the three base representatives of fascist Berlin, and on their abominable accomplice, who are sitting in the dock, to punish them for their bloody crimes, for the sufferings and the blood, for the tears, for the lives of our children, of our wives and mothers, of our sisters and brothers!
>
> Today they are answering to the Soviet Court, to our people, to the whole world, for the felonies they committed on a scale and of a baseness

> far surpassing the blackest pages of human history, the horrors of the Middle Ages and of barbarism! Tomorrow their superiors will have to answer—the chieftains of these bandits who invaded our peaceful, happy land on which our people toiled, reared their children, and built our free State. I accuse Retzlaff, Ritz, Langheld, and Bulanov of the crimes specified in Part I of the Decree of the Presidium of the Supreme Soviet of the U.S.S.R., dated 19th April 1943.
>
> In the name of the law and of justice, in the name of tens of thousands of peoples maimed and tortured to death, in the name of the entire people—I, as State Prosecutor, beg you, citizen judges, to sentence all four base criminals to death by hanging.[39]

Defense counsel did not argue with the prosecution's request for a guilty verdict, only that extenuating circumstances called for the defendants' lives to be spared. Defense counsel Kommodov explained: "[T]hese men were made into assassins by, first of all, killing their souls, and it is this doubt which gives me, comrades, judges, the moral right to pose the question of the possibility of a lesser penalty than that demanded by the Prosecutor."[40] His colleague, defense counsel Kaznacheyev, described the crimes as being committed by an army in which "human feelings were considered a weakness, and ruthlessness and fanaticism a virtue."[41] Focusing on defendant Retzlaff, Kaznacheyev argued that because "Retzlaff . . . is now conscious of what he has done and has undergone a psychological transformation, I consider it possible to ask that his life be spared."[42] With regard to Bulanov, the defense argued that he also had repented, and this should be taken into account in the determination of a final sentence.[43]

The four defendants were allowed to make final statements. Langheld stated: "I do not want to minimize my guilt in any way, but I should like to point out that the underlying reasons for all the atrocities and crimes of the Germans in Russia are to be sought in the German Government. . . . The Hitlerite regime has succeeded in stifling the finest feelings of the German people, by implanting base instincts in them."[44] According to Langheld, who argued that he had to follow the evil "orders or directives" of his superiors, like the deceased, "I was also a victim of these orders and directives."[45] Retzlaff repeated the defense of compulsion: "If I had not obeyed these orders, I would have been put in the same position as my victims."[46] Bulanov begged: "I ask one thing of you, citizen judges, that in passing sentence you spare my life so that I may in the future atone for my guilt before the country."[47]

Ritz, the young lawyer, gave the most eloquent speech in an attempt to save his life. Like Langheld, he argued the defense of duress: "I would like to ask the Court to take into consideration an old principle of Roman Law: Crime under duress. You must believe me that if I had not obeyed orders I should have been arraigned before a German military tribunal and sentenced to death."[48] But he then detailed particular circumstances that led him to commit his crimes:

> I beg you, gentlemen of the Court, also to take into consideration the facts of my life. When the Hitlerite system came to power I was a child of only thirteen. From that time on I was subjected to the systematic and methodical influence of the Hitlerite system and education in the spirit of the legend of the superiority of the German race; an education which taught me that only the German people were destined to rule, and that other nations and races were inferior and should be exterminated. I was subjected to systematic training by such teachers as Hitler, [Alfred] Rosenberg, and Himmler, who educated the whole German people in the same spirit.
>
> At the beginning of the war new propaganda came from these same sources, although these were encountered before the war. I have in mind the idea that the Russian people were uncultured and inferior. That is what they taught us. Then, with total mobilization I was sent to the front. When I reached the Eastern Front I was convinced that there was not a word of truth in these fables of Hitler, Rosenberg, and others; that on the Eastern Front the Germans did not have the slightest understanding of any tenets of international law; that there was no justice here in all the actions of the German authorities. But nothing remained to me but to continue along the same path. On the Eastern Front, I was also convinced of another thing, namely that a system on the banner which is inscribed the words "murder and atrocities" cannot be a right system.
>
> I realize that the destruction of this system would be an act of justice. I am young. Life is still only beginning with me. I request you to spare my life so that I may devote myself to the struggle against that system.[49]

The tribunal judges returned with a verdict later that evening. All four defendants were found guilty. The tribunal described the individual guilt of each defendant as follows:

- Wilhelm Langheld . . . personally fabricated a number of cases in which about 100 perfectly innocent Soviet war prisoners and civilians were shot.
- Hans Ritz . . . directed the shootings carried out by the *S.D. Sonderkommando* in Taganrog, and during the examination of prisoners beat them up with ramrods and rubber truncheons, thus trying to extort from them false statements.
- Reinhard Retzlaff . . . tried to extort from them [Soviet civilians] false statements by means of torture—plucking out their hair and torturing them with needles, drew up fictitious reports in the case of 28 arrested Soviet citizens. . . . He personally drove into the "murder van" Soviet citizens doomed to death, accompanied the "murder van" to the place of unloading and took part in the burning of bodies of asphyxiated people.
- Mikhail Petrovich Bulanov, having betrayed the Socialist motherland, voluntarily sided with the enemy, joined the German service as a chauffeur with the Kharkov Gestapo branch, personally took part in the extermination of Soviet citizens by means of the "murder van," drove peaceful Soviet citizens to the place of shooting and took part in the shooting of sixty children.[50]

All four defendants were sentenced to death by hanging, with no right to appeal. As Stevens observes: "The sentence of hanging was read by the chief judge around midnight, in a final blaze of klieg projectors."[51]

The next morning, on December 19, 1943, at 11 a.m., the defendants were publicly hanged in Kharkov City Square. Stevens describes the hanging:

> It was all over in a few moments. The defendants were hoisted into the back of four open trucks and stood on stools. Then the nooses were looped around their necks. There was no blindfolding. During the preliminaries three of the four prisoners had to be propped up. Bulanov had fainted; Ritz and Retsalu [Retzlaff] had turned pasty white; they drooled at the mouths and their knees gave way. Only Langheld, the old soldier, remained stiff as a ramrod throughout, never once flinching. Once the nooses had been adjusted, at a signal the trucks pulled away and the four were left dangling and kicking in mid air.[52]

In 1944, the Soviet Union released a full-length documentary of the trial, which was screened throughout the Soviet Union and also in London and New York. Seven months after the trial, *Life* magazine published a full two-page spread with photos (taken from the documentary film stills) and brief descriptions of the trial and its participants.

The Kharkov Trial's Three Audiences and the Absence of Jews as Victims

The Soviets organized the Kharkov trial for three audiences: (1) their domestic audience, the Soviet populace fighting for their liberation from Germany; (2) their international audience, the U.S.S.R.'s British and American allies with whom they were in a common cause to defeat Nazi Germany; and (3) their enemy, the German military and German political leaders. In this sense, the Kharkov trial was a "show trial," where political considerations led to the creation of the judicial proceedings. Stalin's strategy towards these three audiences each featured different considerations, and the trial was supposed to satisfy all of these.

On the home front, Stalin used the media to publicize the trial and link it to the victories of the Red Army.[53] Not only did the publicity aim to promote a positive image of the Soviet Union, but also a negative image of the enemy to "satisfy popular demand for revenge and to stimulate further hatred of the enemy."[54] The Soviet Union, in the view of American Ambassador Averell W. Harriman, "meant to show Soviet citizens that the government was sincere in its promise to punish the Germans and to lose no time in doing so."[55] The Soviet official daily *Pravda* declared: "The sword of the Red Army and the armies of our Allies are victoriously preceding the sword of justice. . . . The sword will not be sheathed until the leaders of the cursed Fascist band shall answer with their heads for their crimes against humanity."[56] In effect, Stalin wanted to keep Soviet spirits high in order to ensure success in the war effort.

On the international front, Stalin wanted to exhibit the Soviets' determination to track down, and hold responsible, war criminals.[57] Additionally, Stalin may have wanted to ensure that his allies, the British and Americans, would "keep their pledge about bringing 'war criminals' to trial."[58]

Finally, Stalin sought to deter Germans from creating further harm while they were in retreat from Soviet territory. Harriman asserted that the Soviets sought to create a fear of retribution among the German army ranks and the SS as well as to encourage the Soviet resolve "to hold individual Germans responsible for crimes committed by them even though they were acting on direct orders from their superiors."[59] An article in the *Washington Post* posited at the time: "The Kharkov trial is a warning to th[e German nation], a warning not merely to Hitler and his hierarchy, not merely to Himmler and his menagerie of trained brutes, but also to the rank and file in the German army, to the German officer class, to Germans generally that as far as the Allies are concerned guilt will be personal as well as collective."[60]

In reviewing the Kharkov trial proceedings, we observe one glaring omission: the word *evrei* (Jew) is never uttered during the trial nor does it appear in any court document. Rather, the primary murder victims of the German invaders are described in generic terms as "civilian Soviet people," "Soviet citizens," or "peaceful civilians." The initial indictment termed the herding of the Jews of Kharkov into a ghetto as the "forceful resettlement of Soviet citizens"—hiding the fact that only Jews were forced to ghettoize while the rest of the local population were free, for the most part, to go about their daily lives, albeit under German occupation.

Even when different groups are mentioned, the Jews are specifically omitted. In his closing address, Prosecutor Dunayev refers to the extermination campaign fashioned by the Nazi leaders:

> It is a matter of common knowledge that these [atrocities at Kharkov] are no accidental crimes of individual Germans, but a thoroughly considered, well-worked-out programme for the extermination of the Russian, Ukrainian, Byelorussian, and other peoples, that this was a system of annihilation of the population in the temporary occupied districts of the Soviet Union.[61]

In their verdict, the judges found Langheld guilty of "shooting and atrocities against . . . the civilian population." Ritz was also found guilty of "shooting Soviet civilians." Retzlaff and Bulanov "personally drove into the 'murder van' Soviet citizens doomed to death" and "personally took part in the extermination of Soviet citizens by means of the 'murder van,'" respectively, without mentioning that it was Jews who were in those vans. The verdict also completely de-Judaizes the ghettoization of the Jews of Kharkov and the Drobitsky Yar massacre, referring to "Soviet civilians . . . [being] turned out of their houses in the town into barracks in the area of the Kharkov Tractor Factory. Later they were taken away in groups of two to three hundred to a gully in the vicinity and were shot."[62]

In publicizing the Kharkov trial, noted Soviet war correspondent Ilya Ehrenburg tried to correct this glaring omission against his Jewish brethren by writing in his dispatches "explicitly about the Jewish victims and descri[bing] with contempt how German officers spoke without emotion about helpless [Jewish] women and children, as if hoping they could 'emerge dry from the water.'"[63] Robert Chandler explains the Soviet policy of avoiding the mentioning of Jews as specific targets of the Nazi murder process:

> The official Soviet line . . . was that all nationalities had suffered equally under Hitler; the standard retort to those who emphasized the suffering of the Jews was "Do not divide the dead!" Admitting that Jews constituted the overwhelming majority of the dead would have [also] entailed that other Soviet nationalities—and especially Ukrainians—had been accomplices in the genocide; in any case, Stalin was anti-Semitic.[64]

The omission of Jews from the historiography of the Great Patriotic War continues, unfortunately, to the present day. In 2000, more than a half-century after the trial, the Drobitsky Yar Memorial Committee in Kharkov installed a plaque at the entrance of the Kharkov Theater to commemorate the trial. It reads, in Ukrainian:

> *In this building, on 15–18 December, 1943 there took place the first trial in history of war criminals for atrocities they committed against the civilian population of Kharkov and Kharkov region, who, according to verdict of the Military Tribunal of the 4th Ukrainian Front, were sentenced to death by hanging.*

Was the Kharkov Trial Another Typical Stalinist Show Trial?

The show trial is one of the special hallmarks of the Stalin era and of Stalinism. The first Stalinist purge trial of fellow Communist Party members in August 1936 typifies the process by which Soviet courts became instruments of political repression. Sixteen party leaders were charged in organizing a "terrorist" center on behalf of the exiled Leon Trotsky. After their arrest and interrogation, most confessed to the false charges—a common occurrence in such trials. Stalin's instructions to the secret police, the NKVD, for interrogation were as follows: "Mount your prisoner and do not dismount until they have confessed."[65] Defendants were told (falsely) that if they signed a confession, their lives would be spared. Prosecution witnesses were forced to provide false evidence by the same method.

For those trials, as William Chase notes, Stalin was the producer, controlling the show in the courtroom. For the August 1936 trial, Stalin "helped phrase the charges, decided on the slate of defendants, crafted the [false] evidence, and prescribed the sentences. He even dictated [prosecutor Andrei] Vishinsky's emotional speech as the grand finale of the trial and polished its style." [66]

Considering the pedigree of the trial process in Stalin's Soviet Union and when it took place, it is difficult to see the Kharkov trial as anything other than one more Stalinist show trial. The making of a full-length documentary film on the trial and its screenings in Soviet movie theaters adds to this notion. Even the publication in English in 1944 of the proceedings of the Kharkov trial, to be sold in the United States and the U.K., is further proof that the Kharkov trial followed in the tradition of a typical Stalinist show trial.

With regard to Soviet show trials, Susan Arnold notes that there is a gulf difference between Soviet-style show trials and a true war crimes trial: "A real trial involves risk and assuming that risk is a political decision."[67] Why were the Nuremberg trials not show trials? The consensus is that because not all of the defendants were convicted. As noted by David Luban: "The best proof of the fairness of the Nuremberg Tribunal lies in its acquittal of such major figures of the Third Reich as Fritzsche, Papen, and Schacht."[68]

The "show" element of the trial, however, does not necessarily make the trial unfair. Rather, in addition to providing procedural due process, the trial can be used for a didactic purpose. The Eichmann trial was a show trial in that sense also, since Israeli Prime Minister David Ben-Gurion and prosecutor Gideon Hausner aimed to use the trial of Eichmann to teach both young Israelis and the outside world about the

Holocaust. As Lawrence Douglas observes: "The Eichmann trial, even more explicitly than Nuremberg, was staged to teach history and shape collective memory."[69]

Modern-day proceedings before international criminal tribunals, such as the International Criminal Court and the U.N.-created tribunals for the former Yugoslavia and Rwanda, likewise have an important "show" element to them. As Asli Bâli has noted: "Trials that exemplify international standards of accountability for atrocities are for show in the best possible sense: they provide a public forum for local and international audiences that demonstrates that justice is being served and leaders are being held accountable for their crimes."[70] For this reason, Jeremy Peterson asserts: "[T]his does not mean that all show trials are damnable. It also may be true that some show trials are defensible."[71]

The Kharkov trial can be characterized as such a defensible show trial. As Arieh Kochavi observes:

> American correspondents who followed the trial [in Kharkov] and attended the hanging of the convicted men were generally convinced of the guilt of the accused and of genuineness of the Soviets' charges of organized atrocities. They thought that the Russians had been punctilious in their observance of the legal proprieties of the trial and found no evidence of duress. The self-abasing testimony of the accused, the journalists observed, was reminiscent of the purge trials of the mid-1930s. Still, this was largely attributed to the care that had been exercised in selecting those who were placed on trial.[72]

Unlike a paradigmatic "show trial," whose purpose is to stage-manage falsehoods, the defendants on the dock in Kharkov were indeed guilty of the crimes accused. From the perspective of Greg Dawson, whose mother and aunt are the last-known living survivors of the Drobitsky Yar massacre, the Kharkov trial, "[s]ymbolically at least, was the trial of the men who murdered my grandparents and great-grandparents at Drobitsky Yar. . . . If this was a 'show trial,' it was because the victims were showing the perpetrators far more justice than they deserved."[73] Soviet Jewish lawyer Aaron N. Trainin, in the aftermath of the trial, correctly observed that in the Kharkov trial defendants "were tried for the misdeeds which they themselves committed, with their own hands, for the crimes committed by them personally."[74] Justice, therefore, was meted out in Kharkov by the Soviet judges, albeit through the vehicle most familiar to Soviet jurists at the time, the Stalinist show trial.

The Aftermath

At the outset of the Kharkov trial, Ehrenburg wrote the following while sitting in the press box:

> I waited a long time for this hour. I waited for it on the roads to France. . . . I waited for it in the villages of Belarussia, and in the cities of . . . Ukraine. I waited for the hour when these words would be heard: "The trial begins." Today I heard them. The trial commences. On the dock, beside a traitor, three Germans. These are the first. But these are not the last. We will remember the 15th of December—on this day we stopped speaking about a future trial for the criminals. We began to judge them.[75]

Ehrenburg's words did not come to pass. The Kharkov trial was not succeeded by other Soviet public trials of captured Nazis. After Kharkov, Stalin acceded to Churchill's and Roosevelt's request not to conduct any more high-profile prosecutions of captured Germans for fear that the Nazis would do the same to captured Western POWs. The documentary film of the trial was soon taken off Soviet screens.

For the rest of the war, the Soviets returned to their pre-Kharkov trial behavior of trying captured Nazis and collaborators in secret. The only evidence of such trials was their aftermath: the sudden appearance of gallows with dead men hanging from them.

After the war, the Soviet Union once again began publicly trying war criminals. The first postwar public trial took place in 1947, when ten low-ranking captured Germans were tried in the western Russian city of Smolensk. Other similar trials followed. Prusin notes: "As in the Krasnodar and Kharkov cases, the trials were held to pursue political and ideological objectives. The timing of the trials was chosen carefully to correspond with the Nuremberg Military Tribunal."[76] Sporadic trials of Nazis took place in the Soviet Union well into the 1960s. In total, it appears that the Soviets convicted approximately 25,000 German and Austrian Nazis, with most of the trials taking place within a few years after the end of the war.[77]

Additionally, over a million German POWs in the Soviet Union and other parts of Eastern Europe were used as laborers to rebuild the destruction that resulted from the war. Many of these men were not returned to Germany until many years after the war ended.[78] It would not be until 1955 that the last surviving German POWs returned from the U.S.S.R.

Formation of Holocaust Memory in Soviet and Post-Soviet Eras

In the Soviet Union, immediately after the war, discussion of the mass murder of Soviet Jews during German occupation was repressed, as it had been during the war and at the Kharkov trial. According to Zvi Gitelman, "the term 'Holocaust' [was] completely unknown in the Soviet literature. In discussions of the destruction of the Jews, the terms *unichtozhenie* ('annihilation') or *katastrofa* ('catastrophe') [had] been used."[79] Gitelman adds: "It is only recently [as of 1997] that 'Holocaust,' transliterated from English [as *Holocost/ Холокост*]" appears in the public vocabulary.[80]

Gitelman provides a leading rationale behind the official Soviet policy of treating the suffering of all nationalities and ethnic groups in the Soviet Union under German occupation equally, encapsulated in the above-noted Soviet slogan "Do Not Divide the Dead":

> [N]o country in the West lost as many of its non-Jewish citizens in the war against Nazism as did the U.S.S.R., so that the fate of the Jews in France, Holland, Germany, or Belgium stands in sharper contrast to that of their co-nationals or co-religionists than it does in the East. . . . Thus the Soviet Union did treat the issue differently from the way it was treated in most other countries, whether socialist or not, though the Soviet treatment was not uniform . . . the Holocaust was seen as an integral part of a larger phenomenon—the murder of civilians—whether Russians, Ukrainians, Belorussians, Gypsies, or other nationalities. It was said to be a natural consequence of racist fascism. . . . If the Nazis gave the Jews 'special treatment,' the Soviets would not.[81]

With respect to discussion of the Holocaust of Ukrainian Jews, Dawson explains: "It's been said that history is written by the winners, but in the history of the Holocaust it's as though the chapter on Ukraine had been written by Himmler himself. For all practical purposes, the pages are blank."[82] Dawson reflects:

> The slaughter by gunfire in Ukraine should have become Hitler's original sin and Babi Yar—where 34,000 Jews were murdered in two days—the darkest icon of the Shoah. But when the war ended, Stalin abetted Himmler's cover-ups by throwing an Iron Curtain around his crime scene, off limits to writers, journalists, and historians. The only deaths in the Great War to defend the Motherland would be "Russian" deaths. And so, by default, the liberation of Auschwitz and other camps became the defining images of the Holocaust. Hitler's crime in Ukraine began to fade slowly from public view and consciousness till it became what it is today—barely a footnote in popular understanding of the Holocaust.[83]

After the war, some effort was made by Soviet Jews themselves to bring to light the suffering of the Jewish people at the hands of the Germans and local collaborators. In 1946, Soviet Jewish writers Ilya Ehrenberg and Vassily Grossman published the *Black Book* in the United States and other foreign countries. The *Black Book* became the "best source of primary material on the Holocaust in the Soviet Union,"[84] but was banned from publication in the U.S.S.R. because, in the eyes of Soviet officials, it emphasized that "the Germans murdered and plundered Jews only. The reader unwittingly gets the impression that the Germans fought against the U.S.S.R. for the sole purpose of destroying Jews."[85] The volume only made its appearance in Russia and the other former Soviet states in 1993, after the breakup of the Soviet Union.

Despite attempts by Soviet officials to restrict the memory of the atrocities committed against the Jews during the war, Soviet Jews did attempt to commemorate their special suffering. One of the first gatherings to commemorate Holocaust victims took place in Kharkov in January 1945 to mark the anniversary of the Drobitsky Yar massacre. The Drobitsky Yar commemoration was an exception. Public commemoratory gatherings and burials became forbidden, though "appropriate institutions" such as synagogues were able to hold memorial services.

According to Mordecai Altshuler: "[There is] evidence of extensive Jewish activity in the commemoration of Holocaust victims. Jews from various towns participated in these efforts, and religious circles and prominent figures in the Soviet establishment maintained cooperative relations in their joint endeavors."[86] This commemoration continued even when it was forbidden. Unlike in other European nations where commemoration was allowed, Soviet Jews had to make "strenuous efforts" and "maneuver among various Soviet authorities in order to implement, albeit partly and often unsuccessfully, even a few of their plans in this respect."[87]

Finally, in 1991, with the fall of the Soviet Union, discussion of the "Holocaust" and access to the massive Soviet archives were finally allowed. Reference to the victims of the Holocaust as "Jews" in the monument for Babi Yar was made for the first time. The monument had not even been constructed until 1976, well after Yevgenii Yevtushenko's poem "Babi Yar" brought the world's attention to the massacre (its opening words were: "No monument stands over Babi Yar").

We noted above how the plaque installed in 2000 at the Kharkov Theater noting the trial makes no mention of Jews as victims. However, in 2002 a memorial was dedicated in the presence of Ukraine's president, Leonid Kuchma, at Drobitsky Yar. A nine-foot-tall menorah stands beside the highway at Drobitsky Yar: "To one side, a tree-lined road winds to a massive white arch with the years '1941–1942' framed in a circle on the outside and bright blue Stars of David within. Below the arch is a sculpture depicting the tablets of the Ten Commandments. 'Thou Shall Not Kill' [is] engraved in several languages, including Yiddish and Ukrainian."[88]

And in 1996, the Kharkov Holocaust Museum opened in Kharkov. It contains an exhibit devoted to the murder campaign against the Jews and the trial at Kharkov in 1943, including photos, a documentary of the trials, and other archival materials. The museum remains "the only public Holocaust museum in Ukraine."[89]

Prime Minister Pierre Laval meeting with Reich Marshal Hermann Göring. Photo Archive, Yad Vashem.

2

The Trial of Pierre Laval

Criminal Collaborator or Patriot?

Once Germany began its conquest of Europe, the only European countries that could stop the German military onslaught were the other regional military powers: France, Britain, and the Soviet Union. Nazi Germany never succeeded in conquering Britain and the Soviet Union. It conquered France in just thirty-three days.[1] What came afterwards remains one of the most shameful periods in French history.

Approximately 75,000 Jews were deported from French transit camps to their deaths in occupied Poland between 1942 and the end of German occupation, in December 1944. Almost a third of these were French citizens, and over 8,000 were children under thirteen. The roundup of the Jews was conducted by the French police and pursuant to laws enacted by French authorities. It took over forty years for France to finally acknowledge its role in the Holocaust. In 1995, President Jacques Chirac spoke for the first time about France's responsibility for the deportation of Jews: "The folly of the occupiers was seconded by the French, by the French state,"[2] he said.

President Chirac's statement referred not only the ignoble role France played in the Holocaust, but also the larger shame that a large portion of the French population collaborated with the German occupiers.[3] And this collaboration included much of the French political class. One of those was a major political figure in prewar France: Pierre Laval.

Laval was born in 1883 in Châteldon, a small town in the central Auvergne region of France.[4] His early political affiliations were socialist but, as he commented at the end of his life, he was not a doctrinal socialist but more a socialist of the heart. Laval was first elected to the

French National Assembly at age thirty and simultaneously elected as mayor of Aubervilliers, a working-class suburb of Paris. He held this latter position for over twenty years until he was removed from it in 1944 by the provisional French government of Charles de Gaulle. In addition to success as a politician, Laval was a successful lawyer, representing mainly workers and frequently attaining favorable results. Trials would mark both the beginning and the end of his professional life.

Laval's political career witnessed more electoral wins than losses and, as he moved upward in the French governmental structure, he also drifted to the right. In the 1920s, he occupied subcabinet and cabinet positions in various center-right governments, leading to his selection twice as prime minister of France in the 1930s: from January 1931 to February 1932, and then again from June 1935 to February 1936.

As a government minister, Laval had to deal with many of the issues that arose in the last ten years of the French Third Republic. It appears that Laval's views on Germany and on international relations in general were formulated during this period. These came to shape his conduct as a leading figure in the Vichy regime, which followed the military defeat and collapse of France in 1940, the armistice with Nazi Germany, and the end of the Third Republic.

In his prewar tenures as prime minister, Laval's principal concern with Germany–pre-Hitler Germany–dealt with reparations owed by the Weimar Republic to France, France's debt to the United States, and the burden the international economic crisis imposed on these financial obligations. Laval's efforts in this area resulted in a 1931 trip to the United States, when he met President Herbert Hoover and other leading American political figures. All seemed to have been impressed with his practicality and intelligence.[5] The seven months of Laval's tenure as Vichy France's prime minister, four years later, were in an entirely different world—rendering the financial issues he dealt with in 1931 almost inconsequential, if not even quaint.

Hitler had written in 1925 in *Mein Kampf* that France and Germany were intractable enemies. Once he became Germany's chancellor in 1933, his public message changed. In a 1934 speech to the Reichstag, Hitler announced that there was no reason for France and Germany to remain foes. To demonstrate the absence of tensions between Germany and France, Hitler renounced any claim to Alsace and Lorraine and stated that the only issue between the two countries was the status of the Saar, where a plebiscite was to be held to determine whether it would be French or German territory. That plebiscite, held in 1935, resulted in the Saar reverting to Germany, a result that France and the rest of Europe accepted. Unfortunately, Hitler's statements in *Mein Kampf* presented a far more accurate depiction of his objectives than those in the conciliatory speech before the Reichstag.

Laval's approach to Germany also envisaged cooperation between the two continental powers. His underlying philosophy was that France and Germany, as powerful neighbors, would clash on the battlefield every twenty years unless they reached some long-term accommodation. To keep its belligerent neighbor at bay, Laval sought to isolate Germany from other European powers. Clearly, an alliance between Hitler and the United Kingdom was not realistic. Thus Laval tried to work out an alliance between France and Italy. The latter was an especial focus of his foreign policy, an objective complicated both by Italy's colonial ambitions in North Africa, which conflicted with French interests there, and Italy's expansive policies in Abyssinia (Ethiopia), which generally came in conflict with the position of Western liberal democracies. Nevertheless, Laval felt that a union of France and Italy, coupled perhaps with Nationalist Spain, would preclude Germany from implementing any aggressive objectives. Laval saw himself as a friend to Italy and was convinced that he had an almost unique ability to resolve issues with it, an ability that had to lie dormant during the critical years between his tenure as prime minister, which ended in 1936, and the beginning of the Second World War. There was a certain delusional quality to Laval's conception of himself as a unique facilitator of Italian issues.[6] With or without Laval, during this period Italy drifted inexorably into a military alliance with Germany.

The last part of the 1930s saw increased belligerence and expansionism on the part of Germany. The notion that all Germany wanted was to regain the Saar was quickly shown to be nonsense. In addition to defaulting on its post–First World War reparations obligations, Germany also remilitarized the Rhineland in direct defiance of the Versailles Treaty. This was followed by (1) the annexation of Austria in the spring of 1938, (2) the annexation of the Sudeten region of Czechoslovakia in the fall of 1938, and (3) the annexation of all of Bohemia and Moravia in the spring of 1939. All of these military takeovers went unchecked. Following its August 1939 nonaggression pact with the Soviet Union, Germany invaded Poland the following month. France and the United Kingdom now declared war on Germany and the Second World War began.

Germany's Western front remained quiet for several months as its military efforts, with the assistance of the Soviet Union, were directed to the obliteration of Poland. On May 10, 1940, Germany launched its invasion to the west, attacking first the Low Countries (Belgium and the Netherlands) and then France through the Ardennes, bypassing the purportedly impenetrable barrier of the Maginot Line. Five days later, German tank divisions broke through at Sedan and, in that short time, France's military situation completely deteriorated.

The panicked French government, headed by Prime Minister Paul Reynaud, began making cabinet changes and brought on First World War hero Marshal Philippe Pétain as a deputy prime minister. The French military was placed under the leadership of General Maxime Weygand, also a First World War veteran who had seen success in battle. These changes were useless; the German offensive continued and German troops broke through the French lines in early June.

At this point, the Reynaud government had a choice: it could try to reach an agreement with the Germans or flee and carry out resistance from abroad.[7] Laval urged the government to stay, claiming it would be treason to abandon France to a German *Gauleiter* (regional Nazi Party leader). President Albert Lebrun, on the other hand, strongly urged a government-in-exile. Laval's view prevailed.[8] A few days later, Reynaud resigned and Pétain was asked to form a new government. Pétain offered Laval the Justice Ministry portfolio but Laval declined, since he wanted to be foreign minister. This meant that Laval was not part of the new government, which was immediately tasked with ending hostilities before France was completely crushed militarily.[9]

France received Germany's armistice terms on June 21. If France agreed to the terms, Germany would occupy two-thirds of the country, including the entire Atlantic and English Channel coasts, and France would bear the cost of the occupation. The French military would be reduced to a police force of one hundred thousand, and its weapons and equipment would be made available to Germany. The French naval fleet would be disarmed, except as necessary to protect the colonies, but would remain under French control. Germany would not use the fleet for its military objectives. The French colonial empire would be left intact, and a new and emasculated French government would administer both the occupied and unoccupied zones of France. France would also be obliged to hand over Germans living in France to the Germans; these were essentially German Jews and political opponents who had fled Hitler's Germany for what they had thought was the safe haven of the French Republic.

France signed the armistice agreement on June 22.[10] The following day, Laval was appointed minister of state and several days later, he was made deputy prime minister.[11] Since Paris was in the zone occupied by the Germans, the new French government had to locate elsewhere. It selected the spa town of Vichy, located centrally in France, but in the northern section of the unoccupied zone. The new government then became known as the Vichy government or regime.

The criminal trial against Laval at the end of the war related to his conduct as a minister in the Vichy government. Laval was part of the Vichy government twice: first from June 1940 to December 1940, and then again from April 1942 until the war's end. The following pages focus on Laval's conduct during these two stages, which formed the core of the charges against him. Such conduct was, of course, but a small fraction of what Laval did over the almost three-year period covered by his position of power in the Vichy regime.

Laval as Deputy Minister: June to December 1940

As deputy prime minister, Laval had two primary objectives. The first was to create a governmental structure that differed from that of the just-defeated Third Republic. Convinced that the many changes in government and its leftist tinge had weakened the French state, Laval favored a more authoritarian and right-wing form of government. Second, his long-standing view that Germany and France had to reconcile was now made even more urgent by France's military defeat at the hands of Nazi Germany. In Laval's view, this latest round of European warfare would end in Germany winning the war, including the conquest of England. Moreover, as others mistakenly believed at the time, Laval felt that Hitler could be worked with and perhaps even managed.[12]

The first objective of substituting a more authoritarian form of government for the existing Third Republic did not take long to implement. Pétain shared Laval's notion that the democracy of the Third Republic weakened France and that a stronger, more authoritarian form of government was desirable. On July 10, 1940, Pétain and Laval prevailed upon the French National Assembly to vote itself out of existence, which it did by a vote of 569 to 80. This formally ended the Third Republic. Pétain now launched the *Révolution nationale,* an authoritarian regime aimed at restoring France.[13]

In October, Laval was in Paris when informed by the German ambassador to Vichy France, Otto Abetz, with whom Laval had established a close relationship, that he would soon be meeting the German foreign minister, Joachim Ribbentrop. The meeting turned out to include Hitler as well, who said he would like to meet with Pétain. On October 24, 1940, Hitler, Ribbentrop, Pétain, and Laval met at Montoire, a Parisian suburb. "Montoire," as it was to be known, was more significant for its symbolism than for any concrete results. The German leaders had hoped that France would declare war against England, but Pétain, who still had a semblance of authority, did not accede to the request. Pétain and Laval did agree that France would fight the British to retain control over French colonies.

Shortly after the conference, Pétain made an infamous radio address to the French people in which he announced that he had experienced no pressure from Hitler but that "a collaboration was envisaged between our two countries." Collaboration was undertaken, according to Pétain, to preserve French unity and French sovereignty.[14]

Prior to Montoire, Laval had insisted that the French foreign minister, Paul Baudouin, not attend the meeting. This caused Baudouin to resign. Laval was then named foreign minister, a position from which he could effectuate the goal of cooperation with Germany.[15] Laval was able to quickly resolve two separate issues of importance to Germany. The first related to Belgian gold reserves that had been given to the Bank of France for safekeeping after Germany's occupation of Belgium. Just before the fall of France, these gold reserves were transferred to French West Africa to keep them out of German control. Germany now wanted to ensure that these gold reserves not fall into British hands. Initially, they were to be returned to the Belgian National Bank, and the

Germans insisted that, as an occupying power, they stood in the shoes of the Belgian National Bank. Laval assented to this position.[16]

A second issue after Montoire, again indicating French cooperation with Germany's war effort, involved the French-owned Bor copper mines in Yugoslavia. Because of the need for copper in the production of war materiel, the Germans wanted to purchase these mines. Prior to Montoire, the French government rebuffed these requests. After Montoire, Laval instructed the directors of the French company to sell the Bor mines to the Germans. The sale took place and ownership was placed in German hands.[17]

Laval's first tenure with the Vichy regime was to be of short duration. On December 13, 1940, Pétain asked for the resignation of all his ministers, which he received. He then announced that he accepted the resignations of Laval and one other minister. Why Pétain sacked Laval has been the subject of much speculation over the years. Geoffrey Warner, in his political biography of Laval, concludes it was a personality clash between the military approach of Pétain and the more casual, parliamentary approach of Laval.[18] Pétain liked decision-making along clear lines of authority; Laval tended to make decisions without "going through channels." A more mundane explanation is that Pétain was tired of Laval blowing smoke in his face, something that Laval quite literally is supposed to have done.[19] Whatever the reason, Laval's first association with the Vichy regime ended, and he was to proceed into oblivion for the next sixteen months.[20]

Laval as Prime Minister: April 1942 to April 1944

By April 1942, the nature of the Second World War had changed. Following Japan's attack on Pearl Harbor in December 1941, the United States entered the war. Events on the Soviet front, however, were more likely of concern to Germany. Contrary to the expectations of Hitler and his generals, the invasion of the Soviet Union in June 1941 did not lead to a quick victory. Even though the German military was still on the offensive on its eastern front, the war now promised to be lengthier and more demanding than Hitler and the German military had anticipated. This led to Germany expecting more from France, its vassal ally. Playing on his background as someone who could deal with Germany,

Laval began to orchestrate his return to power by suggesting that only he could finesse the tension between France's independence and its cooperation with Germany.[21]

At this time, the United States still maintained diplomatic relations with the Vichy government. When American diplomats learned of Laval's possible return, they made clear that this move would lead to the rupture of such relations.[22] Once Hitler was informed of American pressure against Laval's return, he "issued an ultimatum of his own to the effect that he would judge France's willingness to collaborate with Germany by the presence or absence of Laval in the French Government."[23] This made Laval's return inevitable.

On April 15, 1942, a new government was formed. Laval was to hold several ministries, including the Foreign Affairs Ministry. Laval was also designated as "head of the government," responsible only to Pétain, now the figurehead head of state.[24] In effect, Laval now ruled Vichy France, with the acquiescence and support of his German overlords.

In one critical sense, cooperation with Germany was more important to Laval in 1942 than it had been in 1940. Two years earlier, it was simply a matter of attempting to ameliorate the harshness of the German occupation and retaining whatever was left of French sovereignty. Now Germany was fighting the Soviet Union, and to Laval this made all the difference. Laval viewed the spread of Soviet communism as a greater threat to France than Germany's National Socialism. Laval was convinced that Germany's defeat at the hands of the Soviets would result in Soviet expansion to the Rhine, leaving France at the mercy of the Soviet Union. As Laval saw it, Germany's interests and France's objectives were now the same: the defeat of the communist Soviet Union.[25]

Thus, Laval's oft-quoted radio statement to the French people, made during his second tenure with the Vichy government: "*je veux la victoire de l'Allemagne*" ("I wish for a German victory"). [26] The statement certainly proved damaging to Laval at his trial in 1945. However, as he saw it, this sentiment made him a French patriot who was acting in his country's best interests.

As of April 1942 no major turning points had been reached in the war. The German army on the Russian front was still on the offensive and a major German victory at Tobruk in North Africa was a month or two in the future. Britain had staved off an invasion by retaining control of the skies over the English Channel, but it surely posed no threat to Germany. The United States was engaged in a full-fledged retreat in the Pacific and its major Pacific naval victories were still months away. But it was to be a long war and the war's duration required virtually complete conscription in Germany, which in turn left its home-based industrial machine understaffed.

Recognizing the need for foreign laborers, Hitler appointed Fritz Sauckel as special labor czar in March 1942. Some of the shortages were to be filled by bringing forced laborers from the East, primarily Slavs, to Germany. But France was not immune. Sauckel set an immediate goal of three hundred thousand workers from both the occupied and unoccupied zones of France to be recruited in the month following May 15, 1942.[27] Laval, however, wanted a *quid quo pro,* in part because the program had to be sold to the French public. The over one million French soldiers who remained POWs since their capture by the Germans in 1940 were of great concern to Laval and the French nation.[28] Laval originally proposed that for every worker sent to Germany, one of these French POWs would be released and returned to France. The Germans refused. Finally, it was agreed that for every three French workers sent to Germany, one prisoner from a farm family would be allowed to return home.[29]

Laval announced this agreement on the radio on June 22, 1942. In his address, he told the French people that his first concern on returning to power was the return of these captured French soldiers. The worker-for-prisoner exchange program, called the *Relève* program, would serve two purposes. First, it would bring POWs back to their families. Second, it would make a significant contribution to end the war. As Laval saw it, France could not remain "indifferent in the face of the huge sacrifices Germany is making to construct a Europe in which we must take our place."[30] In his effort to sell the *Relève* program to the French public, Laval stated in this radio address that he wished for a German victory, insisting that this would give him latitude to obtain future concessions from Germany.[31]

Germany had multiple war objectives. One was to defeat the Allied powers and establish hegemony over Europe. Another related to the extermination of European Jewry, a policy formally implemented in July 1941 when the initial German military successes in the Soviet

Union made clear that the vast majority of Europe's Jews would now be living in places under German occupation.[32]

France first implemented an anti-Jewish policy in the early months of the Vichy regime with the repeal of the "Marchand Law" in August 1940. That statute prohibited the French press from attacking any particular group on grounds of race or religion when the purpose of the attack was to arouse hatred.[33]

Two months later, in October 1940, the *Statut des juifs* was passed—though Laval opposed it. This statute excluded Jews from top positions in the civil service and certain other high-ranking professions. There followed a series of laws permitting the confinement of foreign Jews and a statute stripping Algerian Jews of French citizenship. Postwar inquiry into the passage of these statutes reveals little German pressure towards their enactment; they appear to have been totally French-inspired initiatives.[34]

While there were notorious anti-Semites in France, Laval does not appear to have been one of them.[35] Nevertheless, when it came to implementing the German plan to murder all of European Jewry, Laval participated to a degree; the degree was defined by the difference between Jews in France who were French citizens and those who were refugees from Germany or German-occupied territories. In June 1942, Heinrich Himmler, the head of the SS, announced that all Jews in France were to be deported. Laval became aware of the announcement a month later.[36] By the end of the summer, twenty-seven thousand Jews, mostly foreign Jews, had been deported. Laval was not reluctant to have the French police assist in the round-ups that preceded deportation. When the Catholic Church protested the arrest of foreign Jews, Laval made clear to Otto Abetz, the German ambassador, that he would use the local police to drag Jews out of any church or religious building in which they were given shelter. Indeed, Laval indicated that he was glad for the opportunity to get rid of the foreign Jews, as they had always been a problem in France.

As Germany's military successes became fewer, the intensity of its efforts to murder Jews increased. Laval was somewhat successful in preventing the deportation of Jews who were French citizens when the Germans asked for legislation depriving Jews of citizenship, or at least voiding any citizenship granted as of 1927. Laval actually refused to assent to such legislation.[37] The end result was that of the three hundred thousand Jews in France, about a quarter were sent to Poland, where most were gassed immediately. About a quarter of the seventy-five thousand Jews were French citizens.[38] Therefore, it is safe to say that Laval clearly assisted in the process by which a large number of Jews were killed. His policies, however, undoubtedly also saved a large number of Jews.[39] Laval himself linked the two: "[E]very time a foreign Jew leaves our territory, it's one more gained for France's."[40] Thus, Germany's efforts to eradicate Jewry from the face of Europe received some, but by no means complete, assistance from Laval.

Arrest, Flight, and Prelude to Trial

By mid-1944, the tide turned clearly against Germany. As a consequence, the powers of the Pétain regime and its ability to maneuver vis-à-vis the Germans continued to erode. On August 17, 1944, Laval was in Paris with Abetz, when Abetz, implementing a directive from German Foreign Minister Ribbentrop that the seat of the Vichy government was to be transferred from Vichy to Belfort in eastern France, told Laval he had no discretion on the question. When Laval responded that he would not assent to the transfer, Abetz then had him arrested and transferred to Belfort where, along with Pétain, he was held in custody.[41]

Perhaps Laval's last official act was to turn down a request that he and others meet with Hitler. He indicated that, as a person in custody, he could not negotiate on behalf of France, and that for him to do so would jeopardize his future political career.[42] In the meantime, the Allies were quickly advancing eastward across France. After about a month in Belfort, Laval and others were transferred to a castle in Germany where they remained until the following spring. With the complete collapse of German authority in April 1945, Laval was momentarily free. He flew to Spain, hoping that his earlier support of the Nationalists would convince Francisco Franco, Spain's dictator, to grant him asylum. Franco, sensing the direction in which the war was heading, refused and gave Laval a choice of going to either Ireland or Portugal, both neutral countries. Laval declined and remained in custody in Spain, probably in the hope that Franco would have a change of heart.[43] It was not to be.

General Charles de Gaulle had by then established a government in France. De Gaulle's desire to arrest Laval was communicated to American and British officials, who in turn made it known to Franco. Franco, not inclined to defy the victorious Allies, assented. Consequently, on July 31, Laval was flown to Linz, in the American zone of Austria; he was immediately transferred to a different plane and taken to Innsbruck, where the French authorities arrested him.[44]

On August 1, 1945, Laval was flown to Paris and detained at the Fresnes prison facility. The following seventy-five days were to be full and decisive for Laval. He began by testifying as a defense witness in the trial against Pétain, appearing on the stand within two days of his arrival in France.

Once Paris had been liberated on August 25, 1944, General de Gaulle's government wasted no time in dealing with persons seen as having betrayed France by cooperating with the Germans. It became essential to create a formal mechanism for dealing with "collaborators." The most pressing reason was that vigilante justice was rampant. It is not clear how many persons were killed as collaborators between the successful Allied landing at Normandy on June 6, 1944, and the complete withdrawal of German forces from France several months later. The figures range from as low as nine thousand persons to one hundred thousand.[45] Because the regular courts were slow and heavily laden with judges who functioned during the Vichy regime, an ordinance of November 18, 1944, established special courts to try collaborators: a High Court of Justice for cabinet ministers and a Court of Justice for others. Magistrates for these purge courts were picked from among the less compromised members of the French judiciary. This selection method was driven by the embarrassing fact that only one French magistrate had refused to swear an oath of allegiance to Marshal Pétain.[46] Hundreds of thousands of persons were processed through these courts, and about fifteen hundred executed. Many of the imprisoned received amnesty once the immediate ardor of the postwar period cooled in the early 1950s.[47]

The charges against Pétain, drawn under the same provisions of the penal code that were later applied to Laval, alleged that he acted against the interests of France in creating a form of government similar to the Franco dictatorship in Spain (Article 87) and that he collaborated with the enemy (Article 75).[48] The presiding judge and prosecutor were the same as in the Laval trial and the jury was drawn from two lists: one was comprised of members of the National Assembly who had not voted to end the Third Republic, and the second consisted of names provided by various Resistance networks. Under the French legal system, three judges and a jury deliberate jointly and the verdict is a composite of their votes.

Pétain's trial began on July 23, 1945. As a defense witness, Laval testified that Pétain never desired to set up a dictatorship. Pétain's very able lawyers cross-examined prosecution witnesses and delivered a stirring closing argument, urging that as peace spread throughout Europe at last, France should not bruise itself further by condemning its own. Pétain himself ended the proceeding by saying: "Dispose of me according to your consciences. Mine does not reproach me because during a long life and having arrived by age [he was eighty-nine] at the threshold of death, I affirm that I had no ambition other than to serve France." On August 15, 1945, Pétain was found guilty and sentenced to death. General de Gaulle, however, commuted his sentence to life imprisonment. Pétain was to remain in prison until his death of natural causes in 1951, at the age of ninety-five.[49]

Before turning to the trial against Laval, we briefly set out the basics of the French criminal process. Understanding this process is essential to appreciate how it was ignored in Laval's case. The French system is a two-stage procedure that relies heavily on the judiciary.[50] During the initial investigatory stage, an investigating magistrate collects all relevant evidence, both inculpatory and exculpatory, and then decides whether a prosecution should go forward and a trial take place. In Laval's case, the investigative stage began within three weeks of his testimony in Pétain's trial. The investigative stage is central to the criminal process since it defines the crimes that may be considered at trial. Given its importance and given the complexity of the case against Laval, it is not surprising that on August 21, 1945, his lawyers were promised that the preliminary stage would be lengthy, involving perhaps twenty-five sessions that would take them well into November.[51] Had that procedure been followed, Laval would have been given pertinent documents and participated at length in presenting his defense. Whatever charges were then recommended would be tried by a court with a jury. Laval would be questioned by the court and the prosecution and allowed to call witnesses in his defense. This would be followed by the French equivalent of closing arguments. The process that was promised never materialized.

Early on in the preliminary phase, Laval's lawyers learned through the press that the first stage would be terminated after just five sessions. Several more sessions were quickly arranged, but they were brief and largely ineffective. Laval had a right to review prosecution documents so that he could present a complete defense. When he asked for those documents, Laval was told that the examining magistrate had them in his locked files and was away on vacation. Around the same time, the president of the High Court announced that the trial had to be over by the time of the general elections in France, scheduled for October 21, 1945.[52] The law required that there be more potential jurors than the number ultimately selected, to give the accused an ability to challenge jurors. When the trial began, however, the number of jurors called was exactly the number required, precluding the ability to strike objectionable jurors.[53]

Laval was charged with violations of articles 87 and 75 of the French Penal Code, plotting against the security of the state and collaboration with the enemy (the French term is "*intelligence*").[54] Both the presiding judge in the trial, Pierre Mongibeaux, and the prosecutor, Andrei Mornet, had been active in the judicial process during the Vichy period but, as has been noted, it was impossible to staff a judicial proceeding immediately after liberation without recourse to such jurists. The lawyers assigned to represent Laval, senior counsel Albert Naud and Jacques Baraduc and junior counsel Yves Jaffre, were excellent lawyers. However, given the irregularity of the procedures, they were unable to properly defend their client. The defense lawyers were not given access to key documents, and because the preliminary phase had been completed in such a hurried fashion, they were unable to fully confer with Laval to prepare both him and themselves for trial. The time sequence, with preliminary investigation beginning in late September and trial scheduled for early October, to end before October 21, was just too compressed. Nevertheless, the trial began on October 4, 1945.[55]

As a lawyer with extensive criminal defense experience, Laval was to be active in his own defense. His lawyers, however, felt there was little they could do because of the hurried and aberrational nature of the legal process. The transcript does not reveal any participation by these lawyers from the inception of the first day of trial until its tumultuous adjournment later in the day. The frustration of Laval's lawyers was demonstrated at the opening of the proceedings when the presiding judge read a letter from the lawyers in which they asked to be relieved from the responsibility of representing Laval because of the premature termination of the preliminary stage. In their letter, the lawyers also expressed their concern that the haste which characterized the proceedings was driven not by judicial considerations but politics.[56] The court denied their request. It mattered little, however, since the lawyers were not even present to hear the ruling.

After the charges were read, including a reference to the deportation of Jews, Laval stated that he wished to be judged by the Jews of France. According to Laval, French Jews knew that he saved them.[57] In defending himself against the charge that the termination of the Third Republic constituted plotting against the security of the state, Laval observed that 569 out of 649 deputies voted to end the Third Republic and provisionally substitute the more authoritarian form represented by the Vichy regime.[58] When Laval mentioned that France was now free, a juror shot back: "No thanks to you." This reaction was perhaps an omen of things to come.[59]

It was around this point that events became even more heated. Laval kept complaining that his right to counsel had been denied by the irregularity of the proceedings and their rushed nature. The court responded that it had appointed lawyers to represent Laval and the fault lay with them, since they chose not to involve themselves in his defense.[60] The transparency of this comment, oblivious as it was to the abandonment of procedural norms in the case, seemed to bring Laval to a boil. He then told the court to condemn him right away. Taking this as an insult to the supposed impartiality of the tribunal, the presiding judge instructed the guards to take Laval away.[61] A spectator apparently made a comment supporting Laval, at which point a juror shouted that the spectator should be arrested. Either another or the same juror then shouted: "he [the spectator] deserves 12 bullets in his hide, like Laval."[62] On this foreboding note, the first day's proceedings ended.[63]

It should be clear that regardless of whether Laval was guilty as charged, the proceedings were seriously flawed. The preliminary examination, an integral part of the French criminal process, had been prematurely and unjustifiably terminated. Defense counsel, though able, was thwarted from participating on behalf of Laval because of the truncated nature of the proceedings and the inaccessibility of key documents. The stated determination to finish the trial before the national elections scheduled for October 21 made it impossible for both the charges and Laval's defense to be thoroughly aired, since each would have entailed a detailed and close examination of the Vichy regime. Finally, it was perfectly clear from the comments of the jurors, whose selection was flawed to begin with, that they did not have an open mind and that their expressions to that effect went unnoted by the court.[64]

When the trial resumed the next day, Laval's lawyers again asked to be relieved from representing him. They specifically pointed to the broken promise that the investigatory stage would take place over at least twenty-five sessions. In light of the stated need to end the trial before the elections, then just two weeks away, they felt there was not nearly enough time to present a defense that touched on all facets of France's complex history during the Second World War. Raising the bar, they asked that Laval be given at least the same rights as the "monsters" of the Bergen-Belsen concentration camp, being tried at the same time by the British in occupied Germany[65]

Mornet, the prosecutor, responded that the case was not complex. Rather, it was based almost entirely on documents, specifically Laval's speeches or other public statements that were not disputed and which made France the accomplice of its aggressor and dishonored it in the eyes of the world.[66] The court then took a recess. On its return, the court announced that it did not have the power to reopen the preliminary investigation. The trial would proceed. Laval could raise whatever defenses he felt were appropriate during the course of the trial.[67]

The trial continued with Laval representing himself, with his roles as witness and advocate constantly shifting. The prosecution focused on his involvement in the transport of thousands of French men to work in Germany, a major component of the collaboration charge. Laval had repeatedly justified his involvement by noting that he arranged for the release of French prisoners of war in exchange for sending workers to Germany. In a rejoinder, the prosecution alluded to evidence that Laval said that most French prisoners would have to wait until the end of the war to be released.[68] Agreeing that he signed documents that directed workers to Germany, Laval urged it was important to know why he signed such documents and then restated the moot point that this type of investigation should have been done during the preliminary stage.[69] In a concession to Laval, the court noted that the charge was not that he was complicit in the creation of the new form of government—the National Assembly had voted overwhelmingly in favor of it—rather, he was liable for abuses that occurred under the new form of government.[70]

Laval spent much of the balance of the October 5 session going into extraordinary depth and detail with regard to the history of his leadership. One of his lawyers, present, though not participating in the proceedings, commented that "Laval finished up by being terribly verbose and boring. His interminable expositions on the birth of the Vichy regime were listened to by an icy jury, upon whom no argument seemed to have any effect. . . . [The] hearing which had begun in a high state of excitement ended in somnolence."[71] Of course, this is precisely why ordinarily an accused should not represent himself. It is difficult to remain objective and perceive events through eyes and ears other than one's own if one is also the litigant in the case, with a direct and powerful stake in its outcome.

The following day, October 6, began tranquilly enough. Laval read into evidence correspondence relating to his efforts at having a full preliminary examination and a lengthier trial.[72] His reiteration of a lost issue seemed to have raised the emotions of everyone in court again. The prosecutor asked about the enactment of laws under the Vichy regime that Laval had signed. Laval replied that the prosecutor had applied these laws without objection at the time. The court then rushed to the defense of the prosecutor by warning Laval of the serious consequences of contempt.[73] A dispute then arose when Laval, with his "non-participating" lawyers, added they had been deprived of documents. The prosecutor responded that everything they needed to know was in the indictment. The court then asked several questions, and at one point interrupted Laval's answer by observing that France knew all about what he had done over the four years of the Vichy regime.[74] Laval observed that the court asked the questions and at the same time answered them.[75] Several jurors then shouted that "justice would be done,"[76] and "French justice"[77]—whereupon Laval said he would not answer any further questions. As he did on the trial's first day, the presiding judge directed the guards to remove Laval from the courtroom. Jurors then shouted out "instigator," "a bastard," "twelve bullets," and "he will never change."[78] Laval remarked that this was extraordinary.[79] The wild scene ended with the disturbingly accurate statement by a juror that Laval had already been judged and France had judged him as well.[80]

When the trial resumed later in the afternoon, Mongibeaux, the presiding judge, announced that the court had completed the first phase of the case relating to the charge of plotting against the state. It now turned to the second charge: collaboration with the enemy.[81] This was remarkable since no witnesses had yet been called by the prosecution; the entire process had been a dialogue with Laval resulting in a narrowing of the charge, so as not to include the actual creation of the Vichy regime. Laval responded that in light of the way the court had questioned him and the reactions of some of the jurors, he felt he might be the victim of a judicial crime and, therefore, he would remain silent, not wishing to be an accomplice to the process.[82] The court then directed Mornet to call the first prosecution witness. When Mornet said he had none, Mongibeaux adjourned the proceedings for the day.[83] When the trial resumed the next day, Laval was not present.

The first witness called by the prosecution on the following day was Albert Lebrun, the last president of the Third Republic. Lebrun testified as to Laval's part in the transition from the Third Republic to the Vichy regime. This was odd since the court had previously indicated that Laval's part in the transition would not be part of the charge, but only what he had done afterwards. Lebrun testified it was his view that after the collapse of the French army, it would have been better to have a government-in-exile than a French government that would only be endorsing the policies of the occupier.[84] This was juxtaposed with Laval's view that to leave France was treasonous.[85] Lebrun's testimony ended with a less than ringing endorsement of the prosecution's position. When asked whether the creation of the new government was an abuse of power, Lebrun answered, "If you say so."[86]

The next witness was General Paul André Doyen, director of the French Armistice Commission that formally ended hostilities between Nazi Germany and France in 1940. His testimony was emphatic: Laval's policy of collaboration in 1940 helped Germany in its fight against

England and its allies, and constituted a political crime that dismembered and destroyed France.[87] Laval's rebuttal to this evidence came at the end of the proceeding when he pointed out in a written submission that Doyen had not resigned from the chairmanship of the Armistice Commission until June 1941. Laval then asked how Doyen could have participated so long in a policy he condemned so harshly in his testimony.[88]

Following General Doyen, the prosecution called Henri de Lapommeraye, a former secretary of the dissolved French Senate, who testified that in the fall of 1940, Laval, referring to the new regime, said that "this is how one reverses the Republic."[89] De Lapommeraye, however, did not give Mornet everything he wanted. He described conversations during the same period in which Laval said that France was beaten like never before, England would be brought to her knees in six weeks, and to avoid more brutal treatment, it would be necessary to adapt to German institutions.[90] When the prosecutor asked Mornet whether Laval used the term "national socialism," the witness responded emphatically: "No, Mr. Laval never used that term in front of me."[91]

The prosecution then called Maurice Beauchamp, secretary-general to the National Federation of Deported Workers. He represented 400,000 of the 750,000 workers drafted for work in Germany, including 50,000 who had not returned and were presumed dead. Beauchamp described the brutal conditions French workers faced in Germany: they were underfed, underclothed, and exposed to Allied bombardment. Mornet placed into evidence circulars Beauchamp brought with him soliciting workers for work in Germany, signed by Laval.[92] Upon completion of Beauchamp's brief testimony, the prosecution once again ran out of witnesses. It then read a deposition into evidence, resulting in the gradual withdrawal of the spectators.[93]

The prosecution continued its case by reading into evidence questions put to Laval during the investigative stage and his answers. Laval had responded to most of the questions by deferring his answer to what he thought would be a later stage in the proceeding, which, of course, never came. Nevertheless, by placing into evidence even these truncated exchanges, the prosecution put some of Laval's more inflammatory statements made during the war before the court. Given Laval's failure to deny the facts explicit in the questions, this process had some evidentiary value.

1. Why was he on list of possible ministers for Pétain? Because he had been in many ministries before and had been Prime Minister several times.[94]
2. Wasn't the creation of the new government with extraordinary powers delegated to Pétain an abuse of power? Deferred answer.[95]
3. Did he stop France from instituting a real government abroad by intrigue and threats? Deferred answer.[96]
4. Explain his discharge from the cabinet and subsequent arrest after the meeting with Hitler at Montoire and why he was known as "the Germans' man." Deferred answer.[97]
5. Why did he return to the government in 1942 after his humiliating dismissal in 1940? Deferred answer, except to note that he wasn't humiliated, only those who squeezed him out were.[98]
6. Why did Marshal Pétain send a telegram to the Germans congratulating them on their success in repelling a British raid at Dieppe in August 1942? Answer: He (Laval) had nothing to do with telegram.[99]
7. In the summer of 1942, in an infamous radio address, Laval had said he wished for a German victory.[100] Why did he say that, especially since the United States had joined the war at that point, allied with England, and with the Soviet Union also fighting against Germany? Did he really think Germany would win as he wished? Deferred answer.[101]
8. Later in 1942, did he not say that Germany would win the war, that England had stolen colonies from France, and that the real menace was Bolshevism, and it should not come wrapped in the fur of England and the United States to destroy French civilization? Deferred answer.[102]
9. In a December 1942, press conference, had he not said that France had to choose sides without equivocation and that he wanted the victory of Germany[103] and not that of Bolshevism; and that Roosevelt carried in his baggage the double triumph of the Jews and communists and he must break them at all costs? Deferred answer.[104]
10. Had he not thanked the French volunteers on the German side of the eastern front for fighting with Germany against the Soviet Union in the interests of France, their sacrifices complementing the efforts of the many French citizens working in Germany? Deferred answer.[105]
11. Had he not threatened doctors who provided false certificates to persons facing the draft to work in Germany and also threatened their parents? Deferred answer.[106]

12. Had he not placed the French police at the service of the Gestapo in the arrest of 25,000 Jews in Paris, the nights of July 15 and 16, 1943? Deferred answer.[107]

In elaborating on his deferrals in the interrogatories, Laval added that had he not used the words attributed to him, he would not have been able to resist certain German demands, and, as a result, his actions benefited France.[108] The reading into evidence of Laval's answers to the interrogatories consumed the balance of the October 8 session. The next-to-last interrogatory asked him to explain why he had signed a law on December 12, 1942, requiring Jews, both French nationals and others, to carry cards identifying themselves as Jews. Laval's response was that he had been questioned since 9:00 a.m. with a three-hour break; it was now 5:45 p.m. and he was tired. He again noted his astonishment that the preliminary phase of the case was brusquely closed and demanded that it be continued so that he could defend himself, a right given to all accused. The question posed to him went unanswered.[109]

On October 9, the last day of the trial, the prosecution called Leon Noel, the French ambassador to Poland from 1935 to 1939. Noel noted that his early statements in opposition to the Vichy regime had prematurely ended his diplomatic carrier. In Laval's favor, he noted that Laval had helped Noel secure the freedom of a friend who had been a member of the Resistance and was under arrest. Noel then took a principled position, which precluded any assistance to the prosecution. Since Laval was not present to listen to Noel's testimony, ask him questions, or offer rebuttal, Noel stated he could not in good conscience continue to testify and asked to be excused. The court granted his request.[110]

The case then proceeded to closing arguments, or more accurately, to one closing argument, since Laval and his lawyers were not present. The prosecutor summarized the evidence and asked for the death penalty.[111] Laval, for his part, had submitted a three-and-a-half-page statement, dealing largely with the credibility of prosecution witnesses. The document did not even closely resemble a closing argument. The court then recessed.

The court resumed later in the day. After noting the charges,[112] the court found Laval guilty on both charges, sentenced him to death, and directed that his property be confiscated.

Three days later, on October 12, Laval's three lawyers met with General de Gaulle. They did not ask for a commutation of the death sentence, but rather for a new trial. Defense counsel Albert Naud pointed out that, as a member of the Resistance, he had absolutely nothing in common with Laval. Nevertheless, Naud argued that the trial was conducted in a scandalous fashion and that the execution of a former prime minister after such a trial would be disgraceful and set a dangerous precedent. The three defense lawyers also provided details as to the deficiencies of the trial.

Earlier, Paul-Henri Teitgen, minister of justice in the de Gaulle cabinet, agreed with the defense lawyers on the indefensible nature of the proceedings. However, when later consulted by de Gaulle, Teitgen said that events which took place during the trial were regrettable but that Laval had provoked them.[113]

Unbeknownst to Laval's lawyers, de Gaulle was comparably duplicitous. While he clearly suggested to the defense lawyers that he had not decided what to do prior to the meeting with them, he had already made clear to his fellow ministers that there would not be a new trial. Predictably, the defense request for a new trial was denied.[114]

Three days later, on October 15, Laval faced a firing squad. Even the moment of Laval's death could not pass without high drama. Immediately before his execution, Laval tried to kill himself by taking a cyanide capsule, which he had secreted in his clothes. However, the age of the poison had eroded its effectiveness. Laval was brought before a firing squad still suffering from the nonlethal effects of the poison, revived, and then shot and killed.[115]

In his prison cell, he left the following note: "For my advocates—for their information: to my executioners—for their shame. I refuse to be killed by French bullets. I will not make French soldiers accomplices in a judicial murder. I have chosen my death—the poison of the Romans, which I have carried with me through my long wanderings and which has escaped the searchings of my guards. I wish to be buried with the Tricolor scarf round my neck. I die because I loved my country too much. My last thought is for France."[116]

Was Justice Served?

The narrowly drawn jury pool, the aborted preliminary examination, the hurried nature of the trial itself circumscribed by the arbitrary date of the pending election, the unchecked demonstrations not just of jury bias, but also of court bias, make it impossible to conclude that Laval received fair treatment. The question remains, did the French authorities execute a guilty man or an innocent man?

The charge of plotting against the security of the state (Article 87) seems most problematic. An axiomatic notion in criminal law is that before there can be a crime, there has to be notice that the complained-of conduct is unlawful. The unique situation that France found itself in after its ignoble military defeat at the hands of the Germans makes it difficult to conclude that the actions Laval took amounted to plotting against the security of the French state. Was it in the best interest of the state at that time to avoid a complete German administrative takeover of continental France, or better that its government not be beholden to the German occupiers? A strong argument can be made that everything Laval did, he did to preserve whatever little French sovereignty remained after the armistice with Germany.

This leaves the charge of collaborating with the enemy (Article 75). Was there an enemy? A proponent of Laval's position might argue that the real enemy was the Soviet Union. There are two main difficulties with this argument. First, historically, Laval had no difficulty in trying to come to terms with the Soviet Union. In 1934, while foreign minister, he negotiated a Franco-Soviet protocol with one of Stalin's henchmen: the Soviet commissar for foreign affairs, Maxim Litvinov.[117] Second, there was no state of war between France and the Soviet Union; indeed, during Laval's second tenure at Vichy, the Soviet Union was engaged in a death struggle with France's invader.

In contrast, France had declared war against Germany in September 1939 after Germany's invasion of Poland. The following year, Germany invaded France, crushing its military forces. The terms of the ensuing armistice reflected the hapless French position. While there was a truce or armistice, there was no peace treaty. Absent a peace treaty, Germany and France were at war with one another. This made Germany the enemy.[118]

If one had to point to specific policies Laval pursued as falling under collaboration with the enemy, two would seem the most likely candidates: (1) siphoning French workers to Germany to assist it in its war effort, and (2) facilitating the deportation of Jews in France to help Germany attain its goal of annihilating European Jewry.

Transfer of Workers to Germany

As noted above, as prime minister of Vichy France, Laval reached an agreement in the spring of 1942 with Fritz Sauckel, Hitler's forced-labor czar. Sauckel's responsibilities were simple: to obtain workers from occupied countries to be transported to Germany so that their labor would assist in its war effort. Beauchamp's testimony at Laval's trial was that 400,000 French workers were sent to Germany. That number, however, included only those workers who were members of the organization that Beauchamp represented. General estimates place the number of workers sent to Germany under Laval's aegis at about 700,000, a number consistent with Laval's own estimates.[119] While in prison at Fresnes prior to his trial, Laval prepared extensive notes and memoranda to be used in his defense. In the memorandum relating to the *Relève* program, Laval conceded that 641,500 French workers had been in Germany as of July 30, 1944.[120] Since Sauckel and the Germans agreed that one farm worker prisoner of war could be released for every three workers sent to Germany, Laval apparently considered the exchange beneficial to France. As a result, Laval stated that both he and Pétain were "sincerely grateful" for Hitler's generous gesture[121]—somewhat surprising since Laval had originally asked for a one-for-one exchange.

On its face, it would seem that providing labor to a belligerent power to assist it in continuing its war effort is criminal collaboration. The enemy's goal is to retain an efficient domestic production system while the majority of its working-age men are in the military. That goal is implemented if a large number of foreign workers are imported to staff domestic production. Nor is there anything benign about the massive transfer of civilian populations for use as workers in a foreign country. Sauckel himself was convicted of war crimes at Nuremberg for precisely such conduct and hanged.[122]

There is also evidence that at some point in mid-1943 Laval refused to cooperate further with Sauckel.[123] Logically, however, such a refusal is more inculpatory than exculpatory. First, if there had been collaboration up to the point of refusal, then a subsequent refusal cannot undo what had been done. Second, that Laval was able to say "no" to Sauckel would suggest he could have, and should have, done so earlier. It could be, however, that Laval's refusal was triggered not so much by his newly found backbone, as by the changing wartime conditions, both external and internal. By then the tide of the war had begun to turn against Germany. The French police were no longer as cooperative in implementing the draft of French workers for Germany and the French Resistance was draining off considerable manpower from the French population, making the number of persons available for transport to Germany much smaller.[124] Until this point, however, Laval's actions had served the Germans in their war effort. This is collaboration.

Deportation of Jews

Vichy France passed legislation directed against the Jews during Laval's first tenure with the Vichy regime.[125] Although he opposed such legislation, he nevertheless signed it.[126] Even so, it is a stretch to see domestic legislation, even if anti-Semitic in substance, as amounting to collaboration with Germany. Such legislation was the product of internal motivation, not external pressure from the German occupier.[127] If there was collaboration, it would have to be Laval's role in deporting Jews from France to their deaths as part of the Nazi plan for the extermination of Jews in Europe.

No doubt certain comments Laval made would suggest anti-Semitism on his part, especially his December 1942 statement at a press conference that he wished for a German victory, and that President Roosevelt carried in his baggage the double triumph of Jews and communists. Nevertheless, the general consensus, both by Laval's biographers and by Holocaust historians, is that Laval was not an anti-Semite.[128] In the end, however, his general attitude towards Jews is a side issue since the critical question is his actual involvement in the deportation of Jews to their deaths.

There is no question that a large number of Jews, about 75,000 of the 300,000 in France at the beginning of the war, were sent to Poland, almost all of whom were killed. Certainly, the German effort to deal with Jews in France and the Vichy government's assistance during the period he was out of office—December 1940 to April 1942—cannot be attributed to Laval. German efforts at deporting French Jews did, however, extend well into his second tenure with the Vichy government—and, in fact, became even more intense during that latter period.

On June 23, 1942, Himmler ordered that all Jews of France be deported. When Laval was informed of this shortly afterwards, probably by Adolf Eichmann who came to Paris with that message a week later,[129] Laval saw deporting foreign Jews as his only option, in the hope of saving Jews of French citizenship.[130] Thus, the Vichy regime agreed "to the deportation, as a first step, of all stateless Jews in the Occupied and Unoccupied zones."[131]

In order to deport Jews, they first had to be rounded up and this required the extensive cooperation of the French police who, in the last analysis, were in the administrative hierarchy under Laval and Pétain. The authority to cooperate was given.[132] The July 1942 efforts in Paris yielded about 13,000 Jews. When it became clear that Jews were in danger of arrest and deportation, one of their options was to head for French colonies in Africa. To prevent this, Jews were barred from voluntarily leaving the country. In explaining why, Laval stated that "it would be a violation of the Armistice agreement with Germany to permit Jews to go abroad for fear they would take up arms against Germany."[133] Laval was doing his part.[134]

Considerable controversy related to Jewish children. Initially, after the Parisian roundups and deportations, families were separated, and children left behind, as parents were sent to the death camps. The United States, on October 15, 1942, offered to extend visas to up to 5,000 Jewish children. In negotiations with the United States, Laval insisted that there be no publicity in connection with Jewish children leaving France without parents under such visas.[135] However, once Allied forces landed in North Africa in November 1942, technically an invasion of French colonies, negotiations broke down and no visas were issued. The breakdown of negotiations was probably preordained since Laval, speaking on French radio in mid-September 1942, said that the

Vichy government was prepared to make a concession with regard to the deportation of Jewish children. Henceforth they would be deported together with their parents instead of being separated. He added, however: "No one and nothing can deter us from carrying out the policy of purging France of undesirable elements, without nationality."[136]

Clearly the cooperation of the Vichy regime in the deportation of 75,000 Jews to Poland, where most were murdered, assisted the Germans in implementing their Final Solution. Laval bears responsibility for such cooperation. His explanation, of course, was that his concern was saving French Jews and if that meant sacrificing non-French Jews in France, that was a choice he could reasonably make. It is doubtful whether a defense to a charge of collaboration with the enemy can be that collaboration was committed to avoid more damaging collaboration. And Laval did show that he could say "no" to German demands. In 1943, when Germany wanted legislation to denaturalize any person who had attained French citizenship after 1927, Laval refused. Even though this refusal cast doubt on his commitment to cooperation, the Germans took no action against Laval.

Laval's Motivation

To the end, Laval insisted that he was a patriot who did everything in the best interests of France. It may well be that he genuinely felt that way. But that cannot be the end of the discussion. How does his subjective sincerity bear on the question of whether he collaborated with the enemy, sham trial aside?

Generally, criminal law sees intent and motive as different mental states. Intent is the state of mind at the time of conduct; conduct is intentional if it is done on purpose and not accidentally or negligently. Motive is the underlying reason that spawns the conduct. A man who reveals state secrets may have a benevolent motive. Such motive, however, does not undo the underlying crime. So too with Laval. He provided significant assistance to Germany, France's enemy, on behalf of its two major goals: victory in the war and annihilation of European Jewry. He did it intentionally—clearly aware of the purpose he was serving. Moreover, this intentional conduct was not on its face benevolent: it breached international norms, as expressed in numerous treaties relating to the treatment of civilian populations.[137] Laval's assistance facilitated Germany's attainment of its dual wartime goals. Surely, this is criminal collaboration.

To defend against the collaboration charge, Laval would say that Soviet Bolshevism represented a greater threat to Europe than Germany's Nazism. Even his "I wish for a German victory" statement was tied to the communist threat. Thus, however mistakenly, until the end, Laval felt genuinely that he could negotiate with Hitler while the ideological thrust behind Soviet expansion left no room for negotiation with the Allies. Under these circumstances, as Laval perceived them, France's interests would best be served by a German victory and a Soviet defeat. How could it be a crime to act in France's interest?

Hitler's track record of broken promises makes this position difficult to appreciate, no less to defend. The dismemberment of Czechoslovakia and annexation of Austria came *after* Hitler had said that all he wanted was the Saar—which he had gotten. And, after all, it was the German military that invaded Poland in 1939, without a semblance of provocation, and then thrust across the Ardennes in 1940, utterly humbling France. It was the German, not the Soviet, administration that imposed the harsh armistice conditions on France, and at various places subjected French citizens to the brutality of the SS. In siding with Germany, Laval ignored the pattern of recent events. The only promises Hitler kept were those of death and destruction. On all others, his word was worthless. At some point, Laval's concerns about the theoretical spread of communism in the future had to bump up against the reality of whom he was dealing with—and who was actually harming his country. This was a reality he never squarely faced.

Did Laval just guess wrong as to who would win the war? Given the same information on the war's progress that Laval had, many Frenchmen opted to resist and refused to cooperate with the German occupiers under the Vichy regime. No one forced Laval to lead the collaborationist government. Laval's preeminence in the Third Republic left him with the same choices faced by other former French prime ministers. Unlike other politicians, Laval sided with the Vichy government because he saw an opportunity for political advancement. Laval opted to pursue that opportunity, and it carried a price.

The Sentence

Pétain's death sentence was commuted to life imprisonment, while Laval was sentenced to death. Did Laval deserve a greater punishment than Pétain? This is a difficult question. Pétain was much older and mostly a figurehead in the Vichy regime. Laval, from April 1942 until he was placed in custody, was the *de facto* head of the government. Nevertheless, Pétain's status as a genuine French hero is what gave the Vichy regime a semblance of legitimacy—far more than Laval could have given it. And Pétain had not been reticent about his feelings, having sent a congratulatory note to Germany after its forces successfully repelled the British raid at Dieppe. While Pétain and Laval were both reviled after the war, age alone could form a rational basis for the distinction between the two sentences, coupled also with Pétain's heroism on behalf of France a full generation earlier. Perhaps both should have been executed, but the mercy de Gaulle showed by commuting the death sentence of the eighty-nine-year-old Pétain to life imprisonment does not, on its own, render the sentence imposed on Laval an injustice.

If the question is whether a guilty man was railroaded, the answer is "yes." Laval collaborated with the enemy. It is, however, a stain on the de Gaulle postwar government that it failed to prosecute the leader of the Vichy regime in accordance with its own established procedures. Laval was entitled to a fair trial and he did not receive it. It is unfortunate that when the history of this period is reviewed, a tinge of martyrdom colors Laval's collaboration.[138]

Bodies among the more than 2,000 seen by the U.S. military as it liberated the main Dachau concentration camp. Courtesy of the USHMM.

"Earthholes" at one of the Kaufering camps, satellites of the Dachau concentration camp, set aside mainly for Jews. Courtesy of the USHMM.

Inside an "earth-hole." Courtesy of the USHMM.

3

The Dachau Trial under U.S. Army Jurisdiction

Dachau

In March 1933, shortly after Hitler's ascent to power in Germany, the Nazis opened the concentration camp known as Dachau, which included an entire ring of concentration camps administered from Dachau and encircling it. It remained under German control until the surrender of the main camp to Allied military forces on April 29, 1945. The main Dachau camp was built to accommodate 8,000 inmates; the entire complex was built to hold about 20,000 inmates. At the time of surrender, the main camp held about 30,000 inmates and the entire complex held about 65,000 people.[1]

The original purpose of the camp was to detain politically undesirable persons, mainly political dissidents and those seen as potential threats to Hitler's regime. While Jews were among those brought to Dachau during the first five years of its existence, it was in their role as communists, socialists, or other opponents of National Socialism. Jews as Jews were not detained at Dachau until the immediate aftermath of Kristallnacht in November 1938, when thousands of Jewish men were arrested in Germany and sent to various concentration camps including Dachau.

Dachau was not a killing center in the same sense as Auschwitz, Chelmno, Treblinka, Sobibor, Belzec, and Majdanek were. Unlike those camps in German-occupied Poland where most, if not almost all, persons brought there were immediately murdered, persons brought to Dachau were detained for hard labor and brutal exercise. In another sense, however, Dachau was a more brutal killing center. Though not as efficient, its inmates were overworked, overcrowded, and underfed, resulting in a slow death for thousands through starvation and disease. As the war was coming to an end, the Germans began evacuating camps about to be overrun by the Allies. As a consequence, they funneled inmates of those camps to camps in Germany proper, including Dachau. This resulted in even more overcrowding and the further spread of disease. Incredibly, on cross-examination of one of the prosecution witnesses, counsel for the defendants suggested that the Allies should be blamed for the overcrowding since successful Allied advances, liberating other camps, exacerbated the suffering of inmates at Dachau.[2]

Once the Second World War began in 1939, and certainly after the German invasion of the Soviet Union in June 1941, Dachau's inmate population took on an international face. At the time of liberation, about half the total population came from Eastern Europe; the balance comprised persons from central and southern European countries such as Italy and Germany. Jews were a plurality, constituting slightly over a third of the total.[3] Generally speaking, Jews were confined in Dachau's satellite camps, mainly camps named after the nearby town of Kaufering, where the conditions "were considered the worse from the standpoint of overcrowding, malnutrition, disease and brutality."[4] For example, the beds at Dachau eventually held three men to a bed, while housing, if it could be called that, at the Kaufering subcamps was even more crowded.[5] The allocation of food, well below the caloric and nutritional minimum at Dachau, was even less in the Kaufering subcamps. Thus, it is not surprising that more Jews were murdered at Dachau than any other group of prisoners.

Civilians constituted over 90 percent of the Dachau population. Most of the military inmates were Soviet POWs sent to Dachau in the year after the invasion of the Soviet Union in June 1941. A majority of these men were executed by shooting; some were hanged. The unfortunate Soviet men brought to Dachau were singled out and suffered a higher murder rate than any other group. Nevertheless, because their numbers were smaller, the total killed did not approach the number of Jews killed. This mix of civilian and military inmates was of legal significance in the proceedings that followed because the principles of international law that apply to civilian populations—the vast bulk of Dachau inmates—differ from those that apply to prisoners of war.

The Liberation of Dachau and Summary Executions

Dachau's liberation was a foregone conclusion to the Nazi hierarchy. With Soviet troops advancing from the east and the Americans and British from the west, it was just a question of time before German control of Dachau and its inmates would fall into Allied hands. Consequently, on April 14, 1945, Heinrich Himmler, head of the SS, directed that Dachau be destroyed and its 30,000-plus surviving inmates be murdered to preclude the survival of witnesses to its horrors. Fortunately, by mid-April 1945, the administrative machinery of the Third Reich was sufficiently disrupted and chaotic so that this directive was not carried out to completion. Jews, however, were singled out and constituted the bulk of the 7,000 Dachau inmates selected, on April 26, for a death march to the Tegernsee to the south. Those not able to walk, either at the inception of the march or during the march, were shot on the spot. Others died of exposure and starvation along the way. Survivors were liberated at the Tegernsee a week after leaving Dachau.[6]

American troops liberated Dachau on April 29, 1945. As the American troops arrived at Dachau,[7] they passed an abandoned train on the tracks leading to the main camp. The train contained over 2,000 bodies of emaciated, skeletonlike victims who had been sent from Buchenwald to Dachau in the days before. Most died from starvation and disease; on some the eyes were open, even in death; all contributed to a mosaic of pure horror.[8] It was ghastly even for the American liberators; battle-tested soldiers who had lived with death for weeks, if not months or years. As one account of the introduction by American liberators to Dachau observed:

> If ever the American soldier needed confirmation of the reasons why he was in uniform, why he was at war, why he was required to put his life on the line day after day, enduring all hardships and discomfort and danger, it was contained in these thirty-nine railroad cars. Here was the very embodiment of the evil Nazi regime that he had sworn to vanquish. As they cautiously approached, the familiar, sickening stench of death greeted them. . . . In each railroad car were piles of rotting human

> corpses—a total of 2,310 men, women and children, to be exact, either totally naked or partially clad in blue and white striped concentration camp uniforms. Mainly Poles, most of them had starved to death while being moved from Buchenwald in an effort to keep them from falling into the hands of the approaching Allies. Many others had been killed by their sadistic guards; still others had died while fighting among themselves during the trip. A few with enough strength to attempt escape had been shot down by the SS guards or brutally beaten with file butts, their brains oozing from shaved, emaciated skulls. An order from SS head Heinrich Himmler to destroy evidence of atrocities had gone unfulfilled.[9]

The gruesome scene that prefaced the U.S. Army entry into Dachau set in motion the events that followed. Nothing inside the camp mitigated the initial reaction provided by the train; indeed, seeing thousands upon thousands of living persons emaciated almost to the point of death augmented the anger of the liberating soldiers.

Accounts of what happened on entry to Dachau and its surrender vary, and an attempt to resolve these conflicting accounts is beyond the purview of this chapter. It is clear, however, that the four SS men who came to the American liberators with a white flag of surrender were shot and, if not killed immediately, shot again in the head to ensure their deaths. Other SS men were rounded up and lined up against a wall where they were machine-gunned. Once again, those who survived the machine-gunning were shot in the head, perhaps by Dachau inmates who had been given access to guns. Some SS men were turned over to the inmates. For example, one SS medic, who reportedly had castrated an inmate, was shot in the leg to immobilize him and then left to inmates who pummeled him to death with shovels. One of these inmates was the castration victim.[10] Others were handed to inmates who literally tore them apart. Estimates as to the number of SS men killed following liberation range from a few dozen[11] to about 550.[12] There is some evidence that among the SS killed in this manner, several had just been assigned to Dachau and thus could not, under any conceivable theory of criminal liability, be responsible for its horrors.[13]

On May 2, 1945, shortly after the liberation of Dachau, the assistant inspector general of the Seventh Army, Lieutenant Colonel James Whittaker, at the direction of the Seventh Army's commanding general, conducted an inquiry into the events surrounding Dachau's liberation. In his June 8, 1945, report, he found that SS men at Dachau had indeed been killed without justification by named members of the liberating troops. He also noted that Lieutenant Howard Buechner "violated his duty both as a physician and a soldier [by] . . . ignoring the possibility of saving the wounded but still living prisoners who had been shot."[14] Whittaker's report was filed with General George S. Patton, the head of the Seventh Army and the military governor of Bavaria (where Dachau was located), who simply ignored the report and took no action.[15] Forty years later, Buechner wrote a book about the killing of the SS men by the American military[16] and in 1992, forty-seven years after liberation, the Whittaker report was made public.[17] The number of SS men summarily executed and the question as to whether their execution was at least understandable, though clearly not lawful, remains open.

The Setting for the Trial

Historically, the military has the power to try persons in military courts under a number of circumstances, including warfare conditions where there is no functioning local civilian government.[18] That was certainly the case in Germany in the months after its surrender. The International Military Tribunal (IMT) tried the major Nazi defendants at Nuremberg, and the United States Military Tribunals presided over twelve different trials at Nuremberg after the IMT trial. Those were not the only trials, however. Acting under the same authority, the United States established U.S. Army courts, which sat in Dachau and presided over trials of 1,672 persons in 489 different proceedings from 1945 to 1948. Six of these 489 proceedings related to the administration of six concentration camps: Dachau, Buchenwald, Flossenbürg, Mauthausen, Nordhausen, and Muehldorf. This chapter deals with the trial at Dachau, focusing on the Dachau concentration camp and its satellites.[19]

The substantive law for these military tribunals is (1) violations of the laws and (2) usages of war, both concepts established by various treaties and practices. An initial requirement is that the conduct alleged to have been criminal occurred during an actual war since the laws and usages of war are operative only during an international conflict. Thus, it is not surprising that the Dachau case charge sheet (the equivalent of an indictment) alleges that, between January 1, 1942 (after Pearl Harbor), and Dachau's liberation on April 29, 1945, the forty named accused acted pursuant to a common design and participated in the commission of certain criminal acts.

There were two charges. The first alleged that as part of this common design the defendants subjected the civilians of nations then at war with Germany to cruelties and mistreatment including killings, beatings, tortures, starvation, abuse, and other indignities. The second alleged the same conduct—cruelties, mistreatment, etc.—with respect to members of the armed forces of nations then at war with the German Reich who had surrendered and were unarmed prisoners of war in the custody of the German Reich. The technicalities of the charges required the prosecution to prove both that the defendants acted during wartime and that their acts were directed against either civilians or prisoners of war who were other than of German nationality.[20]

The tribunal consisted of eight army officers, seven colonels, and one brigadier general. Brigadier General John M. Lentz presided. Lieutenant Colonel William Denson, a Harvard Law School graduate, headed the prosecution team. Three captains joined him: William Lines, Richard McKusky, and Philip Heller.[21] Three officers were assigned to specific defendants: Major Maurice McKeon represented fourteen defendants, including the lead defendant, Commandant Martin Weiss. Captain John May represented twelve defendants and Captain Dalvin Niles represented the remaining fourteen.[22] Some of the difficulties with such mass representation by three defense lawyers will surface later in this chapter.

The trial began on November 15, 1945, and ended on December 13, 1945. It followed the usual contour of both military and civilian trials in the United States: preliminary motions, opening statements by both sides, direct and cross-examination of prosecution witnesses, direct and cross-examination of defense witnesses, closing arguments, and then a verdict by the eight officers constituting the court. The prosecution and defense called hundreds of witnesses and most of the forty defendants testified.

Preliminary Motions, Opening Statements, and the Prosecution's Case

There were several facets to the preliminary defense motions. First, counsel argued that the defendants were prisoners of war and as such were entitled to a trial following the rules of the prosecuting power, which was not the case here. The prosecution responded that the accused were charged with violating the laws of war and, as such, were alleged criminals, not entitled to the protections afforded prisoners of war. The defense rejoinder was that as members of the *Waffen-SS*, they were part of the German army. The prosecution reiterated that the allegation that the defendants violated the laws of war trumped any status they might otherwise claim.[23] The judges rejected the defense's argument and noted that no legal rights would be denied the accused.[24]

The defense then asked that the charges be dismissed on two different legal grounds. First, the laws of war required that those injured by violations of those rules had to be nationals of a country other than that of the defendants: the charge made no reference to the nationality of the victims. Second, simply alleging that forty defendants acted pursuant to a common design, as the charge did, was too vague. These motions were denied as well.[25] Finally, the defense lawyers asked the judges to sever the trials of the forty defendants on the grounds that their various defenses were antagonistic—a legitimate ground for a severance request in a conventional criminal case—requiring separate trials for each defendant.[26] Conceding there were many defendants, the prosecution expressed confidence in the ability of the court to properly assess the evidence. The court denied the defense motion.[27]

The prosecution's opening statement in the trial was short, covering barely two pages of transcript.[28] Its first witness, Colonel

Lawrence Ball, was a medical officer who arrived at Dachau on May 2, 1945, three days after its liberation. The defense immediately objected to his testimony, noting that the underlying charge was a common design to violate the laws of war from January 1, 1942 to April 29, 1945, the date of Dachau's liberation. The defense claimed that no accused could be held accountable for the status of the camp at a time when he had no responsibility over it.[29] The objection was patently absurd; camp conditions in the period immediately after liberation could easily lead to an inference as to the conditions just a few days, if not weeks and months, earlier. Obviously, evidence that on May 2, a Dachau inmate was on the verge of death by starvation and disease, weighing less than one-half the inmate's normal weight, could justly lead to an inference (1) that the inmate was not the picture of health three days earlier and (2) that his condition came about while the defendants had responsibility over the camp. Nevertheless, the objection, coming at the very inception of the prosecution's case, must be lauded since it was symptomatic of the vigorous nature of the defense and the extraordinary effort made by defense counsel on behalf of their clients, concededly operators of a vicious and inhumane killing machine.

The prosecution proceeded at two levels: an overview, which dealt with the general population of Dachau and how it was treated, and then the behavior of individual defendants. What follows are the facts established by many of the prosecution witnesses, the general thrust of which was not denied by any of the defendants. Their defenses, as will be seen, consisted not in a denial of the general conditions at Dachau, but rather that they were powerless to do anything other than what they did, since they were simply following orders. It was a repeat of the legal defense the Nazis first raised on trial in 1943 at Kharkov, and echoed again and again in subsequent prosecutions of Nazi defendants, even the high-ranking major war criminals before the International Military Tribunal at Nuremberg. In some instances of particularly horrid brutality, the defendants simply denied their involvement.

Meticulous records the SS kept showed that approximately 250,000 persons were "processed" through Dachau from its inception to its liberation, the vast bulk of whom were processed after the beginning of the Second World War.[30] As noted earlier, Jewish prisoners were usually confined in the satellite camps, principally the Kaufering camps, where living conditions were the worst and the largest number of lives was lost. While the facilities at Dachau consisted of aboveground housing, actual buildings, the living facilities in the Kaufering camps were below ground with a covering over the entry hole. The defendant Otto Foerschner, in charge of the Kaufering camps towards the end of Dachau's use, testified that the inmates lived in "earthholes."[31] Kaufering inmates slept on planks, not beds of any sort, and usually used their shoes as pillows.[32] Not surprisingly, therefore, the death rate among Jews was the highest, approaching one in seven inmates during the seven months before liberation.[33]

Prison blocks built for 400 persons regularly held 800 to 1,200 prisoners during the last months. Sometimes, 2,000 were quartered in accommodations built for 400. Often three persons had to share one bed, really just a cot, and an unwashed blanket, not infrequently embedded with fecal matter from widespread dysentery.[34] Clothing was entirely inadequate and the limited supply of shoes was given to those who could work so that disabled inmates were forced to stand barefoot in snow and sleet. Not surprisingly, washing facilities were horrendous: there were eight latrines to accommodate 300 to 400 prisoners, many of which were inoperable in the winter. Two sinks were meant to serve 800 inmates. As a result, dysentery, tuberculosis, and typhus were rampant and no steps were taken to prevent the spread of contagious diseases.[35]

The daily ration for inmates was designed to starve them to death. Breakfast consisted of a half-liter of synthetic coffee; the midday meal was made up of three-fourths to one liter of "watery soup," which occasionally contained cabbage leaves or rotten potato peeling; and the evening meal consisted of a slice of bread and a thin slice of sausage, cheese or margarine, and a liter of soup. Put together, the maximum daily caloric content of these meals was between 500 to 700 calories, on rare occasion reaching 1,000 calories. According to prosecution witness Dr. Franz Blaha, a Czech physician who worked at Dachau towards the latter part of its existence, sawdust replaced some of the flour in the bread, rendering the overall diet even more void of caloric and nutritional value. The workday of those given these minimal amounts started at four thirty in the morning with a roll call, and ended late at night, with eleven to thirteen hours of physically taxing labor in between.[36] It is a further barometer of the aggressiveness of assigned defense counsel that they objected to Blaha's testimony on the ground that as a Czech, he was a citizen of a country not at war with Germany. The objection was overruled.[37]

A large number of frightening discipline devices were used by the SS guards. These were invoked for the slightest pretext or for no pretext at all. Many of these torture methods were interwoven with severe weather conditions, whether cold, snow, or rain. A representative, though definitely not complete, list of what Dachau prisoners were regularly exposed to, includes:

1. The "twenty-five"—an inmate's feet were locked in place, the inmate bent over, and twenty-five lashes with a whip were applied to the prisoner's buttocks; more, if the prisoner failed to keep count as the punishment was administered or even at the whim of the SS individual administering or ordering the punishment.
2. Hanging by the wrists for an hour to an hour and a half while being beaten. In a situation where simply surviving can be defined as heroism, one instance emerges that, for want of a better term, can be called heroism plus. One of the inmates, Bodigan Krajewski, was born in that part of Poland that was German at the time of his birth—presumably before the creation of Poland in 1918. One of the defendants directed Krajewski to designate himself as a German by birth. Krajewski refused, saying it would bring dishonor to him, that he was a Pole by birth, not a German. Krajewski was then subjected to whipping, while hanging by the wrists, again and again, but maintained his refusal to state he was German. The torture ended without Krajewski having relented.[38]
3. Solitary confinement for days in a dungeon without food or water.
4. Standing in a cell about the size of a coffin not high enough to permit erect standing but too confined to permit resting in a position of comfort.
5. Forcing an inmate to hold a lit cigar in the palms until it burned out completely—called euphemistically the "human ashtray."

Three additional methods went beyond discipline and were designed instead to end in death.

6. Hanging, sometimes with a device so that the choking effect would begin once a prisoner loosened his muscles.
7. Shooting.
8. Medical experiments. These will be discussed in detail with reference to the defendants Weiss and Schilling.[39]

Finally, before turning to some of the individual defendants, we note the ubiquitous trains and their major role in the killing process, representing one of the primary symbols of the Holocaust. Dachau was at both ends of the process by which trains were used to murder and weaken those in the custody of the Third Reich. Persons sent by train *to* Dachau for confinement were cramped into brutally inhumane conditions and kept as such longer than many could possibly tolerate. By the time the trains arrived at Dachau, many had died from suffocation, hunger, thirst, or some combination of these horrors. Similarly, persons were sent *from* Dachau, usually to Auschwitz, for extermination. These involved comparable conditions, but now for inmates on the verge of death. Dachau inmates knew full well that a transport to Auschwitz, many hundreds of miles away, meant almost certain death. Since it was usually the sick and disabled who were sent, resistance was impossible.

It would be impossible in these pages to deal with the evidence as to each of the forty Dachau defendants. With a view to providing as broad a perspective as possible, we have chosen to look at the evidence relating to four defendants: Martin Weiss, commandant at Dachau; Dr. Klaus Schilling, responsible for malaria experiments; Josef Jarolin, an SS officer responsible for discipline; and Emil Mahl, a *kapo*.

Specific Defendants

Martin Weiss: Commandant

Weiss had a long history at Dachau. From 1933 to 1938, he was in charge of technical issues at the camp such as electrical power, heating, etc. From 1938 to 1940, he was adjutant—second in command. For the next two years he was commandant of smaller concentration camps, returning to Dachau is September 1942, where he stayed as commandant until November 1943. To some, Weiss was known as "the good commandant," an image central to his defense.

The major reasons for Weiss's designation as the "good commandant" related to several changes he instituted while in charge. Through Weiss's direct examination, questioning of witnesses called by the defense, and cross-examination of prosecution witnesses, defense counsel brought out that Weiss had discontinued the punishment of hanging by wrists and during his tenure beatings occurred less frequently. Under Weiss, beatings also became less severe: for example, he took special steps to see that twenty-five lashes meant twenty-five, not more as had frequently been the practice. The standing punishments were abandoned;[40] food sent from outside sources was allowed to reach Dachau inmates; and some minimal arrangements for entertainment were made.[41] Nevertheless, the general culture of brutality at Dachau continued during Weiss's fourteen-month tenure as commandant, and some of this brutality was directly linked to him.

As mentioned above, trains played a major role in weakening and killing persons destined for camps in general, and Dachau in particular. A political prisoner, Wilholm Visintainer, stated that towards the end of Weiss's tenure as Dachau commandant, a train arrived with 750 men in boxcars closed by nails and surrounded with barbed wire. A trip that could have taken two days took sixteen; only 219 of the 750 men were still alive. An examination of some of the bodies revealed that they had been mutilated and it became evident that the survivors subsisted on the flesh of the dead. Weiss had those bodies laid out in front of the 219 survivors. He then promised that those who would acknowledge the mutilation would receive food. Seven men stepped forward. They were told to stand behind the bodies, where they were photographed. They were then taken to the Dachau crematorium where they were hanged.[42]

The prosecution showed that numerous executions and beatings took place while Weiss was commandant and that he authorized each of them. Most important, perhaps, the prosecution focused specifically on the medical experiments conducted while he was commandant, each of which he also authorized. These included infecting inmates with malaria and then testing various antidotes, submerging inmates in ice water to test the body's endurance to cold,[43] introducing infectious diseases to skin and other tissue, feeding inmates only salt water, performing liver biopsies without an anesthetic, and withdrawing air from a confined area to test endurance limits in conditions that approached a vacuum.[44] Weiss did not deny that these experiments occurred; rather he claimed that he had no responsibility for them by virtue of direct orders from Heinrich Himmler, head of the Gestapo and SS, which gave the physicians independent authority to conduct the experiments.

Weiss testified that when Himmler visited Dachau, he was summoned to meet him. The meeting occurred at an experiment Dr. Sigmund Rascher was conducting, involving the submersion of inmates in cold water. According to Weiss, he had previously been less than cooperative with Rascher. It appeared that Rascher had told Himmler he had had some trouble with Weiss. Himmler told Weiss not to interfere with Rascher's experiments, explaining that Rascher was not under Weiss's supervision but directly under Himmler. Himmler made it clear to Weiss that he was to comply with every request Rascher made, whether it was for more inmates to experiment on or for more cognac or coffee. The defendant Dr. Klauss Schilling had apparently also complained to Himmler about Weiss's lack of full cooperation in providing inmates for Schilling's experiments. Himmler told Weiss that he was to provide whatever number of inmates Schilling wanted and that any refusal to do so would be viewed as sabotage.[45]

Overall, the prosecution did not controvert evidence that conditions at Dachau under Weiss were somewhat less severe than under either Weiss's predecessor or his successor. Rather, the prosecutors simply ignored the comparative analysis and focused on what took place during the fourteen months Weiss was commandant. In an oblique acknowledgement of Weiss's "improvements," the prosecution noted that starting in late 1942, when Weiss took charge, Germany's wartime fortunes started to change and it became more important to utilize the labor available at Dachau more efficiently. The prosecution argued that whatever changes Weiss may have instituted were done to enhance efficiency.[46]

Dr. Klaus Schilling: Initiator of Medical Experiments

Dr. Klaus Schilling, seventy-four years old at the time of the trial, was a noted bacteriologist connected with the prestigious Robert Koch Institute in Berlin prior to his work at Dachau. He studied under Koch, generally recognized as the founder of modern bacteriology and the recipient of the Nobel Prize for Physiology or Medicine in 1905. Schilling's work focused on tropical diseases. He studied in the United States and received grants from the Rockefeller Foundation for his work in helping to eradicate tropical disease in Africa. By the 1940s, he had retired.[47] Because soldiers in Germany's North Africa campaign were being infected with malaria, Himmler requested that Schilling come out of retirement and work on antidotes. He was sent to Dachau for this purpose.

The malaria experiments at Dachau were brutal. Inmates, frequently Roman Catholic priests,[48] were infected with malaria either by having their thighs bitten by mosquitoes carrying the parasite or through direct injection. Many witnesses testified as to these experiments, including several of the priests who survived them. Dr. Franz Blaha, a Czech prisoner-physician who was required to perform autopsies of those who died, provided the most detailed evidence as follows:

> During my time at Dachau I was familiar with many kinds of medical experiments carried on there on human victims. These persons were never volunteers but were forced to submit to such acts. Malaria experiments on about 1,200 people were conducted by Dr. Klaus Schilling between 1941 and 1945. Schilling was personally ordered by Himmler to conduct these experiments. The victims were either bitten by mosquitoes or given injections of malaria sporozoites taken from mosquitoes. Different kinds of treatment were applied including quinine, pyrifer, neosalvarsan, antipyrin, pyramidon, and a drug called 2516 Behring. I performed autopsies on the bodies of people who died from these malaria experiments. Thirty to 40 died from the malaria itself. Three hundred to

> four hundred died later from diseases which were fatal because of the physical condition resulting from the malaria attacks. In addition there were deaths resulting from poisoning due to overdoses of neosalvarsan and pyramidon. Dr. Schilling was present at my autopsies on the bodies of his patients.[49]

Schilling's defense consisted of several prongs. First, he separated himself from his co-defendants by pointing out he was not a member of the SS, the Nazi Party, or any other Nazi organization. Second, he disputed the facts as stated by Blaha. According to Schilling, he inoculated about 500 persons with malaria—none of whom, he agreed, had consented to the inoculation—and as far as he knew, none of them died.[50] If there was a death attributable either to the inoculation or to an overdose of one of remedies he injected, Schilling claimed it was because that person had typhus and Blaha did not inform him of that. Third, Schilling called character witnesses who testified that his colleagues regarded him as a serious scientist and that his reputation for truth was untouchable.[51] In the cross-examination of one of these witnesses, a nurse whose husband was a physician, the questioning went as follows:

> Q. Mrs. Duerck, do you know what work Dr. Schilling was engaged in here at Dachau?
> A. Yes, I know.
> Q. Would your husband have done the same thing?
> A. No.[52]

Finally, Schilling ended his own direct examination by explaining why he accepted the commission to come to Dachau for purposes of doing medical experiments on its inmates. He said he had placed the concerns a doctor would have before performing experiments with human beings on one side of the scale and on the importance of those experiments on the other. He said that seventeen million annual cases of malaria, as determined by a League of Nations commission of which he was part, "constituted the heavy weight which tipped the scales."[53] Whether it was wise to end his direct examination by acknowledging his willingness to do as charged and to defend his choice as proper is debatable. However one views the wisdom of this approach, it was probably truthful, but probably equally fatal to his position as an accused.

Josef Jarolin: Enforcer

Many examples of cruelty saturate the transcript pages of the Dachau trial. Some examples of what inmates were forced to endure have already been summarized and many witnesses testified as to how many of the accused willingly committed these acts. While it is difficult to contemplate a gradient of cruelty, there seemed to be a consensus that Josef Jarolin was among the cruelest of the SS men at Dachau. Testimony that he regularly beat prisoners to death was not subjected to cross-examination.[54] In his appearance before the court[55] and by his lengthy pretrial interrogation statement, Jarolin had essentially admitted as much.[56]

Jarolin's trial testimony was short and to the point. While he denied some of the testimony tendered against him, he admitted to most. Nonetheless, he stated he was following orders and none of the beatings were spontaneous on his part. In his appearance before the court, he also denied any involvement in the shooting of Russian POWs. His handwritten statement was blatantly in conflict with his statements to the court.

In that handwritten statement, Jarolin wrote that from May 1941 to December 1941 he was responsible for "interrogations." In that capacity he tied up 150 prisoners and beat them with an oxtail whip at the direction of the camp commandant. For two years, beginning in December 1941, it was his responsibility to ensure that punishment orders were carried out correctly. This meant holding a prisoner down, administering twenty-five strokes with the oxtail whip, and requiring the prisoner to count out the number of strokes he was receiving. Later, Jarolin stated that prisoners were required to administer the beatings, and if they did not hit hard enough the stroke did not count. Jarolin was also involved in two other facets of Dachau: medical experiments and the shooting of Soviet POWs. Jarolin stated that he provided inmates for experiments where oxygen was removed from airtight chambers in which inmates were held. He estimated that thirty to forty people died as a result of the experiments.

As to the Soviet POWs, he stated that in the months after the German invasion of the Soviet Union in June 1941 approximately 2,400 Soviet POWs were brought to Dachau. These POWs were told to undress and then taken to the rifle range where they were shot. Jarolin admitted to giving the order to "fire" with respect to about 700 of these 2,400 POWs. After the order to fire had been given, it was his responsibility to go over to the fallen POWs and administer a "mercy" shot to be certain that the person was dead.[57]

Emil Erwin Mahl: Kapo

In Dachau, as in most concentration camps, the administrators used camp inmates to assist in the running of the camp. These "assistants" were known as *kapos*. In the environment of the concentration camps where random beatings and killings were not unusual, it seems clear that the moral dilemma for a person chosen to be a *kapo* was acute. As will be seen in the discussion in some of the later trials, failure by anyone in the Nazi hierarchy to follow orders never resulted in death or serious punishment. However, an inmate had no reason to have such rosy expectations for failure to follow the directives of the SS guards. One of the Dachau *kapos*, Emil Erwin Mahl, was named as an accused.

Mahl was brought to Dachau in 1940 as a German civilian convicted of a crime and remained there until its liberation. He became a *kapo* in mid-1944. The principal evidence against him was his involvement in the execution of French and Soviet POWs. Testimony showed that he placed a noose around the necks of French POWs and then kicked out the supports they were standing on. Witnesses also testified Mahl shot Soviet POWs.[58] Mahl, in testifying, acknowledged placing a noose around the necks of POWs but denied any further involvement in killing. He specifically denied even having a pistol, saying that if he had had one, he would have used it on himself.[59]

Perhaps reflecting the changing nature of his role and which side he was on, Mahl turned out to be helpful to the prosecution on cross-examination. Some of the accused who testified tried to downplay the actual killing of inmates after January 1, 1942, since the core of the prosecution's case was essentially murder during wartime.[60] Mahl expressed great disdain for that notion.[61]

Closing Arguments

The prosecution made its closing argument first, followed by the defense. On December 11, 1945, Lieutenant Colonel Denson gave the principal closing for the prosecution. Anticipating that in their closing defense counsel would rely on evidence that certain defendants were not in Dachau on dates when prosecution witnesses testified that they beat or killed inmates, Denson asked the court to "remember that these persons who testified . . . were prisoners in a concentration camp where they were subjected to more horrors and tortures in various forms than man had up to this time devised—where Monday was not the 19th of December but a day filled with the hanging of young Russians accused of sabotage, the beating of prisoners in the formation place or the wrist hanging of loyal Poles who would not stoop to don the uniform of infamy."[62]

Denson then dealt with the considerable evidence that conditions at Dachau under Weiss had improved. He acknowledged that there were fewer beatings, but argued that this was not because of kindness on anyone's part. Rather, the reality was that as the war progressed Germany had a greater need for labor. While punishments may have become less frequent under Weiss, the total labor output increased: "In his methodic and economic Nazi mind he had determined the maximum output of labor with the least input, the least investment by means of food and maintenance. No regards were had for the fact that by following such procedure total exhaustion and ultimate death was inevitable."[63]

Denson spent considerable effort to stress that the charge was not murder *per se* but participation in a common design to kill, torture, or degrade. This meant the prosecution did not have to prove that a particular defendant committed a particular act, such as a beating or a killing. He cited evidence by witnesses who described the administration of Dachau, the various departments, their functions, and testimony on the interrelated nature of all of them. In that context, he alluded to the murder and beatings of prisoners, referring to Jarolin and to Schilling's "mosquitoes and murderous doses of neosalvarsan and pyramidon [which] meant ultimate death."[64] As to the *kapo* Mahl, Denson was not overly sympathetic: "[T]hese *kapos*, being appointed by SS [were] responsible to SS and therefore . . . come within the provisions of the particulars in these two charges."[65]

Denson ended his closing with references to legal precedent that relegated the defense of following orders to the question of mitigation or punishment; when it came to violations of the laws of war, following orders was not a defense.[66]

> [T]he conduct of these accused will have turned back the clock of civilization at least a thousand years. . . . [The court should make] absolutely clear that such crimes will not be again tolerated on this earth. I believe, and am convinced, that every man in that dock has forfeited his right to mingle in decent society.[67]

Each of the defense attorneys then spoke. Captain May, who represented Mahl and eleven other accused, stressed several points: (1) that the charge of "common design" was as vague at the end of the trial as at the beginning; (2) that many of the accused were at Dachau not by design, but by the direction of persons far superior in the Nazi hierarchy than they; (3) that many of the prosecution witnesses testified as to acts by the accused at times when the accused were not at Dachau, thereby challenging the credibility of these witnesses altogether; and finally, (4) that the accused simply were following orders and had no choice. When it came to the prosecution's denigration of the following-orders defense, May made it personal: had he known orders didn't have to be followed, he wouldn't have obeyed the colonel who directed him to the defense side of the table, "[b]ecause on the defense, the unpopular side in this case, we four have had to walk alone. Ridicule and shame has been heaped upon [us] because we present the defense, through no choosing of our own."[68]

With respect to the *kapo* Mahl, May asked pointedly: "[H]ow could there be a common design between [Mahl] . . . and the SS? How could there be a common design to murder between master and prisoner, between the conqueror and the conquered?" He then compared Mahl's participation with that of the physician and prosecution witness Blaha who performed autopsies on those killed during medical experiments:

"Do you suppose that he [Blaha] wanted to do that? No more than Mahl wanted to put the noose around the neck of others."[69] May ended on an elegant and patriotic note: "[I]n the mad cry for blood, let us not stain our flag with innocent blood. If somebody must hang for Dachau, let's hang him on the truth, and not on vengeance."[70]

Major McKeon, who represented fourteen defendants including Weiss, Schilling, and Jarolin, gave the final defense closing. Like his co-counsel May, McKeon attacked the vague notion of common design, which underlay both charges, and then asked how there can be a common design when persons come and go. His client Weiss, he pointed out, came to Dachau in September 1942 and left a little over a year later. What common design, asked McKeon, did Weiss fit into? How could Weiss, who methodically reduced the number of beatings at Dachau, be part of a common design when someone much lower in the camp hierarchy beat an inmate?[71]

When it came to Schilling, McKeon observed that the doctor was called on to reduce the suffering of troops from malaria. He then raised the fact that, when fighting yellow fever in 1902, Walter Reed also experimented on human beings. McKeon agreed that, in form, participation in Dr. Reed's experiments was voluntary, but then noted that each participant was paid $200. Each subject, according to McKeon, probably had no idea as to what the consequences of the experiment might be and $200 was simply too great of an inducement for them to resist. He then alluded to other experiments that took place in the United States, including other malaria experiments that involved inoculating unknowing subjects.[72] After these references, he distinguished Schilling from the other defendants. He was neither an SS member, nor a member of the Nazi Party, but a man "in the very late fall of life" who was given an opportunity to work on a disease in a manner no different than Dr. Reed or those doctors in the United States who were doing the same thing. He ended his defense of Schilling by noting that the conventional manner of dealing with physicians who act on the border of propriety is to bring them before medical ethics panels to determine whether unethical conduct occurred and whether that person should be precluded from practicing medicine, rather than criminally prosecuting them. Louis Pasteur, McKeon opined, was so treated.[73]

Verdict, Sentences, and Sentence Review

The following day the court returned its verdict: all forty defendants were found guilty as charged.[74] The court then heard arguments with regard to the sentences to be imposed. For Weiss, McKeon noted that it was not just his wife and child—a second was expected the following month—who were dependent on him, but also members of his larger family, which had been decimated by the war.[75] As to Schilling, McKeon made an argument that can at best be called novel or daring, and at worst laced with temerity—Schilling should be spared so that the results of his experiments could be used to better the chances of survival for millions suffering from malaria. Schilling, McKeon presumed, could interpret those results better than any other scientist.[76] McKeon's argument for Jarolin observed that he had no children, but that his aging parents were dependent on him because three of his brothers were "lost" in the war.[77]

May argued for the *kapo* Mahl. It was a strange argument in a setting where the death penalty was more than a theoretical possibility. May stated that Mahl's case was pitiful and that "his life isn't worth much . . . and [he] hasn't much to live for anyway." He then proceeded to spell out the reason for mercy: "he did what they told him, to save his life, in self-defense."[78]

The following day, December 13, 1945, the court pronounced sentence: thirty-six of the forty accused, including the four discussed, were sentenced to death by hanging.[79] Eight of these death penalty sentences, including Mahl's, were later reduced to lesser terms, and on some occasions reduced more than once. Weiss, Schilling, and Jarolin were hanged on May 24, 1946. Those whose sentences were reduced, some to life imprisonment and some to lesser terms, were all released between 1950 and 1955. Mahl was released in 1952.[80] As we discuss in greater detail in chapter 6, Cold War imperatives on the part of the Western Allies led to the early release of the convicted Germans, many of whom rose to prominence in postwar West Germany.

Conclusion

Was this trial fair? On the side of fairness, it is clear from a reading of the transcript that the officers charged with defending the accused did a masterful job. Carrying on a tradition that goes back as far as John Adams representing the British soldiers charged with manslaughter in connection with the Boston Massacre, a charge that had to be tried before a local Boston jury, these officers viewed themselves as carrying on the finest aspects of the American legal tradition. Nothing in the lengthy transcript of this trial suggests that they acted out of anything but a complete commitment to their clients and did so with great ability. And they pulled no punches.

The court, on more than one occasion, also demonstrated its commitment to fair procedure. When the prosecution attempted to elicit negative character evidence about one of the accused—one who had not presented affirmative evidence of that nature—the court excluded the evidence, following the same rules that would be followed in a courtroom in the United States.[81] When one of the defense witnesses, a former Nazi official, declined to testify on behalf of an accused because he felt that the oath of silence he took during the Hitler regime was still binding on him, the court made absolutely clear that such an oath could not be used as barrier to the defense effort to present evidence helpful to the defendant and summarily overrode a claim of privilege that bordered on offensive.[82] Cross-examination of prosecution witnesses was extensive, never curtailed, and each accused had an opportunity to testify and present defense witnesses.

There are a number of considerations that point the other way. First, was it humanly possible for three lawyers to defend forty defendants? A bedrock principle of American justice, whether administered in civilian or military courts, is that guilt is individual. There is no such thing as collective guilt in a criminal case. The officers representing the accused alluded to this point more than once. Could Major McKeon, for example, really give each of the fourteen accused he represented the consideration necessary to deliver an adequate defense for each? This is not meant to suggest that McKeon was in any way deficient in the representation of his fourteen clients; indeed, his severance motion at the beginning asking that each accused be tried separately subsumed much of this point. There is, however, a limit to what one defense counsel can do, no matter how skilled. Representing over a dozen accused in one case may well be beyond that limit.

A subtler problem emerges from this multiple representation. Virtually all of the accused had made statements, some quite lengthy, and in these statements they occasionally implicated others. For example, the accused Redwitz, a fairly high-ranking official at Dachau, subordinate only to the commandant, stated that Weiss ordered him to turn prisoners over to one of the doctors for medical experiments, that death sentences were transmitted through Weiss and Kick, another accused, and that when he told Weiss that the barracks were built for one-third the number of men occupying them, Weiss did nothing. McKeon represented all of these men, Weiss, Redwitz, and Kick. Similarly, Captain Niles represented the accused Niedermeyer, who implicated his codefendant Endres, another of Niles's clients, in the shooting of Russian POWs. Niles also represented the accused Lausterer, who testified about the brutality of another Niles client, defendant Seuss.

Representation under these circumstances clearly presents a conflict of interest. Kick's evidence that he wanted to do something about overcrowding is exculpatory as to him, but inculpatory as to Weiss. This problem would have been more acute had the prosecution not seemed to refrain from exploiting it. For example, Lausterer's comment on Seuss's brutality appears in Lausterer's written statement, which was an exhibit in evidence. Yet when Lausterer testified, the prosecution did not ask about whether Seuss was exceptionally cruel, as it easily could have done based on what Lausterer had previously said. But to mitigate a conflict at the defense table by holding back at the prosecution table is not really the way the system is designed to work.

There is one other facet to the multiple representation problem that is striking. When some of the accused testified, their direct examination took only a page or two of the transcript.[83] Some of the others were not much longer. In a capital case, this seems extremely minimal. To testify and then simply deny the most damning factual allegation against oneself is hardly the kind of defense that will resonate well with the trier of fact. While it is conceivable that the lawyers for these accused made the judgment that any further testimony would be more hurtful than helpful, it seems more plausible that the constraints of time led to such cursory direct examinations.

In any case, the massive multiple representations made adequate preparation impossible. Placing a defendant on the witness stand requires hours of preparation. Evidence against that person must be reviewed and integrated into the direct examination. The direct examination should be gone over until the client is comfortable enough to articulate his testimony, thereby enhancing the likelihood of its acceptance. The defense lawyer must then switch roles and cross-examine the client as a prosecutor would to prepare the client for that facet of his testimony. Part of this mock cross-examination requires that documents relating to the client must be reviewed to keep the client from being blind-sided before the court. There is no way any of the three capable military lawyers could have had the time to conduct this proper preparation for the forty accused.[84]

Given the charge of participation in a common design to kill, torture, starve, and exploit civilian populations and prisoners of war and the evidence produced, it seems fair to say that—perhaps except for the *kapo* Mahl, as discussed below—all of the accused were guilty. But process matters. Regardless of how capable and aggressive the lawyers for the accused are, mass representation under these circumstances is not the kind of process that characterizes a fair proceeding.

As for Mahl, there is a lingering question of his guilt. It may have been this uncertainty that caused the reviewing tribunal to reduce his death penalty sentence to ten years' imprisonment. But was he guilty in the first place? On more than one occasion in the trial, the prosecution stressed that the crime was not one of conduct, but almost the mental process of participating in the common design to starve, torture, and kill. Lives of inmates at Dachau were cheap. For example, inmates who made footwear out of blankets to avoid walking barefoot in the cold were charged with sabotage and executed by the Nazis.[85] Given this raw brutality, an inmate who refused to do as told faced either a horrific beating or death. In this setting, can it be said with any conviction, to say nothing of a level of certainty that transcended reasonable doubt, that Mahl possessed the necessary state of mind to make him part of the broad design to murder, torture, and starve? May referred to Mahl's participation—largely in the execution of prisoners of war—as the product of self-defense. While the criminal law concept of coercion or duress might be more precise, the underlying idea is the same: Mahl did what he did because he felt he had no choice, not because he willingly assented to become part of the Dachau death machinery.[86] Mahl's conviction does not seem warranted. The subsequent reduction of his sentence and even his release, over six years after the trial, only mitigates whatever injustice was involved; it does not undo it. (We take up this subject again in chapter 7, on the trials of the Jewish *kapos*.)

The Dachau trial stands as an effort to bring justice to those who administered a killing machine that, in terms used in another later Nuremberg trial, "curdles the ink of description."[87] That the military undertook such an effort is both understandable and laudable. That U.S. Army officers undertook to represent the defendants and did so with total dedication, to the best of their considerable abilities, is a tribute to their and the military's commitment to fairness. However, the almost summary nature of the proceedings makes these proceedings a less than stellar example of the administration of justice.

A photo of Amon Göth during his trial, 1946. Photo Archive, Yad Vashem.

Amon Göth being led from court after sentencing. Photo Archive, Yad Vashem

4

The Trial of Amon Göth in Postwar Poland

Poland's "Nuremberg"

One of the most notable trials undertaken soon after the end of the Second World War is that of Amon Göth, the brutal commandant of the Płaszów concentration camp on the outskirts of Kraków. While Göth's 1946 trial in newly liberated Poland has largely been forgotten, his cruelty and sadism have gone down in worldwide infamy through his representation by actor Ralph Fiennes in Steven Spielberg's 1993 film *Schindler's List*. David Crowe, in his biography of Oskar Schindler, calls Göth "one of Nazi Germany's more infamous war criminals."[1]

In examining the Göth trial, it should be kept in mind that the thirst for vengeance in Poland was overwhelming. Next to the Soviet Union, no country suffered as much as Poland from German occupation. Poland was in fact more ravaged than the U.S.S.R. While the latter's large territory, spanning eleven time zones, was only partially occupied, all of Poland eventually came under the yoke of Nazi rule. Between 18 and 20 percent of the prewar Polish population perished during the six years of occupation from 1939 to 1945, making Poland the country that suffered proportionally the largest loss of any belligerent during the Second World War.[2]

Polish infrastructure was devastated as well. The capital city of Warsaw was nearly destroyed in its entirety in 1944 in fulfillment of SS chief Heinrich Himmler's order: "The city must completely disappear from the surface of the earth and serve only as a transport station for the *Wehrmacht*. No stone can remain standing. Every building must be razed to its foundation."[3]

The driving force behind Germany's destruction of Poland was the Nazis' racist vision that saw the German "Aryans" as the master race, the Europeans living to the east of Germany as subservient and inferior, and the Jews as subhumans. The belief in the superior Germanic Aryan race meant that the Slavic Poles were to serve as serfs subjugated to their German masters during the "Thousand Year Reich." The western part of Poland, bordering Germany, would be incorporated into the Reich to create *Lebensraum* (living space) for the Germans. The eastern part would become one of Germany's colonies in Europe, with both its peoples and resources exploited for the benefit of the German supermen.

The subjugation of Poland, existing solely to serve the Third Reich's needs, included the need for territory that would serve as Ground Zero for the Holocaust. To fulfill its racist ideology calling for the extinction of the Jewish race, which was cast as the mortal enemy of the German people, the Nazis established some twenty concentration camps and six major human slaughterhouses—all on prewar Polish territory. The names we associate with the Nazi genocide of the Jews—Auschwitz, Belzec, Chelmno, Majdanek, Sobibor, and Treblinka—were all located in the territory of prewar Poland.

The Nazis' anti-Semitic eliminationist policy led to the murder of almost all of the Polish Jews who found themselves under German occupation. Of the prewar Jewish population of 3.5 million, 3 million were murdered by end of the war. Train boxcars brought Jewish men, women, and children into Poland from all parts of Europe, and these Jews, like the Polish Jews, either did not survive the brutal journey, were gassed upon their arrival at the German extermination centers in occupied Poland, or died through the "extermination-through-labor" (*Vernichtung durch Arbeit*) programs established by the Nazis to exploit working-age Jews before their eventual death. Of the 6 million Jews of Europe who had been murdered (1.5 million of them children), more than half had been murdered in Poland, making postwar Poland the site of the world's largest Jewish graveyard. In light of what Poland suffered, and the undisputed role played by Göth in such misery, we must ask: What did his trial and that of other Nazis before Polish courts represent? Was it merely, in the words of Nuremberg chief prosecutor Robert H. Jackson, "a staying of the hand of vengeance," or worse, Soviet-style "judicial theater"? As the discussion below aims to show, the trial of Amon Göth was not a "show trial" but a genuine effort to deliver justice. At the same time, the Poles aimed for the trial to serve as a didactic purpose—a history lesson to run concurrently with the trial process. Moreover, in setting out this history, the Polish judicial authorities did not shy away from calling the victims targeted by Göth by their rightful name—Jews—and the rightful name of this crime against humanity—genocide.[4] Unlike the Kharkov trial conducted by the Soviets in 1943, the murder of the Jews *as Jews* was made an explicit, central feature of the trial. The Göth trial, therefore, was in every sense a trial of the Holocaust, though in 1946 the term not had yet entered common usage.

The Nazi Career of Amon Göth

During the Nazi era, a significant number of high-ranking Nazis were Austrian (Hitler, of course, among them). Though numerically Austrians were a minority among the Nazi elite, the role they played in the murder and destruction of the Jews and other ethnic groups was disproportionately large. Franz Stangl, the commandant of the Treblinka extermination camp, and Siegfried Seidl, commandant of the Theresienstadt concentration camp in Bohemia, were both Austrians. Our subject here, Amon Göth, was another Austrian Nazi.[5]

Amon Leopold Göth was born in Vienna on December 11, 1908, to an upper-class Catholic family involved in publishing. He finished high school and began university studies but never completed them. In 1925, at age seventeen, he joined the youth group of the Austrian version of the Nazi Party. Five years later, in 1930, he became a member of the *Schutzstaffel* (SS), the elite wing of the party. In 1933, as the Austrian authorities were about to arrest Göth for terrorist activity, he fled to Germany where the Nazis were already in power. He settled in Munich and married, but the marriage lasted only a few months. In 1938, after the annexation of Austria, he returned to Vienna and married again. This marriage eventually produced several children. A subsequent relationship with his German secretary Ruth Calder, a former actress he met in Kraków, produced another child born in German-occupied Poland.

Following Germany's invasion of Poland in 1939, Göth left Vienna for Poland where he worked as a full-time SS administrator, focusing on the expulsion of Jews and Poles and resettlement of ethnic Germans in western Poland. In 1942, he was transferred to Lublin in eastern Poland, where he worked with another Austrian Nazi, *SS-Gruppenführer* (major general) Odilo Globocnik, the police chief of occupied Lublin. Under Globocnik, Göth showed his administrative mettle in the roundups and deportations of Jews. After six months, Göth was transferred to Kraków to work for *SS-Sturmbannführer* (major) Willi Haase, who in February 1943 put him in charge of completing the construction of a small forced labor camp on the southeast outskirts of Kraków, in an area known as Płaszów, where a quarry was located. The Germans began construction of the Płaszów labor camp in summer 1940 on the site of two Jewish cemeteries. Jewish gravestones were used for paving the roads. Before the liquidation of the Kraków ghetto, Płaszów held approximately 2,000 prisoners. After the liquidation of the ghetto in March 1943, the population of the Płaszów camp swelled to approximately 12,000. With the deportation of Jews from Hungary by Eichmann in 1944, some of the Hungarian Jews were sent to Płaszów and its population peaked at 22,000.

On January 11, 1944, the Płaszów labor camp was designated a concentration camp, under the authority of the SS Economic Administrative Main Office (WVHA) in Oranienburg, Germany, which controlled the concentration camp system. Göth now became commandant of a concentration camp, and held that post until September 1944. During his time at Płaszów, he was involved in, as added assignments, the closing down (liquidation) of two ghettos, in Tarnow and Kraków, and one labor camp, Szebnie (also spelled Szebnia). Jews in these three places were sent either to extermination camps or forced labor or concentration camps like Płaszów.

Closing Down of the Kraków Ghetto and Other Liquidations

The Jews of Kraków, which the Nazis made the seat of their General Government, had suffered especially brutal persecution. Two-thirds of the Jews were driven out of the city within a few months, and the remainder, beginning in March 1941, was forced to relocate into a walled ghetto in Podgórze, a district of Kraków.

Deportations to extermination camps began in May 1942 as part of the policy instituted by SS chief Heinrich Himmler to make the territory of the General Government *judenrein* (free of Jews). On March 13 and

14, 1943, the closing down of the Kraków ghetto took place. Göth was in charge of the liquidation. In this *Aktion*, the old and weak, as well as the children, were deported to nearby Auschwitz. Those capable of working marched to the nearby Płaszów labor camp. While the Germans tried to hide the fate of most of the Jews by labeling the liquidation a resettlement, and instructing all evacuees to bring their most necessary belongings and two days of provisions, word had leaked out that those being resettled were being sent to Auschwitz. Many tried to hide and escape, and SS raiding parties entered the ghetto to search for those hiding, shooting anyone who resisted. Göth personally participated in the shootings.

Six months later, in September 1943, Göth oversaw the closing down of the Tarnow ghetto, about forty-five miles east of Kraków. At Tarnow, Göth supervised the loading of 10,000 people onto trains headed for Auschwitz. His next assignment was to close down Szebnie, a forced labor camp located fifty miles southeast of Tarnow and holding about 4,000 Jewish and 1,500 Polish prisoners. Between September 1943 and February 1944, Göth ordered the killing of several hundred Jewish prisoners. The remaining prisoners were transported to Auschwitz where most were murdered in gas chambers. The Polish prisoners from Szebnie were shipped to Płaszów or other labor camps.

Life at Płaszów

As violent as these liquidations were, David Crowe writes in his biography of Schindler, "it is not in Szebnie, Tarnow or even Kraków where Amon Göth committed his greatest war crimes. It was in Płaszów."[6] Two days after his arrival in February 1943, Göth ordered two female prisoners hanged because they went back to the ghetto area without permission. This was done to make an example of the new regime that he was instituting. When a group of prisoners returning from work was discovered to be smuggling extra food into camp, he used a bullwhip on them, and then shot two of the prisoners. Killings became a daily occurrence. Mietek Pemper, a Jewish prisoner who worked as Göth's office assistant, testified at trial that the various methods of murder and torture included "shooting, hanging, [and] savaging by dogs." Alexander Biberstein, a Jewish physician in Płaszów, summed up in his testimony Göth's behavior toward the prisoners: "Whenever Göth put in an appearance at the camp, particularly during the morning hours, somebody was always killed."[7] One of the most notorious scenes in *Schindler's List* shows Göth shooting prisoners from the balcony of his villa located just outside of the camp. According to Helen Jonas, one of the two Jewish women who worked for Göth as his house servant:

> He was a madman. He always, from the balcony he watched the camp, and he's standing with the little machine gun through the window. He said, "You see those dumb heads? They're standing, doing nothing." He says, "I'm going to shoot." And you could hear shooting like hell. And I could hear him whistling a happy tune, like he did so well. And this face with such satisfaction![8]

In May 1944, to make more room at Płaszów for incoming Hungarian prisoners, Göth supervised a health *Appell* (roll call), in which 1,400 persons were selected as unsuitable for work and sent to Auschwitz, where the whole transport was gassed on arrival.

Göth also used his various posts to gain enormous wealth. During the liquidations of the ghettos, he took for himself furniture, furs, clothes, and jewelry. At Płaszów, valuable belongings of new prisoners were confiscated and kept by Göth. Gold teeth fillings were removed from any dead prisoner and Göth took much of this gold.

Göth's Arrest by the SS and Then by the Allies

By the summer of 1944, the SS had decided to close down the Płaszów camp, fearing the approach of the Red Army. Corpses were exhumed from the three killing sites near the camp and then burned. Train transports took the prisoners who were still alive to concentration camps farther west. Göth's fortunes also took a turn for the worse. On September 13, 1944, he was abruptly relieved of his command and placed on administrative duties. The next month, he was formally arrested and charged by an SS police court in Kraków with corruption and murder.

On the corruption charge, Göth was accused of violating SS regulations by not turning over to the SS authorities the wealth that had been forcibly taken from Jewish prisoners as well as ghetto and slave labor residents. Stealing from Jews was fine, but keeping the proceeds for personal enrichment was *verboten* (forbidden).

The SS prosecutors also charged Göth with the killing of his personal assistant, Wilek Chilowicz, a Jewish prisoner who fenced Göth's stolen goods on the black market. On August 13, 1944, Göth had Chilowicz, his family members, and immediate Jewish *kapo* assistants killed. This was done because Chilowicz and his *kapo* cronies helped Göth amass his fortune and therefore knew the full extent of his thievery. When Płaszów was closed, Chilowicz would no longer be beholden to Göth for his life and could possibly reveal to German camp authorities Göth's thievery. In the bizarre legal world of Nazi justice, mistreatment of Jewish prisoners was a punishable offense. As David Crowe explains, "The SS drew a fine line between what it justified as politically approved killings and 'selfish sadistic or sexual punishment.'"[9]

After Göth's arrest in September 1944, the investigation continued, but due to the collapse of Germany, it was never completed. In the meantime, Göth was committed to an SS sanitarium in Bad Tölz, Germany. Though not yet forty years old, he suffered from kidney and liver problems in addition to diabetes; no doubt, his heavy drinking and unhealthy diet in Poland contributed to his ill health.

In February 1945, Göth was arrested by General Patton's troops and moved to Dachau, now serving as a camp for German POWs. He tried to hide his identity by pretending to be an officer in the regular German army, the *Wehrmacht*. Four former inmates from Płaszów, however, recognized him. According to Pemper, one even stood in front of Göth, clicked his heels, and announced, "Four Jewish swine reporting for duty, Herr Kommandant!"[10]

The following year, the Americans turned Göth over to the Poles along with Rudolf Höss, the commandant of Auschwitz whom the Americans were also holding. The two former Nazi camp commandants and six other Germans were brought by train to Kraków. In his memoirs, Höss recalls: "On 30 July [1946] I was taken to Kraków with seven other Germans. We had to wait for some time in the station there until the car had arrived. Quite a large crowd collected, and the people hurled insults at us. Göth was recognized at once. If the car had not come soon, they would have stoned us seriously."[11] Göth was incarcerated in Kraków's Montelupich Prison, used by the Germans during the occupation for Polish prisoners. That same day, the indictment against him was filed before the Supreme National Tribunal of Poland.

Poland's Nuremberg: The Supreme National Tribunal of Poland

At this point, it is necessary to explain why Göth was turned over to Polish authorities by his American captors and how he came to be tried before a Polish court called the Supreme National Tribunal, or NTN (*Najwyższy Trybunał Narodowy*). During its two-year existence from 1946 to 1948, the NTN held only seven trials, including Göth's, before it was dissolved by the Polish communist government.

The original impetus for punishing individual Germans for acts committed at the start of the Second World War came from Poland, and specifically the Polish government-in-exile in London. The Polish exile government first raised the issue of individual punishment before its British and American allies in 1940. It received scant attention. As each year of the war brought reports of additional brutalities, the Polish exile government (together with its brethren exiled governments, especially the Czechs) pressed the Allies to announce stronger measures to punish the Germans.

Eventually the Allies began to pay more attention to the question of how to deal with Nazi war criminals. After 1941, Poland had an important ally, the Soviet Union, on its side since the brutalization that began in Poland now extended into Soviet territory, and had intensified with Germany's victories on the Eastern Front.

On December 17, 1942, British Foreign Secretary Anthony Eden stood before the House of Commons and issued a statement on behalf of the Allies, including the United States and the Soviet Union, denouncing the "bestial policy of cold-blooded extermination of Jews in German-occupied Europe." Eden specifically named Nazi-occupied Poland as "the principal Nazi slaughterhouse" for the Jews of Europe. He concluded with the promise: "[T]hose responsible for these crimes shall not escape retribution."[12]

Eden and his foreign minister counterparts from the U.S. and the U.S.S.R. met in Moscow ten months later. At the end of the conference, the three countries issued on November 1, 1943, the so-called Moscow Declaration, which became the first legal basis under international law for the punishment of Nazi war criminals and collaborators. The Allies "speaking in the interest of the thirty-two United Nations," announced that upon an armistice "those German officers and men and members of the Nazi Party who have been responsible for or have taken a consenting part in . . . atrocities, massacres and executions will be sent back to the countries in which their abominable deeds were done in order that they may be judged and punished according to the laws of these liberated countries."

The last paragraph of the Moscow Declaration expressed a caveat to the above language as it pertained to Hitler and the other Nazi leaders: "The above declaration is without prejudice to the case of German criminals whose offenses have no particular geographical localization and who will be punished by joint decision of the Governments of the Allies." The joint decision that the Allies eventually reached after Germany's unconditional surrender in May 1945 was to put Nazi leaders on trial, with the trials to take place, at least with regard to the so-called major war criminals, before the International Military Tribunal (IMT) at Nuremberg.

The Allies also decided that only the "Great Powers" would be represented at the IMT. The Polish delegation was not pleased. Considering the scale of destruction inflicted upon Poland by Nazi Germany, the delegates argued that Poland should also be being given a seat at the prosecutorial table, or on the panel of judges deciding the fate of the Germans in the dock. In response to these slights, the new Soviet-installed Polish government created, pursuant to a decree of January 22, 1946, its own mini-Nuremberg tribunal. Notorious Germans that committed crimes on Polish soil, and were either captured in Poland or sent back to Poland pursuant to the Moscow Declaration, would be tried before this tribunal.

A critical factor in play during the time the NTN would function was the developing rivalry between the Soviet Union and its Western allies. The Red Army's eventual liberation of Poland from Nazi occupation led to a ferocious struggle for power in Poland between the noncommunist underground supporting the London-based government-in-exile and the communist sympathizers supporting the Soviets. The communists triumphed, and the Polish People's Republic (*Polska Rzeczpospolita Ludowa*, or PRL) was formally established in 1952 after they consolidated power.

The postwar Polish communist government, however, did not create the NTN with the intention that it would follow the model of

Soviet-style show tribunals, in which the verdict was determined prior to the trial. Rather, in a bid to consolidate power by gaining domestic legitimacy among the local populace, which frequently viewed the communist leaders as stooges of the Soviet regime, as well as to gain respect by Western powers, which also viewed the communists with suspicion, the NTN was established as a Western-style court. Its founders aimed to have the court operate both on the model of how Polish courts operated before the war and how the IMT tribunal, then in session in Nuremberg, was conducting itself.[13]

As a consequence, the NTN judges, prosecutors, defense attorneys, and other court staff were, save a few exceptions, not Stalinist loyalists. Rather, they came from across the political spectrum, with many individual jurists who were well known before the war. Some had been Polish representatives in Nuremberg or at other international conferences organized by the Allies upon Germany's surrender to decide the great questions of postwar Europe.[14]

Moreover, while hard statistics are not available, we can surmise that a substantial proportion of Poles prosecuting Nazis and collaborators in the immediate postwar years were Jews. The reason Jews became rather visible in the political police of the emerging communist regimes—and the same could be said of judicial personnel—was clear, as Israeli political scientist Shlomo Avineri notes:

> After 1945 the main task of the political police in those countries was to trace their fascist collaborators and bring them to trial, and to prevent the resurgence of fascist and near-fascist movements. Who but the Jews could be trusted not to have been involved in such movements and not to have brothers and cousins and uncles and nephews who were involved? And who but Jewish people has an unquestioned motivation to bring Nazi collaborators and fascists and anti-Semites to trial?[15]

The most notable Polish Jew on the NTN was Judge Emil Stanislaw Rappaport, a noted prewar Polish jurist who remained in Poland after the war.

While hints of communist ideology would sometimes break through, for the most part the NTN was a court where standards of fair play and procedural due process were considered important. For example, even though the Polish communist government granted the NTN the power to try those responsible for prewar "fascistization" of the country and "for the defeat of Poland in September 1939"—meaning the anticommunists who had been in power between 1926 and 1939—the court never took any steps to try anyone of such a crime.

It would be fair to describe the NTN, throughout its seven trials between June 1946 and July 1948,[16] as acting in a cocoon, conducting proceedings more akin to its brethren court in Nuremberg than to the regular Polish courts, including the Supreme Court of Poland, which had become quickly Sovietized upon their postwar reestablishment by the Polish communist regime. The struggle for power that was going on in the streets, government buildings, and other courtrooms in Poland between the communists and anticommunists (including a serious move to make Poland another Soviet socialist republic of the Soviet Union, favored by a large contingent of the Polish communists) was not a part of the NTN's identity during its proceedings. That the decisions of the NTN were final, and not subject to reversal by a higher court, helped to guarantee its independence.

The best indicator that the NTN delivered Western-style justice was the court's acquittal of SS doctor Hans Münch, who served alongside the infamous Dr. Josef Mengele at Auschwitz. Arrested by the Americans, Münch was also turned over to the Poles for trial. He was one of the forty-one defendants on the staff at Auschwitz to be prosecuted in the NTN's fifth trial, focusing on Auschwitz personnel. Münch and SS doctor Johann Kremer were accused by the prosecution in the Polish Auschwitz trial of engaging in gruesome, Mengele-style medical experiments. Unlike Kremer, Münch called a number of Jewish inmates to testify on his behalf. These witnesses attested to his compassion for the inmates and described his professional behavior towards them, akin to that between doctor and patient. They described him as unlike any other SS man they had ever encountered, shaking hands, for instance, with prisoners when he first arrived at the medical laboratory attached to Auschwitz.

The NTN found that none of Münch's experiments on the unwilling prisoners had harmed them. In its judgment of December 22, 1947, the NTN explained that of the forty-one defendants, he was the only one acquitted; "not only because he did not commit any crime of harm against the camp prisoners, but because he had a benevolent attitude toward them."[17] The acquittal was also based on Münch's refusal to participate in the selections.

In every sense, therefore, the seven Polish trials conducted by the NTN were, in Alexander Prusin's words in his study of the tribunal, "Poland's Nuremberg."[18]

Legal Decrees Used by the NTN

As noted above, the legal basis for the establishment of the NTN came from international law: the Moscow Declaration of 1943, which announced that those Germans (and this included Austrians who became subjects of the Third Reich after the *Anschluss*) "responsible will be sent back to the countries in which their abominable deeds were done in order that they may be judged and punished according to the laws of these liberated countries." As a result, between 1945 and 1949, the Allies extradited to Poland approximately eighteen hundred alleged culprits.[19]

During the war, both the Polish communists in Moscow and the government-in-exile in London issued decrees for the punishment of Nazi and Polish collaborators. The decrees issued by the London government, however, were never put in force after liberation, remaining solely footnotes in Polish history. The only laws actually used to prosecute Nazis and collaborators in Poland were the decrees of the competing communist Polish government. Such decrees became so entrenched in Polish law that many remain in force today, even after the end of communism in Poland.

In July 1944, the Red Army liberated a small portion of eastern Poland from German occupation. The Polish communists arrived on the heels of the Red Army and almost immediately created in the liberated city of Lublin a provisional government, the Polish Committee for National Liberation (*Polski Komitet Wyzwolenia Narodowego*, or PKWN), informally known as the Lublin Committee. On August 31, 1944, the Lublin Committee turned to the question of punishing Nazis and collaborators. The decree it issued became the main basis for the Polish prosecution of Nazi-era crimes.[20] Amended by the decree of February 16, 1945, and four times thereafter, the August 31 decree "concern[ed] the punishment of Fascist-Hitlerite criminals guilty of murder and ill-treatment of the civilian population and of prisoners of war, and the punishment of traitors to the Polish Nation."[21] The text of the original decree, before it was made more elegant through various amendments, was both simple and draconian: "Anyone who, being supportive of the German state or any of its allies participated in killing people, whether civilians or military or prisoners of war, shall be liable to the death penalty."[22]

On December 31, 1944, the Soviet Union recognized the Lublin Committee as the provisional government of Poland, while the Western Allies continued to recognize the Polish government-in-exile in London. On January 17, 1945, Soviet troops captured Warsaw and the Lublin Committee moved the provisional government to the capital city. There it issued a more elegant version of its August 1944 decree. Article 1 of the February 16, 1945, amended version, used to prosecute Göth, read as follows:

> Any person who, assisting the German occupation authorities:
> (a) took part in committing acts of murder, ill-treatment or persecution against the civilian population or prisoners of war;
> (b) acted to the detriment of persons wanted or persecuted by the authorities of occupation for whatever reason it may be (with the exception of prosecution for common law crimes), by sentencing, detaining or deporting them is liable to the death penalty.[23]

As with the IMT Charter, the fact that the perpetrator was in the service of the German occupying forces, or employed by the occupying authority, or acted pursuant to orders, or under duress, was not an excuse for the commission of the above-mentioned acts (Article 3).

According to Prusin, the August 31, 1944, decree "was one of the first Allied-issued laws dealing specifically with the prosecution of war criminals; beyond the crime of collaboration, it covered in essence what the International Military Tribunal later would define as war crimes (violations of the rules of warfare) and crimes against humanity (crimes against POWs and civilians—in this case mainly Jews)."[24]

The prosecution of Nazis and collaborators was a popular move in liberated Poland and so the communist provisional government conducted such prosecutions energetically. The trials helped the communists gain support from the local populace who were distrustful of the Polish leaders arriving with the Red Army. The communist government also established the Chief Commission for the Examination of German Crimes in Poland (*Główna Komisja Badania Zbrodni Hitlerowskich w Polsce*, or GKZNwP) within the Ministry of Justice, whose task was the initiation of investigations and prosecutions of Nazi crimes in Poland.[25]

Special summary courts to try Nazi crimes (called in Poland, until the late 1990s, "Hitlerite crimes") were established on September 12, 1944. Each composed of a professional judge and two lay judges, they were to mete out justice in a "just and swift manner." Prusin observes: "Indeed, the courts acted speedily, though hardly fairly. The indictments were delivered to defendants just forty-eight hours before trial, the presence of defense counsel at the trial was not made mandatory, and any sentences of the court were not subject to appeal."[26]

After Germany's surrender in May 1945, the power of these summary courts was turned over on October 17, 1946, to common courts; however, these courts continued to try individuals in summary fashion, akin to typical Soviet-style show trials. The language of the August 1944 decree that called for the punishment of those who "assisted the German occupation authorities" also gave the communists wide latitude to put on trial their political opponents, whom they accused of collaborating with the Nazis. As expressed by one critic: "It seems that the intention of the authors of the August Decree was to limit, if not outright preclude, the possibility of a fair investigation and a fair trial. The objective was to punish 'Nazi collaborators,' whether real or alleged."[27] As a result, of the eighteen thousand individuals prosecuted before Polish courts between 1944 and 1960 under the August 1944 decree, three-quarters were Poles accused of collaboration with the enemy,[28] "fascization" of prewar Poland, or responsibility for Poland's defeat in 1939. It would be fair to assume that a substantial number of these individuals were not actual collaborators but political opponents of the Polish communists.

Keeping in mind the political context surrounding the creation of the NTN, we now return to examine more closely the decrees establishing the court and its grant of special jurisdiction.

The name "Supreme National Tribunal" of course, was misleading since this was not the Supreme Court of Poland, the country's highest appellate court, which was reconstituted after the war. However, like the Supreme Court, the NTN had no superior court above it and was equal to the Supreme Court under the court hierarchy.

The Polish communist government, for reasons discussed earlier, established the NTN on the model of the IMT at Nuremberg. Like the IMT, the NTN was a single-instance court, with no appeal allowed. As a supreme court of the Polish nation, its special jurisdiction over Nazi-era cases assigned to it by the January 22, 1946, decree was exclusive, and *not* subject to review by any other court, including the Supreme Court of Poland.

The substantive criminal statutes that the January 22, 1946, decree mandated the NTN to apply in judging individuals included: (1) the August 31, 1944, decree and (2) specific provisions of the 1932 Polish Criminal Code dealing with common crimes, including murder and theft. In case of conflict, the 1944 decree took precedence over the 1932 penal code.

As noted earlier, the main provision of the original language of the August 31, 1944, decree, found in Article 1, Section 1, was the crime of "participat[ing] in killing people" (the *actus reus* of the crime) as part of the perpetrator's intent of "being supportive of the German state or any of its allies" (the *mens rea* of the crime). The crime originally carried a single penalty: death. Later amendments added an alternative sentence: "imprisonment of up to fifteen years and no less than three years, or for life."

Trial of Amon Göth

Göth's trial began on August 27, 1946, and lasted two weeks. The Amon Göth who appeared on the first day of trial was a leaner, much healthier man than the one arrested by the Americans. As with Hermann Göring, who also became leaner and fitter and was weaned off narcotics during his incarceration, the prison regimen imposed by Göth's American and Polish captors had a beneficial influence. This made him, like Göring before the IMT, a more formidable defendant. Göth was also allowed by the NTN judges to directly cross-examine prosecution witnesses. He was sharp, often catching those testifying against him in small inconsistencies.

The indictment that had been filed against Göth on July 30, 1946, dealt initially with his acts as commandant of Płaszów and accused him of causing the death of "approximately 8,000 [prisoners]." Specifically, he was charged in count one of "personally with his hands killing, or ordering for prisoners to be savaged by dogs, beat[ing], torture[ing and] subject[ing] prisoners to various methods of torture, resulting with the prisoners dying or becoming crippled." The second count accused him of the "final liquidation" of the Kraków ghetto. The third count accused him of the liquidation of the Tarnow ghetto. It added that, during this liquidation, "Göth personally participated in the killing, beating, tormenting many inhabitants, and instructing his assistants to kill likewise." The fourth count accused him of conducting a "progressive liquidation of the forced labor camp at Szebnie." This count repeated the personal participation language of the previous count. The fifth count accused him of theft, specifically "the valuables of the victims, gold, money, and even clothing or furniture, as also any other item of value, which the inhabitants of the various locations had to abandon prior to being forcefully taken away."[29]

Three observations can be made about the indictment. First, it did not seek to accuse Göth of a multitude of crimes but was pared down by the prosecutors to specific criminal acts that could be easily proven through percipient witness testimony. Second, all the crimes he was charged with were committed against Jews. Third, the charges read like those against a common criminal. Nevertheless, because the NTN was operating in the shadows of its big brother tribunal at Nuremberg, references to war crimes, crimes against humanity, and membership in criminal organizations made their way in during the course of the proceedings. The last two crimes—crimes against humanity and membership in a criminal organization—did not exist in Polish domestic law, the decree of August 31, 1944, nor the Polish Criminal Code of 1932. Accordingly, they are the best examples of how the IMT Charter influenced the trial of Göth and others before the NTN. The NTN prosecutors and judges were aiming to work lockstep with those prosecuting and judging contemporaneously the major war criminals at Nuremberg.

Dr. Tadeusz Cyprian, a prosecutor and judge in prewar Poland and a Polish delegate to the United Nations War Crimes Commission, led the prosecution team.[30] In his opening address, he noted that that the acts enumerated in the indictment violated (1) the decree of August 31, 1944, and (2) the corresponding provisions of the Polish Criminal Code of

1932 that related to murder, grievous bodily harm, torture and ill treatment, infringement of personal liberty and appropriation of property.[31] But he did not stop there.

Cyprian also noted that the acts violated international law. He referred to two sources: Article 46 of the Hague Convention of 1907 concerning the Laws and Customs of War on Land, punishing war crimes; and crimes against humanity, the last promulgated as substantive law by the Nuremberg Charter. The prosecution, therefore, accused Göth of being both (1) a common criminal violating Polish law and (2) a war criminal under international law. Another notable feature of Cyprian's opening address is that he described the offenses committed by Göth as the crime of genocide (*ludobójstwo*), claiming it to be one of the crimes against humanity enumerated at Nuremberg.[32]

Though the IMT did not use the term "genocide" in its judgment, the prosecutors at Nuremberg made use of this term in their arguments, and specifically used the term in its physical and biological connotations. The prosecutors at the Göth trial seized upon this formulation and extended it. In his opening address, Cyprian specifically noted that Raphael Lemkin's definition of "genocide" in his 1944 study *Axis Rule in Occupied Europe*[33] described it as encompassing economic, social, and cultural destruction. Genocide, said Lemkin when he coined the word, is "a coordinated plan of different actions aiming at the destruction of essential foundations of the life of national groups, with the aim of annihilating the groups themselves."[34] Lemkin also spoke of genocide as including the destruction of the "culture, language, national feelings, religion" of the target group.[35]

Lemkin, a Jewish refugee from Nazi-occupied Poland living in the United States, looked specifically to what Germany did to his native land as an example of what constitutes genocide. The prosecutors made use of their fellow Pole's description of what acts constituted genocide to argue that all these forms of destruction were manifested in Poland. Therefore, while genocide was not yet a crime on the books in 1946, Lemkin's 1944 description became a useful tool in the Göth trial two years later. One word *ludobójstwo* (from *lud*, "people," and *zabójstwo*, "murder")[36]—now could encapsulate the entire range of destructive measures used by the Germans against both Jews and Slavic Poles in Poland during the six years of occupation. It also distinguished this occupation from the earlier occupations and dismemberments of Poland by its larger neighbors. Only in this occupation was *ludobójstwo* committed.

The prosecution team also borrowed the formulation from the then-ongoing IMT trial to charge not only Göth, but also the entire clique of Hitlerites (to use the favorite term of the Soviets and their communist allies throughout Eastern Europe) responsible for the atrocities committed in Poland and for their "general plan for world domination."[37] Cyprian aimed to make known to the world that large-scale persecutions and wholesale extermination of people, in this instance Jews and Slavic Poles, was standard German policy.[38]

Cyprian also explicitly acknowledged that besides proving the crimes of the accused, this second trial before the NTN also aimed to serve a didactic purpose. Using language akin to that of Justice Jackson's IMT opening address about the purpose of the trial being to prevent such horrid crimes in the future,[39] Cyprian noted that "these proceedings are taking place not just to ensure that the accused is accredited his rightful justice, not only in order to expose the conscience of these Germans, not only to illustrate to the whole world the real face of Nazism but, primarily and above all, to project the important messages of warning to our future generations."[40]

The well-attended trial included foreign observers. Speakers were set up outside the courthouse to broadcast the proceedings for those who could not obtain a seat inside the courtroom, which was capable of seating several hundred. The Polish press did not shy away from expressly mentioning that the most interested in the trial were Jews. According to one contemporaneous account:

> The Jews are the majority of the audience. These are their days. . . . Today they can whisper to their dead beloved ones, that although there is no compensation for their suffering, there is justice. There are many representatives of the press, the Jewish Historical Commission, University Professors, professionals and the great attorneys.[41]

Unlike in the concurrent trial going on at Nuremberg, in the Göth trial, the murder of the Jews was front and center. Every single victim that Göth was charged in either personally killing or ordering to do so was a Jew. The percipient witnesses testifying against him were all Jews. As we discuss below, one of the two expert witnesses at the trial was the head of the Jewish Historical Commission in Kraków, who testified about the persecution and mass extermination policy by the German invader against the Jews of Poland. This was, explicitly, a trial of the Holocaust.

Lastly, Cyprian noted another unique feature of the trial: the defendant in the dock was accused of committing murder with his own hands. Cyprian used as a counterpoint the recently concluded British trial of Bergen-Belsen commandant Joseph Kramer:

> A considerable amount of publicity has been directed recently to the trial in Bergen-Belsen of that camp's commander Joseph Kramer, a professional friend of the accused. This man acquired the nickname "The Beast of Belsen" which illustrated this individual's behaviour. I have taken part in these proceedings in Belsen, representing the Government of Poland, and I can testify that in the case of Kramer, not a single incident of murder by Kramer personally has been proven in court. This in itself clearly illustrates the comparison of these two professional friends. The "Beast of Belsen" pales into insignificance in comparison to the accused Amon Göth.[42]

Even Höss, the Auschwitz camp commandant, tried by the NTN soon after Göth, was never charged with ever personally killing anyone.

To help facilitate a fair trial, Göth was appointed two defense counsel. However, unlike the IMT trial and the subsequent Nuremberg proceedings held by the Americans and British under the IMT jurisprudence—where each defendant was appointed German defense counsel of his choice—here the defense counsel were Polish lawyers. This is in counterpoint also to the Eichmann trial, in which the State of Israel allowed Eichmann to choose a team of German lawyers and paid for the entire defense. The court relied on Article 86 of the Polish Code of Criminal Procedure, which stated that "only . . . persons appearing on the list of advocates in Poland; [and] . . . professors and lecturers in law at one of the Polish universities" could appear in court as counsel.

The two Polish defense attorneys must not have given Göth much comfort when, on the first day of trial, they asked to be relieved from their duties:

> The accused Göth is a German, the accused is a member of a nation that completely without precedent, committed crimes of unheard proportions, with the most serious intention of eliminating whole nations, certainly the citizens of Poland and the Jewish nation in particular. In view of the fact that we belong to the population directly affected, we feel that the responsibility, and duty of the defence, forces us to suppress our personal views, convictions and feelings. The fulfilling of these responsibilities by us, as Poles becomes extremely difficult and that is the reason we beg the court to be relieved from this task.[43]

Before bringing their unusual motion, however, the attorneys met with their client and received a list of witnesses that Göth wanted to call at trial. They submitted this list to the court contemporaneously with their motion to be relieved as his counsel. Their motion to be relieved was denied by the tribunal, and so they continued as defense counsel, but played a passive role in the proceedings. The most telling example is that it was only Göth himself, rather than his appointed defense team, that cross-examined the witnesses testifying for the prosecution. Neither lawyer appeared to be a zealous advocate for his client. This failure to provide Göth with ardent defense counsel is the largest black mark on the proceedings.

The Case for the Prosecution

The prosecution called close to seventy witnesses, almost all former inmates, to testify about Göth's brutality. Words like "sadistic," "psychopath," "horrible," "monster," and the like came up frequently during their retelling of the horrors at Płaszów. One of the most effective witnesses was Mieczyslaw "Mietek" Pemper, a Jewish prisoner who served as Göth's office assistant. Taking the stand on the afternoon of the first day of the trial, Pemper was no longer Göth's "dutiful office slave" (as he describes himself in his memoirs[44]), but a well-dressed young man of twenty-six, who spoke directly and eloquently about the atrocities committed by the defendant. In his memoirs, Pemper states that while testifying, he "assiduously avoided eye contact with Göth. I wanted to remain objective and not get distracted, confused or unnerved."[45] He added that, during a recess, "friends of mine in the audience said, 'You know, he's sitting there between two policemen, at a considerable distance from us. He can't do us any more harm. And yet we're afraid of him.'"[46] Pemper explains why he was such an important witness: "Many inmates had seen Göth torturing or shooting people, but only I was able to describe the entire network of Göth's responsibilities and powers."[47]

Göth participated extensively in his own defense and, as noted, the Polish judges allowed him to cross-examine witnesses. Pemper recalls that Göth tried "to discredit what other witnesses said on the basis of tiny details and small inaccuracies. . . . He was without a doubt in full possession of his faculties and had a very good memory. . . . He followed the proceedings attentively and took extensive notes."[48]

The trial even featured a moment of humor, elicited during Göth's cross-examination of the former inmate Wilhelm Kranz. As a member of the *Ordungsdienst*, the Jewish inmate security force, Kranz was in charge of the camp's detention center, and so had regular contacts with Göth. As related by Pemper: "After the war, Kranz developed an enormous appetite and by the time of the trial had gained about forty-five pounds. Göth, on the other hand, had become remarkably slim. 'I can recall the Jewish *Ordungsdienst* man you're talking about very well,' Göth said, 'even though I can't remember his name. But it definitely was not this witness.' When the judge asked Kranz what he had to say, he replied, 'It's simple. Back then I was as skinny as Göth is now, and now I'm as fat as Göth was then.'"[49]

The prosecution also relied on the testimony of two expert witnesses. The first, Michał Borwicz, was the director of the Jewish Historical Commission in Kraków; he described the general policy and system of exterminating Jews in Poland.[50] The prosecution's use of Borwicz demonstrated how an important part of the trial was to present evidence about the genocide of the Jews in Poland. The Commission, in turn, published the following year the text of the proceedings and copies of documents introduced at the trial.[51]

The second expert witness, Dr. Ludwik Ehrlich, was a professor of international law at the University of Kraków. Ehrlich testified on the recent developments in international law concerning the trials of war criminals, including the enactment of the Allies of the London Charter for the Nuremberg trials.

As noted, the court allowed Göth to cross-examine prosecution witnesses himself. The following is a portion of the cross-examination by Göth of Pemper regarding a transport to Auschwitz on May 14, 1944.

DEFENDANT: The witness was a clerk in the camp for a year and a half and also conducted secret correspondence?

WITNESS: Yes, in part.

DEFENDANT: Whence does the witness know that those sent to Auschwitz reached [Auschwitz] and were exterminated there?

PRESIDING JUDGE (to the interpreter): Please call it to the defendant's attention that in respect to the questions he has asked the witness, the defendant, who has been interrogated by the Court, has stated that the Auschwitz camp was an extermination camp. Everyone in the SS knew this.

DEFENDANT: Only part of it was that kind of camp.

PRESIDING JUDGE: Please tell the defendant that his deposition says: "I knew, and it was known among us, that in 1940 to 1943 the Auschwitz camp was an extermination camp."

[The presiding judge allowed Göth to proceed with his cross-examination.]

DEFENDANT: Does the witness state that the transport of May 14 [1944] left for Auschwitz and was exterminated there?

WITNESS: That is correct.

DEFENDANT: If so, how can it be that the cook, a prisoner named Meier, received a letter from his wife and children several weeks later?

WITNESS: It is difficult to explain cases like those, which are self-explanatory. Maybe it was done especially to make the cook happy, maybe because he behaved well.

DEFENDANT: The fact is, he received the letter and ran all over the camp with it.

WITNESS: I can say nothing in this matter; I only know [that] no one survived.[52]

The Defense Case

After the prosecution rested its case, Göth took the stand in his own defense. Unlike Auschwitz camp commandant Rudolf Höss, who candidly admitted the mass killings at Auschwitz and his responsibility for them,[53] Göth remained as defiant as ever. He denied certain facts and tried to diminish the extent and seriousness of the crimes alleged against him. He testified that only six to eight people were hanged during his tenure as commandant of Płaszów camp.

PRESIDING JUDGE: The accused has stated that in Płaszów only 6–8 persons have been hung, and besides this he has not heard anything about hanging. Could the accused name the incidents, which are known to him, about executions in Płaszów?

DEFENDANT: The surnames I do not know but there were two women who escaped. In that case they were arrested by police before their escape was known in the camp. The police established that they had contacts with underground bands [partisan units], and ordered execution.

Göth admitted to depriving individuals of their life but only if they were found to be in possession of explosives. He also denied that torture ever took place in the camp and there was no way that the guards could have tortured any prisoners without his knowledge.

JUDGE: Has the accused deprived someone of his life?

DEFENDANT: Yes.

JUDGE: What were such cases, how many and for what reason?

DEFENDANT: In that case, if they did not obey the established rules, if a prisoner was found in possession of explosives.

JUDGE: Did the accused kill with his own hands?

DEFENDANT: Yes, several people.

JUDGE: In how many cases have you ordered for someone to be deprived of his life?

DEFENDANT: Also in several cases, but this I do not remember, I cannot say.

JUDGE: For what reason?

DEFENDANT: For the same reasons as I have stated earlier.

JUDGE: Has any member of the camp guards without your knowledge killed any prisoner?

DEFENDANT: No, I do not believe that was so. In any event I am not aware of such a case. If there were such cases, they were reported to the chief of the police.

JUDGE: Were the prisoners tortured in the camp, if so, by what means?

DEFENDANT: None were used.

JUDGE: Maybe without your knowledge, by the guards on their own?

ACCUSED: Likewise no.

PROSECUTOR SIEWIERSKI: Who was authorised to sentence anyone to death, in cases [where] as you have stated, it was considered legal to do so, as for example in cases of possession of explosive materials?

DEFENDANT: I myself.

PROSECUTOR: Did you have any procedure, which was followed, in the process of sentencing someone to death?

DEFENDANT: No.

PROSECUTOR: Was this the case when the camp was a labour camp, as well as when it was elevated to the status of a concentration camp? Were you therefore authorised to sentence prisoners to death?

DEFENDANT: Yes, I have been authorised, but before doing so I had to make a report, as happened in the case of Chilowicz.

PROSECUTOR: So first you had to have a decision, and only thereafter you carried this decision out?

ACCUSED: Yes.

PROSECUTOR: The cases [where], as you have testified, you were authorised to give the sentence of death, did they include the cases of hanging which you have reported?

DEFENDANT: These incidents happened not in 1943, but in 1944 when I have no longer been in the camp.

Göth also denied that he personally participated in the shootings in Tarnow and Kraków during their liquidations and claimed he never killed anyone during the liquidation of Tarnow.

PROSECUTOR: Were you responsible for the methods deployed in the process of the liquidation of the Ghetto in Kraków?

DEFENDANT: I have not been responsible for the liquidation, nor for any matters in the Ghetto, as everything [*sic*] to the Ghetto in Kraków, was the exclusive domain of [*SS-Sturmbannführer* Willi] Haase.

PROSECUTOR: What were you doing in the Ghetto during this liquidation?

DEFENDANT: Accompanied by my unit, my responsibility was limited to the transfer of people, from those blocks in the Ghetto which were due to be liquidated. The searches in the Ghetto were carried out by the SS.

PROSECUTOR: Did members of your unit participate in the killing of Jews, yes or no?

ACCUSED: My unit was stationed in front of the Jewish Council building. As far as I know, no one was shot there.

PROSECUTOR: Did you personally liquidate the Ghetto in Tarnow?

ACCUSED: Yes.

PROSECUTOR: Were there many people killed there?

DEFENDANT: As far as I know not many.

PROSECUTOR: Have you at any time killed, or ordered to kill a child?

ACCUSED: No.

Göth maintained that any death sentence that was carried out was done so with the knowledge and authorization of his superiors.

PROSECUTOR: Today, from a purely human point of view, does the defendant consider his conduct in Płaszów as having been normal?

DEFENDANT: At that time human considerations or any other sentiment were beside the point. I strove only to achieve my objectives.

PROSECUTOR: Does the defendant think that to reach such objectives even inhuman methods were acceptable?

DEFENDANT: Such methods were practiced during the war.[54]

Göth's defense witnesses were of little help to him. The former inmates whom he hoped would testify about his acts of kindness confirmed his brutality instead. Other witnesses that he had on this list, including Oskar Schindler, whom he hoped would attest to his good deeds, did not appear. It is doubtful that Schindler would have helped his case. David Crowe notes, "From Amon Göth's perspective, Oskar was his friend. In reality, it was a relationship, at least from Oskar's perspective, based purely on necessity. All Oskar's post-war statements about Göth center around two topics: the bribes he paid him and his brutality."[55]

We noted earlier the meager help that Göth's Polish defense attorneys offered him. However, they did raise a credible legal point, arguing that Poland's prosecution was legally defective because the August 1944 decree, as amended on February 16, 1945, applied only to Polish collaborators, and did not cover Germans who committed acts on Polish soil. In other words, there was no valid Polish law or decree permitting Göth's trial. As support, they pointed to the decree's language subjecting to prosecution "[a]ny person who, assisting the German occupation authorities, . . ." They observed that the decree on its face covered only those who assisted the German authorities, and not the German authorities themselves. Göth, as a German authority, was not covered by the decree.

The Verdict

The court found Göth guilty on all counts of the indictment. In its verdict, the court rejected his defense of military necessity. It did so on the grounds that there was no justification under the law of war for the liquidation of defenseless civilians. The tribunal also rejected the defense of superior orders in accordance with Article 4 of the August 1944 decree, stating: "The fact that any of the crimes envisaged in Articles 1 and 2 of the Decree was committed while in service of the enemy authority of occupation or on its orders, or under duress, does not exempt from criminal responsibility."[56]

The tribunal likewise rejected the argument that the August 1944 decree referred only to Poles and not to Germans, finding that the purpose of the decree was to cover all perpetrators. Moreover, it found that Göth's acts of murder were also crimes under preexisting legislation—the murder, bodily injury, and theft provisions of the Polish Criminal Code of 1932. Göth, though a foreigner, had committed these acts on Polish soil, and therefore was subject to Polish law that made his acts illegal.[57]

The tribunal convicted Göth of having "personally issued orders to deprive of freedom, ill-treat and exterminate individuals and whole groups of people, and himself murdered, injured and ill-treated Jews and Poles as well as people of other nationalities.[58]

As noted earlier, the prosecution argued that Germany committed genocide in Poland. The NTN agreed, and found that the genocide was of both Jews and of non-Jewish Poles:

> The policy of extermination was in the first place directed against the Jewish and Polish nations. . . . This criminal organization did not reject

> any means of furthering their aim at destroying the Jewish nation. The wholesale extermination of Jews and also of Poles had all the characteristics of genocide in the biological meaning of this term, and embraced in addition the destruction of the cultural life of these nations.[59]

A month earlier, on July 9, 1946, the NTN's first judgment likewise used the word "genocide" to describe the acts committed by defendant Arthur Greiser, though in more circumspect terms.[60] It is a fitting tribute to Lemkin that it would be his countrymen's courts that would utilize the term.

The tribunal sentenced Göth to death by hanging. In accordance with its procedures, Göth was not allowed to appeal the merits of his case, but was allowed to ask for a pardon. The president of the State National Council did not grant his appeal for mercy.

Two months earlier, in July 1946, Arthur Greiser, the first defendant found guilty by the NTN, was publicly hanged before fifteen thousand people in Poznan. Greiser's was the last public hanging in Poland, akin to the public hanging of the defendants in the Kharkov trial discussed in our earlier chapter. For this trial, and the five that followed, public hangings were abandoned, to fit within the decorum of the IMT. As a result, Göth was privately hanged on the grounds of the Płaszów labor camp.

The execution took place on September 13, 1946, two years to the day after he was arrested by the SS for corruption. At his execution, Göth's hands were tied behind his back. The executioners twice miscalculated the length of rope necessary to hang him (he was six feet, four inches tall), and it was only on the third attempt that the execution was successful. According to Ruth Kalder Göth—his mistress at Płaszów, who took on his name—her beloved Amon died "at peace, a political soldier."[61]

Photo of the defendants at the Ravensbrück trial, Hamburg, 1947 (l to r): Dorothea Binz, Margarete Mewes, Greta Bösel, and Eugenia von Skene. © Imperial War Museum (HU 42874).

5

The Hamburg Ravensbrück Trials in British-Occupied Germany

Women as Perpetrators, Women as Victims

After Nazi Germany's defeat, each of the four major Allied powers conducted trials in their respective zones of occupied Germany, with the British holding 358 trials in their zone. British military courts convicted 1,085 individuals, with 240 receiving death sentences.[1] Two hundred were actually executed, and this included at least 20 women. Albert Pierrepoint, the United Kingdom's official hangman, was flown in from London for each execution or set of executions.[2]

The British trials involved prosecutions of (1) crimes committed during wartime in the now British zone of occupation, (2) crimes committed elsewhere (including those on the Eastern Front) by perpetrators who fled to the British zone after Germany's surrender, and (3) individuals extradited to the British zone to stand trial for crimes committed against British military and civilian personnel, including POWs.

This chapter focuses on one set of such trials held by the British military in occupied Germany: the seven trials of thirty-eight Ravensbrück concentration camp personnel, including camp leaders, guards, doctors, and fellow inmates, who brutalized and murdered camp prisoners.[3] Because the trials took place in Hamburg, located in the British occupied zone, they are often referred to as "the Hamburg Ravensbrück trials." This also helps distinguish them from the trials of Ravensbrück camp staff that took place at other times and in other places, such as in the French zone of occupied Germany, Poland, and the United States. In this chapter, we will refer to the seven trials that took place in the British zone of occupied Germany simply as the "Ravensbrück trials."

One trial that notably did not take place in the British zone was that of *SS-Sturmbannführer* (major) Fritz Suhren, who served as commandant until the camp's liberation in April 1945. To the great embarrassment of the British, Suhren escaped from military custody in November 1946 as he was being readied to be the lead defendant in the First Hamburg Ravensbrück trial. On the run for three years, he was finally captured by the Americans and turned over to the French, who were holding another trial of Ravensbrück personnel in the German city of Rastatt. A French military court convicted Suhren of war crimes and sentenced him to death. He was executed in June 1950.

The Ravensbrück trials feature four notable characteristics. First, the *Frauenkonzentrationslager Ravensbrück* (Ravensbrück women's concentration camp) was the only Nazi concentration camp to hold almost exclusively female prisoners. As a result, all of the victims featured in the Ravensbrück trials were women. The unique experience of women during the war has emerged as a special field of interest in Holocaust studies in recent years, and the revelations from the Ravensbrück trials are an indispensable source of information about the experiences of women prisoners in concentration camps.

Second, since the Ravensbrück staff was comprised of mainly female guards, the trials highlighted the role of women as Nazi war criminals. Of the thirty-eight defendants in the dock, twenty-one were women.

As Daniel Patrick Brown writes in *The Camp Women*: "[W]omen in the Third Reich were never intended to play a direct role in any aspect of administration [of the Nazi regime]. . . . [T]he SS did not train the female auxiliaries to become administrators of the camps; in fact, even FKL-Ravensbrück, the only major women's camp in the Nazi empire, was managed by males."[4] Nevertheless, even if they did not hold top positions in camp administration, female guards, doctors, and nurses dealt directly with the concentration camp inmates and so had a direct hand in determining who would live and who would die. As Claudia Taake has noted: "[T]he *SS- Aufseherinnen* [female guards] were often as brutal as their male counterparts in the concentration camps even though they were at the bottom of the hierarchy within the SS."[5] The hierarchy used for the SS female guards at concentration camps went as follows:[6]

- *Erste Oberaufseherin* or "chief senior guard"; also translated as "chief senior supervisor," "chief senior overseer" or "chief senior warden"
- *Oberaufseherin*, or "senior guard"
- *Aufseherin*, or "guard" (literally "female overseer"); also translated as "supervisor," "wardress," or "matron"

There were only four women to achieve the rank of *Erste Oberaufseherin*, and two of them were tried in the seventh Ravensbrück trial.

The third notable characteristic of the Ravensbrück trials is that they feature another aspect of Nazi policy put on trial after the war: the medical crimes committed during the National Socialist era. A substantial portion of the defendants at Hamburg were medical personnel, charged with involvement in the gruesome medical experiments conducted at Ravensbrück upon unwilling female prisoners, both Jews and non-Jews.

The "deadly medicine" practiced by German doctors during the Nazi era led to the drafting of the postwar "Nuremberg Code," which medical professionals are supposed to follow when conducting medical research. The reference to Nuremberg in these standards is somewhat of a misnomer, however, since much of the evidence of the practice of "deadly medicine" was uncovered by British war crimes investigators in preparation for the trials at Hamburg.[7]

Finally, like the American military trials at Dachau, much of the impetus for the holding of the Ravensbrück trials came from the immediate reaction to the Allied discovery of the horrors inside the Nazi concentration camps. This information became imprinted in the public's mind "back home" through newsreels and newspaper stories. Bradley F. Smith observes: "The American leaders needed an outlet to register their abhorrence of Nazi atrocities, and they were quick to see that the public outcry regarding the concentration camps provided such an opportunity."[8] The same went for the British leaders.

The "concentration camp" trials conducted shortly after the cessation of hostilities took place as the full scope of the Nazi conspiracy to exterminate the Jews of Europe was still coming to light. Hence, these trials reflected how the murderous policies of the Germans were viewed at the time. Unlike today, the Jews, if mentioned at all, were just one category of victims of the Nazis. Donald Bloxham notes that "[t]he indictment [at the Belsen trial] made no mention of Jews"[9] and so he speaks of a "dejudaized Belsen"[10] in the evidence presented by the prosecution at the Belsen trial in 1945. By the time of the Ravensbrück trials in 1946–48, the dejudaization is less obvious, with a greater focus being placed on the Jews as victims. We are seeing here the slow formation of memory about the murder of the Jews of Europe that would emerge years later as the "Holocaust."

Governing Law: The Royal Warrant of 1945

A little over a month after Germany's unconditional surrender, British military courts in occupied Germany were given jurisdiction to convene tribunals for the trials of suspected war criminals. The entire process took place pursuant to a legal mechanism known as the Royal Warrant, dated June 14, 1945.[11] The Royal Warrant was based on the Royal Prerogative, described as "nothing else than the residue of arbitrary authority which at any given time is legally left in the hands of the Crown."[12] It was expressed in the "will and pleasure" of the British monarch "for the custody, trial, and punishment [of] violations of the laws and usages of war committed during any war in which WE (His Majesty) have been or may be engaged at any time after the 2nd of September, 1939."[13] The Royal Warrant trials program could be quickly implemented because it did not require parliamentary assent. Instead, it emanated directly from the wishes of the wartime cabinet, acting in the name of the monarch.

The Royal Warrant trials were prosecuted by the British Army's Department of the Judge Advocate General (JAG) under the auspices of the United Kingdom's National Office of the United Nations War Crimes Commission. The British military tribunals followed the general procedures of British military law. Each was composed of at least three military officers, including a resident and a so-called convening officer. Since the military men acting as judges in most instances were not learned in the law, a legally-trained JAG officer, known as the judge advocate, would advise the court on matters of substantive and procedural law. The judge advocate was impartial and his advice did not have to be accepted by the court.

The Royal Warrant permitted representation by defense counsel either from Britain or by any person qualified as a lawyer in another jurisdiction. In the Hamburg proceedings, all defense counsel were German and their fees were paid by the British military.

The Royal Warrant provided that a death sentence must be unanimous (or by two-thirds of the members if the panel consisted of more than three judges). While there was no right to appeal to a higher court, the accused was permitted to submit a petition for review, which would be referred, together with the trial proceedings, to the judge advocate general or to any deputy for advice and report. All of the defendants sentenced to death at Hamburg submitted such petitions, and were reviewed by Brigadier R. C. Halse, deputy judge advocate general. Halse's reports demonstrate a thorough review of each death sentence, including the accompanying affidavits and letters on behalf of the defendants explaining why the death sentence should not be carried out.

Life at Ravensbrück Concentration Camp

The village of Ravensbrück is located in northern Germany near the town of Fürstenberg, about fifty-five miles north of Berlin. This tranquil and picturesque setting became the site for the largest female prison ever constructed.[14]

Construction began in May 1939, and at the outset, 867 female prisoners were transferred there from an already-existing concentration camp at Lichtenburg. The facility was originally intended as a female work camp. Inside the main camp, women prisoners worked at garment factories that produced various products including fur coats for the wives of SS officers, military uniforms for the SS, and striped prisoner garb. Other women were selected strictly for outdoor work, including cutting trees, moving logs, carrying dead bodies from barracks, and, for the enviable few, work in the various gardens around the camp. In 1942, Siemens constructed a factory next to the camp to build rocket parts for V-1 and V-2 rockets and "rented" the women from the SS.

Both the workload and the brutality at the camp increased as the war progressed. Over time, Ravensbrück also became a site for (1) conducting insidious medical experiments on unwilling female prisoners in the camp's *Revier* (hospital block), (2) a killing facility with its own gas chambers and crematoria, and (3) a site for training female guards. Other experiments were conducted at a laboratory outside the camp with the women prisoners of Ravensbrück as involuntary subjects, or *lapins* (French for "rabbits") as they were known.

Even though Ravensbrück was primarily an all-women prisoner camp,[15] the patriarchal Nazi social structure meant that the camp commandant would be a man. *SS-Hauptsturmführer* (captain) Max Kogel, commandant at Lichtenburg, became the first commandant of Ravensbrück. He was replaced in 1942 by Fritz Suhren. As in other Nazi camps operated by the SS, the commandant was assisted by various German staff, both male and female. In this camp, however, a large portion of supervisors and guards were female.

Ravensbrück also served as a training facility for female SS supervisors and guards for the entire SS camp system. The guards "were trained in treating the prisoners to a constant barrage of foul language and threats, blows to face, head, and body by using fists and truncheons, kicking them with their booted feet, or setting their dogs at the prisoners to bite their legs."[16] Germaine Tillion, a French Resistance fighter arrested and sent to Ravensbrück in 1942, recounts in her memoirs the guard training she witnessed there:

> The beginners usually appeared frightened upon first contact with the camp, and it took some time to attain the level of cruelty and debauchery of their seniors. Some of us made a rather grim little game of measuring the time it took for a new *Aufseherin* to win her stripes. One little *Aufseherin*, twenty years old, who was first so ignorant of proper camp "manners" that she said "excuse me" when walking in front of a prisoner, needed exactly four days to adopt her requisite manner, although it was totally new to her.
>
> It would be a reasonable estimate that about half of the guards took visible pleasure in striking and terrorizing their prisoners, especially the weak, ill, and frightened. Others dealt their blows with the coarseness and simplicity of a peasant whipping her donkey, some simply acted for the sake of conformity particularly in front of their colleagues or the SS men. In any case, even the best of them showed no adverse reaction when a prisoner was beaten in their presence.[17]

Assignment as a camp guard offered secure employment and good pay, and the SS placed newspaper ads recruiting female volunteers. Of the approximate 50,000 concentration camp guards at various camps run by the SS, over 3,500 were women.[18] Almost all received their training at Ravensbrück. Female prisoners were also selected to assist the prison administration, and granted special privileges for such work. These female prisoner-functionaries could be as brutal as any prison guard, and some were included as defendants in the trials after the war.

Ravensbrück was originally built to hold 3,000 prisoners, but by 1942 the inmate population had reached almost 11,000. It continued to expand, reaching its maximum population of close to 30,000 in 1944. The camp grew so large that it eventually had thirty-four satellite camps.

During the six years of its existence, over 132,000 women representing over a dozen nations and various ethnic and religious groups were shipped to Ravensbrück. The largest contingent, over 40 percent, was native Slavs, with the largest nationality being Polish. Approximately 20 percent of the population was Jewish. Five percent of the prisoners were Roma (Gypsies). Rochelle Saidel, in her study *The Jewish Women of Ravensbrück Concentration Camp,* labels the camp "a special hell for women."[19] Saidel sets out the myriad of ways that the women of Ravensbrück could die: "hard slave labor, torture, shooting (in a specially designed alley), lethal injection, 'medical' experiments, starvation, or gassing, both inside and outside the camp."[20] As the camp expanded, overcrowding became a major source of illness and death.

One of the most despicable legacies of Ravensbrück is the medical experiments conducted there on unwilling prisoners. Experimentation began in the summer of 1942 to determine the best way to treat battlefield wounds. With that purpose, prisoners were infected with bacterial wounds and then administered a new antibacterial drug, sulphonamide, to determine its effectiveness in stopping the infections. Discovered a few years earlier by Bayer AG, sulphonamide was the antibiotic of choice during the Second World War before the discovery of penicillin.

Among the variety of ways that inmates at Ravensbrück were deliberately killed, the initial method was to shoot them in the back of the neck. Prisoners too ill to work were killed on site with phenol injections. Condemned prisoners were also shipped to places like Auschwitz or to the Bernburg euthanasia center to be gassed. In early 1942, about 1,500 women were gassed at Bernburg, half of them Jewish. Later that year, about the same number was sent to Auschwitz on two train transports. By April 1943, Ravensbrück had its own crematorium. In November 1944, the SS installed gas chambers at Ravensbrück, with Uckermark, a former female juvenile camp for "asocial" girls located nearby, used as a way station for women selected to die. By the time of liberation in April 1945, approximately 5,000 had been gassed at Ravensbrück, with three ovens operating as a crematorium. Of the 4,000 women moved to Uckermark, only 1,000 survived.

The most prominent person to have been imprisoned in Ravensbrück was Gemma LaGuardia Gluck, sister of New York City Mayor Fiorello LaGuardia. The LaGuardias had a Jewish mother, and Gemma had moved to Budapest after marrying a Hungarian Jew. Gemma was arrested in June 1944 on direct instructions from Himmler and brought to Ravensbrück, where she was designated a "special prisoner." Though considered Jewish under the Nazi Aryan racial laws, she was exempt from the customary twelve-hour shifts at hard labor and also given rations designated for non-Jewish prisoners. In her memoir, Gemma noted that "the Jewish women had the worst and dirtiest work to do. Their block was the most unhealthy and dirtiest, with no electric lights. They were treated like animals and not like human beings."[21] Because the Jewish prisoners were subject to the harshest treatment, they constituted the largest group of those who perished at the camp.

In January 1945, with the Red Army on its doorstep in Poland, the Germans evacuated Auschwitz, sending thousands of Jewish women in open railroad cars during the dead of winter to Ravensbrück. Most of the Jewish women who survived Ravensbrück came from that last Auschwitz group. In March and early April 1945, with the Red Army now in Germany, the Germans began to evacuate Ravensbrück, and over 20,000 prisoners were put on a forced "death march" westward. Those considered unable to make the march were immediately gassed. Early in April 1945, in a bid by Himmler to curry favor with the Allies, 7,500 women prisoners were handed over to the Swedish Red Cross and transported to Sweden. Later, many of these women came to testify at the Ravensbrück trials.

On the night of April 29–30, 1945, Soviet forces liberated Ravensbrück and found 3,500 sick female prisoners. Earlier, the SS tried to destroy much of the physical evidence of their crimes. They blew up the gas chamber on either April 22 or 23 and burned arrival lists, transfer lists, gas-chamber death lists, and the central index of the camp.[22] For this reason, most of the crucial evidence offered at the Ravensbrück trials came from witness testimony, unlike at Nuremberg, where the defendants were found guilty primarily on the basis of documentary evidence.

The Seven Hamburg Ravensbrück Trials

The seven Royal Warrant Ravensbrück trials all took place between the end of 1946 and the beginning of 1948 in a building known as the Curiohaus, located in the Rotherbaum quarter of Hamburg. The JAG selected the Curiohaus because it already had a courtroom and, like the Palace of Justice at Nuremberg, was still standing in the aftermath of Allied bombings. The British viewed the trials as both a means to mete out justice and a didactic event, by which the local residents could learn first-hand about the terrible crimes committed by fellow Germans on behalf of the German people.

Hamburg, which ended up in the British zone of occupation, was 180 miles from Ravensbrück, located in the Soviet zone. Though the Soviets were formally responsible for establishing trials for war crimes committed at Ravensbrück, Moscow did not show any interest. Its reasons were practical: most Ravensbrück war criminals fled to the West in northern Germany. Moreover, Poland also wanted some of the accused for its own trials, since many of the victims were Poles. The potential conflict with the Soviet-backed Polish government and the additional requirement of submitting extradition requests to the British led the Soviets to decline taking over the trials. The British, however, were not ready to turn over defendants in their custody to Warsaw since they viewed the Soviet-backed Polish government with suspicion. The chief of staff of the British Army of the Rhine (BAOR) stated that each nation "should try in its own courts the persons it already hold[s] for war crimes committed at Ravensbrück."[23] Six days before the United States opened its Nazi doctors' trial in Nuremberg, the first Hamburg Ravensbrück trial was underway.

The First Ravensbrück Trial

The first Ravensbrück trial began on December 5, 1946, and lasted close to sixty days. The trial received intensive press and radio coverage, not only in Britain, but also in many other countries, as Ravensbrück victims came from all parts of German-occupied Europe. Sixteen defendants were selected for the first trial, seven female and nine male. The defendants were placed in two rows of seats, similar to the dock constructed at the IMT. There were five guards, five medical doctors, three inmates, one nurse, one Gestapo inspector, and the lead defendant, deputy camp commandant Johannes Schwarzhuber. As noted earlier, Schwarzhuber became lead defendant when camp commandant Fritz Suhren escaped from British custody on the eve of the trial. With so many in the dock, it was difficult to keep track of the identity of each defendant; the solution was to have each defendant wear a number that would be used as a referent along with his or her name.

Before the trial began, British intelligence under the BAOR set up small War Crimes Investigation Teams whose task was to collect evidence for prosecutions under the Royal Warrant. One team, consisting of seven individuals of various ranks, was specifically assigned to obtain evidence for the prosecution of the Ravensbrück staff. The team obtained statements from former prisoners and interrogated camp personnel, including the accused, whose deposition testimony would be used at trial. The depositions began with the following language:

> I have been warned that I am not compelled to make a statement unless I wish so, but that any such statement made, will be written down and may be used as evidence in the future. I make this statement voluntarily without the use of force or threat of force or the promise of personal advantages.[24]

Attorneys for each defendant were given the opportunity to contact potential defense witnesses who would testify on behalf of each accused, but faced a practical problem: most potential witnesses were either not located or unwilling to testify. Very few witnesses who were not already defendants were willing to make statements or appear at trial.

There were three prosecuting officers, two British males and a French female attorney. The lead prosecutor was Stephen Stewart, born Stefan Strauss in Vienna in 1914. Strauss had fled Austria in 1938 soon after the Nazi takeover, upon learning that the Nazis were about to arrest him. He ended up in England and joined the British military in 1939. He was assigned to the JAG services because of his Austrian training as a lawyer and by the end of the war had risen to the rank of JAG major. In occupied Germany, he participated in a variety of war crimes trials. He was first a member of the prosecution team at the Belsen trial, then an assistant prosecutor at the Neuengamme trial in Hamburg, and finally appointed chief prosecuting officer at the first Ravensbrück trial. Stewart's junior counsel was John da Cunha, a Cambridge-trained barrister who first joined JAG as an investigator.[25] The French member of the prosecution team was Madame Aline Chalufour, one of the few women lawyers to participate in Nazi war crimes trials. She had earlier been part of the French prosecuting team at the IMT. The sixteen defendants had twelve German defense counsel between them. The panel judging the defendants was composed of seven military officers: five British, one French, and one Polish. The non-British members of the prosecution and the court were added in recognition that many of the victims were either Polish or French.

In his opening address, Stewart focused on the ill treatment of Ravensbrück inmates. His legal argument was straightforward: the killings at Ravensbrück and the ill treatment of inmates, including the medical experiments committed upon them, amounted to war crimes.[26]

Lead defendant Johannes Schwarzhuber, deputy commandant of the camp, had been arrested by the British on April 29, 1945, after he fled to the British zone.[27] Witnesses at the trial provided varying descriptions of Schwarzhuber. He could send thousands to their death and, at the same time, made efforts to save certain persons by removing their names from the gas chamber lists. Schwarzhuber did not try to exculpate himself. He testified:

> I attended one gassing. 150 women at a time were forced into a gas chamber. *Hauptscharführer* Moll ordered the women to undress, as they were

> to be deloused. They were then taken into the gas chamber and the door was locked. A male inmate climbed on to the roof and threw a gas container into the room through a window which he again closed immediately. I could hear groaning and whimpering inside. After 2-3 minutes, all was quiet. Whether the women were dead or just unconscious I could not say as I was not present when the chamber was cleared out.[28]

Defendant Ludwig Ramdohr, a Gestapo *Kriminalsekretär* (detective sergeant) in charge of interrogations at the camp, admitted that in connection with his work he would beat prisoners, have them injected with narcotics, and deprive them of food and water. During interrogations, he would bend prisoners over a table with their hands tied behind their backs, and force their head into a large bowl of water.[29]

Prisoners interrogated by Ramdohr testified to treatment that was much worse. A female Polish prisoner, Stanislawa Szeweczkowa, testified about a form of torture devised by Ramdohr called euphemistically the "water douche" or the "cold water treatment." It consisted of shooting icy cold water from multiple pipes at high pressure onto a naked prisoner.

Defendant Gustav Binder was the head of one of the clothing workshops at Ravensbrück. Binder drove the women mercilessly with twelve-hour shifts at sewing machines. According to Lord Russell, who oversaw British war crimes trials and later wrote a book on Nazi crimes (see later discussion): "[Binder] was responsible for the deaths of many women by forcing them to work when no longer fit do so, and making them stand outside in the rain stark naked, often for more than an hour at a time."[30]

Of the female defendants, the most notable was senior guard Dorothea Binz. Twenty-seven years old at trial, she denied participating in the maltreatment of the prisoners and claimed to have performed only her duties. Former inmates testified that Binz would beat, whip, stomp, or kick prisoners on a regular basis. Lord Russell, from trial testimony, relates a particular incident of cruelty: "[O]nce, outside the camp when she was visiting a work party in the forest, she felled a woman with a pickaxe and continued hitting her with it until, covered with blood, the woman moved no more. Binz then mounted her bicycle and pedaled back to camp."[31]

Russell summarizes Binz's notoriety: "It is impossible to give more than a rough sketch of this girl's activities at Ravensbrück. She came to the camp on the first day of the war and remained there until the end. . . . For over five years she struck terror into the hearts of thousands of wretches in her power."[32]

Though the fourth Ravensbrück trial would focus strictly on medical personnel, the first trial also featured notable medical defendants, both doctors and nurses. Lead among these was Percy Treite, the doctor in charge of selections. Treite was found guilty and sentenced to death but committed suicide on April 8, 1947. Another doctor, defendant Adolf Winkelmann, died during the trial on February 1, 1947.

Defendant Martin Hellinger conceded in his pretrial deposition that one of his duties was to remove gold teeth from the mouths of corpses, which he performed himself or had one of the prisoner assistants perform. He also conceded that he waited in the crematorium while the dead bodies of just-executed prisoners were brought in so that gold could be removed from their mouths before the mass cremations.[33]

Defendant Elisabeth Marschall was the head nurse at Ravensbrück from April 1943 until the camp's liberation in 1945. Her duties included assisting the physicians with the medical experiments, selecting sick prisoners for execution, and selecting those that would be shipped off to Auschwitz. According to one witness: "It was a perfectly normal thing for the Schwester [nurse] to beat the sick, indeed I have seen Schwester Lisa beating sick women without any reason at all."[34]

Defendant Greta Bösel, a trained nurse, at age thirty-six became a guard at Ravensbrück, supervising work teams. She participated in the selection process of those to be gassed or shipped off to Uckermark for eventual death by neglect. At trial, she denied participating in the selection process.

Three of the female defendants were themselves prisoners in the camp, accused of mistreatment of fellow prisoners. In a later chapter, we discuss the trials in Israel of Jewish prisoners who, in exchange for special privileges, became prisoner-functionaries in the Nazi concentration camp system. Under the SS-organized system of administration of the camps, both non-Jewish and Jewish prisoner-functionaries, known in camp slang as *kapos*, worked under their German overseers to enforce the brutal camp order. The *kapos* on trial in Hamburg were all non-Jews. Their stories are full of tragic irony, since they themselves were initially arrested for defying the Nazi system, but then became instruments for carrying out the brutality of that system inside the camp.

Defendant Carmen Mory was a Swiss journalist who began working for the SS in occupied Czechoslovakia in 1941 in order to pass on information to the Czech resistance. Arrested by the Gestapo, she was sent to Ravensbrück, where she began working as a *kapo.* According to her trial testimony, she did so to survive. She also asserted that if she did not treat prisoners cruelly, she would have been removed from her position. One witness testified that Mory "behaved like a real SS."[35] According to Lord Russell: "The Belgian women in the camp called Mory 'The Monster.' She used to drag sick women, half-dead, out of their beds . . . have them pulled into the washhouse, dumped on the cold stones, and have buckets of cold water poured over them saying, 'Now you will be clean.'"[36]

Former French prisoner Violette Le Coq implicated Mory in murder:

> One night we were awakened by shouting which came from the room where the insane prisoners were housed. Carmen Mory, a student of medicine, a French nurse and myself got up and went to the room to see what was happening. We opened the door and saw two women fighting with each other. One of these was apparently a Russian. Mory took one of the leather belts which were always hanging there and started belaboring both the women. She sent the medical student to get some ampoules, and then gave both the women injections. The following morning I returned to the room where I saw five women lying dead, including the two women whom Mory had injected the night before.[37]

Defendant Vera Salvequart was a prison nurse working in the *Revier.* Lord Russell describes Salvequart as "[o]ne of the most sinister figures in th[e] camp."[38] Born in Czechoslovakia of German background, Salvequart was arrested by the Nazis for having relationships with Jewish men in violation of the Nazi race laws, released, and then arrested again for helping five detained officers to escape.[39] Twenty-seven years old at the time of trial, Salvequart was accused of mistreating and administering poison to patients, and inspecting cadavers for gold teeth. She likewise denied all accusations. Former inmate Lotte Sontag, whom Salvequart called in her defense, ended up helping the prosecution by confirming testimony of other witnesses that Salvequart administered poison to sick prisoners: "I was told by Vera Salvequart herself that the women were partly killed by poisoning with a white powder by her and partly murdered by injections which were administered by the SS men Koeller and Rapp."[40] Sontag testified that the prisoners were suspicious of receiving treatment from any nonprisoner staff, but since Salvequart "was herself a prisoner with a kind voice and apparently friendly to them they took the powder thinking they were taking medicine."[41]

On January 30, 1947, the prosecution and defense attorneys began their closing arguments. Major Stewart began his closing argument as follows: "May it please the court. It is not the duty of the prosecutor before a British court either to press the court for a conviction or to ask you for a finding or a sentence; it is merely my duty to put before you, now that you have heard the whole of the evidence, once more the contentions of the prosecution, and impartially to view the whole of the evidence in order to show how it supports, as I say, the case for the prosecution."[42]

On February 3, 1947, the seven-member panel issued its verdicts. All sixteen defendants were found guilty of war crimes. Eleven were sentenced to death, including four female defendants. All four SS doctors—Rolf Rosenthal, Gerhard Schidlausky, Adolf Winkelmann, and Percy Treite—were sentenced to death, but only two were actually executed. As noted above, Winkelmann died on the day the verdicts were announced, and Treite committed suicide two months later.

On May 2–3, 1947, the defendants were hanged at Hameln Prison. Their bodies were buried in a nearby cemetery. Defendant Marschall, age sixty, was the oldest female to be executed as a Nazi war criminal.

The execution of former *kapo* Vera Salvequart was stayed because she petitioned the British monarch for a reconsideration of her sentence. Granted a stay while the Royal Prerogative was being considered, her appeal was eventually rejected and she was executed on June 2, 1947. Carmen Mory, the *kapo* originally from Switzerland who spied for the Czechs, was also sentenced to death. She committed suicide on April 9, 1947, by cutting her wrists with a razor blade hidden in her shoe.

The remaining defendants received various prison terms, ranging from ten to fifteen years' imprisonment. Martin Hellinger, the dentist, was sentenced to fifteen years' imprisonment but was released in May 1955. Eugenia von Skene, another *kapo*, received a sentence of ten years and was released early in 1951. Defendant Heinrich Peters, an SS camp supervisor, received a fifteen-year sentence and was released in 1955. Defendant Margarete Mewes, a guard, received a ten-year sentence and was released five years later, in February 1952.

The Fourth Ravensbrück Trial

Because all five defendants at the fourth Ravensbrück trial were medical personnel, it has been called the "Doctors and Nurses Case." The trial began on May 5, 1948, before five British military officers and ended a month later. Deputy Judge Advocate Halse, reviewing the fairness of the fourth trial a month after its conclusion, summarized:

> Ravensbrück Concentration Camp has now become a matter of notoriety and it has been proved time and again in war crimes trials and again in this trial that many thousands of female allied nationals passed through its gates . . . and a very large proportion of these nationals either never came out of the camp alive or only came out of the camp in order to be taken to a place of destruction. . . .
>
> There was, in my opinion, in this case ample evidence of physical ill-treatment of both the fit and the sick internees. In addition, evidence was given in connection with medical experiments carried out in the most brutal manner by doctors who were apparently stationed there for the purpose of experimenting on human guinea pigs. There was further evidence that lethal injections were given to inmates who were too sick to be of any further use to the German war machine and also evidence of operations carried out in order to procure abortions in respect of any woman who were expectant mothers in the camp.[43]

The case was based on the testimony of twenty-four witnesses, all but one of whom were former female inmates. As noted earlier, because the Germans destroyed almost all of the records at Ravensbrück, the prosecution's case rested almost exclusively on testimony of these former female prisoners.

Defendant Benno Orendi, age thirty at trial, was a medical doctor accused of assisting Percy Treite, the doctor sentenced to death at the first trial, in conducting medical experiments and participating in the selection of prisoners for the extermination transports. Inmates described Orendi as "inhuman, brutal, vulgar, and rough."[44] Other doctors testified that "he knew nothing about the art of medicine and was allowed to gain experience on the bodies of internees who had no way of complaining."[45] Witnesses also testified that he "prepared the lists for the selections and indeed suggested that certain persons should be included on that that list who had not previously been included."[46]

Upon taking the stand, Orendi refused to "make a [sworn] statement, saying that he considered he was still bound by his oath of allegiance to the late Adolf Hitler."[47] Instead, in a short unsworn statement he "den[ied] that he ever ill-treated anyone and . . . never worked independently but always did what he was told by Dr. Treite who was then senior doctor."[48] Two former prisoners testified on the defendant's behalf claiming that, though present, he did not participate in the selections and was kind to prisoners.

Orendi was found guilty of what the prosecutors called the "omnibus charge" of mistreating prisoners and also for murder. Accordingly, he was sentenced to death. In reviewing his sentence, Deputy Judge Advocate Halse noted: "There is no doubt that this man was only a minor cog in the machine. He has never, however, put forward the plea that he was acting under superior orders. Indeed, he could not, since he denied ever having had anything to do with the selections."[49]

A procedural dispute during trial indicated the extent to which the British aimed to make their trials fair. Orendi complained during the course of the trial that his appointed German counsel "was not doing everything he could"[50] and asked for another attorney. Orendi's sister also wrote to the British military authorities claiming that the attorney tried to extract payment from her. After an investigation, the judge advocate found "that this accused's original counsel was doing his utmost for the accused and that he was acting in accordance with the traditions of the

German bar."[51] Though rules for the tribunals did not allow such objections and substitutions, the judge advocate nevertheless allowed another attorney to take over the case. During the postconviction review process, Halse reviewed whether this change of counsel during the course of the trial prejudiced Orendi. He determined that "the accused did not suffer as a result of the change of counsel nor was he prejudiced in the early stages by being represented by counsel who he subsequently said did not satisfy him."[52] Orendi was hanged on September 17, 1948.

Defendant Walter Sonntag, age forty-one at time of trial, was a senior medical doctor also accused of participating in medical experiments. In his postconviction report, Halse summarized the evidence against Sonntag: "A number of witnesses spoke of him allowing flogging to take place in respect of women who were quite clearly physically incapable of receiving corporal punishment. He was described as one of the most brutal men in the camp and he frequently kicked inmates . . . particularly those of the Jewish faith."[53] On the accusations of murder, witnesses, including other defendants, confirmed that Sonntag made selections of those who would be sent for extermination and also administered lethal injections. Sentenced to death, Sonntag was executed on September 17, 1948.

Defendant Lisbeth Krzok, age thirty-nine at the time of trial, was a registered nurse. "Witnesses for the prosecution described her as the 'camp horror' and very cruel."[54] Initially denying she beat prisoners in her pretrial statement, she admitted doing so at trial. Krzok was sentenced to four years' imprisonment on July 3, 1948, and released in 1951.

Defendant Martha Haake, a registered nurse age thirty-three at the time of trial, testified: "The medical treatment was good. The food in Ravensbrück concentration camp was at least as good and the same quantity as in this Internment Camp. . . . I cannot remember that anybody was punished in the *Revier.* I have never beaten a prisoner . . . nor have I seen anybody beaten. . . . Every patient had his own bed. . . . [I]n winter every patient had 3–4 blankets. All beds were covered with linen, a white sheet, chequered bolstors, and coverlet."[55]

The court found her testimony not credible. Witnesses "spoke of this woman having treated Allied nationals most brutally and she appeared to have a particular dislike for French internees."[56] Haake was sentenced to ten years of imprisonment for her mistreatment of prisoners. While Haake and Kezok both worked as nurses, the court found Haake more culpable because she administered heavy doses of lethal medications to internees. She was released in 1951 for medical reasons.

The last defendant, forty-year-old Gerda Ganzer, was a prisoner-nurse arrested by the Gestapo in 1938 for making anti-Nazi statements. She spent the remainder of the Nazi years in various German camps, including Auschwitz. In 1942, she was transferred to Ravensbrück, where she worked as the senior prisoner-nurse at the *Revier*. Arrested by the British in 1947, Ganzer was accused of "killing by lethal injections . . . a number of female Allied internees" and "[t]he killing of a newly born child of an unknown female Allied internee . . . on a day between September 1941 and December 1942."[57] The latter was based on pretrial testimony given by a fellow prisoner.

While at the *Revier*, Ganzer entered into a romantic relationship with SS physician Rolf Rosenthal, who was tried and sentenced to death in the first Ravensbrück trial. The court sentenced her to death, but her sentence was reduced to life imprisonment pursuant to Halse's recommendation:

> [O]n the one hand there was, in my opinion, ample evidence to show that she administered lethal doses to the inmates. On the other hand she was undoubtedly under the influence of her lover and witnesses have said that on a number of occasions she helped them where she was able to do so. . . . It must also be borne in mind that this woman was not a Nazi. In fact she was at the time of the commission of the crimes an inmate of the camp because of her objection to the Nazi regime.[58]

In 1950, the British reduced Ganzer's sentence to twenty-one years' imprisonment, and then finally in 1954 to twelve years. She was released in 1961.

The Other Ravensbrück Trials

The other Ravensbrück trials followed the patterns of the two trials previously discussed. The second Ravensbrück trial began on November

5, 1947, and involved only one defendant, Friedrich Opitz, a Nazi Party member in charge of all the clothing manufacture shops at Ravensbrück. Opitz was charged with three war crimes: ill-treatment of prisoners; sending prisoners to Uckermark, knowing their impending death; and the killing of an unknown female Czech prisoner by kicking her in the stomach so severely she died a week later.[59] According to Halse upon reviewing Opitz's sentence:

> [T]he punishment meted out by the accused and his henchmen was barbaric in the extreme. Evidence was called that the accused had been seen hitting workers with a stick, belt and with his hand, that he encouraged his henchmen to ill-treat workers in a similar way, he frequently increased the output of the shops and if the inmates did not keep up the output, they were deprived of the small quantity of food which they normally received and were forced to stand for long periods in the open.[60]

A former female prisoner testified that she "prepared [for Opitz] lists of useless workers" to be sent for extermination at Uckermark and "it was common knowledge that anybody who went to the youth camp would be gassed."[61]

Opitz denied beating any prisoners, "but admitted that he might have slapped their faces because of thefts."[62] With regard to the deadly kicking of the Czech prisoner, Opitz claimed on the stand that it was a case of mistaken identity. The prosecution witness was then recalled to the stand to confirm that it was indeed Opitz who committed the killing. The five-person military court (with all British personnel) convicted Opitz on all three counts and sentenced him to death; he was executed on January 26, 1948.

The third Ravensbrück trial, also referred to as the "Uckermark trial," began on April 14, 1948, and was based on the actions that took place at Uckermark, the former camp for "asocial" female juveniles. After the juvenile camp was closed in January 1945, approximately 4,000 women from nearby Ravensbrück were moved there, over a period of six weeks, to die when they were determined unfit for work; approximately 1,000 survived.

Five female camp officials of the Uckermark concentration camp were indicted for mistreatment of prisoners and participation in the selection of prisoners for gassing. Three defendants were found guilty and received prison terms. Two were acquitted because the court determined they had worked at Uckermark only while it was still a camp for German girls.

The fifth Ravensbrück trial began on June 16, 1948, and lasted thirteen days. It involved three male defendants, all former guards at Ravensbrück. All were found guilty.

The sixth Ravensbrück trial began on July 1, 1948, and lasted twenty-five days. On trial were two male defendants, a guard who operated the main gates of the concentration camp and a professional tailor who helped supervise another clothing workshop. Both were found guilty, given prison terms, and then released early in the 1950s.

The seventh and final Ravensbrück trial began on July 2, 1948, and lasted for sixteen days. It involved six female defendants who served either as wardens or chief wardens at Ravensbrück. All were accused of mistreating prisoners and also participating in the selection of prisoners for gassing. Of the four found guilty, two were sentenced to death by hanging and two were given prison terms; and two were acquitted. This trial featured the only two female guards to have attained the rank of *Erste Oberaufseherin*. One of these, Anna Friederike Mathilde Klein, was acquitted due to lack of evidence. The other, Luise Brunner, was sentenced to three years of imprisonment, since evidence of her participation in the selections for gassing was lacking.

Was Justice Served?

The trial records and other documentation from the Ravensbrück trials show a strict devotion to fairness, both procedural and substantive, on the part of the prosecutors and the tribunal officers.

Pretrial investigations were thorough, and no one accused was convicted based on testimony of just one witness. Though evidence of prisoner mistreatment at Ravensbrück was legion, the seven tribunals all focused on whether sufficient evidence existed to find guilty each defendant of the specific accusations of war crimes lodged against them. Almost all defendants, for example, were charged with the so-called "omnibus charge" of ill treatment of prisoners, but only those that were shown themselves to have committed such ill treatment were convicted of this charge. Medical personnel accused of selections and involvement in experiments were found guilty only when credible witness testimony that a defendant actually participated in the selections and experimentation was produced. If a defendant was convicted of murder, specific identifiable acts of murder had to be proven.

As noted earlier, the German defense counsel had difficulty in getting potential witnesses who would purportedly testify on behalf of the accused to appear at trial, which presented the possibility that exculpatory evidence was not introduced. On the other hand, for those found guilty, especially those sentenced to death, numerous witnesses corroborated acts of murder or participation in murder. Moreover, in some cases when witnesses sought by the defense did appear, they ended up hurting the defense by corroborating testimony given by prosecution witnesses.

Court records reflect that for those who received the death sentence, defense counsel often submitted witness statements postconviction seemingly helpful to the defendant, and these were considered during the review of the sentence.

While those convicted could not appeal to British courts, the detailed reviews conducted by Deputy Judge Advocate Halse of each trial were akin to a review by a British judicial officer. Those who were sentenced to death had multiple reviews of their sentences, including a final review by the British military governor in occupied Germany.

Whenever questions arose as to whether a certain defendant was treated fairly, the Office of the Judge Advocate investigated the matter. An example previously discussed is defendant Orendi's accusation in the fourth trial of inadequate representation. That led to an investigation, and though not required, Orendi was appointed new counsel. A complaint by an English barrister observing how defendant Gerda Ganzer was treated, though unsubstantiated, was also taken seriously and investigated.[63]

The archival trial records contain letters of appeal for defendants sentenced to death from former prisoners who dispute the statements made by prosecution witnesses. Some accuse the prosecution witnesses of bias, alleging that they were communists and so ready to testify against any German on the dock. Others state that some prosecution witnesses, as a result of their suffering, were ready to implicate all those accused. Defense counsel Dr. A. Meyer-Labastille, in the appeal of the sentence of his client Orendi, illustrates this contention:

> [O]wing to their own bad experiences in Ravensbrueck, and through pamphlets which appeared in great number, and finally, through frequent discussion of concentration camps these [prosecution] witnesses have become prejudiced against the administrative personnel of concentration camp to such an extent that they tend to confuse their own experiences with those of other prisoners and they mistake one person for another. But the worst of it is that they are no longer capable of distinguishing responsibility of an individual for specific criminal acts from the guilty responsibility of a criminal clique for the generally known inhuman conditions at Ravensbrueck.
>
> As is humanly entirely conceivable—every member of the camp-administration is in their eyes a criminal. One cannot blame these women having been ill-treated for years that their thinking is being guided by such elementary emotions. . . . One therefore should mistrust in principle the statements of former prisoners.[64]

It is difficult to assess these letters, especially since they paint such a different picture of the convicted defendants presented at trial. Because they are written statements of former prisoners who did not testify, their versions cannot be subject to cross-examination. What can be said is that the prosecution witnesses who did testify were closely questioned by the tribunal judges and also cross-examined by the German defense attorneys. We can only surmise that if the prosecution witnesses' testimony was discredited, the defendants would not have been convicted. In fact, when the charges were not adequately substantiated during the trial, military officers either acquitted the defendant of that specific charge or issued a complete acquittal. Of the thirty-eight defendants during these seven trials, the court completely acquitted four.

Most remarkable are the verdicts against the highest-ranking female guards, Luise Brunner and Anna Klein. Klein was acquitted and Brunner sentenced to three years. These verdicts starkly demonstrate that military judges were indeed looking at individual culpability rather than imposing group guilt. Being a female guard at a concentration camp, even a chief supervisor, was not made a crime; only those guards who were proven to have directly mistreated prisoners were punished. The principle of command responsibility was not used by the judges to convict Brunner and Klein for acts done by others who were under their command.

Our only criticisms are of the death sentences issued for some of the *kapos*, since those sentences did not take into account the defendants' status as prisoners. However, as shown in the case of Gerda Ganzer, the death sentences for some of these former prisoners were commuted on review.

On the other hand, there are some who criticize the trials as having issued sentences that were much too lenient. American historian Adam Brown, speaking of all the British war crime trials in occupied Germany, states: "The lenient attitude of the British is baffling. The sentences meted out were frequently downright asinine. It often appeared that an SS woman had to be in charge of large-scale 'selections,' sending masses of helpless people to their deaths to merit the death penalty themselves. The letters sent to the British government protesting the unjust verdicts are filled with contempt for such ridiculously lenient punishments."[65]

Geneviève de Gaulle Anthonioz, the niece of General de Gaulle who was deported to Ravensbrück, wrote of her experiences not long after the war and made the same critique, asserting that the British failed to appreciate the brutality that took place at the camp. As proof, she noted that military judges repeatedly demanded former inmates who testified as witnesses to provide exact dates for when they were beaten by a certain defendant and when certain camp operations took place.[66] This accusation demonstrates to us the devotion of the British judges to fairness by testing the credibility of the witnesses. Only through the use of relevant, reliable, and credible testimony could a proper and just verdict be reached. In the same vein, Brown's description of the verdicts as "asinine" is also off the mark. Eighteen of the thirty-eight defendants from Ravensbrück were sentenced to death; surely, this is not an indication of leniency.

The Aftermath

Great Britain's great experiment in post-Holocaust justice came to an end as quickly as it was implemented. From the end of the 1940s and definitely by the 1950s, the British public no longer wanted to hear about the war. The focus of British politicians, like those of the other Western Allies, likewise turned to the establishment of an economically strong and militarily rearmed Federal Republic of Germany, created out of the American, British, and French zones, as a bulwark against Soviet expansionism. As Donald Bloxham points out: "[T]he war-time alliance had turned on its head, and convicted war criminals were an irksome reminder of the time when Germany was the sworn enemy of the 'big three.' . . . At a time when memories were short and perceptions unclear, it was comparatively easy to ignore the past for the purposes of the present."[67]

While the story of the premature release of war criminals by the Americans is well known, Bloxham notes that the British record of letting convicted war criminals going free is, as he puts it, "even less impressive than that of the United States."[68] It is surprising how the atrocities that so shocked the British, when they began revealing themselves upon the liberation of the camps in late 1944 and until surrender in May 1945, so quickly passed into memory.

In May 1948, during a debate in the House of Lords, the lord chancellor, Lord Jowitt, expressed the prevailing opinion of the time—both among the majority of the politicians and the British people—by noting that "the indefinite prolongation of the trials is not performing a useful or a desirable purpose."[69] Winston Churchill, now head of the opposition, concurred, and in his lyrical style declared: "Revenge is, of all satisfactions, the most costly and long drawn out; retributive persecution is, of all policies, the most pernicious."[70] This, from the British leader who just four years back was calling for the creation of drumhead courts martial for captured German leaders that would convene in the mornings and conclude with the expected executions by sunset.[71]

On September 1, 1948, two months after the last Ravensbrück trial concluded, Clement Attlee's ruling Labour government announced that the British would not hold any further trials. The still-ongoing trials were quickly concluded and the war crimes trials program shut down. With the establishment of the Federal Republic of Germany in 1949, prosecution of Nazi war criminals in the former British zone was taken over by the new West German criminal justice system. By the time Winston Churchill and the Tories returned to power in 1951, the war crime trials and the crimes against the Jews first highlighted during the trials appeared to be old history. Churchill, who had now made a complete about-face on punishment of Nazis, moved to release those in British custody, first the generals and then the lower-ranking personnel. By 1957, all convicted war criminals in British custody had been released, a year before the Americans released their last German prisoner.

Not that there wasn't resistance to the mood for forgetfulness in the service of fighting the Cold War. In 1954, Lord Russell of Liverpool, who as deputy attorney advocate general of the British Army of the Rhine oversaw all the trials by British military courts of German war criminals, wrote *Scourge of the Swastika*, which recounted in graphic detail the crimes of the Nazis. As suggested earlier, a substantial portion of Russell's indictment of National Socialism in the book recounts the testimony of victims and defendants at the first Ravensbrück trial.

Russell, still in government service when he sought to publish his book, was informed by the lord chancellor, Lord Simonds, that the book was incendiary since it put Britain's new ally, West Germany, in a horrible light. Russell was given a choice to suppress the book or resign. He chose the latter. The concise tome, about two hundred pages, became a bestseller. In the political arena, Labour Party politician Nye Bevan rallied against "Guns for the Huns," aiming to stop or least to slow down the rearmament of Germany.

Labeled by their opponents as inveterate German-haters, Russell and others like him were soon drowned out by the mandarins of the Cold War Anglo-American policy, who aimed to get West Germany rearmed and economically strong as rapidly as possible. The *autobahn* away from Nuremberg now led directly to a West Germany full of former high- (and not so high-) ranking Nazis regaining their foothold as part of the postwar ruling class.

In East Germany, prosecution of German female concentration camp guards went through two stages. Initially, the role of female Nazi perpetrators was diminished, and so the sentences handed out against the former Ravensbrück female guards tried by the Soviets or East German courts were quite lenient.[72] Ravensbrück Memorial Director Insa Eschebach, who has examined the East German files of these proceedings, speaks of "three main devices used in legal discourse in order to exonerate those women: first, the emphasis was put on the youthfulness of the accused; second, their activities were described as a moral lapse; and third—and here the particular nature of legal texts of the Soviet zone becomes apparent—the working class status of the accused was highlighted."[73] As a result, of the thirty-eight women charged in the Soviet zone of occupation before 1950, eight were acquitted or given suspended sentences. The majority of those convicted were sentenced to a few months imprisonment. For example, the SS camp leader of a Ravensbrück satellite armaments work camp received a suspended sentence. The court emphasized that she was guilty only of "a few moral lapses."[74] Eschebach points out that *entgleisung*, or "moral lapse," was a term frequently used in the early proceedings in East Germany against former female guards.

With the founding of the German Democratic Republic in October 1949, and in the context of the Cold War, the situation changed. East Germany now sought to burnish its antifascist credentials vis-à-vis the perceived fascist-dominated Federal Republic of Germany. As a result, "the judgments became increasingly dominated by the negative image of the SS-beast and the SS-[female]hyena. The severity of sentences increased drastically: five of the eight former women guards sentenced after 1950 received life imprisonment, and in one case the death penalty."[75]

The story of the prosecutions of female perpetrators from Ravensbrück resumes decades later, not via the British or Germans but the Americans. On March 14, 1973, Hermine Braunsteiner Ryan, a former *Aufseherin* at Ravensbrück who later moved on to Majdanek, was extradited by the United States back to Germany to stand trial.[76] She became the first female Nazi criminal to be extradited from the United States.

After the war, Ryan married Russell Ryan, a U.S. Air Force mechanic stationed in Germany. She came to the United States in 1959 and became a U.S. citizen in 1963, living the life of a suburban housewife in Queens.

Braunsteiner Ryan was tracked down by Simon Wiesenthal, who was told about her by female survivors living in Israel. She was called by prisoners the "Stomping Mare" for her brutality and was accused of "whipping women to death, seizing children by their hair and throwing them on trucks to take them to the gas chamber, kicking away a stool to hang a young girl, and stomping old women to death with her [steel-studded] jackboots, among other cruelties."[77] Her husband, in an interview, told a journalist: "My wife, sir, wouldn't hurt a fly."[78]

In Germany, following extradition, Braunsteiner Ryan was put on trial with fifteen other defendants from Majdanek. Found guilty of murdering 80 people and abetting the murder of more than 100 children and about 1,000 adult inmates, she was sentenced in 1980 to life imprisonment. Released sixteen years later on the grounds of ill health, she died in 1999.

The discovery of Braunsteiner Ryan, and that of other hidden Nazis and collaborators living quietly in the United States, led to the establishment in 1979 of the U.S. Justice Department's Office of Special Investigations (OSI). This, in turn, led to the deportation twenty-seven years later of another former *Aufseherin* from Ravensbrück: Elfriede Huth Rinkel, who became the 103d former Nazi perpetrator (and the only other woman) to be denaturalized in a case brought by the OSI.

Born in 1922 in Leipzig, Rinkel served as a guard and *Hundeführerin* (dog handler) at Ravensbrück during the last nine months of the war, when the worst atrocities were committed there. In 1959, she immigrated to the United States to join her brother in San Francisco. There she married Fred (born Fritz) Rinkel, a Jewish refugee from Germany who lost both parents in the Holocaust. Fred Rinkel died in 2004, apparently never knowing his wife's secret past.

OSI discovered her whereabouts through an obituary notice of her husband's death listing her as the surviving spouse and her maiden name. According to her lawyer, "She married a Jewish man and gave to Jewish charities. She was trying to atone for her actions."[79] Eli Rosenbaum, head of OSI, counters: "No statement of remorse was volunteered to me. She shed no tears as her past was exposed."[80] When interviewed by Rosenbaum in her San Francisco apartment, Rinkel "walked across the room and she came back with a photograph of her husband's tombstone at the Jewish cemetery near San Francisco. It showed both her name and his on the tombstone with a Star of David above. She said her wish had been to be buried next to him."[81]

After OSI came knocking on her door, the eighty-four-year-old Rinkel quietly moved back to Germany in 2006 rather than challenge the about-to-be-instituted denaturalization proceedings against her. She returned to her hometown of Willich, near Düsseldorf, to live in a retirement home there. Reached on the telephone in 2007 by a reporter from the London *Times* who tried to interview her, she replied in German-accented English, "Forget it. There is nothing to say. Forget it," and slammed down the phone.[82]

Chief Prosecutor Benjamin B. Ferencz, flanked by defense attorneys Dr. Friedrich Bergold (at his right) and Dr. Rudolf Aschenauer. Courtesy of U.S. Holocaust Memorial Museum.

Otto Ohlendorf, main defendant at the *Einsatzgruppen* trial. Courtesy of U.S. Holocaust Memorial Museum.

6

The *Einsatzgruppen* Trial at Nuremberg

Did Anyone Have to Follow Orders to Kill?

The Nuremberg Idea

This book is about Holocaust trials that have, in large part, fallen below the public radar. While there may be some difference of opinion about which trials fall into that category, it is clear that the first Nuremberg trial held before the International Military Tribunal (IMT) in 1945–46 and the Eichmann trial held in Jerusalem in 1961 do not. Lesser-known trials are not as easily grouped together. Certainly, for most of the general public, all the trials after the first Nuremberg trial have descended into varying degrees of obscurity. That many refer to the first Nuremberg trial as "the" Nuremberg trial underscores the notion that the later Nuremberg trials are relatively unknown. In fact, between 1946 and 1948 there were twelve trials held at Nuremberg after the IMT proceeding. The ninth of these was called the *Einsatzgruppen* trial, the subject of this chapter. How did it come about?

Almost immediately after the invasion of Poland on September 1, 1939, that marked the beginning of the Second World War, it was clear that Germany was not complying with the rules of war. Its grave breaches of the traditional rules of warfare, rules that go back to the Middle Ages, were accentuated after the invasion of the Soviet Union in June 1941 when the massive Jewish population centers of eastern Poland and western Russia came under German control. This meant that Hitler's dire January 30, 1939, prophecy that a world war would mark the annihilation of European Jewry could now be implemented.[1]

It is in this context that one of the more amazing documents of the war was issued. In the Proclamation of St. James, dated January 13, 1942, the exile governments of the nine European countries then occupied by Germany announced that at the end of the war those responsible for war crimes would be punished. Coming at a time when German military success made victory over Germany seem almost hopeless, the Proclamation, issued in London, was not just a warning to Germany, but an expression of hope and the determination to triumph. Ironically, the Proclamation came just one week before the infamous Wannsee Conference. At that gathering, Reinhard Heydrich, the high-ranking SS officer whom Göring placed in charge of implementing the "Final Solution to the Jewish question," ensured that the German bureaucracy was to cooperate fully with the Final Solution. Forty months later, in May of 1945, Germany surrendered unconditionally.

The victorious Allied powers could not leave Germany's starting the war and manner of conducting it unaddressed, a determination underscored by the experience a generation earlier. After the First World War, the victors had acquiesced in allowing Germany to handle its own prosecutions, a decision that led to the Leipzig trials. In 1918, the expansionist threat posed by the new communist behemoth to the east and the conceived need to contain it played some role in this decision.[2] Aside from German pressure to try its own, the absence of any international mechanism for prosecution became an additional reason to permit Weimar Germany to deal with its own accused war criminals. The end result did not spawn confidence in the process of a defeated power trying its own nationals for war crimes. The Leipzig prosecutions, dealing with clear violations of the rules of war, resulted in many acquittals, light sentences in the event of conviction, and convenient escapes from prison for those sentenced.

With the defeat of Nazi Germany imminent, it became obvious that the victorious Allies would not follow the Leipzig precedent. First, the unfortunate results of the Leipzig prosecutions cautioned against a repeat of that process. Second, the enormity of German crimes eclipsed anything even alleged in the aftermath of the First World War. Finally, there was the Kellog-Briand Pact of 1925, which outlawed aggressive war. Germany was one of the signatories to this multilateral pact. Up to and through the First World War, nations saw war as a legitimate instrument of foreign policy. The carnage of the First World War changed that. As the Second World War neared its end, the complete illegitimacy of Germany's naked aggression became the glowing target for prosecution, even more so than war crimes and the soon-to-be-defined concept of "crimes against humanity." The enormity of the latter two was only slowly beginning to come to the surface.[3] Some of the concentration camps, for example, were not liberated until a week or two before the war in Europe ended. It was inconceivable that what remained of the German judiciary—judges who had implemented Nazi laws—would preside over the high-level defendants who were to be tried.

The victorious Allies differed in how to approach German atrocities. While the United States and British shared a common law system, the French system was entirely different as was the Soviets'. The Nuremberg process emerged from these differences, most of which were resolved in favor of the United States. The French had the least say as their military contribution to the Allied victory was minimal and the Soviets simply lacked jurisdiction over the main Nazi defendants, most of whom had surrendered to either the British or the United States.

Under the Nuremberg Charter, an international tribunal composed of judges from France, the Soviet Union, the United Kingdom, and the United States would preside over charges brought under the Charter, which gave the IMT jurisdiction over four categories of crimes: crimes against the peace, war crimes, crimes against humanity, and conspiracy to commit crimes against the peace.[4] The Charter gave defendants the right to counsel, to cross-examine witnesses, to call their own witnesses, to testify on their own behalf, and to have access to prosecution documents before they were introduced in evidence. Hearsay would be permitted under limited circumstances. President Harry Truman appointed United States Supreme Court Justice Robert H. Jackson as chief United States prosecutor, lending enormous prestige to the Nuremberg effort. Telford Taylor was to be his principal assistant and to take his place once Jackson returned to the United States after the IMT trial.

The persons guiding the Nuremberg process, mostly Americans, envisioned the first trial as only the beginning of a lengthy process that would mete out justice to both first-ranking and second-ranking perpetrators of the Nazi regime. A Pentagon lawyer, Colonel Murray Bernays, conceived a plan by which various Nazi organizations such as the SS and the Gestapo would be included as defendants before the IMT. They would be charged as criminal organizations for having participated in the crimes that fell within the Nuremberg mandate. If they were convicted, then in the future any person alleged to have been a member of such a criminal organization could be charged simply with membership. Once membership was proven, the degree of involvement would bear on the sentence to be imposed; the underlying criminality of the organization would not have to be relitigated. Bernays' broad approach was adopted in the Nuremberg Charter.[5] The Americans were clearly planning a major and sustained effort at prosecuting the criminality of the Third Reich.

The Fortuity of the *Einsatzgruppen* Trial

By mid-1946, the Americans had decided that there would be no further international proceedings in Nuremberg. Cooperation with the Soviets had become much more difficult than in the days immediately following the war. Instead, all subsequent trials in Nuremberg would be strictly an American affair, presided over by American judges, not international tribunals.

Even though the trials the Americans had planned would touch only the bare surface of Third Reich criminality, they were still a massive undertaking. Under Taylor, the American prosecutors planned a set of trials targeting the German high command, German doctors, judges, industrialists, concentration camp administrators, and slave labor organizers. They also contemplated trials against those involved in forced resettlement on racial grounds, including the kidnapping of children for racial purposes. Last, the American lawyers looked to charge those who had implemented the use and mistreatment of hostages.[6]

Benjamin Ferencz was a young attorney working for Taylor. During the war, Ferencz had fought in General Patton's Army. In 1946 he was hired by Taylor and became responsible for gathering evidence in connection with the post-IMT Nuremberg trials then underway.[7] Much of the documentary evidence that could be helpful was archived in Berlin. In early 1947, Fred Burin, a Swiss national and one of Ferencz's researchers, in going through those archives, found a series of remarkable documents: reports sent by German forces from the field on the Eastern Front to major Nazi officials containing descriptions of the massive atrocities then being committed.[8]

The reports described the activity of special units called *Einsatzgruppen*, broken into four units, *A*, *B*, *C*, and *D*, with each unit consisting of five hundred to eight hundred men. The reports were highly detailed, indicating exactly how many "Bolsheviks," "Jews," and "Gypsies" they killed, including the dates of killings and their locations. The earliest of these reports of mass murder was dated shortly after the German invasion of the Soviet Union on June 21, 1941. The reports went on for almost two years. When Ferencz started to total up the number of persons murdered reported in these documents he stopped at one million and flew to Nuremberg. There he proposed to Taylor that an additional trial be added to those already planned.[9]

By this point, in early 1947, prosecution of Nazi war criminals was no longer a national priority in the United States.[10] In addition, funding for the prosecutions was limited. Ferencz, however, made an eloquent case to Taylor that one could not simply overlook the murder of over a million civilians, especially where the documentary evidence of these crimes was so strong and where those implicated were already in American custody or possibly could be located. Taylor assented to the idea of an additional trial—but only if Ferencz, then a twenty-seven-year-old Harvard Law School graduate without any trial experience, would take on the job of being the chief prosecutor in this new trial. Ferencz agreed.

The Charge, the Court, Prosecutors, and Defendants

Since the evidence revealed unambiguously that the Nazis had executed an incredibly large number of civilians, it was not difficult to establish bases for the charges of war crimes and crimes against humanity. The reports made clear that the *Einsatzgruppen* consisted of men from the SS (*Schutzstaffel*, originally responsible for Hitler's security, then expanded to implement his policies), the SD (*Sicherheitsdienst*, responsible for security and neutralizing enemies and opponents of the Third Reich), and the Gestapo (*Geheime Staatspolizei*, the State Secret Police, parallel to the SS and after September 1939, included within the SD.) The IMT had found all these organizations criminal in its judgment of October 1, 1946. Consequently, all defendants also were charged with membership in one or more of these criminal organizations. (All were members of the SS, some had belonged to the SD, and some were in the Gestapo. A few were in all three organizations.)

The indictment, filed on July 3, 1947, and amended a few weeks later, named 24 defendants. Twenty-three actually went to trial since one committed suicide prior to arraignment.[11] The case went to verdict as to 22 defendants; one was removed mid-trial for medical reasons.[12] Each of the defendants had been part of one of four *Einsatz* units, each of which performed its gruesome task in a different geographical area: *Einsatzgruppe A* worked in the Baltic states and White Russia, *Einsatzgruppe B* in central Russia, *Einsatzgruppe C* in Ukraine and White Russia, and *Einsatzgruppe D* at the southeastern perimeter of the German advance into the Soviet Union. Of the 23 defendants who went to trial many were well educated. Eleven had post-secondary degrees in law; three in economics, political science and history, and education and language; and one had been trained at a theological seminary.[13]

Four other lawyers joined Ferencz as prosecutors, requisitioned from other Nuremberg cases: Peter Walton from Georgia, John Glancy from New York, James Heath from Virginia, and Arnost Horlik-Hochwald, a Czech. Ferencz's boss, Taylor, delivered much of the closing argument. As chief prosecutor, however, the twenty-seven-year-old Ferencz was largely responsible for the conduct of the prosecution. Each defendant was represented by counsel—in almost all cases, by two German lawyers; some had represented defendants in earlier Nuremberg proceedings and were well versed in the Nuremberg process. Since documents were at the core of the prosecution's case, it was important that the defense have the ability to review them and the prosecution provided the necessary access.

Three American judges presided over the trial: Judge Richard Dixon, formerly a North Carolina judge; Judge John Speight, a prominent member of the Alabama bar; and Chief Judge Michael Musmanno, who served as a trial judge in Pennsylvania before the war. Ferencz does not remember Dixon or Speight saying much during the trial; Musmanno dominated.[14] Musmanno had been a Navy captain during the war. After the war, as a volunteer, he interviewed about two hundred persons in an effort to document Hitler's last days and to verify his death. The highlight of his legal career, prior to Nuremberg, had been his assistance to Sacco and Vanzetti in their appellate efforts after conviction. Their subsequent execution made him a lifelong opponent of the death penalty.[15] Unlike the other two judges, Musmanno took an extremely active role in questioning witnesses.[16]

Because he had testified dramatically at the IMT trial and was an intelligent, articulate, and committed defender of his and his troops' conduct during the war, the prosecution made SS Brigadier General

Otto Ohlendorf the principal and first-named defendant. Thus, the case is known as *United States v. Otto Ohlendorf*.[17] Ohlendorf commanded *Einsatzgruppe D*, which operated in the furthest reaches of the German advance towards Stalingrad, and he testified about its conduct at the IMT trial. His testimony was relevant because his position in the SS put him in the chain of command that began with Heinrich Himmler, head of the SS, and continued to him through Ernst Kaltenbrunner, the only SS person on trial before the IMT. (Kaltenbrunner was the head of the Main Security Office of the Reich [*Reichsicherheitshauptamt*], an umbrella group that encompassed the SS, SD, and Gestapo, among other organizations.)

To prove its case against Kaltenbrunner at the IMT trial, the prosecutors called Ohlendorf, who was in American custody. In contrast to Kaltenbrunner's brutish appearance, Ohlendorf was almost elegant. He provided clear testimony and exuded intelligence in the precision of his answers. Everything about him contrasted sharply with the horrifying nature of his testimony. For example, he calmly described his responsibility for the murder of ninety thousand civilians. He had reviewed the field reports and was certain that his numbers were accurate. Ohlendorf's testimony had a dramatic impact at the IMT trial as it connected Nazi propaganda, vicious in itself, to actual murders. The theoretical became the real. That the vehicle that transformed the theoretical into the real was a calm, articulate, and apparently intelligent man amplified the shock value of his testimony. At the time, however, the full extent of *Einsatzgruppen* activities was still unknown. Given Ohlendorf's complete cooperation with the Allies while in custody, it was by no means certain that he would be prosecuted.[18] The discovery of the *Einsatzgruppen* reports changed that.

The Trial: Prosecution's Case

Shortly after the trial began on September 15, 1947, Ferencz began the prosecution's case with simple elegance.

> May it please your Honors: It is with sorrow and with hope that we here disclose the deliberate slaughter of more than a million innocent and defenseless men, women, and children. This was the tragic fulfillment of a program of intolerance and arrogance. Vengeance is not our goal, nor

do we seek merely a just retribution. We ask this Court to affirm by international penal action man's right to live in peace and dignity regardless of his race or creed. The case we present is a plea of humanity to law.[19]

In his opening, Ferencz used the word "genocide," a termed coined by the Polish-Jewish lawyer Raphael Lemkin in his 1944 tome, *Axis Rule in Occupied Europe*. Lemkin thrust the book into Ferencz's hands at the Nuremberg courthouse.[20] As a tribute to and mark of respect for Lemkin, Ferencz referred to "genocide" in his opening statement, in a case horrifically suited to that word.[21]

In what the Associated Press called "the greatest murder trial in history,"[22] it took just two days for the prosecution to put its case into evidence. It was comprised entirely of documentary evidence: largely the *Einsatz* reports found in the Berlin archives, in which field commanders reported back to Berlin on their successes in killing Bolsheviks, Gypsies, and Jews. Part of an actual report follows. It reveals that forty copies were made. It seems implausible that the Nazis could have destroyed such a large number of copies in the hectic finale to the war when they tried to destroy evidence documenting mass murders. The extraordinary bureaucratization of the Final Solution thus formed the core of the prosecution's case against its perpetrators. In addition to the reports, the prosecution placed several affidavits into evidence.

EXTRACTS FROM REPORT OF EINSATZGRUPPE A COVERING THE PERIOD FROM 23 JUNE 1941 TO 15 OCTOBER 1941

[Pencilled] Personal property of SS Lieutenant General [Obergruppenfuehrer] Wv. 31 January 1942

[Rubber stamp] Top Secret

40 copies

23d copy *EINSATZGRUPPE A*

Comprehensive Report up to 15 October 1941

3. Action against Jewry

From the beginning, it was to be expected that the Jewish problem in the East could not be solved by pogroms alone. In accordance with the basic orders received, however, the clearing activities of the security police had to aim at a complete annihilation of the Jews. Sonderkommandos reinforced by selected units—in Lithuania including partisan detachments, in Latvia units of the Latvian auxiliary police—therefore performed extensive executions both in the towns and in rural areas. The operations of the execution detachments were performed smoothly. When attaching Lithuanian and Latvian detachments to the execution squads, men were chosen whose relatives had been murdered or deported by the Russians.

Especially severe and extensive measures became necessary in Lithuania. In some places—especially in Kovno—the Jews had armed themselves and participated actively in guerrilla warfare and committed arson. Besides these activities, the Jews in Lithuania had collaborated most actively hand in glove with the Soviets.

The sum total of the Jews liquidated in Lithuania amounts to 71,105. During the pogroms in Kovno, 3,800 Jews were eliminated, in the smaller towns about 1,200 Jews.

In Latvia as well the Jews participated in acts of sabotage and arson after the invasion of the German Armed Forces. In Daugavpils [Dvinsk] so many fires were started by the Jews that a large part of the town was lost. The electric power station burned down to a mere shell. The streets which were mainly inhabited by Jews remained unscathed.

In Latvia up to now 30,000 Jews were executed in all. Five hundred were rendered harmless by pogroms in Riga.

Most of the 4,500 Jews living in Estonia at the beginning of the eastern campaign fled with the retreating Red Army. About 200 stayed behind. In Tallin alone there lived about 1,000 Jews.

***

The number of Jews executed up to the present may be seen in the schedule on enclosure 8.[23]

Enclosure 8

Total	Jews	Communists	Total
Lithuania	80,311	860	81,171
Latvia	30,025	1,845	31,868
Estonia	474	684	1,158
White Ruthenia	7,620	—	7,620
Total	118,430	3,387	121,817

If one adds to this report the numbers in other reports, paralleling what Ferencz did when he began the investigation, that addition yields a seven-digit number—the total killed by the *Einsatzgruppen*. A mass murder trial of historic dimension.

Each of the defendants was linked to these reports by virtue of the structure of the *Einsatzgruppen*. Each group, *A*, *B*, *C*, and *D*, consisted of multiple "*Kommando*" units, known as either "*Einsatzkommandos*" or "operation forces commandos," which were numbered. Each defendant was tied to either the larger group or the sub-group. Ohlendorf, for example, was the head of *Einsatzgruppe D*; Otto Rasch the head of *Einsatzgruppe B* and, at a different time, *Einsatzgruppe C*. Paul Blobel was the head of the Special Commando unit 4A under *Einsatzgruppe C* and as such, was responsible for the massacre at the Babi Yar ravine outside Kiev where 33,000 Jews were murdered in the space of two days. Thus, every defendant was linked to at least one massacre and most were linked to several.

Ferencz decided not to use live witnesses—even if he was aware of their existence in the short period since the war had ended—because he felt that their testimony might be shaky. Further, it was extremely unlikely that any of them would identify any of the defendants on trial; most were the officers who gave the orders, not the persons doing the actual shooting.[24] The end result vindicated this tactical decision. However, since the balance of this chapter deals with reports, defenses, and rebuttals, something is amiss if the sheer horror of victimhood revealed in this trial is lost in the descriptive process.[25]

Astonishingly, Ohlendorf thought he was acting humanely in circumscribing the manner in which his victims were killed. He stated that he would not permit his men to bash the heads of infants against hard surfaces, but rather had his men instruct mothers to hold their children close to their chests so that one bullet through the head of the child would kill both the child and mother.[26] But "humanity" to hapless victims was not his concern. The defendant Heinz Schubert, an Ohlendorf subordinate and a descendant of the great composer,[27] noted that "it was of the greatest importance to Ohlendorf to have the persons who were to be shot killed in the most humane and military manner possible, because otherwise . . . the moral strain would have been too great for the execution squad."[28]

What preceded the kinds of executions Ohlendorf prided himself on was anything but neat or humane. Civilian populations—largely Jews—would be marched or driven to the outskirts of their towns to open pits where they were made to undress and then shot, so that the momentum of the bullet would cause them to fall into the pit. Most of the time they were shot in the head. When conducted on such a large scale, this method of killing became less precise. Perhaps after several hundred killings in a day, an *Einsatz* officer would shoot slightly off-target, grazing a victim's skull. This might cause the victim to fall into the pit while only superficially wounded. As a consequence, a very small number of victims survived the killing process; those who survived the war lived to tell about it.

The following testimony is taken from the Eichmann trial held in Jerusalem fifteen years after the *Einsatzgruppen* trial. This entire chapter on the trial of the *Einsatzgruppen* should be read with this testimony in mind. The testimony describes the fate of an extended family of about ten people—parents, grandparent, siblings, nephews, nieces, and daughters. The image it evokes should be multiplied by 150,000.

ATTORNEY GENERAL: I call Mrs. Rivka Yoselewska.
PRESIDING JUDGE: Certainly. [To the witness:] Do you speak Hebrew?
WITNESS: Yiddish.
[The witness is sworn.]
PRESIDING JUDGE: Please be seated and speak as calmly as you can.
ATTORNEY GENERAL: You live in Ramat Gan, 57 Bialik Street?
WITNESS YOSELEWSKA: Yes.
Q. Were you born in the townlet of Powost in the Pinsk district?
A. Powost-Zagorodski.
Q. In Yiddish it was called Powost?
A. Yes.
Q. Your father had a leather goods shop there and was considered one of the notables of the townlet?
A. Yes.
PRESIDING JUDGE: How many Jews lived in the townlet?
WITNESS YOSELEWSKA: About five hundred families.
ATTORNEY GENERAL: You also had two sisters, Chaya and Feige?
WITNESS YOSELEWSKA: Yes.

Q. And you have a brother named Moshe who was saved and lives in the United States?

A. Yes.

Q. You were married in 1934?

A. Yes.

Q. And you had a daughter named Marka of this marriage?

A. Yes.

Q. Mrs. Yoselewska, when the Germans entered in 1941, what happened to your synagogue?

A. They turned it at once into a stable for horses.

Q. When you say "they," who were they?

A. Germans, for the most part they were SS men.

Q. You remember Saturday, the first of the month of Elul, 1942?

[Yoselewska then describes how the Jews were made to stand in the ghetto square as they were told to bring all valuables, none of which were left as all had already been taken. The gates of the ghetto were then opened and a truck entered.]

Q. They filled up the truck. What happened to those who had no room on the truck?

A. The rest they made run after the truck.

Q. And you were running with your little girl?

A. I was holding my little girl and running after the truck, too. Many mothers had two or three children. All the way we had to run. When somebody fell down, they wouldn't let him get up; they shot him on the spot. All my family was there. We arrived at the place. Those who had been on the truck had already got down, undressed and stood in a row.

Q. Where was it?

A. It was about three kilometers away from our town. There was a hill and a little below it they had dug something like a ditch. They made us walk up to the hill, in rows of four, and the four whom we likened to Angels of Death shot each one of us separately.

Q. What German unit did these four belong to?

A. The SS. They were SS men. They carried several guns with plenty of ammunition pouches, real Angels of Death.

Q. What did you see when you came there?

A. When we arrived at this place, we saw naked people standing there already, so we thought maybe they are being tormented, perhaps there was still hope we would remain alive. To get away was impossible. I was curious to see whether anybody was below that hill where the people had to stand and I made a quick turn. I saw three or four rows, twelve people already killed. I wish to add that when they lined us up in the ghetto my little daughter asked: "Mother why are you wearing your Sabbath dress, they are going to kill us?" Even when we stood near the ditch she said: "What are we waiting for, come let's escape." Some of the younger ones tried to run away. They hardly managed a few steps, they were caught and shot. Then came our turn. It was difficult to hold the children, they were shaking. We took turns. Parents took the children, took other people's children. This was to help us to get through it all; to get it over with, and not see the children suffer. Mothers took leave of their children, the mothers, the parents.

PRESIDING JUDGE: How did you survive all this killing?

WITNESS YOSELEWSKA: We were lined up in fours. We stood there naked. Our clothing was taken away. My father didn't want to undress completely and kept on his underwear. When he was lined up for the shooting and was told to undress, he refused; he was beaten. We begged him: "Take off your clothes. Enough of suffering." No. He insisted on dying in his underwear.

Q. And then the Germans tore it off?

A. They tore his things off and shot him.

Q. And he fell into the pit?

A. I saw it. Then they took Mother. She didn't want to go, but wanted us to go first. Yet we made her go first. They grabbed her and shot her. There was my father's mother who was 80 with two grandchildren in her arms. My father's sister was also there. She, too, was shot with children in her arms.

Q. Then your turn came?

A. Then my turn came. My younger sister also. She had suffered so much in the ghetto, and yet at the last moment she wanted to stay alive, and begged the German to let her live. She was standing there naked holding on to her girl friend. So he looked at her and shot them both. Both of them fell, my sister and her girl friend. My other sister was next. Then he got ready to shoot me.

Q. Did he ask for something?

A . We stood there facing the ditch. I turned my head. He asked, "Whom do I shoot first?" I didn't answer. He tore the child away from me. I heard her last cry and he shot her. Then he got ready to kill me, grabbed my hair and turned my head about. I remained standing and heard a shot but I didn't move. He turned me around, loaded his pistol, so that I could see what he was doing. Then he again turned me around and shot me. I fell down.

Q. And then you fell into the pit?

A. I felt nothing. At that moment I felt that something was weighing me down. I thought that I was dead, but that I could feel something even though I was dead. I couldn't believe that I was alive. I felt I was suffocating, bodies had fallen on me. I felt I was drowning. But still I could move and felt I was alive and tried to get up. I was choking, I heard shots, and again somebody falling down. I twisted and turned, but I could not. I felt I was going to suffocate. I had no strength left. But then I felt that somehow I was crawling upwards. As I climbed up, people grabbed me, hit me, dragged me downwards, but I pulled myself up with the last bit of strength. When I reached the top I looked around but I couldn't recognize the place. Corpses strewn all over, there was no end to the bodies. You could hear people moaning in their death agony. Some children were running around naked and screaming, "Mama, Papa." I couldn't get up.

PRESIDING JUDGE: The Germans were still there, at that time?

WITNESS YOSELEWSK: No. The Germans were not there. No one was there.

ATTORNEY GENERAL: You were naked and covered with blood.

WITNESS YOSELEWSKA: I got out naked covered with blood from the corpses whose bellies had burst.

Q. What did you have on your head?

A. When he shot me I was wounded in the head. I still have a big scar on my head, where I was wounded by the Germans. [The witness shows the scar.] I got to my feet to see that horrible scene. The screaming was unbearable, the children shouting "Mama, Papa." I ran over to the children, maybe my daughter was there. I called out, "Markele." I didn't see her.

[She then describes how she met other women and remained unobtrusive; Germans came and left.]

A. When I saw they were gone I dragged myself over to the grave and wanted to jump in. I thought the grave would open up and let me fall inside alive. I envied everyone for whom it was already over, while I was still alive. Where should I go? What should I do? Blood was spouting. Nowadays, when I pass a water fountain I can still see the blood spouting from the grave. The earth rose and heaved. I sat there on the grave and tried to dig my way in with my hands. I continued digging as hard as I could. The earth didn't open up. I shouted to Mother and Father, why I was left alive. What did I do to deserve this? Where shall I go? To whom can I turn? I have nobody. I saw everything; I saw everybody killed. No one answered. I remained sprawled on the grave three days and three nights.

Q. And then a peasant passed by and took pity on you?

A. I remained not far from the grave. A peasant saw me. I had been wandering around there for several weeks. He saw me.

Q. He took pity on you and gave you food, and then you joined a group of Jews in the forest and stayed with them till the Soviets came?

A. Till the end I stayed with them.

Q. And now you are married and you have two children?

A. Yes.

PRESIDING JUDGE: Do you have any questions to the witness, Dr. Servatius?

DR. SERVATIUS: I have no questions.

PRESIDING JUDGE: Thank you, Mrs. Yoselewska, you have completed your testimony.

An alternative method of killing used sporadically was mobile death vans. Victims, again mainly Jews, were herded into a van, which was then sealed. A tube running from the exhaust was then attached to an opening in the van, resulting in carbon monoxide streaming into the van once it was in motion, and killing those trapped inside. There were several problems with this method of murder. First, periodically, someone would still be alive once the engine was stopped and the van opened. In addition, bodies had to be taken from the van and placed into graves. Traces of carbon monoxide around the dead bodies created physical problems. As Ohlendorf, who refused to use the vans, saw it,[29] the burden on his men of removing and disposing of dead bodies was so great he could not impose it on them.[30] Once again, sympathy for the murderers and no thought about the victims.

The Defense Case

While the prosecution's case, resting as it did exclusively on documents, took just two days to present, the defense case took over four months.[31] Over a period of 136 days, the defendants raised numerous exculpatory claims. These can be divided into two categories: narrow factual defenses and broader conceptual defenses.

Narrow Defenses

The narrow defenses included: (1) challenging the authenticity of the documents underlying the prosecution's case; (2) claiming that the numbers on the documents were exaggerated; (3) presenting alibis: evidence that on the date of a particular massacre the defendant was elsewhere—in Berlin, for example, receiving medical treatment; and (4) claiming an unawareness of what was happening. The latter, of course, was palpably absurd. Given the explicit nature of the reports, detailing to the person the large number of civilians killed, reports, which by their own terms were sent to at least forty persons in the Third Reich, it is ludicrous to think that a defendant on the scene at the time was unaware of the killings. Even the local populations knew. For example, the use of the mobile gas vans was so well known to the local population that a subordinate to Ohlendorf reported to an intermediate officer in *Einsatzgruppe D* that he had ordered the group's vans to be camouflaged as house trailers by putting one set of window shutters on each side of the small van and two on each side of the larger vans, such as one often sees on farm houses in the country. "The vans became so well known, that not only the authorities, but also the civilian population called the van 'death van,' as soon as one of these vehicles appeared. It is my opinion that the van cannot be kept secret for any length of time, not even camouflaged."[32]

As to the authenticity of the documents, the burden on the defendants was insurmountable, given how the documents were discovered.[33]

Testimony that the documents were found in the Berlin archives, and accidentally to boot, could not be seriously challenged. In addition, the detailed information on the documents and the large number of them made it virtually inconceivable that they were fabricated. Although the defendants received duplicates, the prosecution also allowed them to see the original documents, a process that undercut any significant effort at challenging authenticity. Notwithstanding initial claims of fabrication, by the time the case went to closing argument, authenticity was no longer an issue.[34]

The defense of "exaggeration" was presented perhaps most forcefully by defendant Blobel, who claimed that reports of the Babi Yar massacre exaggerated the number of people killed by a factor of two. He claimed that officers falsified reports of massacres to indicate greater success than the actual number killed, in an effort to gain the accolades of the higher-ups in Berlin. There was, however, considerable evidence to the contrary that officers strove to report events accurately. At one point, Ohlendorf, for example, stood by the accuracy of his reports and, based on his knowledge of other *Einsatz* officers, also vouched for the accuracy of their reports.[35] More basically, it is hardly a defense to a charge of murdering thirty-three thousand Jews to urge that only half that number was killed.

As to alibis, none was convincing and the court rejected almost all of them. It is probably of little interest at this point to delve into the degree of proof necessary to show that on the date of a particular massacre an *Einsatzgruppen* defendant was in Berlin receiving medical treatment. Ferencz points out that, periodically, when a defendant claimed to have been at a place other than at a massacre charged to him, the prosecution was able to produce letters written by the defendant, bragging about the number of Jews he had just eliminated.[36] In many cases, there was more than an ample basis for the court to reject almost all evidence of an alibi.

In this connection, the "Penguin Rule" should be mentioned. Judge Musmanno and his colleagues gave the defense great latitude, a fact evinced by the 136 court days it took for the defense to present its case. The judges permitted virtually any potential defense material into evidence. At one point Musmanno indicated that his concept of latitude for the defense was so broad that even if they thought it relevant to introduce the mating habits of Antarctic penguins as evidence, he would admit it. His liberality towards the defense became known as the Penguin Rule. According to Musmanno, at the end of the trial, Ohlendorf even "express[ed] . . . [his] gratitude for the very generous way . . . [the court] dealt with the problems [he] regarded as important to these proceedings."[37]

The reality of the Penguin Rule is somewhat harsher. The court was sitting without a jury. In his opening, Ferencz eloquently summarized the damning documentary evidence of the massive criminality charged. The few affidavits the prosecution relied on supplemented the *Einsatz* reports' cold depictions of mass murders and gave further life to the atrocities. It would not be unreasonable to assume that after the *Einsatz* reports had been reviewed, and the affidavits read—including Ohlendorf's affidavit in which he described his efforts at making the mass murders of civilians humane by shooting them military style—that the judges, including Musmanno, tentatively, at least, concluded that the defendants were guilty. From any perspective, Ohlendorf's explanation of his "humanely" directed killings could hardly be seen as exculpatory. Having thus tentatively decided that the defendants were guilty, why not permit them extraordinary latitude in the presentation of their evidence? Any experienced trial lawyer who has tried non-jury cases would recognize that this extreme liberality towards the defense portended a verdict of guilty.[38]

Broader Defenses

The defendants, individually and collectively, raised five broad conceptual defenses: (1) the varieties of conduct alleged—war crimes, crimes against humanity, and membership in a criminal organization—were not crimes under the laws of any country; (2) even if the crimes alleged existed, they were not in existence at the time of the underlying events, and therefore violated the fundamental legal principle against *ex post facto* laws; (3) the crimes the defendants were charged with—murder of civilians—were no different from conduct the Allies engaged in, particularly the Soviets; (4) all civilians were partisans and more generally, the security of the Third Reich required that all potential enemies be eliminated, thus a "self-defense" defense; and (5) the defendants were simply following orders.

The court readily rejected the first two of these defenses on the basis of precedent established at the IMT trial. IMT defendants had unsuccessfully raised each of these defenses. In responding to the claim that the defendants had not violated any laws, and that any laws claimed to exist in 1945 at the onset of the trials were not in force in the preceding years, Justice Jackson noted that the common theme of murder ran through all the allegations and that murder had been a crime since Cain slew Abel. Somewhat more formally, the IMT judges noted that treaties to which Germany was a party prohibited the conduct charged as unlawful, and that these treaties provided the legitimate bases for the charges.[39] The panel of judges in the *Einsatzgruppen* trial was not about to reject the precedent the IMT had set less than two years earlier.

THE "YOU TOO" ARGUMENT

The "You Too" (*tu quoque*) argument was advanced in considerable detail. The defendant Brigadier General Erich Naumann, who headed *Einsatzgruppe B*, argued that the Allies had destroyed his hometown of Dresden, which he said housed no factories or installations of war importance. In that attack, he said, two hundred thousand civilians were killed, cruelly burned, or otherwise wounded. He also alluded to the thousands of civilians killed by the dropping of atom bombs in Japan and argued that "even the unborn generation will have to suffer."[40]

Ohlendorf was quite explicit in trying to draw a moral analogy between killing civilians by shooting or by bombing:

> The fact that individual men killed civilians face to face is looked upon as terrible and is pictured as specially gruesome because the order was clearly given to kill these people; but I cannot morally evaluate a deed any better, a deed which makes it possible, by pushing of a button, to kill a much larger number of civilians, men, women, and children, even to hurt them for generations, than those deeds of individual people who for the same purpose, namely, to achieve the goal of the war, must shoot individual persons.[41]

When asked whether he did not see a difference between a bomber pilot who hoped, when dropping bombs, that children would not be killed and those such as him and his SS men who intentionally shot children, Ohlendorf responded:

> I cannot imagine that those planes which systematically covered a city that was a fortified city, square meter for square meter, with incendiaries and explosive bombs and again with phosphorus bombs, and this done from block to block, and then as I have seen it in Dresden likewise the squares where the civilian population had fled to—that these men could possibly hope not to kill any civilian population, and no children.[42]

Taylor, in responding to these arguments, pointed out that the laws of war did not embrace aerial warfare[43] and that, in any event, Germany had been the first to bomb and one could hardly expect the Allies to refrain from using airpower.

> The first cities to undergo the terror of modern air raids suffered under German bombs, Warsaw, Rotterdam, and London were badly mauled while there was still hardly a scratch on any city in Germany. Nor can there be any suggestion that the major criminal ventures of the Third Reich—the slave labor program, the extermination of the Jews, or any other crime of similar magnitude—were planned or committed in retaliation for Allied bombing. All of these programs were well under way and on the high road to consummation long before Allied bombing had had any appreciable effect on life in Germany.[44]

In rejecting the "You Too" argument, the court went beyond Taylor's contentions. The court acknowledged that "the bombing of Berlin, Dresden, Hamburg, Cologne, and other German cities followed the bombing of London, Coventry, Rotterdam, Warsaw, and other Allied cities."[45] But there was a more significant distinction between the Allied bombings of German cities and even the use of the atom bomb and what the *Einsatz* defendants did. "[T]he one and only purpose of the bombing is to effect the surrender of the bombed nation. The people of that nation, through their representatives, may surrender and, with the surrender, the bombing ceases, the killing is ended." The killing of Jews was itself the objective and had no connection to the legitimate war aim of victory. Jews were killed in countries after they surrendered (France, Norway, Holland, etc.) and in countries that fought (the Soviet Union). There was simply no war objective to the killing of Jews—it was an end in itself.[46]

SELF-DEFENSE

To fully understand the arguments subsumed under the concept of "self-defense" it is helpful to try to understand the mindset that enveloped the defendants in their formative years. All but three of the defendants were born in the period between 1900 and the outbreak of the First World War.[47] Thus, they witnessed Germany's defeat in a war that ended without the occupation of any German territory by the victorious Allies, but that saw Germany (1) lose Alsace and Lorraine, (2) lose considerable territory to the reconstituted nation of Poland, (3) obligated to make substantial reparations payments, and (4) endure significant constraints on internal affairs. These individuals were thus susceptible to the argument advanced by the German Right, that Germany had been sold out and that the betrayers were the Jews. This chapter is not the place to go into detail on the vicious propaganda against Jews that characterized the years prior to the Second World War. Suffice it to say, the machinery of the state was committed to convincing its populace, in words commonly used then, that "the Jews are our misfortune."[48]

Equating Jews with Bolshevism (and pernicious capitalism, if it was handy) was also standard in Nazi propaganda. As of June 1941, there was a war against the Bolsheviks, and from that it followed that the Jews were the enemy. This concept was articulated by many of the defendants, perhaps most brutally by Ohlendorf when he was asked on cross-examination how he could justify the killing of Jewish children on the theory that they represented a threat to Germany.

> Q. [Mr. Heath] Mr. Ohlendorf, what happened to the Jewish children, the gypsy children?
>
> A. [Ohlendorf] According to orders they were to be killed just like their parents.
>
> . . .
>
> Q. Will you agree that there was absolutely no rational basis for killing children except genocide and the killing of races?
>
> A. I believe that it is very simple to explain if one starts from the fact that this order did not only try to achieve security, but also permanent security because the children would grow up and surely, being the children of parents who had been killed, they would constitute a danger no smaller than that of the parents.[49]

Ohlendorf's answers blended a series of defenses: the enemy was not the invaded country—the Soviet Union—but its governing political philosophy, Bolshevism, and the Jews behind it. These entities posed a threat to Germany and, therefore, had to be eliminated. Ohlendorf relied on a July 3, 1941, speech by Josef Stalin, made shortly after the German invasion, in which Stalin urged that in occupied territory all efforts including sabotage had to be undertaken to fight the occupying forces.[50] From this, the defendants contended that they believed that all Jews would follow this directive; therefore, they were all partisans. Of course, under the rules of war, partisans have to be tried in some form of military tribunal before they can be punished. This never happened, and none of the defendants, in the several-month-long exposition of their defenses, even hinted that Jews, "as partisans," had anything close to a hearing to determine their status. Their pertinent status was pre-established: they were Jews and, therefore, they had to be killed. Taylor dealt with the entire concept most succinctly in his closing when he noted: "In short, the crimes of the *Einsatzgruppen* were not, fundamentally, military crimes at all. They were not committed in order to make military victory possible. On the contrary, military victory was sought in order to put the victors in a position where these crimes could be committed. These crimes were a war objective, not a military means."[51]

FOLLOWING ORDERS

The most significant part of the *Einsatzgruppen* trial is what it revealed about the defense of "following orders." Many defendants advanced this defense and, as in Ohlendorf's case, claimed specifically that the failure to follow orders would result in death.

> The men of my group who are under indictment here were under my military command. If they had not executed the orders which they were given, they would have been ordered by me to execute them. . . . Whoever refused anything in the front lines would have met immediate death. If the refusal would have come about in any other way, a court martial of the Higher SS and Police Leader would have brought about the same consequences. The jurisdiction of courts martial was great, but the sentences of the SS were gruesome.[52]

In framing the Nuremberg Charter, the Allies had obviously foreseen the defense of "following orders" and consequently, the Charter specifically provided that following orders was not a defense to any charge, but rather could only be considered as mitigation at the penalty stage of the proceeding.[53] Since none of the Nuremberg trials divided the guilt stage from the penalty stage, the question of whether defendants were simply following orders was legitimately in issue. This permitted the defendants to raise the issue for sentencing purposes. As a result, a part of the trial was devoted specifically to this question. While the Nuremberg Charter stated as a matter of law that following orders was not a defense, the *Einsatzgruppen* trial went a step further. As this review of the trial shows, the *Einsatzgruppen* trial is significant historically for its finding that, *as a factual matter*, none of the defendants had to follow orders to kill Jews.

Perhaps the first crack in the "following orders" defense came when the defendants were asked to personalize it. Unsurprisingly, Ohlendorf, without hesitation, admitted that if directed to kill his sister, he would have done so.[54] It came out a little differently with the defendant Colonel Willy Seibert, an SS officer directly under Ohlendorf in *Einsatzgruppe D*. On direct examination, his attorney asked him about a statement by the German Kaiser on the need to obey orders, in which the Kaiser reportedly said that, if necessary, a soldier would have to obey the directive to shoot his own parents. Judge Musmanno then intervened and asked whether Seibert would follow such an order. To the surprise of most, Seibert said he did not know and needed time to consider the question. Musmanno then followed a most logical course: he gave Seibert time and adjourned the trial to the following day. The following day the question was posed again and Seibert, undoubtedly to the consternation of most of his co-defendants, answered he would not follow that order. He was then asked if he would follow the order to shoot Jewish parents whose child was standing nearby if the parents had not done anything wrong and were to be shot simply because they were Jews. Seibert at least was logical; he replied he would not obey the order to shoot.[55]

The Seibert sequence was personal, of course, but it was the crack in the door that led to a virtual cascade of evidence that failure to follow orders did not result in severe consequences for those directed to murder Jews. While questioning the defendant Captain Felix Ruehl, an officer in one of the *Sonderkommando* units under Ohlendorf in *Einsatzgruppe D*, the prosecutor asked Ruehl to confirm that his commanding officer was at times drunk, in an effort to show that Ruehl actually took command of the unit. Ruehl indignantly denied the suggestion about the deceased superior and added that he "strongly objected to that in the interest of the deceased." He went on, "And I can assure you that if such a thing had occurred, even once, Herr Ohlendorf wouldn't have stood for this. That would have been the end of his career as a Kommando leader, insofar as I got to know Herr Ohlendorf."[56] In short, as Judge Musmanno observed, if an SS officer in these units was not anxious to shoot eight-year-old children in the back of the head, all he would have had to do was drink a bottle of schnapps.[57]

Ohlendorf's testimony on the subject was similar, more artful, but completely in sync with the notion that anyone wanting to avoid participation had it within his power to do so. Asked whether he could not have avoided the responsibility of shooting defenseless civilians by feigning illness, he said he could have done so. However, it would have meant betraying his men since he had no assurance that his successor would treat them as well as he did. He said that caring for his men was more important than the "cheap applause" he could have gotten by simulating illness.[58]

A witness called by the defense, Albert Hartel, shed further light on the factual fragility of the "following orders" defense. Hartel, an SS officer in Kiev, testified that General Max Thomas, at the time the head of *Einsatzgruppe C* but not a defendant at Nuremberg,[59] issued an order that those who could not reconcile the duties of the *Einsatzgruppen* with their conscience should so indicate and they would be sent back to Germany. According to Hartel, a number of persons, including some commanders, did so and they returned to Berlin. This was not disputed evidence since Ohlendorf himself said that he sent back to Germany those who could not obey the directive to kill civilians. It seems clear therefore, that removal from the SS would in all likelihood entail a transfer to the *Wehrmacht*, the regular German army, where the transferee would be obliged to fight against an armed enemy, as opposed to shooting defenseless civilians. But surely that alternative was not one that granted legitimacy to "following orders," as a defense, even for the limited purpose of mitigating a sentence.

The experience of Lieutenant General Gustav Noßke (anglicized as Nosske), a lawyer by training, is also instructive as to the need to obey orders. Noßke headed one of the *Einsatzkommando* units in *Einsatzgruppe D* under Ohlendorf and was responsible for the murder of thousand of Jews. Evidence presented by Noßke at the trial—presumably, in his defense—showed that, after he ended his tour with *Einsatzgruppe D*, he returned to Düsseldorf in Germany, where he was directed to round up Jews and half-Jews for execution. Apparently, Noßke's social circle included persons who had both Christian and Jewish ancestry, so he protested the order and refused to follow it. This created some very minor difficulties for him, but he was not severely punished nor even demoted for his failure to follow orders.[60]

Noßke submitted this evidence in an effort to show that his stridence as a Nazi was not total. Yet, as the evidence showed his complicity in the murder of thousands of innocent civilians, the refusal to arrest a few persons whose ancestors were both Christian and Jewish is hardly a significant mitigator. The evidence, therefore, had far more bearing on the "following orders" issue than it did on lessening Noßke's guilt.[61]

The case of the defendant Mathias Graf provides even more direct proof that the failure to obey an order to kill defenseless civilians did not carry draconian consequences. Defendant Graf was a master sergeant in *Einsatzkommando 6* of *Einsatzgrupppe C*. When assigned to the command of a sub-*Kommando* group, Graf simply refused to accept the assignment. For this, he was placed in custody pending disciplinary proceedings, but subsequently released when those proceedings were dropped and he was sent back to Germany.[62] There was no evidence linking Graf to any of the massacres. He presented evidence the court found credible that for significant periods of time he was, in fact, in Germany and not working with his *Einsatzgruppe*. The court found his membership in the SS was involuntary and his membership in the SD perfunctory. As a result, the court acquitted Graf of the war crimes charge and also of the crimes against humanity charge, but convicted Graf of being a member of a criminal organization—the SD. The court sentenced him to time served, which meant he was released on the day of the sentence.[63]

Finally, a more general point on the defense of following orders. Ohlendorf had testified that any SS officer who refused to follow orders would have been subjected to discipline and that SS discipline on this point was "gruesome."[64] Was he correct? In the 136 days of defense evidence and 159 exhibits introduced by the defense, was there any evidence that corroborated Ohlendorf's statement? There were twenty defendants in the case; did any of them testify as to "gruesome" consequences for those refusing to follow orders? The answer to all these questions is "no." Given the large number of defendants and their lengthy service with the SS or SD, one would think that if there had been any executions for failure to follow orders—an event that makes sense only if it is publicized, so as to deter others from similar conduct—it would have been brought to the court's attention. To the contrary, the only actual evidence of failure to follow orders that was presented to the court was the experience of Mathias Graf. For his failure to take command of a sub-*Kommando* as ordered, he was placed into custody for a short period and then sent back to Germany. This is hardly a "gruesome" consequence.

Response to the Defense of Following Orders

Five defendants—Ohlendorf, Naumann, Blume, Braune, and Ott—claimed they acted under the compulsion of a superior's orders.[65] In addition to the factual weakness of the claim, it had no basis under German law. Both Taylor, in his closing argument, and the court, in its decision, relied on German precedent, thus undercutting any claim by the defendants that novel and alien principles of law were unfairly applied to them.

While the results in the Leipzig trials were not what the Allies had expected after the First World War, the principle of law that emerged from the trials was helpful to the prosecution in this case. Taylor, in his closing, quoted from the decision by the German Supreme Court in Leipzig in the *Llandovery Castle* case (1921) as follows:

> It is certainly to be urged in favor of the military subordinates, that they are under no obligation to question the order of their superior officer, and they can count upon its legality. But no such confidence can be held to exist, if such an order is universally known to everybody, including also the accused, to be without any doubt whatever against the law. This happens only in rare and exceptional cases. But this case was precisely one

> of them. For in the present instance, it was perfectly clear to the accused that killing defenseless people in the lifeboats could be nothing else but a breach of law. As naval officers by profession, they were well aware, as the naval expert has strikingly stated, that one is not legally authorized to kill defenseless people. They well know that this was the case here.[66]

Taylor then blended these principles of German law with the facts of the case and the earlier decision by the IMT. He observed that the defendants were not "uneducated juveniles," ignorant of the objectives of the Third Reich, but rather were selected because of their commitment to its objectives; they were "lawyers, teachers, artists, and a former clergyman. They [were], in short, men of education, who were in full possession of their faculties and who fully understood the grave and sinister significance of the program they embarked upon."[67] He continued:

> These crimes were committed in execution of deliberate plans laid months earlier. And the crime itself is of staggering enormity–the annihilation of entire racial and national groups—such as Jews and gypsies—and all leading government and party officials. Questions of guilt or innocence of the victims played absolutely no part; this was massacre for its own sake and the intended victims numbered in the millions. This case, therefore, falls well within the conclusion reached by the IMT in passing judgment on [the members of the German High Command, defendants Keitel and Jodl, citing the IMT decision]. . . . There is nothing in mitigation. Superior orders, even to a soldier, cannot be considered in mitigation where crimes as shocking and extensive have been committed consciously, ruthlessly, and without military excuse or justification.[68]

The court blended references to German and Austrian law to the facts developed at the trial. It cited: (1) the 1845 Prussian Military Code, which provided that a soldier/subordinate would be punished "if he executed an order knowing that it 'related to an act which obviously aimed at a crime'"; (2) the 1855 Military Code of the Austrian Empire, which provided that "a subordinate is not guilty of failing to follow orders if the order pertains to an act or omission in which evidently a crime or an offense is to be recognized"; and (3) article 47 of the

German Military Code, adopted in 1872, which provided that a subordinate officer was guilty "if he knew that the order of the superior concerned an act which aimed at a civil or military crime or offense."

The court then summarized some of the evidence that specifically showed orders did not have to be followed: it noted Ohlendorf's testimony about not compelling anyone to kill civilians, the Hartel testimony about General Thomas's offer to excuse those not wanting to shoot civilians, Noßke's experience in disregarding the direction to round up Jews and half-Jews, and, finally, Braune's complete superimposition of what he thought would further the German occupation of Norway over what he had been told to do.[69] In that regard, the court observed that what characterized both the Noßke and Braune situations is that where the defendants did not agree with an order, they ignored it; where they agreed, they followed it.[70]

Towards the end of its discussion of the "following orders" defense, the court quoted lines from Lord Tennyson's famous poem in which he described the cavalry charge at Balaklava in the Crimea:

> Theirs not to make reply
> Theirs not to reason why
> Theirs but to do and die

The court observed that many of the *Einsatzgruppen* operated in the same area almost one hundred years later, but "the *Einsatz* battalions were not being called upon to face shot and shell. They were not ordered to charge into the mouths of cannons. They were called upon to shoot unarmed civilians standing over their graves." The court concluded on this subject: "No soldier or officer attempting escape from such a task would be pleading avoidance of a military obligation. He would simply be requesting not to be made an assassin. And if the leaders of the *Einsatzgruppen* had all indicated their unwillingness to play the assassin's part, this black page in German history would not have been written."[71]

Verdict, Sentence, and Release

Judge Musmanno was clearly the moving force among the judges. As noted earlier, Ferencz does not recall any of the other judges actively participating[72] and the transcript reveals numerous instances of Musmanno's involvement in the questioning. While there are no notes of the deliberations among the judges, it seems clear from Musmanno's participation in the evidence-gathering portion of the trial that he was a major force in the judgment of the court. The manner in which the opinion was written, the hypotheticals used, the parts of the record alluded to, and the insertion of Lord Tennyson's poem all smack of Michael Musmanno.[73]

Musmanno, as has been noted, represented Sacco and Vanzetti as an appellate attorney and was an opponent of the death penalty. In a sense, the *Einsatzgruppen* trial was the perfect case for a death penalty opponent—if the death penalty were to be applied to anyone, it would be those convicted of an almost uncountable number of homicides. In his book on the trial, Musmanno revealed that during a break in the trial, he retreated to a Cistercian monastery about thirty miles from Nuremberg, on the advice of an army chaplain. There, a German priest who spoke Italian, as Musmanno also did, was placed at his disposal. He spent several days in the idyllic setting of the monastery, then took communion, and returned to Nuremberg.[74]

When the court resumed, it found all defendants guilty and imposed sentences varying from time served to death by hanging. The sentences of the court were as follows:

Biberstein, Ernst	Death
Blobel, Paul	Death
Blume, Walter	Death
Braune, Werner	Death
Fendler, Lothar	Ten years
Graf, Matthias	Time served
Haensch, Walter	Death
Jost, Heinz	Life imprisonment
Klingelhofer, Waldemar	Death
Naumann, Erich	Death
Noßke, Gustav	Life imprisonment
Ohlendorf, Otto	Death
Ott, Adolf	Death
Radetzky, Waldemar von	Twenty years

Ruhl, Felix	Ten years
Sandberger, Martin	Death
Schubert, Heinz	Death
Schultz, Erwin	Twenty years
Seibert, Willy	Death
Six, Franz	Twenty years
Steimle, Eugen	Death
Strauch, Eduard	Death

Fourteen defendants were sentenced to death, two to life imprisonment, five to ten- or twenty-year terms of imprisonment, and one, Graf, to time served. The first question that comes to mind is why, given the mass murders committed by all of these defendants (with the exception of Graf and perhaps Ruehl[75]) were they not *all* sentenced to death? In most jurisdictions with the death penalty, then and now, a completely senseless killing of a totally innocent person would qualify for the death penalty; if there were multiple such killings, it would be a powerful case for the ultimate punishment. To this end, one need only recall Rifka Yoselewska's testimony, describing how her grandmother, parents, siblings, nephew, niece, and child were all murdered, and then multiply that scenario by about 150,000.

Hilary Earl, in her thorough examination of the *Einsatzgruppen* trial, makes an acute observation: all of the defendants sentenced to death acknowledged their involvement in murder.[76] Blobel, for example, whose *Einsatz* unit was responsible for the massacre at Babi Yar, claimed that it wasn't 33,000 people who were murdered, but about half that. Ohlendorf had vouched for the accuracy of the count of 90,000 deaths attributable to his unit. Those who denied participation in actual killing, notwithstanding the evidence, received lesser sentences. The plausible inference that arises from Earl's observation is that Musmanno resolved his objections to the death penalty with his obligations as a judge by only sentencing to death those whose statements acknowledged that they had committed mass murder.

However satisfying this may have been for Musmanno and his fellow jurists, it is at odds with the conventional sentencing process. Once the question of guilt is determined, the sentence must be based on the conduct of the defendant as reflected by the verdict. If the candor explicit in an acknowledgement of guilt is relevant at all in the sentencing process, it is precisely the other way around: such candor may be, but does not have to be, considered as a reason for leniency.

As it turned out, any acknowledgement of participation in mass murder was the worst route for a defendant to take in these cases. In the ten years that followed the 1948 verdicts and sentences, the fourteen death sentences were reduced to just four. By mid-1958, the remaining sixteen defendants were either paroled or released to spend the balance of their lives in freedom. The end result was that those who denied their guilt were freed sooner. How could the perpetrators of the crimes of the *Einsatzgruppen* be treated so generously and their enormous crimes ignored?

This reality had nothing to do with sentencing parameters and much to do with the changing political climate. The last half of the 1940s witnessed a major change in the world's alignment of powers. In mid-1945, when the Nuremberg trials began, there was still a semblance of unity among the victorious Allies, and a general commitment to deal with Germany and its leaders who had brought such carnage to the world. The Bernays idea—defining organizations such as the SS as criminal organizations and then later trying individuals on the sole issue of membership—obviously contemplated a prolonged and extensive process of dealing with Nazi criminality. As it turned out, there was no prosecution brought after the Nuremberg trials by the United States in which just membership in a criminal organization was alleged.

Winston Churchill's historic Fulton, Missouri, speech in March 1946, proclaiming that an iron curtain had descended over Europe, was probably the death knell to plans for a thorough and lengthy series of prosecutions, although it would take a while before the full impact of that observation and the events that precipitated it would be felt. Ironically, Hermann Göring, the principal defendant in the first Nuremberg trial, hailed Churchill's speech as precisely the point he had been urging, that the West should unite against the common foe, the expansionist Soviet Union. While the Cold War did not come in time to save Göring, it did lead to the wholesale release of all *Einsatzgruppen* defendants, excepting the four whose death sentences were not reduced.

Article 29 of the IMT Charter allowed for a reduction of sentence. A separate set of rules was created for the subsequent trials since they were not presided over by an international tribunal of four judges, but rather by a tribunal composed of three American judges. Known as Ordinance No. 7, sentence reductions became the sole prerogative of the American Military Governor. Under Article 18 of Ordinance No. 7, the death penalty could not be carried out in any case, unless confirmed in writing by the military governor.[77]

Advocates for the convicted defendants, which included prominent German clergy, were persistent in claiming that the entire Nuremberg process was unfair, resulting in long delays in the implementation of the sentences imposed. These efforts by clergy, some who were imprisoned during the war and some who were closely identified with the Nazi regime, dovetailed with the perceived need for West Germany to serve as a bulwark against an expansionist Soviet Union. This heightened the need to placate growing sentiment in West Germany that all of the trials were unjust and simply the imposition of victor's justice.[78] There can be no question that for the second time in a generation, the "Soviet card" was played effectively.

Initially, U.S. High Commissioner General Lucius Clay decided not to commute any of the sentences of *Einsatzgruppen* defendants. In 1949, John McCloy replaced Clay. Clay had been somewhat of a hardliner when it came to prosecution. McCloy, on the other hand, believed that prosecution interests had to be subordinated to the need to ensure that West Germany was firmly committed to the West and served as an effective buffer to Soviet expansion. McCloy appointed an advisory board to assist him with respect to petitions for clemency. Justice David Peck of the New York State Appellate Division chaired the board composed of three Americans, which was hence known as the "Peck Commission." This advisory board reviewed the numerous petitions advanced by *Einsatzgruppen* defendants and their many supporters, but did not consult Ferencz or any of the prosecutors or seek their input.[79] Naturally, this resulted in recommendations that were, to say the least, bizarre. For example, in the case of the defendant Brigadier General Franz Six, whose attempted alibi in connection with a massacre of Jews at Smolensk the prosecution had refuted, the Peck Commission, without reviewing the transcript or prosecution evidence, found on the basis of his submission that there was a question as to his guilt, and so recommended that his twenty-year sentence be reduced to time served.

The Peck Commission also used its review powers to view evidence differently than how the trial judges had viewed it. In the case of defendant Gustav Noßke, Judge Musmanno saw his refusal to implement orders relating to Germans of mixed Christian and Jewish parentage as strong evidence that he followed only those orders he agreed with, and did not feel obliged to follow all orders. The Peck Commission perceived Noßke's failure to follow orders relating to Germans of mixed Christian and Jewish background as exculpatory and recommended that his sentence be reduced to ten years.[80]

McCloy did not follow Peck Commission recommendations in their entirety. The following table shows the sentences imposed by the tribunal, the Peck Commission recommendations, and McCloy's modifications of both the original sentences and the recommendations. Once these sentences were reduced as reflected by the chart, the four remaining death sentences were carried out. On June 7, 1951, Ohlendorf, Blobel, Braune, and Naumann were executed by hanging.[81]

The pressure for further reductions in sentence did not, however, subside and ultimately prevailed completely. By mid-1958, just ten years after the trial ended, all the remaining defendants were free, either because they had served the reduced time McCloy had granted or were released outright from having to serve the balance of their sentences.

To give some idea of who was released, we can take the first of these defendants, Ernst Biberstein, a former Lutheran clergyman who renounced his ties to the Lutheran Church and in 1935 became a Gestapo chief. Documents tied Biberstein to numerous mass slayings, but he steadfastly maintained that he did not know of the plan to murder Jews until the trial. In every instance in which he was involved in executions, he claimed that there had been an investigation into the activities of the victim and, of course, in all instances, the results of the investigation required execution. He finally acknowledged, and this is no doubt why the court sentenced him to death, that in one execution of sixty-five persons in which he participated, as far as he knew, there had been no investigation.[82] In 1958, Biberstein was released. He lived in freedom for another twenty-eight years.

The last of the *Einsatzgruppen* defendants released was Adolph Ott. On May 9, 1958, he was set free, ten years and a month to the day after

	Original Tribunal	Peck Commission	McCloy Decision
Biberstein, Ernst	Death	Fifteen years	Life imprisonment
Blobel, Paul	Death	Death	Death
Blume, Walter	Death	Twenty years	Twenty-five years
Braune, Werner	Death	Death	Death
Fendler, Lothar	Ten years	Time served	Eight years
Graf, Matthias	Time served	—	—
Haensch, Walter	Death	Fifteen years	Fifteen years
Jost, Heinz	Life imprisonment	Ten years	Ten years
Klingelhofer, Waldemar	Death	Death	Life imprisonment
Naumann, Erich	Death	Death	Death
Noßke, Gustav	Life imprisonment	Ten years	Ten years
Ohlendorf, Otto	Death	Death	Death
Ott, Adolf	Death	Death	Life imprisonment
Radetzky, Waldemar von	Twenty years	Time served	Time served
Ruhl, Felix	Ten years	Time served	Time served
Sandberger, Martin	Death	Death	Life imprisonment
Schubert, Heinz	Death	Time served	Ten years
Schultz, Erwin	Twenty years	Ten years	Fifteen years
Seibert, Willy	Death	Time served	Fifteen years
Six, Franz	Twenty years	Time served	Ten years
Steimle, Eugen	Death	Fifteen years	Twenty years
Strauch, Eduard*	Death	—	—

*Strauch was not executed but transferred to Belgium where he was tried. Found guilty, he was again sentenced to death. He remained in custody until his death in 1955 in a Belgian hospital.

the court's verdict. Ott admitted that Hitler's order was that all Jews, whether partisans or not, had to be executed, and he acknowledged that he had killed Jews pursuant to that order. Specifically, he testified, "I told my sub-*Kommando* leaders that Jews, after they are seized and do not belong to a partisan movement or sabotage organization, must be shot on the basis of Hitler's order." When an incredulous court asked him if he meant this, he responded: "it is correct."[83]

Ferencz, upon learning of the early releases, expressed his frustration in a letter to his former boss Taylor in December 1951:

> I notice in this morning paper's that a group of our Landsberg friends have been given their freedom as a Christmas present. These include... three Einsatzgruppen boys, Schubert, Jost and Nosske. Schubert confessed to personally supervising the execution of about 800 Jews in a humane manner to avoid the moral strain on the execution squad. You may recall that the deadline for cleaning up Simferopol was Christmas 1941 and that Schubert managed to kill all the Jews by then. So for Christmas ten years later he goes Scot free. Who says there is no Santa Klaus? Nosske was the one whom the other defendants called the biggest bloodhound of the day after the sentences were imposed and [he] only received twenty years. Now Nosske is free to join former Gen. Jost whose command ordered a fourth gas van when the three in operation executing women and children were insufficient to do the job properly. Noel, Noel, what the hell.[84]

Conclusion

The *Einsatzgruppen* trial demonstrates the inability of the law to serve the interests of justice alone. In the last analysis, any legal system is the product of the politics that create it. And with the power to create comes the power to destroy. The politics of 1945 led to what was at the time an aggressive, thorough, and ambitious plan to deal with the atrocities of the Third Reich. Five years later, the political scene was very different and that change undeniably undercut the hopes spawned by the ideals of 1945. The mass release of *Einsatzgruppen* defendants significantly undermined whatever justice the trial had attained. If indeed this was the greatest murder case ever tried, then the release of these mass murderers must also mark one of the largest failures of justice. Law is subservient to politics. Sometimes, however, that subservience comes at a steep price.

The Kapo and Those Subservient to Him, a painting by Auschwitz survivor Jan Komski. Courtesy of the Ghetto Fighters' House Museum

7

The Jewish *Kapo* Trials in Israel

Is There a Place for the Law in the Gray Zone?

Kapos were Jewish and non-Jewish prisoners in the concentration camps appointed by the German authorities to maintain order and oversee the fulfillment of work quotas. An unofficial term, the word is usually described as deriving from the Italian word *capo*, meaning "head." According to *The Holocaust Encyclopedia*, a *kapo* was the "[h]ead of a unit in a concentration camp."[1] We use the term in its wider sense, referring to any prisoner in a concentration or labor camp given some supervisory function by the German administrators. Initially, the Nazis chose *kapos* from the ranks of common criminals, and later, political prisoners. Jews were appointed *kapos* in camps where the prisoner population was predominantly Jewish and Jewish *kapos* almost invariably were in charge only of other Jews.

Kapos were part of the day-to-day running of the camps. They ranged from low-ranking functionaries in camp offices, kitchens, and infirmaries, to chiefs in charge of work gangs and barracks who were expected to deal out punishments and beatings. All were, in a sense, collaborators in the system, and all were prisoners themselves—ultimately subject to the same fate as everyone else.

The perfidy of the Nazi regime was in forcing the Jewish victims to be instruments of their own destruction. Jews were at the bottom of the hierarchy in the Nazi concentration camps, with the lowest food rations and selected for the most brutal labor. Jewish *kapos* were just one rung above the miserable existence of the ordinary Jewish prisoner. Legal scholar Lisa Yavnai explains that for Jewish inmates becoming a *kapo* often meant choosing between the possibility of life and almost certain death. In exchange for complete obedience to the SS, *kapos* received more food, warmer clothing, and better sleeping accommodations. According to Yavnai, these amenities increased a Jewish *kapo*'s likelihood of survival tenfold.[2]

Primo Levi, an Italian Jewish survivor of Auschwitz and one of the most incisive chroniclers of the concentration camp experience, referred to the murky area between victim and perpetrator occupied by the Jewish *kapos* as a "gray zone": "The hybrid class of the prisoner-functionary constitutes [the] armature [of the camp (*Lager*)] and at the same time its most disquieting feature," he writes. "It is a gray zone, poorly defined, where the two camps of masters and servants both diverge and converge. This gray zone possesses an incredibly complicated internal structure and contains within itself enough to confuse our need to judge."[3]

While in some cases of collaboration with the German occupier it was easier to establish criminal wrongdoing and guilt (for example, a non-Jewish collaborator who joined the local auxiliary force that assisted the *Einsatzgruppen* in the mass shootings of Jewish civilians), when it comes to the Jewish *kapos* it is particularly difficult, if not impossible, to draw such legal lines. As Lawrence Langer notes, for Jewish *kapos,* these were "choiceless choices . . . imposed by a situation that was in no way of the victim's own choosing."[4]

Levi writes about the "gray zone" in terms of moral judgment, but this chapter considers these issues from a legal perspective. We do so since the new State of Israel and its legal system entered this grim landscape to judge Jewish survivors through its criminal law for acts committed by them while acting as *kapos*. It did so with the passage in 1950 by the Israeli Knesset (parliament) of the Nazi and Nazi Collaborators Law, which we will explore in depth.

Of all the trials discussed in this volume, the *kapo* trials in Israel best fit the moniker "forgotten trials of the Holocaust." Unlike all the other trials, the records of these trials in Israel have been sealed, to be opened seventy years after each of the trials took place. We do not even know exactly how many trials took place. Based upon the meager information available, Israeli scholars estimate that between thirty and forty individuals were prosecuted, with most found guilty. Since information about these trials is limited, and primary documents for the most part are not available, we rely primarily on discussions by Israeli scholars.[5]

Orna Ben-Naftali and Yogev Tuval, the authors of the most detailed study of the *kapo* trials in Israel, explain: "[The trials are] not part of the curriculum in the Israeli educational system. Indeed, over the past four years, we have regularly asked students at [our] law school whether they are familiar with these trials. Not one person was aware of them."[6] This is not surprising, considering the official ban imposed on access to the trials' records. They view the ban in symbolic terms: "[T]he present difficulties of accessing these documents provide a poignant metaphor for the difficulties that the judiciary faced in its own difficult task of passing judgment on these issues."[7]

The sensitivity of the subject was also demonstrated to the author of this chapter (Michael Bazyler) in the course of its writing. Survivors I spoke to urged me to avoid examining this "gray zone," and surprisingly, in contrast to the other chapters, my co-author and I could not agree on a joint conclusion. Therefore, I take full responsibility for the analysis and conclusions in this essay.

The Kapo Phenomenon

A common refrain heard from Jewish survivors of the camps is the cruelty of the Jewish *kapos*. Survivor memoirs invariably include details of killings, participation in selection of prisoners for extermination, beatings, theft, and humiliation imposed by Jewish *kapos* on their fellow Jewish prisoners. A frequent charge is that the Jewish *kapos* behaved "worse than the Germans"—and this statement reflects in large part the bitterness and shame felt by the authors of such statements towards their Jewish brethren. It also reflects the reality of camp life under a system where much of the "dirty work" would be done by prisoners. On a day-to-day basis, Jewish prisoners would have many more encounters with their Jewish prisoner-bosses than with the Germans.

Holocaust scholar Christopher Browning, in his book *Remembering Survival*, describes the complicated views that Jewish inmates held towards the privileged Jewish prisoners—in this case, the camp police (*Lagerpolizei*) at the labor camp in Starachowice, Poland:

> Several survivors bitterly and hyperbolically characterize the camp police as "worse than the Germans." Others took a more differentiated view, noting that some of the police were nice and "a few" were not, "some were bastards and some were good," and "at least some were not unkind" while others "degenerated" and "abused their power unnecessarily." This last phrase about the *unnecessary* abuse of power is significant. This same survivor expressed a quite representative view: "The general feeling in the camp was that a genuinely fine person did not become the policeman for the Germans for any reason."[8]

Jewish survivors of other *Lagers* remember *kapos* who were relatively innocuous, and others who vented their rage upon the inmates directly under their control. Primo Levi recalls their unlimited power vis-à-vis other prisoners: "[T]hey were free to commit the worst atrocities on their subjects as punishment for any transgressions, or even without any motive whatsoever. . . . [I]t was not unusual for a prisoner to be beaten to death by a *kapo* without the latter having to fear any sanctions."[9]

After the war, survivors recognized former *kapos* under different circumstances—in the displaced persons (DP) camps in Europe, in new immigrant communities around the world, and in the young State of Israel, which received more than four hundred thousand Jewish refugees from Europe following the end of the Second World War.

Kapo Trials in Europe and the United States

A common phenomenon throughout Europe after liberation was to exact vengeance upon those who collaborated with the German occupier. Cases of vigilante justice would take place as soon as a particular region was liberated, usually followed by trials of collaborators in newly reconstituted domestic courts, or special courts established to try collaborators when civil order was restored. Some of those put on trial were Jews. No study has yet examined how many of the postwar collaborator trials specifically prosecuted Jewish *kapos*.[10] Two such trials, however, illustrate that vengeance was the primary driving force for punishing *kapos*, which sometimes translated itself into the grotesque result of the Jewish *kapo* receiving harsher punishment than the German principal on whose behalf the *kapo* was acting.

In 1949, a postwar French military court tried Joseph Weiszl, one of Eichmann's Austrian lieutenants, for his role in organizing the selections of Jews to be sent from the French transit camp of Drancy to Auschwitz and other camps in Poland. One of Weiszl's co-defendants was Oscar Reich, a Viennese Jew who had fled to France, but then was interned at Drancy after Germany's occupation of France. Reich, under threat of being deported himself, assisted with the selections. In the postwar trial, the French judges showed no mercy towards Reich. Found guilty of collaboration with the enemy, he was executed on July 5, 1949.[11] The sheer injustice of this verdict is heightened by the fact that the *same* court sentenced Weiszl to life imprisonment, although Weiszl—as pointed out by German Holocaust historian Hans Safrian in *Eichmann's Men*—"had categorized thousands as able to be transported, and so had aided and abetted their murder in the annihilation camps."[12] To add to the travesty, the French authorities released Weiszl six years later. A lifetime pension from the postwar Austrian government awaited him upon his return to his native Vienna in 1955.

A fate similar to Reich's befell Leon Gross, a Polish Jewish prisoner-physician at the Płaszów concentration camp in Poland who worked under commandant Amon Göth (see chapter 4). Göth assigned Dr. Gross the unenviable task of selecting Jewish inmates to be murdered because they were too feeble or ill to work. Rescued for a time by Oskar Schindler, Gross's skills as a physician led him to be transferred to Auschwitz, where he again assisted with selections. Arrested by the Poles after liberation, Gross was found guilty of collaboration by a regular Polish court and sentenced to death. He was hanged on December 22, 1946, three months after Göth's execution.[13]

As noted earlier, in the newly liberated countries, as well as in displaced persons camps in Germany, vengeance killings by Jews against their former fellow prisoner-tormentors, both Jewish and non-Jewish, were not uncommon, as the latter suddenly found themselves at the mercy of their former charges. A more common route, however, for dealing with Jewish *kapos* was to adjudge them through the so-called Jewish "community honor courts." These self-constituted *ad hoc* tribunals, not sanctioned by any state authority, would hold a trial in which the fate of the former Jewish *kapo* would be in the hands of other survivors acting as judges. Survivors offered evidence, both accusatory and exculpatory, which could be presented either through oral testimony during the trial hearing or through signed statements or letters. The most common punishment for those found culpable was to bar the former collaborator from any position of authority in the Jewish community. An additional punishment was the denial of aid and immigration assistance that Jewish relief agencies were offering at the time to Holocaust survivors. In more serious cases, a survivor adjudged to be a "traitor to the Jewish people" would be banished from the community, but such banishments were rare. Interestingly, in some cases a survivor under suspicion of committing brutalities against fellow Jews in the camp, or as a member of the *Judenrat,* the ghetto administration (most often the ghetto policemen), would request a tribunal to clear his or her name and restore their honor in the community.[14]

These postwar Jewish community honor courts did not mete out some form of vigilante justice. Rather, in the postwar havoc of a liberated Europe, the surviving Jews formed their own self-governing and self-sustaining communities, whether in the DP camps in Germany or in cities throughout Europe where Jews began their new lives after the war. The courts would go by such names as the Court of Honor and Rehabilitation of the Union of Liberated Jews in the American Zone of Germany and the Court of Honor at the Central Organization of Survivors in Italy. As a result, these honor courts acted in a manner befitting regularly constituted state tribunals. The local Jewish community organization would often have a legal department, staffed by Jewish lawyers who survived the war. The legal department would investigate complaints of collaboration, decide whether to bring formal charges, and then formally begin proceedings by constituting an honor tribunal, usually consisting of three members. Isaiah Trunk, who has reviewed the archival records of these courts, concludes: "The Courts of Honor gained high moral standing. Their sentences were binding and recognized by the displaced persons community, except for one known case where an attempt was made to charge a court with lack of authority to pass judgment."[15]

Turning to the United States, approximately 140,000 Jewish survivors of the war came to American shores as refugees between 1946 and 1954.[16] Among those, invariably, were former *kapos*. There has been only a single trial, however, of a Jewish *kapo* in the United States. In 1987, the U.S. Department of Justice Office of Special Investigations (OSI) brought denaturalization proceedings in a Brooklyn federal court against naturalized American citizen and Holocaust survivor Jacob Tannenbaum. OSI sought to have Tannenbaum, a former Jewish *kapo* at the Görlitz concentration camp in Germany, stripped of his citizenship and deported. What brought Tannenbaum to the attention of the OSI were detailed statements obtained in Israel and the United States from Jewish concentration camp survivors describing Tannenbaum's brutality.

Under a plea deal reached with the OSI, and approved by a Brooklyn federal judge, the seventy-seven-year-old Tannenbaum agreed to surrender his citizenship but was allowed to live out the rest of his life as a free man in the United States. Tannenbaum's defense attorney, Elihu Massel, explained why this arrangement was the best solution: "It [would] avoid a truly ghastly trial in which Jews would have had to testify against Jews, none of whom really want to remember."[17] Tannenbaum died five years later.

Israel Enters the Gray Zone

The modern State of Israel was born of two powerful impulses. First was the dream of the Zionist pioneers, starting in the late nineteenth century, to return to the ancient Jewish homeland, cultivate the land, and create a new kind of Jew—strong and proud—in an independent state of their own. Second was the growing need for a place of refuge for persecuted Jews from Europe, beginning in the 1930s. While immigration was restricted through the war years by the British, with Israel's Declaration of Independence on May 15, 1948, the floodgates opened. By the end of the 1950s, close to half a million survivors were living in the new State of Israel, constituting one quarter of the country's population.

An analysis of the Nazi and Nazi Collaborators (Punishment) Law (NNCL), passed by Israel's first Knesset in August 1950, has to take note of the relationship between these two communities: the European Jews who settled in Palestine out of Zionist convictions prior to the Second World War—and built what eventually became the State of Israel—and the Jews who came as refugees and survivors of the Holocaust.

The purpose of the NNCL has been hotly debated and criticized. According to one Israeli Supreme Court decision, "The law in question is designed to make it possible to try, in Israel, Nazis, their associates and their collaborators for the murder of the Jewish people . . . and for crimes against humanity as a whole."[18] While this purpose may seem straightforward enough, Israeli scholars do not agree on the *motivations* behind creating this legal remedy.

Israeli journalist Tom Segev provides a plausible explanation for how the NNCL came on the books. He notes that after the war had ended, Jews who were recognized as *kapos* by their victims in liberated Europe were physically assaulted, with some even being murdered.[19] With the establishment of the State of Israel, survivors living in the Jewish state turned to the police. But, as Segev explains: "[T]he police were powerless—there was no law that covered this situation or allowed them to arrest the suspects. As a result, the Ministry of Justice introduced an 'Act against Jewish War Criminals' in August 1949 but did not push for immediate enactment [by the Knesset.]"[20] After ten months, the contemplated Act against Jewish War Criminals was introduced into the Knesset, but with a new name—Nazi and Nazi Collaborators Law—and expanded jurisdiction, targeting not only so-called "Jewish war criminals" but also Nazis and their non-Jewish collaborators who murdered Jews. On August 1, 1950, it won Knesset approval and became law.

While acknowledging some influence of initial survivor complaints, Israeli historian Idith Zertal questions the degree to which such complaints by Holocaust survivors themselves motivated the law:

> The police were under some pressure from survivors—a few dozen in all—who demanded justice and action against "collaborators." According to this quasi-official narrative, the "predicament" of the survivors is therefore what expedited the legislative process. The Justice and Police Ministries joined forces to draft an appropriate law based on the

> complaints of a handful (out of more than a quarter of a million) of survivors against other survivors. Thus, a law was promulgated against "war criminals" and the perpetrators of "crimes against humanity," which, in practice, targeted Jews, themselves Holocaust victims.[21]

Although it was no longer called the Act against Jewish War Criminals, everyone was aware that the main target of the NNCL was Jewish collaborators and not Nazis.

A major proponent of the law was Pinchas Rosen, Israel's first minister of justice. Rosen, born Felix Rosenblüth in Germany in 1887, was already an experienced lawyer when he came to Mandate Palestine in 1926, motivated by his long-standing Zionist commitment. Elected to the first Knesset, he was appointed to serve as minister of justice by Israel's first prime minister, David Ben-Gurion. In that capacity, on March 27, 1950, Rosen testified at Knesset Session 131, during the first reading of the bill, and explained the need for this law to the parliamentarians: "While other nations legislated laws immediately following the war, and some of them even beforehand, concerning bringing the Nazi and their collaborators to justice, the Jewish people, the people whose grievance against the Nazi is the most severe, was deprived until the creation of the state of the authority to bring the Nazi criminals and their collaborators to justice. . . . This will be changed now [with this proposed law]."[22]

But Rosen acknowledged that the NNCL was not just a symbolic gesture by Israel to make what the Nazis did to the Jews a crime under Israeli law. The real thrust of the law came out at the end of his presentation:

> It is assumed that Nazi criminals, who could be charged on the basis of the crimes included in the Law, would not dare come to Israel. But the Law applies also to Nazi collaborators, and, unfortunately, we cannot be certain that such people would not be found in our camp, even if their numbers are probably not many. . . . The proposed Law may also contribute to the cleansing of the atmosphere amongst the survivors who immigrated to the land of Israel. Whoever knows their problems, knows how painfully embedded in them is the question of suspicions and

> reciprocal accusations . . . the police could not, given the absence of the proposed Law, commence an investigation. . . . Let our camp be pure.[23]

The last sentence is from the Bible: "let your camp be holy; let Him not find anything unseemly among you and turn away" (Deut. 23:14). But which "camp" or community was Rosen seeking to purify? There are three possibilities. First, the "camp of Holocaust survivors living in Israel," who themselves had recently emerged from another category of camps—concentration and labor camps—in Nazi-occupied Europe to return to the Jewish homeland built for them by their brethren who came before the war. Second, it could mean the entire "camp of the State of Israel," that is, the Jewish pioneers from around the world that shared the Zionist dream and made the decision both before and after the war to return to their ancient homeland. Third, it could have been a reference to the camp comprising all Jews throughout the world.

Certainly, it was not the last, since Israel did not seek to cleanse the Jewish people worldwide of those who collaborated with the Nazi oppressors. That it was not so intended is illustrated by the fact that the law was not drafted as an extraterritorial statute that would reach out and punish also *kapos* who stayed in Europe or found refuge in North America, Australia, or other parts of the world. The impurity of these camps was of no concern to Rosen.

Taken at face value, Rosen in Session 131 appears to be addressing the community of survivors in Israel, saying: "We are doing this for you." As he said to Knesset members: "Anyone familiar with the problems [of the survivors] knows how painful [for them] are the mutual suspicion and recrimination that, to this day, hover over some of Israel's immigrants who were liberated from camps and ghettos; in some cases perhaps—because they have not been given an opportunity to prove their innocence before an authorized court."[24]

A plausible argument can be made, therefore, that the proposed law came into being in response to demands by the survivors themselves, seeking to purify their community and to do so through a legally sanctioned court process that would fairly separate among their ranks the guilty from the innocent. I am somewhat suspicious, however, that the motivation behind the NNCL was in fact to calm the wrath of the survivors and avenge their suffering. Out of the two hundred thousand or so survivors living in Israel at the time, the police received "a few dozen complaints." A few dozen complaints do not amount to a popular demand.

Rather, it seems that the law was enacted for the psychological benefit of the community of *non-survivors*, the prewar population in Israel. Its intention most likely was to distance Israelis from what they regarded as the shameful response of Europe's Jews to their destruction. As Zertal explains:

> While the social predicament of survivors who found themselves sharing a new country with former petty tormentors may well have added impetus for devising that law, it seems unlikely that this alone would have set into motion so grave and complex a legislative process. . . . Above all . . . as the early trials demonstrated, the law was meant to appease society's disgust at "Jewish conduct" during the Holocaust. Israel introduced an anomaly into its legal code not in order to confront Nazism, . . . but to purge the new and "pure" state of Jewish shame. . . . Jews who had not been in Nazi-occupied Europe brought to justice Jews who had been . . . and conducted trials that, in every sense of the word, were purges.[25]

The greater Israeli society, a majority of whom were *not* survivors, exhibited considerable disdain for the Jews of Europe for not standing up to the Nazi onslaught, but instead, as the narrative went, meekly going to their deaths like "sheep to slaughter." Otherwise, how could the Nazis have succeeded in murdering six million Jews in Europe? As Israeli sociologist Judith Buber Agassi writes, "In the early years after the War, all survivors of the Holocaust who came to Israel were regarded with suspicion as possible collaborators."[26] Female survivors had an additional accusation thrust at them. According to Agassi, "In the case of female survivors, a most unfortunate myth had developed: it was additionally claimed that some Jewish women—especially young and pretty ones—had survived because they had been prostitutes in the brothels of the German forces, and that they had even been tattooed as such."[27]

Ayala H. Emmett relates her memories as the daughter of Holocaust survivors growing up in the new Israel: "What I hated and dreaded most when I was a child was summertime. It was a time when the numbers on my mother's arm would be there for all to see and people would know that she was a survivor and was one of the despised people. People like my parents were despised in Israel, and I was ashamed of them."[28]

In the new Israel, the narrative adopted by Israelis towards the survivors, articulated by one parliamentarian during the debate on the NNCL, was that "had there been the slightest sign of physical resistance, it would not have been possible to murder six million Jews."[29] This narrative pitted Israeli heroism in the face of extinction by her Arab enemies against the perceived "submissive meekness" of Diaspora Jews.[30] The survivors were scornfully referred to as *sabonim* (soap), a reference to the widely held belief at the time that the Nazis manufactured bars of soap out the remains of murdered Jews.

And if survivors as a group were disrespected, then those that collaborated were doubly so. During the debate on the law, one parliamentarian expressed what was probably the view of others in the Knesset: "[O]ne cannot turn a blind eye on the fact that collaboration is what assisted the Nazis to realize their objective. . . . Collaboration applies to anyone who joins the *Judenrat* or becomes a *kapo*, believing that thereby he would save himself. . . . If one was a *kapo* for two or three years he could not have been anything but a criminal."[31]

In enacting the NNCL, it would seem that the MKs were not responding with compassion and empathy for those who survived, as they claimed, but shame that they did not resist and a belief that they might have survived because they collaborated. "For those who survived without putting up a fight, their very survival became suspect, smacked of opportunism, and was certainly not worthy of attention, let alone respect," according to Ben-Naftali and Tuval. "If the Law could be used as a mechanism to cleanse this community of those members whose survival could be attributed to some function or privilege, the survival of the rest could be tolerated."[32] Unlike Zertal, Ben-Naftali and Tuval do not explicitly use the word "purge" to characterize the purpose of NNCL, but the import is the same.

Crimes and Punishment under the NNCL

Minister of Justice Rosen's presentation before the Knesset and the first reading of the bill took place on March 27, 1950. On August 9, the bill became law.[33] By all counts, it was "an odd legislative creation."[34] As discussed, the law was not conceived in order to punish actual Nazis, but rather, their so-called Jewish "collaborators" now living in Israel, who were persecuted survivors themselves. However, nowhere did the NNCL define "a collaborator" and how that individual is to be distinguished from a Nazi. In effect, by failing to distinguish between Nazis and collaborators, the NNCL conflated and appeared to equate their behavior.

This, however, was not the only exceptionality of the law. It was also unique in its *post facto* orientation. Unlike the domestic genocide statute, the Crime of Genocide (Prevention and Punishment) Law (passed by the Knesset five months earlier, on March 29, 1950, after Israel became a party to the U.N. Genocide Convention and which was aimed at the future), this genocide law—the NNCL—looked strictly to the past, targeting those who committed or assisted in the genocide of the Jewish people during the Nazi era. What follows is a brief summary of the various provisions of the NNCL.

ARTICLE 1: CRIMES AGAINST HUMANITY, WAR CRIMES, AND CRIMES AGAINST THE JEWISH PEOPLE

The NNCL introduced three principal crimes enumerated in Article 1 of the law: (1) crimes against humanity, (2) war crimes, and (3) crimes against the Jewish people. It then mandated the death penalty for all three.[35] Israeli judges hearing these cases were specifically denied any room for mercy: a Holocaust survivor found guilty of any of these three crimes must be put to death. In limited circumstances (see below), punishment can be imprisonment of at least ten years.

The first two NNCL crimes—*crimes against humanity* and *war crimes*—are substantially similar to the crimes of the same names enumerated in the Nuremberg Charter. *Crimes against the Jewish people* is a *sui generis* crime, with a formulation not found in the criminal code of any other state (there is, for example, no offense in Polish law of "crime against the Polish people"). The definition of the crime closely tracks the definition of the crime of genocide in the U.N. Genocide Convention but limits its application to only one victim group (the Jews), one location (Europe), and one time period (the years of Nazi rule).[36]

The NNCL then tracks the *actus reus* (conduct) elements of the U.N. Genocide Convention but limits these acts to Jewish victims during the Nazi era: (1) killing Jews; (2) causing serious bodily or mental harm to Jews; (3) placing Jews in living conditions calculated to bring about their physical destruction; (4) imposing measures intended to prevent births among Jews; (5) forcibly transferring Jewish children to another national or religious group; (6) destroying or desecrating Jewish religious or cultural assets or values; and (7) inciting hatred of Jews.[37]

ARTICLES 2–6: OTHER CRIMES

Apart from the three crimes for which the death penalty was obligatory (Article 1), the NNCL included a series of crimes for which imprisonment would be the expected punishment (Articles 2–6). These included: crimes against persecuted persons (Article 2); membership in an enemy organization (Article 3); offenses in places of confinement (Article 4); delivering up persecuted persons to enemy administration (Article 5); and blackmailing persecuted persons (Article 6). While some were charged with an Article 1 crime, all but one of the *kapos* was convicted of crimes under Articles 2 or 4.

DEFENSES AND MITIGATION

As noted earlier, for the three crimes enumerated in Article 1, those found guilty must be put to death. Articles 10 and 11, however, provide affirmative defenses and mitigating circumstances to the crimes set out in Articles 2–6 (unless the crime was murder as defined under Israeli law). The Israeli legislators, therefore, contemplated specific situations where acquittal or a lesser penalty is possible for Article 2–6 crimes, even though the *prima facie* elements of these crimes have been proven.

Article 10 calls for acquittal for these non-capital crimes if the person who committed the crime (a) did so "to save himself from the danger of immediate death threatening him and the court is satisfied that he did his best to avert the consequences of the act or the omission"; and

(b) when the actor's reason for committing the crime was "with intent to avert consequences more serious than those which resulted from the act or omission, and actually averted them."

Article 11 permits the judges to take into account two mitigating circumstances when considering punishment: (a) "that the person committed the offence under conditions which . . . would have exempted him from criminal responsibility or constituted a reason for pardoning the offence, and that he did his best to reduce the gravity of the consequences of the offence"; and (b) "that the offence was committed with intent to avert, and was indeed calculated to avert, consequences more serious than those which resulted from the offence."

This last set of mitigating circumstances *can* be considered for Article 1 offenses, but then limited the judges to imposing a sentence of at least ten years' imprisonment ("in the case of an offence under section 1, the court shall not impose on the offender a lighter punishment than imprisonment for a term of ten years").

The Kapo Trials under the NNCL

Unlike the other trials covered in this volume, we do not know the exact number of *kapo* trials that took place in Israel. As noted earlier, the records of these trials remain sealed and will only be opened seventy years after each of the trials has taken place. According to Israeli scholars, about thirty to forty prosecutions took place between 1951 and 1964, but these are rough estimates.

As for the verdicts, Ben-Naftali and Tuval summarize: "The available, though incomplete, sources suggest that fifteen of a total of about forty cases ended in convictions. The sentences tended to be light, and only rarely was a person sentenced to prison for a period exceeding the time he had already been in detention awaiting verdict."[38] Zertal points out that "*not one* of the defendants tried under the law was charged with or found guilty of directly or indirectly causing the death of a single person."[39]

In stark contrast to the eventual results, the prosecutor's initial charges tended to be harsh, with a number of the known cases showing individuals being charged with war crimes or crimes against humanity.[40] In one case, a Jewish survivor indicted for crimes against humanity was convicted of that crime. Pursuant to the mandatory provisions of the NNCL, he was sentenced to death. However, as discussed below, it appears that this conviction was overturned on appeal.

Despite the sealing of these records, which "lie like corpses in the obscurity of Israel's legal archives,"[41] some information about the *kapo* trials turned up in the papers of Asher Levitzi, a lawyer who represented some of the *kapos*. After his death, his family donated his files to the State Archive, and the sealing order failed to include the Levitzi papers. These papers contain extensive information about three of the trials and sparse information about some other cases. Israeli scholars' descriptions of the trials are based, for the most part, on the Levitzi papers and newspaper coverage. Relying on the latter, however, presents another problem since scant media attention was given to the *kapo* trials. As Segev remarks, "Only a few trials were covered by the press, some not at all. A *kapo* trial was a filthy and embarrassing story, and the papers did not want to get caught up in it."[42]

Though newspapers had a choice whether or not to "get caught up in" these "filthy and embarrassing stor[ies]," the Israeli courts and judges sitting on them did not. Soon after the law came into effect, Israeli prosecutors began charging individuals with crimes under the NNCL. The Israeli legal system does not have jury trials, and all decisions are rendered by professional judges, lawyers of long-time experience appointed to the bench. The pool from which these judges came at the time was the same as that of the Knesset: European Jews who had emigrated to Mandate Palestine before the war. In fact, one of the judges to preside over a *kapo* trial, Yosef-Michael Lamm, was a former lawyer in Vienna who had been arrested and sent to Dachau in 1938, but was able to flee to Mandate Palestine in 1939. He was a member of the Knesset when the law was promulgated. But writing a general law to prosecute perceived criminals is different than sitting in judgment over specific individuals and learning how their conduct took place under unimaginable circumstances. As a result, Segev explains, "[t]he trials required the judges to make extraordinary ethical and historical decisions that often fell outside their areas of expertise. They had to decide whether a man could refuse to accept the post of *kapo*, and to what extent the job required cruelty. They tended not to punish a person for simply being a *kapo*, only for not having been a decent one."[43]

Segev quotes Supreme Court Justice Moshe Silberg, who felt that punishing *kapos* was detracting from the horror perpetrated by the Nazis: "It is hard for us, the judges of Israel, to free ourselves of the feeling that, in punishing a worm of this sort, we are diminishing, even if by only a trace, the abysmal guilt of the Nazis themselves."[44] In sum, despite the eagerness of the Knesset to prosecute these individuals, Israeli judges found it extremely difficult to apply the NNCL to actual cases that manifested the "choiceless choices" faced by individual *kapos*.

Let us now take a look at some of the more notable trials.

Tarnek Trial—1951

One of the earliest trials involved a former female Jewish *kapo*. In December 1951, Else Tarnek (also referred to as "Elsa Trank"), stood trial at age twenty-six for alleged crimes she had committed at age eighteen in her capacity as "block commander" at Auschwitz-Birkenau.[45] The state prosecutors displayed conduct bordering on callousness in seeking the death penalty. They did so by charging Tarnek with both war crimes and crimes against humanity, even though the most serious accusations against her involved beating other inmates. None of the victims were alleged to have died from the beatings. Furthermore, the position of commander of Block 7 in the female section in Auschwitz was imposed on Tarnek. As a result, it became her responsibility to "maintain order and discipline, to assemble the women for roll call as the Germans ordered, and to supervise the fair distribution of food. In so doing, she hit several women 'with her hands' and forced recalcitrant prisoners to kneel, a common camp punishment also before her arrival."[46]

The judges rejected most of the prosecution's claims. Tranek was acquitted of both war crimes and crimes against humanity but found guilty of two lesser counts. In their decision, the judges recognized the untenable position of the female *kapos* at Auschwitz and demonstrated an understanding of, and almost empathy for, Tarnek's actions in Block 7:

> We must take the circumstances under consideration: the defendant was placed in charge, against her will, of a block where 1,000 persecuted women lived. She herself was a persecuted person, just as they were. Her functions were to take care of the distribution of meager and horrible food and to ensure that the inmates would attend the twice daily parade. . . . During the time the food was distributed, the inmates fought to get their portion, or even a double portion. Experience had taught the defendant that consequently some inmates would be left without even one portion. She herself experienced hunger as a result of disorderly distribution of food. The defendants battled against these disorders by slaps, which were the quickest and most effective weapon under the circumstances . . . there were surely times where an innocent inmate got hit.

Focusing on the *mens rea* (mental state) of the defendant, the judges explained:

> It was not proven to us that the defendant identified in any of her acts with the Germans . . . the defendant herself had been interned under much harder conditions since 1942, before she was placed in charge of other inmates, and suffered a great deal.[47]

Finding Tranek guilty of assault and battery, the judges sentenced her to two years' imprisonment with credit for time served. As Zertal observes: "The sentence was not arbitrary. It was exactly two years since her arrest; Elsa Trank was released the same day."[48]

Enigster Trial—1952

The Enigster trial was decided by the District Court of Tel-Aviv on January 4, 1952.[49] Yehezkel Enigster (also transliterated as Anigster) had been a chief *kapo* in the labor camps at Graeditz and Fauelbruch from 1943 to 1944. Of the known cases, Enigster's case showed the most brutal behavior by a Jewish *kapo*. Enigster was described in his role as *kapo* as follows: "[A] heavy man, a red-neck, dressed in a leather jacket and boots, walking with a wire-club covered with rubber, which he used to hit whoever happens to cross his path, whenever he pleased."[50] Witness testimony including the following descriptions of his behavior:

> "He used to hit us like a man hitting his enemy . . . he would beat us for no reason."
>
> "I spent three years in the camps and never encountered a *kapo* who behaved as badly . . . towards Jews."
>
> "He used to lash with his club at the weak and the fainting . . . he severely beat any prisoner whose posture he didn't like."
>
> "I was in 19 camps and the worst hell was when I was working for the defendant. . . . On the day that he and 25 *kapos* . . . were sent away from the camp, people danced with joy."[51]

Enigster was charged with five counts: (1) one count of committing a "war crime"; (2) one count of "crime against humanity"; and (3) three counts of "grave . . . and deliberate bodily harm . . . to a persecuted individual."[52] As noted earlier, if convicted of either of the first two counts the NNCL mandated that Enigster receive the death penalty.

In its verdict, the trial court refused to accept Enigster's claims that he was forced to accept the job of *kapo* and that he hit people only to stop them from fighting with each other. With regard to coercion, the majority decision stated that "[a]ccepting the job was not coerced and . . . if the job was not done to the satisfaction of the Germans, the consequences would have been no more severe than being put out of the job and resuming the life of an ordinary inmate."[53] The factual basis for this conclusion was not given.

In a 2–1 decision, the court convicted Enigster of one count of committing a crime against humanity and also of three other lesser counts. Nevertheless, the majority judges did not want to impose the mandatory death penalty and bemoaned that the NNCL did not give them a choice. It would have been better, they stated, had "the legislator left sentencing to the courts."[54] The majority pointed out that there could be no comparison between a German SS cadre working in the camp and the Jewish prison-functionary. Moreover, they explained that not all crimes against humanity are equal. In the case before them evidence was proffered that some Jewish *kapos* acted even more cruelly than

Enigster. Consequently, they would have preferred a sentence of ten years' imprisonment for crimes against humanity, and briefer concurrent prison terms for the other offenses.

Judge Yosef-Michael Lamm dissented. Lamm, who, as noted, was a member of the first Knesset that passed the NNCL, would not have convicted Enigster of crimes against humanity, but for one of the lesser crimes instead. He also would have sentenced the defendant to ten years' imprisonment. Since Enigster, by the time of trial, had become severely ill, the judges unanimously agreed to recommend that the president of Israel mitigate the sentence.[55]

What happened next remains sketchy. It appears that Enigster's appeal was heard by the Supreme Court of Israel, but that decision is not available. Secondary sources state that the court reduced his sentence to two years' imprisonment from the day of his arrest. Enigster died shortly afterwards.[56]

Berenblatt Trial—1963

Hirsch Berenblatt (also spelled Berenblat) technically was not a *kapo* but served as a Jewish police commander of the Polish town of Bedzin. He emigrated to Israel after the war and, at the time of his arrest, was the assistant conductor at the Tel Aviv Opera House. Berenblatt was brought before the Tel Aviv District Court in the early 1960s and charged under Article 5 of the NNCL: "delivering up persecuted persons to enemy administration."[57] His was one of the last cases to be heard, filed before the Eichmann trial, but decided soon after the Eichmann proceedings.

Berenblatt was convicted in early 1963 of having assisted the Germans in rounding up the town's Jews for a selection. The most serious charge against him was of having "rounded up and arrested, together with others, dozens of Jewish children from the municipal orphanage . . . and [of having] handed them over to the Gestapo." The conviction was based on the testimony of a single witness, whom the court found reliable, and Berenblatt was sentenced to five years' imprisonment.

On appeal, the Supreme Court in 1964 reversed and acquitted Berenblatt of all charges.[58] The court did so by relying on the complete defenses provided in Article 10 discussed above. Justice Moshe Landau, who had earlier presided over the Eichmann trial, noted that it would be "presumptuous and self-righteous on our part, us who never walked in the shoes of those [who were there] . . . to be critical of these 'small people' who were incapable of transcending into an ultimate level of morality. . . . [C]riminal law prohibitions, including the Nazi and Nazi Collaborators Law, were not written for exceptional heroes, but for ordinary mortals, with their ordinary weaknesses." He then added, striking at the heart of the matter: "Let us not delude ourselves that if we subject the acts committed by our persecuted brethren there to criminal justice on the basis of pure moral standards, we would ease the weight of the distress in our heart regarding the horrid blow our people suffered."[59] Another justice, Yakov Ulshan, concurred: "[T]his is a question for history and not for the courts."[60]

Was Justice Served?

My analysis of the *kapo* trials leads me to question the legal foundations for the *kapo* prosecutions in Israel. I submit a new legal basis in order to more accurately examine these trials and their consequences. Building upon the metaphor of "Planet Auschwitz" that Holocaust survivor and author Yehiel Dinur (writing as "Ka. Tzetnik 135633") presented in his written works and in his court testimony, including at the Eichmann trial, I propose that the *kapos* cannot be judged under commonly understood standards of decency that translate themselves into secular legal norms, and by which the *kapos* were judged. International law, in setting out conduct that binds all states and individuals, speaks of "civilized legal systems" as the basis for these universal norms. The most notable characteristic of the world of the Nazi camps, however, is the very absence of this "civilization."

Primo Levi, in his Holocaust memoir *Survival in Auschwitz,* relates this well when he describes an incident when he broke an icicle hanging from a barracks window to quench his thirst and was promptly punished by a nearby guard who snatched the icicle from him. Asking "*Warum?*" (Why?), the answer he receives is "*Hier ist kein Warum*" (Here there is no why).[61]

Levi recognized that when examining behavior of individuals in the gray zone the natural desire is to make judgments about that behavior. And yet he calls for resisting that desire, specifically because places like Auschwitz "confuse our need to judge."[62]

In writing about the *kapos*, Levi does not let us forget that the real culprits were the Nazis who deliberately created environments to break down the human spirit. In an important elucidation, he notes: "It is naïve, absurd, and historically false to believe that an infernal system such as National Socialism sanctifies its victims; on the contrary, it degrades them, it makes them resemble itself."[63] The *Lager,* he writes, was designed to bring out the worst in human nature:

> If one offers a position of privilege to a few individuals in a state of slavery, exacting in exchange the betrayal of a natural solidarity with their comrades, there will certainly be someone who will accept. He will be withdrawn from the common law and will become untouchable; the more power that he is given, the more he will be consequently hateful and hated. . . . [H]e will be cruel and tyrannical, because he will understand that if he is not sufficiently so, someone else, judged more suitable, will take over his post. . . . [H]is capacity for hatred, unfulfilled in the direction of the oppressors, will double back, beyond all reason, on the oppressed; and he will only be satisfied when he has unloaded on to his underlings the injury received from above.[64]

In his last book, *The Drowned and the Saved,* Levi gives one of the harshest and most unflinching accounts of the Jewish *kapos* and their treatment of their fellow prisoners in all of Holocaust literature. At the same time, he cautions against hasty moral judgments:

> Certainly, the greatest responsibility lies with the system, the very structure of the totalitarian state; the concurrent guilt on the part of individual big and small collaborators (never likable, never transparent!) is always difficult to evaluate. It is a judgment that we would like to entrust only to those who found themselves in similar circumstances and had the opportunity to test for themselves what it means to act in a state of coercion.[65]

For this reason, Levi called for suspension of *moral* judgments in the Nazi-created gray zones. But if moral judgments cannot be made, then how are *legal* judgments even possible? And yet this is exactly what Israel aimed to make with the passage of the NNCL.

Benjamin Ferencz, the chief prosecutor of the *Einsatzgruppen* trial at Nuremberg, was able to see the helplessness of the law when, as a young war crimes investigator, he was one of the first American lawyers to come face-to-face with the gray zone. In a letter written in April 1945 from the just-liberated Flossenbürg concentration camp to his future wife, Gertrude, he described what he encountered:

> Many of the prisoner guards had been recruited from the prisoners themselves. These "trustees" had been even more brutal than the SS men. What was to be done about them? At first I thought that we would handle them the same way we intended to handle war criminals. . . . The first one was accused, by several witnesses, of beating a sick Frenchman to death with a rubber hose. I called in the perpetrator and confronted him with the facts I had gathered. The man had been a prisoner there for six years. He had sought to curry favor and perhaps a few privileges from the Nazis by his mistreatment of his fellow prisoners. He denied everything but was obviously lying. What punishment does that man deserve? It was established against another prisoner that, while he was a hospital orderly, he had killed a few patients by beating them and then putting a rubber hose in their mouths and turning the water on full pressure. Brutal you say? That perpetrator had been in prison there for four years. . . . Elsewhere in the world these things would undoubtedly have been charged with murder . . . but in a context where murder is as common as eating, how responsible is a persecuted victim who does only what he sees being done day in and day out? Can we apply the values and standards of a civilized world to people who have been subjected to a murder camp for four or six years?[66]

Ferencz saw the impotence of the law in the gray zone through the eyes of a twenty-five-year-old war crimes investigator learning about the hell of a concentration camp and trying to figure out what normative rules should apply there. Italian philosopher Giorgio Agamben, examining the phenomena of the camps from the comfort of his study a half-century later, comes to the same conclusion: "[E]very question concerning the legality or illegality of what happened there simply makes no sense."[67]

The Jewish Law Alternative: Krieger v. Mittelman in a New York Beit Din 1950

If there is no place for the law in the gray zone that Jewish *kapos* inhabited in the *Lagers*, how are they to be judged? And is it even fair to judge them? My answer is an actual counternarrative to how Israel treated the *kapos*: another forgotten trial of the Holocaust, and specifically a trial of a Jewish *kapo*. But this trial did not take place in a state court of law, but before a *beit din*, a Jewish religious court (literally, a house of judgment). Interestingly, the *beit din* trial took place in 1950, two months after Israel enacted the NNCL.

At the time, *Life* magazine featured a detailed story, including courtroom-style illustration drawings, about the proceedings, authored by noted writer and journalist Loudon S. Wainwright.[68] The story relates the proceedings in 1950 of a *beit din* in New York hearing a matter brought by a survivor who was accused of beating a Jewish prisoner to death. The charge of murder came from Benjamin Krieger, a Holocaust survivor "who swore that five years ago his brother had been killed in a Nazi concentration camp—by [Majer Mittelman,] a Jewish religious leader."[69] Krieger came to the United States in 1949 with his second wife (his first wife and children were murdered in Auschwitz). He opened a fish store in Brooklyn. On the morning of June 20, 1950, walking outside his store was a man he recognized. Krieger ran out and confronted the man, "Were you a *Blockschrieber* [registrar or barrack clerk] at Mühldorf?" Without waiting for an answer, Krieger screamed, "Then you are the man who killed my brother!" and hit Mittelman.

Mühldorf, forty miles northeast of Munich, was a satellite camp of Dachau. Prisoners there worked at an underground installation for the production of the Messerschmitt 262 (Me-262), a jet fighter designed to challenge Allied air superiority over Germany.

Majer (or Meyer) Mittelman was thrity-four years old at the time. He came to the U.S. in 1947 and lived with his wife and two children in Olyphant, Pennsylvania, where he worked as a butcher in a kosher slaughterhouse. Mittelman, who lost forty-five members of his extended family, confirmed that he had been at Mühldorf, but denied ever meeting Benjamin Krieger or his late brother Zalman.

According to Krieger, sometime in early 1945, he stood in the food line behind Zalman, waiting for the meager portions of soup both were about to receive. Keeping the line in order was Mittelman. When Zalman pushed his metal plate forward for food, Mittelman apparently grabbed the plate and hit him with it over the head. Zalman eventually died as a result of the blow.

The police were called and both men were taken to a Brooklyn police station. Mittelman agreed not to press charges against Krieger for the assault. Local papers, however, ran stories about the incident the next day. Mittelman's congregation, where he led services, now learned that he had been accused of murder. With the intervention of the American Jewish Congress (AJCongress), both parties agreed to have the matter heard before a *beit din* convened by the AJCongress.

A prominent member of his community, Mittelman wanted his name cleared, and similar to the *kapos* in postwar Europe who sought the assistance of honor courts, he turned to the *beit din* for the same. Krieger's motivation is unknown, but we assume that he saw little chance of getting American prosecutors to come to his assistance when the events in question took place in Europe and where both the victim and alleged perpetrator had no link at the time to the United States.

The religious tribunal's proceedings began on October 10, 1950. They were held at the Manhattan headquarters of the AJCongress and lasted for three days. The tribunal was composed of two rabbis and an attorney: Rabbi Simon Federbush, formerly the chief rabbi of Finland; Rabbi Joseph Lookstein, a professor of Jewish Law at Yeshiva University; and attorney Leo Pfeffer, assistant general counsel of AJCongress, who presided over the hearing. Both parties were represented by counsel, who took on the cases *pro bono*.

The complainant Krieger took the stand first. He explained that one of the duties of the *Blockschreiber* would be at mealtimes to check off the prisoners' numbers from a list so that everyone received just one portion of the bread and watery soup. Krieger then recalled the incident, which he remembered taking place only about four to five weeks before the camp's liberation on May 1, 1945.

> It came the turn on the line of my brother, so he [Mittelman] said to him you already took soup. So he said "I did not yet" and remained standing. So

> he takes the plate and gives him a crash on the head. It is a sort of a bowl, and he fell down and the blood began pouring. So I came over to him and asked him why did you hit him? And he gave me a punch in the heart. So I picked up my brother and I wiped him off. And I brought him into the barracks and went to get the meal. I went to take myself the meal my brother didn't take already. . . . [Later, t]hey took my brother to the hospital and they took down his record. He was there a few days and he died.[70]

On cross-examination, Simeon Gross, one of Mittelman's attorneys, tried to establish how Krieger knew that it was the person now sitting at the defense table who hit his brother five years earlier.

> GROSS: What impressed Mr. Mittelman's face in your memory?
> KRIEGER: I recognized him by his crooked nose.
> GROSS: In Mühldorf, was Mittelman an overseer for each day for giving out food?
> KRIEGER: Yes, he was the Blockschreiber. I saw him at mealtimes. He looked at your face and directed whether you should be served from the bottom or top [of the soup pot].[71]

In support of his client's testimony, Krieger's attorney called Jacob Rubenstein, age forty-one, who stated that he and the Krieger brothers had been fellow inmates at Mühldorf.

> BERGER: Was Mr. Mittelman a Blockschreiber?
> RUBENSTEIN: When I was [at Mühldorf] he was the Blockschreiber.
> BERGER: Did you know the deceased Zalman Krieger?
> RUBENSTEIN: Yes. He slept near me in the same barracks.
> BERGER: Were you in the line with Mr. Krieger at the time the alleged incident happened?
> RUBENSTEIN: Yes.
> BERGER: Will you explain to this tribunal what happened?
> RUBENSTEIN: One thing I know: that he smote him during the distribution of food because I stood behind him, and he fell.
> BERGER: You said "he." Who is "he"?
> RUBENSTEIN: He (pointing to Mittelman). He hit him and I also have signs from [other] beatings he gave me.

One of the judges asked Rubenstein why he was sure that he was now identifying correctly Mittelman as the man back at the camp. He replied: "I will tell you. If you see what a man has done to someone else, you may not recognize him later. But if you went through his hands yourself and his hands are still on your bones, then you have memories to this date. I definitely recognize him."[72]

The first attack on Krieger's testimony came from a defense witness, Jacob Grossinger, age forty-six, of Brooklyn, who had also been imprisoned at Mühldorf with Mittelman. He testified that Mittelman was severely ill and confined to his barracks a great deal of the time that he was at Mühldorf. Another witness, Dr. Alexander Schonfeld of East St. Louis, Illinois, confirmed Grossinger's testimony. Schonfeld had been the chief Jewish doctor and testified that Mittelman had in fact been seriously ill in the second half of February 1945, and that he ministered him for "periproctal abscess-infection of the entire lower body. He had a septic condition; pus went through his body."[73] According to Schonfeld, Mittelman began recovering sometime around the Jewish holiday of Passover, at the end of March, when the septic condition "busted itself. . . . One day . . . he said he feels a little bit lighter. Later he started a little bit walking, but he was very sick."[74]

Schonfeld also testified that he was in charge of all admissions and did not remember anyone being admitted to the hospital with a fractured skull or suffering a hemorrhage from a blow to the head between March and April 1945. Asked by Harry Berger, Krieger's attorney, on cross-examination, "[w]hy are you so positive Zalman did not die, Schonfeld, referencing the SS obsession to account for every person in a camp, replied: 'It would not have escaped our attention. He couldn't die secretly.'"[75]

In total, the tribunal heard a total of twelve witnesses, each of whom corroborated the testimony of the party that had called that witness to testify, including a rabbi who corroborated Dr. Schonfeld's testimony. Even though the events had taken place just five years earlier, the starkly different recollections of these Holocaust survivors appeared irreconcilable.

Mittelman finally took the stand at the last session, which took place a week later. On direct questioning from his attorney, he confirmed that he had been a prisoner at Mühldorf and had been transferred to Block

8, the same block that Krieger said he was part of. Mittelman testified that he did not remember the Krieger brothers and that there was no *Blockschreiber* for Block 8. He also testified that he had been ill most of the time and confined to his bunk, where he was treated by Dr. Schonfeld. Simeon Gross, Mittleman's attorney, then asked his client the critical question:

> GROSS: Mr. Mittelman, did you at any time, either four weeks or five weeks or six weeks before the liberation, strike anybody on the head in the food line at the evening meal?
>
> MITTELMAN: I never raised my hand over a Jew. There were no non-Jews.[76]

The tribunal followed up with questions on two subjects. First, in response to Mittelman's testimony that he had attended three yeshivas (rabbinical seminaries) in Czechoslovakia before the war and had been ordained a rabbi, the two rabbis on the *beit din* tested him on his religious knowledge. According to Wainwright, "Surprisingly, they found that the accused showed a marked hesitancy and confusion when asked certain questions on religious law which, as a rabbi and student, he should have known."[77] They also asked why he did not go to the camp hospital to be treated for his serious illness. According to Mittelman, "I knew what the result of being in the hospital was. . . . A woman doctor used to come with a higher-rank SS man. . . . They would suddenly come into the hospital and whoever appealed to her was taken from the bed and taken to Dachau, and they are no longer on this earth. Therefore, I asked Dr. Schonfeld . . . that he should have mercy on me."[78] Asked to explain how he could avoid working and stay in his bunk, Mittelman testified that he was warned by block leaders, who were friends, whenever a German was coming in and would get up and sit by a table and pretend to do clerical work. Earlier, another witness confirmed this statement.

Rabbi Federbush of the *beit din* also asked another critical question: "How do you explain that Mr. Krieger recognized you and asked you whether you were from Mühldorf?"

> MITTELMAN: I cannot answer the question. . . . There wasn't a Jew in the entire camp who didn't know me by the name of Majer. Majer the

> Rebbe [the religious one]. . . . [They called me that] because in the morning every time I went to work I prayed, and in the evening when I came back, I prayed, so they called me Majer the Rebbe.[79]

Krieger's attorney cross-examined Mittelman for six hours. Under persistent questioning, Mittelman admitted that he sometimes did check the food line, but was never a *Blockschreiber*, though he did state, as we note above, that he pretended to do clerical work when his barrack was visited by a German. Asked by Rabbi Lookstein in a follow-up question to try to remember approximately how many times he was in charge of checking the food line—"once, twice, three times—ten times?" Mittelman replied: "The rabbi should pardon me. If I wasn't tired . . . I tried to be the first one so I should get some soup first. Everybody got soup, everybody got a portion, but if you got there first it was better."[80]

Six more witnesses followed Mittelman, and then Chairman Pfeffer finally closed the proceedings at 12:45 a.m. on October 30. By that time, Krieger was gone, excusing himself earlier because he needed to open up his fish market the next morning.

It took the *beit din* a month to issue its ruling. In its five-page decision, the judges expressed their belief that Krieger has been absolutely sincere in his accusations. They also felt certain that Zalman died in the concentration camp, probably as the result of a beating. However, they acquitted Mittelman, based on insufficient evidence. In their view, Krieger was mistaken when he identified Mittelman as Zalman's killer.

The tribunal also held that Mittelman had not been completely truthful. They found that, contrary to his denials and those of others, Mittelman had in fact been a *Blockschreiber*. They also ruled that he was not, as he represented himself, ever an ordained rabbi. These latter findings, however, did not take away from their conclusion.

Conclusion

We do not know whatever became of Krieger and Mittelman. Their willingness, however, to resolve this matter outside the bounds of the criminal justice system and turn to a religious court provides a worthy counterpoint to how Israel handled its accusations of brutality against *kapos*. As we noted earlier, it is the contention of the author of this chapter that municipal law or international law has no place in the gray zone. The process undertaken by this one forgotten *beit din* in 1950 in New York, the same year that the Knesset decided to criminally prosecute *kapos,* starkly demonstrates the mistaken route taken by the modern State of Israel in dealing with those Jews who became the so-called *prominents* in the *Lagers* and then, upon surviving the Holocaust, came to the land of Israel for shelter and succor.

The NNCL—in targeting Jewish collaborators—was a bad law that should never have been passed by the Knesset. If the community of survivors fortunate enough to make it to Israel after the war wanted to establish their own informal "honor courts"—of the kind that just-liberated inmates created in Europe both in and outside the DP camps—this would have been a reasonable way to deal with the perceived dishonor brought to the community by some of the *kapos.* Even turning to the *beit din,* as the Mittelman matter illustrates, would have been a reasonable option. Invoking the criminal sanction and involving the newly established regular courts of Israel in this internal messy business was a mistake.

I would not agree with the criminal prosecution of any Jewish survivor who acted as a *kapo.* I do not believe that the laws of a secular state should have been applied to this situation because of the extreme, in fact, inconceivable circumstances of Jews in the concentration camps. In my view, this issue should have been kept out of the state courts of Israel. Israeli legislators should have answered any request to criminally prosecute former *kapos* with the answer given by Elie Wiesel, when asked about the Jewish *kapos:* "[T]he *kapos* were victims. They were chosen by their enemies. It is true that some were very, very cruel, but even those were acting as instruments of the enemy."[81]

As noted earlier, my co-author of this volume, Frank Tuerkheimer, disagrees with my conclusion. Here is his dissent:

The trials we have covered in this book contain the testimony of concentration camp survivors who said they knew when a kapo did the minimum—a good kapo—and when a kapo went beyond that minimum, even in the absence of a Gestapo or an SS onlooker. Browning notes a similar phenomenon by observing that some kapos were "worse than the Germans." Ben Ferencz suggests that in the brutal and inhumane environment of a concentration camp, where killing was as routine as eating, excess brutality can be excused. The fact remains that notwithstanding the horror of the camps, some kapos did just the minimum while others acted with brutality and cruelty beyond what was required. Thus, even in the horrid environment of the camp, kapos could make choices. Those who opted for the brutal should not escape punishment simply because they were Jews or concentration camp inmates. This is not say that their punishment should be the same as that for an SS guard doing the same thing. Their status as kapos should be a mitigator in terms of sentence but not an exoneration for excess and needless brutality.

Robert Mulka, adjutant at Auschwitz, main defendant at Frankfurt Auschwitz trial. Courtesy of Yad Vashem.

Fritz Bauer, attorney general for the State of Hesse and principal mover behind the Frankfurt Auschwitz trial. Courtesy of the Fritz Bauer Institute, Frankfurt am Main.

8

The Frankfurt Auschwitz Trial

The Germans Trying Germans under German Law

On December 20, 1963, a court in Frankfurt began a trial of twenty-two defendants, all connected with the administration of the Auschwitz concentration camp. The trial ended exactly twenty months later, on August 20, 1965. This trial was the most significant postwar prosecution brought under German law for crimes committed during the Second World War. Before examining this trial, we first place it into the context of both the killing process and the efforts by German prosecutors to deal with death camp administrators.

Between 1939 and 1945, many Jews were killed through random shootings, beatings, and forced labor. More organized efforts at mass murder can be divided roughly into three somewhat overlapping phases. First there are the *Einsatzgruppen* shootings, reviewed in chapter 6. A second phase can loosely be described as the "carbon monoxide" phase, in which Jews were placed in confined places and then gassed with carbon monoxide. This was briefly alluded to in the *Einsatzgruppen* chapter, in particular, during the discussion of Otto Ohlendorf's refusal to continue using mobile gas vans for the mass murder of Jews in the Soviet Union because of the effect it had on his men. A more organized form of such gassings took place at four of the death camps located in territory of prewar Poland: Chelmno, Belzec, Sobibor, and Treblinka.[1] In Chelmno, at least 200,000 Jews, mostly from the nearby Łódź ghetto, were gassed in mobile vans. Chlemno was in full operation from December 1941 to April 1943, and only two persons survived this death camp.[2] In Sobibor, Belzec, and Treblinka, carbon monoxide was also used, but in large chambers, rather than trucks, resulting in a more efficient killing operation, as more victims could be herded into a gas chamber. Belzec was in operation mainly in 1942, from March to December. During that period, the Germans murdered between 500,000 and 600,000 Jews from Lublin, Lwów, Kraków, and Radom there. Sobibor, where the Germans murdered about 200,000 to 250,000 Jews, was in operation from May 1942 until October 1943. A revolt in October 1943 resulted in mass escapes and then the destruction of the camp.[3] Treblinka, the largest of these camps, was also the most lethal. The denaturalization proceeding against Feodor Fedorenko is the subject of chapter 9 where the horrors of Treblinka are visited in detail. It is estimated that the Germans murdered about 900,000 Jews at the camp. There was also an escape from Treblinka and those who escaped and survived formed the core of potential witnesses in future prosecutions. Treblinka was also closed down after the escape.

The third phase of the organized killing reflects the switch from carbon monoxide to Zyklon B poison. Used both at Auschwitz and the Majdanek camp near Lublin, Zyklon B poisoning was the most effective method of mass murder. Majdanek was in operation from October 1941 until its liberation by the Soviet army in July 1944. The number of Jews killed at Majdanek has never been pinpointed with precision, with estimates running from the five digits to several hundreds of thousands.

West German courts were the situs for a number of trials against those who ran these death camps. In 1962–63, twelve guards and administrators at Chelmno were placed on trial. Those the court found guilty were sentenced to period of imprisonment ranging from one to thirteen years.[4] Trials of persons running Belzec, Sobibor, Treblinka, and Majdanek were held in West German courts from the 1950s through to the 1970s. Munich was the situs of a Belzec trial in 1964–65; Berlin and Frankfurt in 1950 and Hagen in 1965–66 were the situs of Sobibor trials;[5] administrators of Treblinka were tried in Frankfurt in 1950 and then in Düsseldorf in 1964-65. Franz Stangl, Treblinka's chief administrator, was tried there in 1970. Most of those charged were convicted; some were sentenced to life imprisonment. For those receiving lesser prison terms, the sentences seemed incredibly lenient in light of what they had participated in.[6]

All of these cases were brought under domestic German law, in particular, the 1871 Penal Code, as amended. This is the same code that formed the basis of the charges tried in the Frankfurt Auschwitz trial. Rather than reviewing each of these sentences, many of which seem absurdly lax, one particular case best illustrates the difficulty in the application of the existing German Penal Code, as a prelude to the Frankfurt Auschwitz trial. Whatever its limitations and, as will be seen, there were many, its application at least definitively put to rest any claim of an *ex post facto* violation.

The 1871 German law on murder differs considerably from homicide statutes in the United States in that it delves extensively into motive. Under Section 211 of the 1871 Code, anyone who killed another without the prerequisite motive was guilty of the lesser offense of manslaughter (*Totschlag*), which is punishable by five years' imprisonment except in particularly grave cases, where a term of life imprisonment may be imposed. As applied to administrators of death camps, the applicable parts of Section 211 would appear to be killing from "thirst for blood or base motives." "Thirst for blood" has been applied to someone who has killed a person from an abnormal pleasure in destroying human life." Motives are deemed "base" if they are derived from racial hatred."[7] The prosecution had to prove one of these to prove murder, and given the personal and subjective nature of motive, this was not a simple matter.

Nothing better illustrates this difficulty than the case of Gustav Münzberger, a Sudeten German who was appointed warder at the entrance of the building in Treblinka that housed the gas chambers. His responsibility was to herd people into the gas chamber as quickly and efficiently as possible, for which he used his whip and pistol. When children became separated from their parents, Münzberger literally threw them into the gas chambers over the heads of adults, thereby permitting still more persons to be squeezed in because less floor space was taken. Given the time he spent at Treblinka, it was estimated that he was complicit in the deaths of at least 300,000 people. For his complicity in these murders, a court in Düsseldorf sentenced him to twelve years' imprisonment in 1965.[8] How could this happen?

As directed by the Penal Code, the court was required to delve deeply into Münzberger's motivations: what exactly was in his head and heart as he was herding countless thousands to their deaths and brutally tossing children into the chambers to die? The court found him to be inordinately deferential to authority (*Autoritätsgläubikeit*), with a corresponding proclivity to follow orders. In addition, he was found to have an unusually high regard for Hitler, who had brought the Sudeten Germans "home" (referring to Hitler's unlawful 1938 invasion and annexation of part of Czechoslovakia known as the Sudetenland, the population of which included Czech nationals who were "ethnic" Germans). Finding that duty and deference motivated his conduct, the Düsseldorf court determined that Münzberger's conduct did not meet the elements of murder defined in Section 211. Specifically, the court found there was no proof that he acted out of racial hatred (the necessary "base motive") or that he took inordinate pleasure in the destruction of human life. Instead, a sense of duty toward the revered Adolf Hitler drove him and nothing else. It is this extreme focus on a prescribed mental state that underlay the Münzberger sentence, as well as many of the other sentences imposed by the German courts on wartime perpetrators. Much of this type of reasoning came into play at the Frankfurt Auschwitz trial.

Two excellent books—*The Frankfurt Auschwitz Trial, 1963–1965*, by Devin Pendas, (Cambridge University Press, 2006) and *Beyond Justice*, by Rebecca Wittmann (Harvard University Press, 2005)—provide excellent and detailed narratives of how the Frankfurt Auschwitz trial came about; analyses of applicable German criminal law, German criminal procedure, and the various forces at work in the West German Republic in the 1950s and early 1960s that led to the prosecution; and detailed studies of the trial itself. These books, together with a DVD documentary, *Auschwitz vor dem Frankfurter Schwurgericht, Der Frankfurter Auschwitz Prozess, 1963–1965*, are the basis for the discussion below. The presiding judge at the trial, Hans Hofmeyer, permitted filming for only the first fifteen minutes of the trial. However, the testimony of the witnesses was recorded, unless a witness objected. A significant portion of these recordings is captured in the documentary, which consequently provides first-hand evidence of the trial itself.[9] The documentary also includes numerous interviews with prosecutors in the case.[10]

The two persons most responsible for the Frankfurt Auschwitz trial are Hermann Langbein and Fritz Bauer. Langbein was a non-Jewish political prisoner at Auschwitz who committed his post-Auschwitz life to insuring that its horrors were made known to an increasingly indifferent world. Langbein served as secretary to the International Auschwitz Committee, an organization whose mission was to provide information on what happened at Auschwitz, to look after the interests of its survivors, and to encourage and support contact between the various national Auschwitz committees formed in the years after liberation.[11] Given Langbein's activities, it was not surprising then that in 1958 an inmate in a German prison in Bruchsal, Adolph Rögner, wrote to Langbein to advise him of the whereabouts of Wilhelm Boger, one of the more notorious Auschwitz personnel. Boger had been an interrogator at Auschwitz, responsible for administering excruciatingly painful torture on those unfortunates to come before him.

Langbein passed this information on to the authorities in Stuttgart, then responsible for collecting evidence on Nazi criminality. This was not, however, a straightforward matter. As a convicted criminal, Rögner was a highly suspicious source, and his stated intent to leave the Federal Republic for East Germany upon release did not lend credence to the information he had provided. Meanwhile, in the period following the targeting of Boger, documents relating to Auschwitz were found in Breslau and turned over to the prosecutor in the state of Hesse. This resulted in the transfer of the entire investigation relating to Auschwitz from the relatively cumbersome office in Stuttgart to the attorney general's office at Hesse. This meant that the investigation was now under the aegis of Fritz Bauer, Hesse's chief prosecutor.

The Nazis arrested Bauer, a Social Democrat and a Jew, in 1933. He was not detained for long. Upon his release, he went to Denmark and then to neutral Sweden where he spent the balance of the Second World War. Eleven years after his return to Germany, he became the chief state prosecutor of Hesse, a position he held until his death in 1968. His involvement in the arrest of Adolf Eichmann offers perhaps the best insight into Bauer's approach to Nazi criminality. He is generally credited with tipping off the Israeli government as to the whereabouts of Eichmann in Argentina and then advising the chief of Mossad (Israeli intelligence), Isser Harrel, not to proceed with formal extradition. Bauer conveyed his lack of trust in the German bureaucracy to Harrel and made clear that the German embassy in Argentina could not be relied on for the kind of cooperation necessary to get Eichmann to Israel.[12] For his personal involvement in making sure the Auschwitz investigation continued and his strategic planning in assigning an excellent and young staff to the case, Wittmann correctly assesses Bauer as "the decisive force shaping the [Frankfurt Auschwitz] trial."[13]

Germany's criminal procedure involves a lengthy pretrial investigation by a magistrate. In this case, Magistrate Heinz Dux heard several hundred witnesses over an almost five-year period. Some were from Germany; others, mainly survivors, were from Israel, Poland, the United States, and other countries. The testimony of women who transcribed interrogations at Auschwitz was of particular value since they witnessed the interrogations and so had first-hand knowledge of incidents that formed the basis of the charges against some defendants. The investigation led to the indictment of twenty-four persons, including Richard Baer, the last commandant at Auschwitz. His arrest was perhaps the crowning moment of the investigative process, a relatively short-lived peak, however, since he died of a heart attack in custody, six months before the trial began. That left Robert Mulka, an adjutant at Auschwitz, as the lead defendant. As second in command of Auschwitz, he was responsible for much of its day-to-day administration.

Magistrate Dux submitted a seven-hundred-page report to his superiors, which included suggested defendants and charges. The court had the authority to review charges on the basis of the evidence presented, as well as the power to reduce those charges. In several instances, the court reduced a murder charge to a lesser offense, including the charge of participating in murder. While an accomplice could, in theory, be sentenced as a principal, this was not the custom under German law.

The trial started on December 20, 1963, five years after the investigation had begun. It went on before three judges (two alternates) and six jurors (three alternates), against twenty-two defendants (twenty by the end of the trial, due to physical infirmities). The participants included four prosecutors, nineteen defense lawyers, and three lawyers representing civil litigants.[14] Under German law, judges and jurors had an equal voice on the final verdict, which required an absolute majority of five. Judges alone, however, determined the admissibility of evidence.[15]

It would be impossible in the pages allocated in this book to do justice to a record that covers a twenty-month trial. On the other hand, by focusing on just one or a handful of defendants, some of the larger picture is lost. To present both a broad picture but also one of individual responsibility, in this chapter we will first deal with some of the evidence depicting the Auschwitz trial in general, and then focus on five defendants, each from different sections of the Auschwitz administration. These five are: Robert Mulka, second in command of Auschwitz; Wilhelm Boger, responsible for security; Viktor Capesius, charged with selection at the ramp and the administration of Zyklon B at the gas chambers; Josef Klehr, medical orderly charged with the killing of medically ill inmates; and Oswald Kaduk, responsible for punishing "misconduct" by inmates, including attempted escapes.

An Overview

The presence of Mulka as defendant, if nothing else, justified the prosecution's decision to bring the entire story of Auschwitz before the court. Chronologically, this began with the Nuremberg testimony of Rudolf Höss, the first commandant at Auschwitz, who testified for the prosecution at the first Nuremberg trial. Höss was subsequently found guilty of many crimes by the Poles and executed, fittingly, at Auschwitz. The film of his Nuremberg testimony was presented in these proceedings. In it, Höss described how in the summer of 1941, around the same time Hermann Göring placed Heydrich in charge of implementing the Final Solution to the Jewish question, Heinrich Himmler, head of the combined SS and Gestapo, summoned Höss to

Berlin and told him that the Führer had given the order to implement the Final Solution, and it was the SS that would carry out the order. Himmler also told Höss that Auschwitz had been selected as a killing center because of its easy access by rail. In addition, its flat topography contributed to its isolation, making escape almost completely impossible. Höss estimated that until his departure from Auschwitz in December 1943, two million persons were executed there and another 500,000 died of starvation and disease. He estimated that after he left in November 1943, another 500,000 individuals, made up of 400,000 Hungarian Jews and 100,000 German Jews, were executed, bringing the total to three million.[16]

Rudolph Vrba, the famed escapee from Auschwitz, testified at the Frankfurt trial about the extensive theft at Auschwitz and the methodical manner in which Jews were robbed of their clothes and belongings.[17] At the time the camp was liberated, 393,000 men's suits were found, 863,000 women's dresses, and massive amounts of gold teeth that had been extracted from the mouths of murdered victims.[18] These numbers, of course, do not account for the many shipments of stolen goods sent back to Germany in the preceding years.[19]

The dramatic testimony of Konrad Morgen established the linkage between murder and robbery. Authorities in Berlin were concerned that the amount of extracted gold and other valuable items sent back to Germany did not total the amount they had anticipated, and so they sent Konrad Morgen, an SS judge with training in investigations, to Auschwitz to conduct an audit. Morgen testified as to what he saw when he visited the camp, testimony that prosecutor Joachim Kugler specifically credited as the testimony of an honest man.[20] Morgen testified that on his audit visit to Auschwitz he witnessed the process of murder and thievery. He saw where the trains arrived and how the victims were taken to a room where they were told to undress. He testified they were told to put their clothes on hooks with numbers and to remember the numbers so they could retrieve their clothes after they had showered. They then went into the gas chambers, following an arrow that pointed to the "shower room." Morgen observed the crematoria and noted how absolutely clean they were—not a trace of anything—something that struck him later in his tour.

While walking through Auschwitz, Morgen saw apparently hungover SS men being fed potato pancakes by young women who appeared to be Jewish inmates. When he commented on the sorry state of the SS men, his guide shrugged his shoulders and told him they had had a rough night, as several transports had arrived which had to be processed. Morgen recalled the immaculate crematoria and shuddered at the total absence of evidence of the thousands slain the night before.[21]

The murder of Hungarian Jews, starting in the spring of 1944, placed a great burden on the killing machine at Auschwitz. Four hundred thousand Jews from Hungary were killed in a short period of time, sometimes 10,000 a day. Since the crematoria were inadequate to handle all the murdered Jews, five massive pits were ordered dug. For a period, bodies were disposed of by burning in the open pits. Dov Paisikovic was a *Sonderkommando*, a Jewish inmate selected to dispose of the dead, and he testified as to the burning of the bodies. He also testified how even some of the *Sonderkommandos*, whose lives had temporarily been spared, jumped into the burning fires to end their ordeal.[22]

A non-inmate provided unusual testimony as to those fires. Elise Hainish-Utner was a German dentist living and working in the nearby Polish town of Oświęcim, which the Germans called Auschwitz. She saw the fires at night and unabashedly testified that her first concern was that there might be a revolt by the Jews at Auschwitz, and that they might come to the town, only three miles away, and overrun it. She asked a local policeman to call and after he did, he reassured her there was nothing to worry about. The following day one of her patients, an SS officer who worked at the camp, attributed the fires to the burning of potatoes in the presence of Hainish-Utner's Polish assistant. Hainish-Utner responded that if all the potatoes in Silesia were burned, it would not account for the flames she saw. She and the officer then met afterwards in private and he told her the fires she saw came from the bodies of Jews who had been gassed. When she said that was not possible, he reassured her that it was and that these were Jews from Romania and Hungary. He told her that even the children had been thrown into the fires alive. He then predicted there would be two fires that night and Hainish-Utner testified that he was right.[23]

Two witnesses testified with regard to the fates of newborn children. Langbein, who had played a pivotal role in bringing about the trial, stated that among the worst things he saw was a visit to the place where Gypsy inmates were giving birth. He described how the infants were tattooed on their thighs because their arms were too small and how mounds of dead infants were stacked in a room ravaged by rats.[24] Dr. Ella Lingens,[25] a physician sent to Auschwitz for having helped Jews evade the Gestapo, provided similar testimony. She described the horrendous conditions in the women's camp, which resulted in 10,000 deaths in the space of a few months, the terrible diseases occurring in the barracks, and the pitiful need to place newborn infants into such conditions. She explained that on one occasion, Mrs. Höss, wife of the commandant, in a mind-boggling example of unawareness, sent a pink sweater to the barracks, presumably a gift for an infant girl. Lingens also testified that those inmates not selected for gassing received seven to eight hundred calories of food per day, a caloric intake that permitted survival for no more than four months. Somewhere in that period of time, the dreadful combination of starvation and disease brought life to a tortured end.[26] Particularly in light of the inadequate clothing provided to inmates and taxing work demanded of them, numerous witnesses confirmed the meager caloric content of the food—often just a portion of watery soup and a piece of bread.

No judge or juror of the Frankfurt Auschwitz trial could form a complete picture of the conditions at the camp without actually visiting Auschwitz. Several former inmates had testified that many executions had taken place along a particular wall. Questions asked on cross-examination were designed to show that it was impossible for them to have seen what they said they saw. Obviously, a simple way to resolve the dispute was to take a look. That was not so simple, however, because the Federal Republic had no diplomatic relations with any country that recognized East Germany, including Poland, part of the Soviet bloc. Nevertheless, largely at the instance of an attorney for the civil plaintiffs,[27] the court arranged a visit. One of the judges, Walter Hetz, together with the lawyers, an unincarcerated defendant, Dr. Franz Lucas (later found guilty as an accomplice to murder), and an enormous press corps went to Auschwitz for what was an unprecedented contact between West

Germany and Poland. The visit corroborated the testimony of those survivors who claimed to have witnessed the executions.

Individual Defendants

The operation at Auschwitz was divided into five groupings: Executive Administration, which included the adjutant (Mulka); Protective Custody, responsible for preventing escapes (Kaduk); the Political Division, responsible for gathering information from inmates (Boger); the Medical Service, erroneously self-explanatory (Capesius and Klehr); and *kapos*. We will cover one example from each of the first four of these groups. Only one defendant, Emil Bednarek, was charged in the fifth category as a non-Jewish *kapo*. The court found that he was personally responsible for fourteen deaths and had killed randomly and sadistically, creating pure terror wherever he went. Bednarek was found guilty and sentenced to life imprisonment.[28]

Robert Mulka

Unquestionably, after the death of Richard Baer, Robert Mulka was the principal defendant at the trial. As adjutant, he was responsible for day-to-day camp administration. His signature was on numerous documents relating to the administration of the camp, including requisitions for Zyklon B. The purpose of Zyklon B was noted on documents as being for "resettlement of Jews."[29] In addition, Mulka signed documents that authorized the sick to be taken to the gas chambers.[30]

On the question of knowledge of the killings, however, Mulka took an incredible position. To the astonishment of everyone at the trial, including the press that reported his testimony with disbelief, he denied any knowledge of the killings at Auschwitz. Kugler, the principal prosecutor, specifically asked him if he knew that persons were taken to the gas chambers by truck. Mulka calmly replied that he had nothing to do with gassing.[31] Kugler persisted, responding that he hadn't asked Mulka whether he had anything to do with it, but whether he knew about it. Mulka replied that he was not informed about gassing and didn't know anything about it.[32] While it was hardly necessary, the prosecution called a witness who testified that he became aware of the gassing soon after arriving at Auschwitz and that even a young and somewhat naïve young boy he encountered knew about it as well.[33]

It was standard for all persons working at Auschwitz to participate in the selection process—Höss, as commandant, acknowledged doing it frequently. Thus, the court could comfortably infer that Mulka had been there as well.[34] It had more than an inference to go on, however, to reach that conclusion. Vrba, the Auschwitz escapee whom the court specifically credited as making an excellent and intelligent impression, testified that he had seen Mulka at the ramp.[35] When defendant Kaduk testified, he also said that Mulka and others supervised the selection process.[36]

The documentary evidence of Mulka's overall responsibility for the camp, his lengthy tenure as adjutant coupled with his signature on requisitions and authorizations for the instruments of murder, and his participation in selections at the ramp more than established his complicity in mass homicide.

Wilhelm Boger

Boger, an SS interrogator, was notorious for the infamous "Boger swing." The "swing" constituted of a bar over which inmates were draped, exposing their buttocks and genital area to severe and painful beatings. Boger did not deny his connection to the swing, but claimed he never seriously hurt anyone.[37] Many witnesses, however, testified that they saw Boger kill inmates. Herbert Kurz, a prisoner, testified as to most of these killings, which took place execution-style along the infamous Black Wall, in a courtyard adjacent to the block that housed inmates who were being interrogated. Kurz testified that while he was being held in Block 21, he saw Boger shoot fifty to sixty persons in the back of the neck as they were brought to him, two at a time, in that courtyard. Questions about Kurz's ability to see what he claimed he saw were resolved in his favor later in the trial when the judge visiting Auschwitz went to Block 21. The block was still standing and the judge could see clearly from there to the Black Wall in the courtyard.[38]

Other witnesses testified as to other killings. Stefan Boratynski said he saw Boger shoot ten people on one occasion.[39] The witness Jozef

Piwko testified that he saw Boger murder Gypsy children by taking them by the legs and slamming their heads against a wall.[40] Boger was also implicated in the clearing out of a bunker occupied by Polish inmates by shooting them in the neck.[41]

Given his responsibility as an interrogator, it is not surprising that Boger was directly implicated in measures of brutality designed to get information. Erna Kraft, a political prisoner, explained what happened when she was taken to his office. Boger took a whip and twice whipped her across the face, essentially removing most of the skin tissue from her face. Upon seeing him in the dock, Kraft stated that if Boger were released she would find him and reciprocate. After hearing this dramatic testimony from Kraft, the prosecutor, Kugler, asked Boger if he had anything to say. Boger responded in the negative.[42] He later said he was just following orders. As noted above, he denied killing anyone and claimed that none of his interrogations, which he found distasteful, resulted in serious injury. He explained that everything he did at Auschwitz was because he was told to, not because he wanted to.[43]

Viktor Capesius

Viktor Capesius was a pharmacist from the Transylvanian town of Cluj, "Clausenberg" in German, who was charged with participating in the selection process at the ramp where new arrivals were sent either to the gas chambers or to work. Two Jews who arrived at Auschwitz recognized Capesius and survived to tell about it. Sara Nebel, a resident of Cluj, identified Capesius while being dragged from the train at Auschwitz and testified that he was involved in the selection process.[44]

The testimony of Mauritius Berner was even more poignant. Berner arrived at Auschwitz with his wife and three daughters, two of whom were twins. He was immediately separated from them as men and women were placed in different lines, and he then joined a small number of other men where doctors and pharmacists were being grouped separately. At that point, he recognized Capesius as an I.G. Farben representative whom he had previously seen when Capesius had come to him marketing I.G. Farben products. Berner told Capesius at the ramp he had twin daughters who needed special medical attention and Capesius told Berner to call his family back. He readily did so and the twins were then presented to a man Berner later identified as Josef Mengele, who said he had no time. The twins, as well as their sister and mother, were then sent back to the women's line. Capesius assured Berner he would see them in an hour, since they were just getting a shower. Of course, Berner never saw them again.[45] In addition to convincing evidence of Capesius's presence at the selection ramp, there was also evidence that Capesius stole gold fillings taken from the murdered corpses at Auschwitz. This theft turned out to be of great value to him in establishing a prosperous pharmacy after the war.[46]

Participating in selection constitutes complicity in murder on its face. Capesius's lawyer, Dr. Hans Laternser, dealt with this evidence in his closing in a somewhat imaginative manner. Laternser argued that those arriving at Auschwitz were as good as dead, since Hitler had ordered that all Jews be killed. This meant, Laternser posited, that anyone involved in the selection process was actually saving lives, and therefore selection itself could not be considered complicity in murder. According to Laternser, every person selected to go to the camp, as opposed to the gas chambers, was a life saved.[47] Ironically, this ingenious but shallow argument did Capesius little good since he maintained factually that he was not involved in selection, but rather that he was at the place where the trains arrived in order to pick up pharmaceuticals.[48]

Richard Klehr

Klehr was an orderly who worked in the infirmary. Obviously many of those confined at Auschwitz became ill and it takes no great imagination to envisage that any infirmary at the camp was invariably jammed with ailing inmates. The evidence showed that the simple expedient used to deal with such overcrowding was to kill the very sick and Klehr's involvement in these killings. The witness Imre Gonczi, an infirmary worker, testified[49] that Klehr, who was not a doctor, would enter the room dressed in a physician's white frock where a selectee was lying on a couch. While another person held the infirm individual down, Klehr would inject phenol directly into the victim's heart, causing instant death. Gonczi then described how he was forced to drag the victims to a room and at the end of the day take all the bodies to the crematoria, where they would be incinerated.[50]

The evidence against Klehr also directly implicated him in the mass killing process. Karl Lill, a political prisoner, testified that on numerous occasions he had seen Klehr, along with others, climb atop the bunker where the gas chambers were, open a canister of Zyklon B, and empty it into the gas chambers. Shortly thereafter, Lill would hear a cry, muffled by the concrete, and then many screaming voices. This was followed by a puff of smoke coming from the chimney of the gas chamber.[51]

Klehr's defense was simple: he said he felt nothing but sympathy for his victims but was just following orders. Klehr said that when he complained to the physician in charge at the infirmary about administering lethal injections to the sick, he was ordered to continue administering the injections for the next three months.[52] Klehr's lawyers argued that while his eyes were now open, at the time of the underlying events he was overwhelmed and could not tell right from wrong.[53]

Oswald Kaduk

Kaduk, an SS interrogator responsible for punishing rule violations and escape attempts was, like Boger, known for his brutality. Kaduk's specialty was killing inmates by forcing them to lie on the ground on their backs and then placing a board across their throats, which he would then stand on, thereby choking them to death.[54] Fillip Müller testified as to more collective cruelty. He had seen Kaduk take Jewish women who had just arrived from the transports, threaten them with a gun to force them to beg for their lives, and then start shooting them, first at the feet, then other parts of the body, until he finally killed them. This was done *in seriatum* so that those destined to be shot witnessed the earlier shootings.[55] Ludwig Worl, a political prisoner, testified that he had seen Kaduk drive about a dozen children into the gas chamber at gunpoint. Kaduk then shouted that this was untrue and refused to calm down, even when the court threatened him with ejection. At this point, Worl, who appeared matter of fact about the confrontation, calmly told him: "Kaduk, you are no longer facing me with a pistol in your hand."[56]

In his final statement to the court, Kaduk argued that his previous conviction by the Soviets, which had resulted in the death penalty but was later reduced to eleven years of incarceration and then release, had been punishment enough.[57]

Convictions, Sentences, and Afterthoughts

There were twenty defendants whose cases went to a verdict. Three were acquitted[58] and seven were found guilty of murder. One of those found guilty of murder, Han Stark, was a juvenile under German law at the time of his participation at Auschwitz and so his sentence was limited to ten years' imprisonment. The other six found guilty of murder were sentenced to terms of life imprisonment. The remaining ten were found guilty of being accessories to murder. Their sentences ranged from thirty-nine months' imprisonment to nine years.[59]

The verdicts as to the five defendants we have focused on are illustrative of the larger sentencing pattern. Those sentences are as follows:

- Mulka was found guilty as an accomplice to murder and sentenced to fourteen years' imprisonment. After serving three years of the sentence, he was released in 1968 on compassionate grounds of being unfit for further detention. He died a year later.
- Boger was found guilty of several murder counts and sentenced to several life imprisonment terms. He died in prison in 1977, twelve years after the trial.
- Klehr was also found guilty of murder and sentenced to life imprisonment. He was released to a nursing home in 1988 and died shortly afterward.
- Capesius was found guilty as an accomplice and sentenced to nine years' imprisonment. After his release in 1974, he lived for another eleven years and died in 1985.
- Kaduk was found guilty of murder and sentenced to life imprisonment. He was released to a nursing home in 1988 after serving twenty-three years of his life sentence and lived for another nine years, dying in 1997.

What can explain these sentences? To begin with, it should be noted that whatever broader purposes the prosecution or civil plaintiffs had in mind for the case, for instance, public education or preservation of the historical record, the presiding judge, Hans Hofmeyer, did not share in such a mission. On more than one occasion he stated that this was not a trial of the mass murder process at Auschwitz, but rather a trial against Mulka and other individuals for acts that, allegedly, they specifically committed.[60] This observation, however, is of only superficial relevance. Yes, indeed, this was a trial of Mulka, Capesius, and others, but the evidence showed that Mulka, Capesius, and others were complicit in the murder of many thousands, if not hundreds of thousands of persons. Even if this was a case against specific individuals, if Mulka and the others were mass murderers, then it was a case trying them for mass murder. In light of the conclusion by the judges and jurors that these men were responsible for mass murder, even if as accomplices rather than as principals, why, given the range of sentences permissible under German law, did the court not sentence Mulka and Capesius to life imprisonment, as it clearly had the power to do?

Mulka was the adjutant of Auschwitz responsible for its administration for a year, beginning in early 1942, and as such he was the person who signed several requisitions for Zyklon B. His denial of knowledge that Jews were gassed at Auschwitz was a lie of such magnitude that it would evoke laughter if only the context permitted it. Capesius's even lighter sentence should be seen in the context that his conviction as an accomplice to murder was based largely on the testimony of several credible witnesses that he participated in the selection of Jews at the ramp, a process integral to the dreadful killings that followed. Both Mulka and Capesius, therefore, were shown by credible evidence to have been complicit in a truly massive number of killings.

Whatever the merits are under the German Penal Code of finding that two such major operatives at Auschwitz were guilty only as accomplices and not as principals—and accepting that conclusion—the simple fact remains that under German law, each could have been sentenced as a principal.[61] To be sure, precedent suggested that sentences meted out to accomplices should be lighter than those for principals, but where was a precedent involving this many murders? If the law permitted the ultimate punishment—life imprisonment—for accomplices, exactly what kind of case was the German judiciary waiting for to impose such a sentence? It borders on inconceivable that the court could have had imagined a crime *worse* than Auschwitz. The individual focus that Judge Hofmeyer was so insistent on, rightly so, did not, however, alter the unprecedented mass murder such a focus revealed. The sentences should have been commensurate with that the enormity of the crimes committed.

Both Wittmann and Pendas discuss this issue. Pendas, in contrasting the life sentences for the brutal Klehr, Boger, and Kaduk with the far more lenient sentences for Mulka and Capesius, summarizes the difference succinctly: torture of a handful of persons was viewed as more serious than the killing of many. Wittmann, quoting some of the comments after the trial (including an important written exchange between Judge Hofmeyer, who was unhappy that so many defendants were being tried simultaneously, and prosecutor Bauer, who felt it was an appropriate way to proceed),[62] points to the historically narrow focus on the criminal law by the German legal establishment.

The judges, including Hofmeyer, had been part of the judiciary in the Third Reich. While there was no indication that Hofmeyer had done anything as a judge during the 1933–45 period to suggest that he was ardently implementing National Socialist objectives in political cases or anything that was cruel or sadistic, the fact remains that he willingly remained a cog in the machinery of the Third Reich.[63] No one could describe Mulka as having engaged in conduct that was personally savage or brutal, as opposed to the violent and sadistic conduct of Boger and Kaduk. Therefore, when it came to judges like Hofmeyer, perhaps Mulka's participation hit a little closer to home.

Mulka and Capesius each lived out their lives as free men. They have been dead for many years now, so there is no ongoing injustice with respect to them. But time tends to minimize unjustified leniencies, so the clock must be wound backward to see what impact their relatively mild terms of imprisonment had in 1965.

Over two hundred Auschwitz survivors testified at the trial[64] and they knew better than anyone what it was like to be part of a bureaucratized murder machine, made only more venal by its businesslike operation. It is true that the Kaduks and Bogers created a truly frightening aura of terror, but that was not the core of Auschwitz. The true horror of Auschwitz was the efficiency of the gas chambers—where victims gasped for air to breathe, frantically, in pain, and futilely, knowing that death was inevitable for them and their loved ones. The operation of the gas chambers vastly eclipses the aura of terror created by sadists like Boger and Kaduk. No one knew this better than the survivors. They lived in the shadow of the gas chambers and knew that it took only the arbitrary whim of an SS camp officer to place them there. Some had to endure the rejection of their testimony, perhaps even with the justification that their emotions and the passage of time had clouded their memory, and so their testimony was not as clear as the court required it to be. But all the survivors had to live with the knowledge that, at some point, those found guilty of implementing this horrid machinery of death were to once again share the planet with them and walk as free men. That was not a burden they should have had to bear.

Feodor Fedorenko attending his trial in Fort Lauderdale. Courtesy Lou Toman/*South Florida Sun-Sentinel*.

Franz Stangl, commandant at Treblinka. Photo Archive, Yad Vashem.

9

The Trial of Feodor Fedorenko

Treblinka Relived in a Florida Courtroom

The trial against Feodor Fedorenko in Fort Lauderdale in 1978 was part of an effort by the U.S. Justice Department to rid the United States of persons who had participated in Hitler's death machinery. In 1979, the creation of the Office of Special Investigations (OSI) in the Criminal Division of the Justice Department as a dedicated Nazi-hunting unit formalized that effort. OSI took over the Fedorenko case through its various posttrial appeals and hearings.

In its over thirty-year existence, OSI has successfully deported over one hundred persons who participated in the Holocaust. It has also successfully prevented an additional two hundred such persons from entering the United States.[1] Over time, as most of the victims who survived Nazism have died, the class of perpetrators still living has also dwindled. In 2010, in recognition of this new reality, the Obama administration's Justice Department merged OSI with the Domestic Security Section (also in the Criminal Division) to form the Human Rights and Special Prosecutions Section (HRSP). The HRSP will now have an expanded mandate, focusing not just on ferreting out the few Holocaust perpetrators who remain in the United States, but also preventing the United States from becoming a safe haven for those engaged in modern-era genocides and other mass atrocities.[2]

The process by which the Justice Department discovers and then expels Nazis consists of two stages: first, denaturalizing a suspected person, and second, deporting that individual. Most of those targeted have been citizens. Naturalized citizens have an absolute right to bar deportation. It is only once citizenship has been taken away that suspects are legally vulnerable to deportation.[3] The denaturalization proceeding is usually the more complex part of this process and is mostly based on misrepresentations made by the target of the case when he or she gained entry into the United States. For example, if a target served as a guard at a concentration camp (as in the Fedorenko case we are about to discuss) and provided false information as to his or her whereabouts during the Second World War—"I was shipped to Nazi Germany as a forced laborer"—then the government must prove that the information provided to immigration authorities was untruthful.

Since the denaturalization process is not a criminal matter, but rather a civil proceeding, there is no right to a trial by jury. Nevertheless, because citizenship is sacrosanct, the burden on the government in cases of this sort is extremely high. The United States Supreme Court has said it this way: "[W]here citizenship is at stake the Government carries the heavy burden of proving its case by 'clear, unequivocal, convincing evidence' which does not leave 'the issue in doubt.'"[4]

In Fedorenko's case, the government had to prove (1) that Fedorenko lied in the entry process to the United States in 1950, and (2) that he was indeed a guard at the Treblinka concentration camp. Showing that he was such a guard would warrant deprivation of his citizenship under a provision of U.S. law which permits cancellation of citizenship if "illegally procured or . . . procured by concealment of a material fact or by willful misrepresentation."[5] In addition, the government claimed that Fedorenko was not admissible into the United States under the Displaced Persons Act (DPA), the vehicle by which he obtained entry, because the act excluded from its scope persons who had "assisted the enemy in persecuting [civilians]."[6] The upshot of these relatively technical statutory terms is simple: to obtain Fedorenko's denaturalization, the government had to prove in court that he was a prison guard at Treblinka. As it turned out, the path to proving this by "clear, unequivocal, convincing evidence" was neither simple nor direct.

Before turning to the trial, a brief review of facts not in dispute.

The Horror of Treblinka

Prosecutions against those allegedly involved in the murder of nine hundred thousand Jews in the death camp Treblinka have been relatively rare, mainly because not many victims survived its savagery. At the end of the Second World War, Treblinka survivors probably numbered less than a hundred, a number pared down significantly by the time of Fedorenko's trial in 1978. The combination of age and the burden of testifying about the horrors of Treblinka reduced the pool of potential witnesses still further, a burden made even more difficult because most survivors were in Israel, meaning that testifying required a trip to the United States. Thus, it is not surprising that the number of Treblinka survivors who testified against Fedorenko was in the single digits—six.[7]

While it is difficult to place death camps in any particular order of horror, Treblinka may well have been the worst.[8] This is so for two reasons: first, of all the camps, only at Auschwitz were more people murdered; second, unlike Auschwitz, Treblinka's sole purpose was for the murder of Jews. Everyone brought to Treblinka was to die; the only persons spared immediate killing were those selected to assist in the killing process or in the theft of valuables from the murdered Jews. These *Sonderkommandos* were also regularly slated for execution. The almost endless supply of human beings shipped to Treblinka for extermination guaranteed a vast source of replacements for these hapless prisoner-workers.

Treblinka, located about sixty miles northeast of Warsaw, was built in 1942 after it had become obvious that the method of killing Jews by bullet—the "*Einsatzgruppen* method"—was both inefficient and simply incapable of doing the job. It was one thing to shoot Jewish inhabitants of villages and small towns where their numbers were in the hundreds and perhaps occasionally thousands. Once the Final Solution was directed at Jews living in large population centers of Europe—Warsaw, Łódź, Vilna, Paris, Amsterdam, and later Budapest—where the number of victims for each locale was in the tens and sometimes hundreds of thousands,[9] a different method of extermination had to be used.

Treblinka was divided into two subcamps, Treblinka I and II. Treblinka I was the administrative section and included barracks for the SS troops in charge of the camp, the guards, and others used to assist in running the camp. It also included the railroad station where victims were unloaded. Two buildings near the station were used to house belongings stolen from victims prior to their murder; a third building was used to store victims' clothes. In a fourth building, women were forced to undress and submit to having their hair cut.

A road the SS called *Himmelstrasse*, the "Street to Heaven," went from the railroad depot at Treblinka I to the gas chambers in Treblinka II. A place euphemistically called the *Lazarett* (infirmary) was located along the road to the gas chambers.[10] The *Lazarett* was nothing other than a huge pit where those unable to make it to the gas chambers were taken to be shot. Bodies in the pit were then burned. Many of those temporarily spared from the gas chambers were responsible for gathering wood in the nearby forests to keep the fires burning. There was a pit behind the gas chambers as well where the gassed bodies were dumped and burned, a process later replaced by ovens.

A startlingly small number of people managed the death machinery at Treblinka, relative to the huge number of victims murdered there. Thirty SS overseers, mainly Germans and Austrians, made up the top level of the administration. A camp commandant supervised them. About one hundred guards, largely of nationalities other than German or Austrian—native Russians, Ukrainians, Balts, and persons from the Central Asian republics—assisted the administrators of the camp. These included Red Army soldiers who had been captured during the war and specially trained for guard service at Trawniki, a nearby town.

The eight hundred or so Jews spared from immediate execution were divided into different groups: those who undressed new arrivals and stored their clothes; those who took and stored belongings such as jewelry, cash, and tangibles other than clothing; those who removed dead bodies from the gas chambers; "dentists" (not necessarily professionals) who extracted gold fillings from the dead; those who gathered wood from the nearby forest to keep the pyres burning; and a small, select number who had specific tasks such as smelting the gold and cutting the hair of women about to be killed.

When a train arrived at Treblinka, the doors were opened to let out as many victims as could be handled by the relatively small number of Germans and guards on hand. Once those victims were gassed, more train doors were opened to release the next set of victims—this continued until everyone on the train, other than a very small number selected to assist in the killing process, had been gassed. The Treblinka human slaughterhouse was in operation from the spring of 1942 to the fall of 1943. During this period, the Germans murdered nine hundred thousand Jews; on average, almost two thousand people were murdered each day.

Treblinka's closure came shortly after a successful escape by its inmates. On August 2, 1943, the prisoner-workers succeeded in breaching Treblinka's security. One prisoner made the key to the ammunition room from a wax image of the lock. This gave the inmates access to small arms and some flammables. Having picked a time when most of the SS men were bathing at a nearby river, the prisoners surprised those guarding the camp and about two hundred succeeded in fleeing into the nearby Polish forest. Some were caught by patrols sent to search for escapees. Others, lost in the forest, wandered back to Treblinka. Still others were murdered by unsympathetic Polish partisans who refused them refuge. Less than half of the roughly two hundred escapees ultimately succeeded in getting away, and it is largely through them that the ghastly details of Treblinka are known today.[11]

Feodor Fedorenko's Background

With the contingent of German and Austrian administrators so small, the guards obviously played a key role in assuring the effectiveness of Treblinka as a death camp. Feodor Fedorenko was one of these guards. He was born in 1907 in Ukraine, then part of Czarist Russia. He attended school for only three years, from age eight to age eleven. As an adult, he led an uneventful life: he married, had two children, and worked as a truck driver. Following Germany's invasion of the Soviet Union in June 1941, he was drafted into the Red Army. The massive defeats suffered by the Red Army in the aftermath of the surprise invasion led to the capture of hundreds of thousands of Soviet soldiers by the German military. Fedorenko was one of them; he was captured within a month of his mobilization.

He was then moved from one prisoner of war facility to another. These facilities were crude: food and shelter were well below what was required by international treaties governing POWs. Early on, tens of thousands of soldiers died of starvation. Fedorenko, as he described it, supplemented his near-starvation diet by eating grass and roots. According to Fedorenko, the Germans also beat him for attempting to eat anything other than the food they "officially" provided. There is no reason to disbelieve him. The brutal treatment of Soviet prisoners by their German captors is well documented and an accepted part of the history of the Second World War (see chapter 1). It was not uncommon for the Germans simply to let Soviet soldiers perish from hunger or cold. As summer turned to fall and fall to winter, many Soviet POWs were left to the elements after their capture. As a result, of close to five million Soviet solders and officers captured by the Germans, about two million survived to the end of the war.[12]

At one point in early 1942, Fedorenko, along with other Soviet prisoners, was selected for guard training at Trawniki, not far from Lublin. The Germans provided a uniform, trained him in firing rifles, and allowed him visits to a nearby village. They made clear to the trainees that failure to return to guard camp after such a visit would result in death upon capture. From Trawniki, he was sent to Lublin, where he was issued a rifle and instructed to guard Jewish homes that had been left vacant when the Jews in the Lublin ghetto had been deported. The purpose was to prevent unauthorized looting of "abandoned" Jewish property by native Poles. From Lublin, he was sent to Warsaw and from there, in September 1942, to Treblinka. Federal judge Norman Roettger, who presided over the Fedorenko trial in 1978, referred to Fedorenko as a "prisoner-guard" at Treblinka.

At Treblinka, Fedorenko retained his uniform and was given a pistol. He and other non-SS guards at Treblinka were given regular leaves, enabling them to visit a nearby town when not on duty. According to his trial testimony, about twenty of his Ukrainian compatriots working as guards at Treblinka did not return from such leaves. Of these twenty, four were captured by the Germans and shot. It appears, therefore, that the Ukrainian guards had a viable opportunity to escape from their functions at Treblinka. Escape entailed some risk, but if sixteen out of twenty were able to avoid capture, the risk was not overwhelming.[13]

Fedorenko came to the United States under the DPA in 1949 as a Soviet refugee from Germany and settled in Connecticut. He worked as a laborer in a local foundry for twenty years until his retirement. Having been told by his two brothers at the time he was a prisoner that his wife and sons in Ukraine had been killed, once in the United States he remarried. Several years after his American wife died in 1960, he learned that his Ukrainian family was indeed alive and he visited them several times in the 1970s. After retiring, he moved from Connecticut to Florida, where he was living at the time of the denaturalization proceedings against him.[14] Between 1950 and the time of the trial, he had been a law-abiding resident and citizen; his only brush with the law consisted of one ticket for parking illegally.[15] The move to Miami, however, led to his undoing. Living amidst a large Jewish population in southern Florida, he was identified as a Treblinka guard. Once the Justice Department was made aware of Fedorenko and his whereabouts, it moved against him.

The Trial

The judge who presided over Fedorenko's federal denaturalization trial in 1978 was Norman Roettger. Judge Roettger had been a practitioner in southern Florida when President Nixon appointed him to a federal judgeship for the Southern District of Florida in 1972, at the relatively young age of forty-two. Roettger was on the bench for many years, serving eventually as chief judge of the Fort Lauderdale Division from 1991 to 1997, when he became a senior judge. He remained a senior judge until his death in 2003, at the age of seventy-two.

There were several lawyers at the government table. The head of the four-person prosecution team was the chief assistant U.S. attorney for the Southern District of Florida, Jon Sale. Sale had been an assistant special Watergate prosecutor prior to moving to Florida and earlier had been an assistant U.S. attorney for the Southern District of New York. He went on to a successful criminal defense practice after leaving the U.S. attorney's office, and at the time of this writing is still engaged in that practice. Gregg Pomeroy, Fedorenko's attorney, had been in the local public defender's Office from 1974 to 1975 and was in private practice when Fedorenko hired him. He is still actively practicing in southern Florida.

The Government's Case

The government's burden was to show by clear and convincing evidence (1) that Fedorenko lied to the U.S. immigration authorities on his entry application when he sought entry into the United States as a person displaced by the war and (2) that the truth would have had a significant impact on the authorities' decision to admit him. The underlying federal statute, section 1451 of Title 8 of the United States Code, provides that it is the "duty" of United States attorneys to bring actions to cancel a citizen's certificate of naturalization on the ground that the certificate was "procured by concealment of a material fact or by willful misrepresentation."[16]

Initially, a criminal investigator with the U.S. Immigration and Naturalization Service (INS) located Fedorenko's original application from INS archival files. The application included a photograph of Fedorenko taken in 1947, the time of his application for entry to the United States. Fedorenko did not dispute the authenticity of the entry application *or of the photograph* and did not challenge their admissibility. This was extremely significant in terms of the identification process. The trial was held thirty-five years after the events in question, a period long enough to present formidable obstacles to eyewitness identification. Those obstacles never materialized. Treblinka survivors did not need to identify a seventy-one-year-old Fedorenko as the thirty-five-year-old Treblinka guard. Rather, the identification process turned on that 1947 photograph of Fedorenko, taken less than five years after his work as a guard at Treblinka. If eyewitnesses could identify Fedorenko from the 1947 photograph as the person they remembered from Treblinka in 1942–43, then nothing further was needed in terms of identification.

The government called six Treblinka survivors to testify; all were Israeli citizens, probably a high percentage of Treblinka survivors alive at the time. The first was Eugun Turkowski, born in Łódź, Poland, in 1914.[17] Other members of his family had already been deported when Turkowski arrived at Treblinka in a cattle car with his three-year-old son in a backpack. Father and son were immediately separated and Turkowski later learned that the son had been killed soon after. Someone told the German guards that Turkowski was a mechanic and so his life was spared for the time being. Turkowski spent the remainder of his time at Treblinka working as a mechanic. His skills as a mechanic were put to a much more benign use than just the upkeep of machinery used to murder Jews. Turkowski made the keys for the room where ammunition was stored. This allowed him to gain access to guns and ammunition at the inception of the uprising, leading to his successful escape.

Now over thirty-five years later, the sixty-four-year-old Turkowski was sitting in a Fort Lauderdale courtroom, recounting the horrors of Treblinka in Hebrew, through an interpreter. In addition to his personal story, he initially described for Judge Roettger how Jews were murdered at Treblinka. Once trains arrived, passengers were beaten as they unloaded. Almost all were sent directly to the gas chambers. As noted earlier, those too infirm to reach the gas chambers were taken to the *Lazarett* and shot.

Turkowski specifically remembered Fedorenko from Treblinka. He testified that he knew Fedorenko by name because the two regularly met at the repair shop where Turkowski worked. He also testified that he saw Fedorenko beat people as they got off the train, shoot people at the *Lazarett*, and bring back escaped prisoners from the nearby forest to shoot them. He noted that Fedorenko wore a uniform, carried a pistol and a whip, and occasionally gave orders to other Ukrainian guards.

Up to this point, Turkowski was doing well as a government witness. However, when it came to the question of in-court identification he stumbled terribly. In-court identification is usually one of the high points of a witness's testimony, dramatically linking the direct examination narrative to a real person sitting in the courtroom. Conceptually, there was no need for in-court identification. Turkowski had identified Fedorenko from a photo spread shown to him in court, as he had done earlier when shown the spread in Israel. This was certainly enough to tie his testimony to Fedorenko. Nevertheless, understandably, the government asked him whether he saw Fedorenko in court. Fedorenko was sitting at counsel table. Turkowski, however, picked a spectator in the middle of the third row of the spectator section. The government then briefly went over his prior identifications of Fedorenko's photograph. The direct examination soon ended, obviously on a low point, casting a pall over the testimony that preceded the misidentification.

Pomeroy's cross-examination of Turkowski portended not only the cross-examination of other Treblinka survivors, but also a major component of Fedorenko's defense.[18] Pomeroy first established the obvious: Turkowski worked as a mechanic because if he had refused, he would have been killed. When asked specifically if disobedience meant death, Turkowski responded truthfully and about as favorably as the defense could have wished: "No one disobeyed."[19] Pomeroy then tried to have Turkowski admit that Jewish *kapos* in the camp beat fellow Jewish prisoners. Turkowski denied this, saying that the Jewish *kapos* simulated beatings and never hurt anyone. But the thrust of Pomeroy's cross-examination made clear that a major component of the defense would be that Fedorenko did what he did under coercion, much as the Jewish workers and the *kapos* had.

At this point, a somewhat foreboding dialogue took place between Judge Roettger and Don Boswell, one of the government lawyers. After the defense previewed by Turkowski's cross-examination, namely that disobedience meant death, and the fiasco that was Turkowski's in-court identification, there were some minor evidentiary rulings by the court conveying a less than sympathetic view of the government's case. Trying to ensure what he felt was the proper focus, Boswell articulated the government's theory of the case by observing that any "defense" by Fedorenko was irrelevant once he admitted, as he did, that he was a Treblinka guard. Boswell advised the court that a consular official would testify that if Fedorenko's history as a guard at Treblinka were known, on that basis alone he would not have been allowed to enter the United States as a refugee after the war. Thus, according to the government, any defense based on a denial of what government witnesses said Fedorenko did at Treblinka, or a claim of coercion, was, strictly speaking, irrelevant. Judge Roettger's reaction to this legal argument was tellingly dismissive: "It does not compliment the United States Government to be suggesting that an American citizen is not entitled to bring all the evidence he can to his defense."[20] There was clearly a major disconnect between the court and the prosecution. This disconnect would not be aligned for several years.

The second government witness was Shalom Kohn.[21] Kohn had served in the Polish military and after its rapid defeat by the Germans in the September 1939 invasion, he returned to his hometown of Łódź and eventually ended up in the ghetto in Czestochowa, about seventy-five miles to the south. In October 1942, German, Ukrainian, and Latvian troops surrounded the Czestochowa ghetto and loaded its Jews onto cattle cars. Kohn, his wife, and his mother-in-law were among them. They were told they were going to a labor camp in the east. There was no food or water on the train and when they arrived at their destination, Treblinka, they were yelled at and beaten as they got off the train. Men and women were separated and forced to undress. Kohn was fortunate because he was directed to guard a pile of clothes taken from the prisoners. His wife and mother-in-law were immediately sent to the gas chambers.

Kohn testified that Fedorenko, whom the Germans called by name, had been at the depot with a pistol and a whip. Kohn had previously identified the 1947 photograph of Fedorenko in the spread shown to him in Israel and repeated that identification at the trial. In a somewhat risky move after the Turkowski experience, the government asked Kohn if he saw Fedorenko in the courtroom. After walking around, undoubtedly to the great relief of the government lawyers, he identified Fedorenko.

Kohn also testified he had extensive contact with Fedorenko. One of Kohn's duties was to drag the bodies of people who had died on the train to the *Lazarett*. He testified that Fedorenko whipped him if he thought Kohn was not moving quickly enough and also saw him beat others under similar circumstances. Kohn testified that he was at the *Lazarett* frequently, either to dump bodies of persons who had died on the train or to bring wood from the nearby forest to keep the fires burning. On several of these occasions, he saw Fedorenko shoot people in the back, causing them to fall into the *Lazarett*.

On cross-examination by Pomeroy, Kohn conceded that if he had he not assisted the Germans he would have been killed, thereby lending support to the duress concept central to the defense. In response to a question from Judge Roettger, Kohn denied that he had spoken to anyone about the identification process itself and denied that he had learned that a previous witness misidentified a spectator as Fedorenko. Roettger seemed to be troubled by the identification process.

The next government witness was Josef Czarny.[22] As a thirteen-year-old, he lived with his parents in Warsaw. Once the war began with Germany's invasion of Poland, they were taken to the Warsaw ghetto, where his parents died. Thereafter, he and others were loaded onto cattle cars for deportation from the ghetto to Treblinka. The trip from Warsaw to Treblinka, a mere sixty-two miles, should have taken just a few hours at most. Instead, it took three days with no water or food given to those jammed into the cattle cars. The Germans thus effectively ensured that those who survived the ordeal from ghetto to concentration camp would be totally debilitated on arrival and in no position to organize any kind of resistance to the fate that awaited them.

Czarny remembered that on his arrival at Treblinka he saw and heard Ukrainian guards yelling at those getting off the trains. He testified that he was one of two people among the thousands unloaded from the train that day who was not gassed, but put to work instead. In court, he identified Fedorenko from the photographic spread, which, like other witnesses, he had also done in Israel. He said that he saw Fedorenko every day at Treblinka and witnessed him beating new arrivals and shouting at them as they emerged from the trains. On one occasion, he saw Fedorenko shoot a person at the *Lazarett*.

Judge Roettger then asked Czarny how 30 SS men and about 150 Ukrainians could effectively control several thousand people coming off a train.[23] From this question, it appeared that Roettger simply did not grasp the disorienting impact of three days without food or water while jammed into an overcrowded cattle car. Czarny did not answer the judge's question.

The next government witness was Gustaw Boraks. Boraks, his wife, and two sons were taken to Treblinka in the fall of 1942.[24] His wife and sons were immediately gassed. Because he was a barber, he was added to the crew of about twenty barbers whose job it was to cut the hair of arriving women. Boraks testified that women slated to die—almost all new arrivals—were forced to undress. Then, completely naked, the women were forced to walk through a line of barbers who removed the hair from their heads within one minute. At that point, the women were led down the street called *Himmelstrasse*, directly into the gas chamber.

Boraks remembered Fedorenko from Treblinka, identified him from the photo spread, and described him as one of the Ukrainians who carried a pistol. He also saw Fedorenko on several occasions chasing newly arrived victims off trains with a whip. On one occasion, while on the barbers' line, he heard a shot from the undressing area. He ran into the area and saw a woman on the floor surrounded by several Ukrainians, one of whom was Fedorenko, holding his pistol. Soon after he cut her hair, Boraks asked the woman why she had been shot. She said she had refused to take off her clothes. The wounded woman, like the others with her in line, was then marched to the gas chamber and killed.

It was highly likely after enough trains had come, that the barbers would see someone in line that they knew, perhaps a relative. On one occasion, Boraks saw a cousin and spoke with her briefly. This was a capital offense. On seeing Boraks talking with the woman, an SS guard ordered him to get in the line of men headed for the gas chambers.

Another SS guard intervened and saved him. Over twenty years later, when Boraks testified at the trial of Treblinka guards held in Düsseldorf, he mentioned the incident. As a consequence, the guard who saved his life received a considerably reduced sentence.[25]

On cross-examination, Boraks acknowledged that he did not see Fedorenko shoot the woman who had refused to undress. He also acknowledged that he could not say for sure that Fedorenko hurt anyone when using his whip while forcing people off the train. At the end of the examination, Judge Roettger commented that Boraks had been a candid witness.[26]

The prosecution then broke the stream of Treblinka survivors by calling Kempton Jenkins, a retired U.S. Foreign Service officer who worked at the displaced persons camp in Munich in 1950.[27] Jenkins's responsibilities as vice consul at the camp included the issuance of visas under the DPA, the statute under which Fedorenko gained admission to the United States. Jenkins's testimony ultimately turned out to be key evidence against Fedorenko.

Jenkins's background as well as the act he administered were the subjects of extensive inquiry by both the government and defense lawyers. The DPA was a humanitarian law designed to favor admission to the United States of persons uprooted by the Second World War with no place to go back to. Discretion was to be exercised in favor of admittance and not all acts of "misconduct" would bar admission. Stealing firewood in the midst of a harsh winter, for example, would not preclude admission. Assisting the enemy in the persecution of civilian populations, however, disqualified an applicant. Jenkins was qualified as an expert on the implementation of the DPA as it applied to Europeans in the period after the Second World War.

Though Jenkins had no specific knowledge of Fedorenko, he knew that Ukrainian guards at concentration camps wore uniforms, carried weapons, had leave prerogatives to nearby towns, and were given decent housing and food. The most important part of Jenkins's testimony, however, was his emphatic statement that an applicant who had been a concentration camp guard would not have been admitted to the United States under the DPA. He also noted that Fedorenko said in his application that he worked as a farmer in Sarny from 1937 to 1942 and then was a forced laborer. Thus, according to Jenkins, there were two clear bases to deny Fedorenko admission to the United States: he had assisted in the persecution of civilian populations and he lied on his visa application.

Pomeroy's cross-examination of Jenkins established he had no knowledge of Fedorenko and no personal involvement in the review of his application. While Jenkins acknowledged that involuntary military service might not be fatal to an application, he knew of no case where a concentration camp guard received favorable consideration under the DPA. He also acknowledged that vice consuls had some discretion, but added that such discretion did not include admission of a former concentration camp guard.

The significance of Jenkins's testimony cannot be underplayed. In one sense, it rendered the testimony of the Treblinka survivors irrelevant, since no matter what Fedorenko did or did not do at the camp, his concealment of the fact that he was a Treblinka guard alone disqualified him from entry to the United States. In addition, he was disqualified for entry because of his false statement as to his whereabouts during the war. In a broader sense, Jenkins's testimony had the effect of reducing the significance of Judge Roettger's assessments of the credibility of prosecution witnesses to almost zero. If all that mattered was that Fedorenko was a guard at Treblinka and that he misrepresented his Second World War activities in his visa application, what difference did it make whether he shot a person at the *Lazarett*, as Kohn had testified? Roettger was not insensitive to the impact of Jenkins's testimony, stating at one point that he was not about to "give his robe to Jenkins."[28] No one would expect a judge to give his robes to anyone. If, however, the impact of a witness's testimony under the law is to compel a particular result, then the judge's distaste for that result should play no part in the decision-making process.

At this point, the relationship between Judge Roettger and the government team became testier. Sale said that he wanted to call additional survivor witnesses; Roettger replied that he would preclude the government from simply presenting cumulative evidence of what it had already placed into evidence. In light of Roettger's intimations that he had issues with the credibility of witnesses that had been called, his stated attempt to prevent additional survivor testimony had no basis in fairness or logic. The court does have the power to prevent any litigant from presenting cumulative evidence.[29] However, this power is ordinarily triggered if the evidence that has been presented has convinced the court of some key fact. If Roettger was not convinced by the witnesses already called that Fedorenko had personally been involved in killing or beating Treblinka victims, then how could he legitimately prevent the government from calling more witnesses to prove that? The only basis to exclude further evidence of that nature is if such evidence is not to be given any credence, the kind of prejudgment that is impermissible. Sale, by virtue of his good judgment and extensive trial experience, was aware of Roettger's growing hostility. He saw the major disconnect in Roettger's pronouncement and acquiesced slightly to the pressure from the court by indicating he would reduce the number of witnesses to be called to three, instead of twice that number. Roettger then backed down; he would not exclude testimony on the ground that it was cumulative.

Sonia Lewkowicz, the next government witness, was twenty years old when she was taken to Treblinka in 1942.[30] Her testimony was both articulate and concise. When told to undress, at the whispered advice of one of the Jewish inmates, she said she was a laundress. As a result, she was assigned to work in the laundry and her life was saved. She escaped the following year. With regard to Fedorenko, Lewkowicz testified that once, while she was carrying laundry, she saw him shoot a prisoner. Though subjected to a lengthy cross-examination, Lewkowicz maintained the accuracy of her testimony.

The testimony of Pincas Epstein was far more provocative. Epstein testified he was brought to Treblinka in 1942 at age seventeen with his parents, two brothers, and a sister, all of whom were killed.[31] Epstein's life was spared because he was assigned the task of removing dead bodies from the gas chambers and placing them in the pit where they were to be burned, a function he exercised until he escaped during the uprising. He testified that he knew Fedorenko's name because he heard other guards address him as "Fedorenko." Epstein then testified that on one occasion when taking dead bodies from the gas chamber to the pit, he saw a prisoner named Laibel next to the pit, naked and on his hands and knees, with Fedorenko next to him. Fedorenko then shot Laibel, who fell over dead. Epstein had known Laibel from their hometown.

As was also the case with other witnesses, Epstein identified Fedorenko from a spread shown to him in Israel, in his case, by an investigator named Kolar. The defense had Kolar's report and nothing in it referred to the Laibel shooting. Understandably, Pomeroy brought out on cross-examination that Epstein had made no reference to the Laibel shooting when Kolar had questioned him. Epstein tried to explain that he had an enormous catalog of bad memories from Treblinka and that Kolar's questions were of a more general nature. Nevertheless, since the Kolar interview was conducted with a view to see whether Epstein would be a witness against Fedorenko, the omission of the Laibel shooting in the interview was clearly noteworthy.[32]

In the midst of Epstein's cross-examination, Judge Roettger finally lost his temper. He noted that Fedorenko was simply a poor foundry worker, a hard-working American, and that in an effort to denaturalize him, the government had committed a "small fortune" to the case. He noted that it had brought witnesses to the United States from Israel, had asked for a daily copy of the transcript—something Roettger said he had not seen before—and had a large number of lawyers at counsel table. Under such circumstances, he said it would be disgraceful if he permitted such extravagant use of government resources and not give Fedorenko every opportunity to defend himself. Not to give him that opportunity, Roettger said, would be inconsistent with notions of American justice.[33]

The last prosecution witness was Harry Zimon, a naturalization examiner working in the Boston area who handled Fedorenko's citizenship application.[34] Zimon testified that if Fedorenko had disclosed that he was a guard at Treblinka, he would not have recommended him for citizenship. He agreed on cross-examination that the naturalization process was not particularly thorough since Fedorenko had stated he was a Ukrainian citizen in his naturalization request, whereas his entry papers said he was Polish. This discrepancy did not trigger further review. Pomeroy asked whether involuntary service as a prison guard would disqualify Fedorenko from naturalization. Zimon responded that an applicant for citizenship had the burden of showing good moral character and that employment as a guard in a Nazi camp, even under such circumstances, would demonstrate poor moral character.

The government then rested its case and asked the court to end the trial summarily on the ground the government had proven its case. The government argued that based on the testimony of its witnesses,

Fedorenko had clearly lied on his entry papers and therefore the court should enter a judgment to denaturalize him. Pomeroy countered that the witnesses the prosecution called had all been traumatized by their Treblinka experience and would do what was necessary to convince an American court that anyone associated with the administration of Treblinka was an evil person. Not surprisingly, Judge Roettger denied the government's request for a summary judgment and the trial moved to the defense portion of the case.

Fedorenko's Case

Fedorenko's defense was divisible into two parts. The first consisted of three character witnesses, persons who had known Fedorenko for a long time and found him to be an upright, honest, law-abiding person.[35] The testimony of one of these three, Nadia Huczar, had some significance beyond her statement that Fedorenko was a man of good character. She explained that for Ukrainians in British or American custody after the war, there was a fear of repatriation to the Soviet Union, which, it was thought, carried the risk of banishment to Siberia. Consequently, she said, when faced with the possibility of returning to the Soviet Union, some Ukrainians killed themselves.[36]

Fedorenko then took the stand. After relating details of his life before Treblinka, he testified that upon arrival at Treblinka from Trawniki in August 1942, he was among eighty to one hundred Ukrainian guards. Given a uniform, his initial responsibility was to guard Jews who went to the woods to gather branches to keep fires burning. While trains came periodically to Treblinka, that did not concern him. He said he met the trains once, standing about twenty to twenty-five meters away and simply acting as a guard. He then went to his barracks. Fedorenko's testimony was unclear as to whether he was present when victims were forced to undress before being gassed. He said that after he had been at Treblinka for some time, he was given a pistol, but he was never given a whip.[37]

When asked about the gas chambers, Fedorenko testified that he never went near them although he could see them from the guard tower, where he was stationed occasionally. He further testified that he once saw dead people loaded onto a stretcher and then put into a hole.

He denied that he ever whipped or shot a prisoner. To the contrary, he said once when he saw an elderly Jew being beaten, he inquired why and asked that the Jew be left alone. As to the infamous *Lazarett*, he said he saw it once, there was no fire in it, and he never saw anyone killed there. At the time of the uprising, when Treblinka inmates escaped by running into the forest, he shot at the escaping prisoners on orders from a superior, but he did not hit anyone.[38]

On cross-examination Fedorenko stated that he considered himself a prisoner of war throughout his time at Treblinka, though he did acknowledge that the Germans gave him a gun and the right to take regular leaves to the nearby town. His self-classification as a POW, however, clashed with his deposition, in which he referred to himself as a private in the German army.[39]

Fedorenko continued to distance himself from Treblinka atrocities, saying that other Ukrainians were ordered to shoot at people at the *Lazarett*, but he was never instructed to do so. In an apparent response to Borak's testimony that he saw Fedorenko standing next to a woman who had been shot with a gun in his hand, he testified that he never saw Jews forced to undress on arrival at Treblinka. As to his misstatements at the time he requested entry to the United States, he said he had made them to avoid repatriation to the Soviet Union.[40]

Perhaps the most significant—and surreal—part of Fedorenko's testimony came after the lawyers had finished their examinations. At this point, Judge Roettger asked him specifically whether he did any of the shootings or beatings that government witnesses had testified to seeing. Fedorenko said he did not. Roettger then asked Fedorenko to look him in the eye and to respond "*da*" or "*nyet*" to the question. Fedorenko looked Roettger in the eye and responded "*nyet*."[41]

Up to this point there had been considerable dialogue between Judge Roettger and the attorneys about the taking of depositions of other Treblinka guards who, Fedorenko said, would support him. Fedorenko had been back to the Soviet Union three times in the 1970s. On one of these occasions, he was apparently detained by Soviet authorities who, after questioning him and taking statements from six other persons, exonerated him. He wanted those six witnesses to testify, a process that raised severe logistical problems since they were all located in the Soviet Union. Suddenly, after Fedorenko testified, Roettger announced that testimony from the six former Treblinka guards in the Soviet Union would not be necessary. Sale, fully realizing the impact of that statement, expressed his disbelief that he had heard correctly and asked the court to repeat what it had said, which Roettger did. Since Fedorenko claimed the testimony of the six guards was favorable to him, Roettger's statement that their testimony would not be necessary could only mean that he believed Fedorenko's denial of wrongdoing at Treblinka. Given the court's limited view of the Jenkins testimony—"[the judge] would not give his robe to Jenkins"—Sale correctly perceived how Roettger would decide the case.

Closing Arguments

In a case such as this, tried before the court, closing arguments tend to have less impact on the end result than closing arguments made to a jury. A judge is presumed to have a full grasp of the case and is not as likely to be swayed by a lawyer's final arguments as would a jury. Judge Roettger's extensive involvement in the questioning demonstrated he was on top of the case and had a sense of where it was headed. Nevertheless, each side made its closing arguments.

Pomeroy pointed to the inconsistencies in the testimony of government witnesses, the vagueness of some of their testimony, and the time that had lapsed between the events at Treblinka in 1942–43 and the trial, over thirty-five years later. The government relied on Jenkins's testimony, which government attorney Boswell contended rendered legally insignificant the details as to what Fedorenko did or did not do at Treblinka—an argument that Judge Roettger made clear he did not accept. Boswell also urged that the testimony of the survivor witnesses was credible.

One of the differences between closing arguments to jurors and to the court is that judges frequently ask questions and often those questions give a clear idea of which way the judge is leaning. That was certainly true in this case. After pointing out that under Justice Department policies, denaturalization proceedings are to be brought to better the citizenry of the United States, Judge Roettger asked how it bettered the United States to expel a man who in thirty years had accumulated one parking ticket. He went on to suggest that the Justice Department, in bringing the denaturalization case against Fedorenko, was failing to follow its own policies.[42]

Court Decisions

Judge Roettger's Decision

Judge Roettger's decision, clearly portended by his trial comments and rulings, was emphatically in Fedorenko's favor.[43] He rejected the testimony of the Treblinka survivors on three grounds. First, he found that the photographic spread shown to them in Israel was unduly suggestive, inasmuch as it consisted, for some of the witnesses, of only three photographs. Also, the photo of Fedorenko together with one other guard was bigger, framed with black, and clearer than others. Most spreads used in criminal cases have at least six photographs. He also discounted the in-court identifications of Fedorenko since Fedorenko was the only person of an age in the well of the courtroom old enough to have been a Treblinka guard thirty-five years earlier.

Second, Judge Roettger found that the description some of the survivors gave that Fedorenko had a cruel visage was simply not correct: he detected no such component to Fedorenko's face, which he actually found sympathetic. He also found a conflict in the description of Fedorenko's uniform, some of which was inaccurate in light of the evidence he accepted. He pointed out that one of the witnesses, when asked to identify Fedorenko in the courtroom, initially picked out a man sitting in the back of the spectator section. Finally, Roettger concluded, more on conjecture than any hard evidence, that the witnesses had colluded on the identification question—or perhaps had been coached by the Israeli investigators working on the case.

At the same time, he credited Fedorenko's testimony. He found him to be a simple man who wanted to please and be helpful to the prosecution when he was being cross-examined. He seemed impressed by the fact that Fedorenko was living on his social security pension and a pension from his former employer, that he owned no real estate other than a cemetery plot, owned neither a car nor a house, and had life savings of $5,000. Although the comparison had no logical connection to his credibility, Roettger contrasted Fedorenko's lack of significant resources with the prosecution's efforts. He observed that in his six years as a federal district court judge he had never seen the government order a daily copy of the transcript nor have four lawyers at counsel table, even though during those six years he had presided over a trial of a Mafia don and the trial of a narcotics "hit man."[44]

However, there was one part of Fedorenko's testimony that Judge Roettger did not credit. Fedorenko painted himself as a "do no evil" Treblinka guard. Fedorenko said he was never at the barracks where women were forced to undress—contradicting the testimony of Borak, whom Roettger had found to be the most credible of the survivor witnesses. If Fedorenko were to be believed, he was out in the fields on the perimeter of Treblinka guarding inmates collecting wood; he never whipped anyone, shot anyone, or committed any act of brutality towards any of the inmates. And during the escape, he shot in the air. Roettger found this specific testimony not credible. He never took the next step of inferring that if Fedorenko was untruthful about his general role as a Treblinka guard, then perhaps his denial of what witnesses said about him was also untrue.

Having resolved credibility issues in favor of Fedorenko, there were two legal obstacles Judge Roettger had to overcome. First, the prosecution's argument that the false statement to the consular official at the time Fedorenko applied for his entry visa alone disqualified him. Jenkins had testified that a Ukrainian guard at Treblinka would not have been permitted to come to the United States; therefore, the false statement on Fedorenko's application required denaturalization. The second obstacle for Roettger lay in the DPA, which provided the legal backbone for the entire entry process. The act had two specific exclusions: (1) those who had "assisted the enemy in persecuting [civilians]" and (2) those who had "voluntarily assisted the enemy forces . . . in their operations." The first of these exclusions, on its face, would certainly seem to have rendered Fedorenko ineligible and required his denaturalization. Roettger overcame both these obstacles.

He dealt with Jenkins's testimony that if Fedorenko had told the truth—that he was Ukrainian and a guard at Treblinka—he would not have been admitted, in two ways. After pointing to what he thought were inaccuracies in Jenkins's testimony, he addressed the question of materiality. Obviously, not every false statement in the entry process would disqualify an applicant. Misstating a birthday by a month or the number of one's siblings would not disqualify an applicant because those misstatements would make no difference in the judgmental process involved in permitting entry, or as the law would term it, those misstatements would not be material. Materiality, as the judge defined it for purposes of entry, meant that a true statement would have led to the discovery of facts that would disqualify the applicant. Roettger then went on to find that an inquiry at the time of Fedorenko's entry application would have shown that he was forced to work as a guard at Treblinka, under penalty of death, and there was nothing to indicate that credible evidence would have materialized that he engaged in any acts of brutality. Hence, his false statement indicating that he was at places other than at Treblinka during the war was not material.

The wording of the DPA, disqualifying those who assisted the enemy in the persecution of civilians, raised an even more formidable difficulty on Judge Roettger's delineated path to upholding Fedorenko's citizenship. Thus, we come back to the *kapos*, Jewish prisoners at Treblinka who were temporarily salvaged by the Germans from the gas chamber, to assist in the killing process. Pomeroy, in cross-examining Treblinka survivors, tried to equate Fedorenko with the *kapos*. For example, Boraks, the barber whom Roettger found credible, "assisted" the enemy by cutting off women's hair just prior to their fateful walk to the gas chambers. Such persons, Roettger concluded, could not conceivably be excluded from entry to the United States under the DPA.

Working on the theory that someone like Boraks could not possibly have been intended to be barred from United States entry, Judge Roettger concluded that that part of the act that excluded those who "assisted the enemy" had to mean those who *voluntarily* assisted the enemy. This was not a simple matter of statutory interpretation for the court since, as noted above, the very next exclusion specifically read, "voluntarily assisted the enemy forces." Basic rules of statutory construction suggest that if the term "voluntary" was used in the second exclusion, but not in the first, its omission from the first was by design. Roettger, however, in contemplating how the act would have been applied, said that literally applied, it would have barred "every Jewish prisoner who survived Treblinka because each one of them assisted the SS in the operation of the camp."[45] Indeed, he went on, those Treblinka survivors who were citizens of the United States would have their status imperiled if the word "voluntary" were not read into the act.[46]

Judge Roettger had one last arrow in his quiver on Fedorenko's behalf. There is a historical division between concepts of law and equity. When a court sits as a court in equity, it is entitled to arrive at a result that is equitable or fair, even if that is not the result the law might require. Observing that in a denaturalization proceeding he was sitting as a court of equity,

Roettger found that aside from the law, it was inequitable to strip citizenship from a man who had led an exemplary life for almost thirty years in the United States, had worked hard, was respected by co-workers and neighbors, and whose only antisocial conduct in almost three decades was one parking ticket. Under these circumstances, Roettger held that for equitable reasons, he would not strip Fedorenko of his citizenship because of his status as a guard at Treblinka over thirty-five years earlier. He noted it was undisputed that Fedorenko was not given a choice about being a Treblinka guard; he was at the camp only because that is where the Germans put him, and had he refused, he would have been killed. While Roettger acknowledged that Fedorenko was able to leave Treblinka for visits to a nearby village, he found that the Germans did this to keep the Ukrainian guards' morale at a level that would preclude their rebelling.

The Court of Appeals and Supreme Court Decisions

The government appealed its loss to the Court of Appeals. On June 28, 1979, the Court of Appeals reversed Judge Roettger's order denying the government's request to strip Fedorenko of his citizenship. It ruled that he applied an incorrect test on materiality: it was not whether a truthful statement on the application *would* have led to facts that would have disqualified him from entry to the United States, but rather whether such an inquiry *might have* led to such facts.[47] From the record, it was clear to the appellate court that such facts might have been found, resulting in a denial of Fedorenko's entry application. The Court of Appeals also held that Roettger was mistaken when he determined that he could invoke equitable principles in ruling on the denaturalization request. Congress had created specific rules for entry to the United States and the courts did not have the power to override congressional will, as expressed in the statutes, by applying the court's concept of what was equitable.

Having lost in the Court of Appeals, Fedorenko petitioned to the United States Supreme Court, which agreed to hear the case.[48] On January 21, 1981, the Supreme Court affirmed Fedorenko's denaturalization. In its decision, authored by Justice Thurgood Marshall, the court did not decide the case on "materiality" grounds, as had the lower appellate court. Instead, Justice Marshall's opinion focused on the DPA and the prohibition against entry for any person who assisted in the persecution of civilian populations.[49] The Court highlighted Jenkins's credentials as someone who personally handled over five thousand entry requests at the time and then referred to his testimony that Fedorenko, as an armed guard at Treblinka, would have been found to have assisted in the persecution of civilians—a "uniformly accepted" reading of the act. The Court also observed that Jenkins knew of no concentration camp guard who was admitted to the United States under the DPA. The Court then completely vindicated Jenkins's position by stating that once it was shown that Fedorenko lied in his entry application and the truth was that he had been an armed guard at Treblinka, as Fedorenko acknowledged, as a matter of law he was then ineligible for entry to the United States. Materiality was irrelevant.[50] This, of course, brings us back to the *kapos* and Judge Roettger's observation that even Treblinka survivors would have been ineligible to enter the U.S. under the DPA because of their involuntary assistance in the administration of Treblinka.

The Supreme Court dealt with this argument summarily. It noted the obvious: the DPA used the term "voluntarily" in the second exclusion when it dealt with assisting enemy forces; no such qualification was based on the persecution of civilians. It distinguished (1) a guard, given a uniform, a weapon, a stipend, afforded leave and someone who shot at escaping prisoners under order from a superior, from (2) an inmate slated for death but provisionally assigned to cut the hair of female inmates. As to *kapos* or others whose involvement in the killing process was more direct, the Court simply deferred those issues until they would arise: "Other cases may present more difficult line-drawing problems but we need decide only this case."[51] The Court went on to agree with the appellate court that these cases, dealing with specific statutory provisions barring entry of certain persons to the United States, did not provide a court with the power to make judgments based on equity. An equitable decision could not validate entry into the United States by those Congress specifically had barred. The final order, therefore, was that Fedorenko's citizenship be stripped on the ground that it was illegally procured.

After Denaturalization

The Supreme Court made its decision directing that Fedorenko be denaturalized in 1981, three years after formal proceedings against him had begun. The Justice Department then took the next step of expelling the now stateless Fedorenko. In 1984, he was ordered to leave the United States to any country that would take him. Since his original family was still alive in the Soviet Union and since he had visited them several times in the 1970s, he opted for deportation to the Soviet Union. The Soviet Union agreed to accept him. As a result, in 1984, he rejoined his first wife in Dzhankoi in the Crimea and lived with her for about a year. He was then arrested and brought to trial in the Soviet Union as a war criminal. He pled guilty, and in 1986, he was sentenced to death. Tass, the official Soviet news agency, reported Fedorenko's execution on July 27, 1987.[52]

As far as we are aware, the Ukrainian archives containing the details of Fedorenko's proceedings have not yet been opened. Consequently, we know less about this Soviet case in the 1980s of a Nazi collaborator than we do about the Kharkov trial (also in Ukraine) of Nazi collaborators in the 1940s (see chapter 1). However, Fedorenko's denaturalization file in the United States contains one document that may shed some light on the Soviet proceedings. Until Judge Roettger concluded that he found Fedorenko's denials credible by having Fedorenko look him in the eye and say "*nyet*," there was an issue of whether witnesses from the Soviet Union would testify. Roettger's decision mentions these potential Soviet witnesses by name; one was a former Treblinka guard named Korotkey. A translation of Korotkey's April 21, 1950, interrogation by an investigator from the Ukrainian Ministry of State Security is in the Soviet case file and it is anything but exculpatory of Fedorenko.[53]

Korotkey's interrogation report shows that, like Fedorenko, he was sent to Treblinka where he worked until the liquidation of the camp in 1943. He was asked to name all the Ukrainian guards he remembered. He then described only Fedorenko, whose birth year he estimated as about 1910. (It was 1907.) He said he met Fedorenko at Trawniki, where they were both trained as camp guards and then worked together as guards at Treblinka. Korotkey then described the killing process at Treblinka in the kind of chilling detail only either a survivor or participant could know. According to Korotkey, Fedorenko's role as a guard was specifically to guard the passage extending from the undressing area to the gas chambers. In that role, Fedorenko stood in the cordon of guards to prevent individuals sent to the gas chambers from escaping through the barbed wire. Korotkey also stated that Fedorenko participated in the unloading of trains that arrived with Jews to be killed. Korotkey's interrogation statements are dramatically inconsistent with Fedorenko's denials in his Florida trial, and are consistent with the testimony of government witnesses, namely that Fedorenko was directly involved in the mass murders at Treblinka.

Conclusion

The ultimate purpose behind Fedorenko's denaturalization trial was to achieve his subsequent deportation. The idea both behind the underlying statute and the government's case was to rid the United States of persons who engaged in the persecution of civilians during the Second World War. It is really simple: that the diverse polity that makes up American society should not include those who participated in the Holocaust.

Judge Roettger never seemed to grasp this fundamental idea. Actually, it was not really his to grasp. Congress passed the law setting out the concept and the Executive was to enforce it. Even if Roettger felt differently, it was not his call. And while it is no doubt true that Jewish Defense League protests and perhaps the occasional outbursts of the courtroom crowd were unpleasant and extremely disturbing to the judge, they should have played no role, one way or the other, in his decision. The same is also certainly true for the number of lawyers sitting at government counsel table. How the Executive chooses to utilize its resources is its decision and should not be of any evidentiary significance to a judge trying a case.

Was it fair to deport Fedorenko to the Soviet Union, whose judicial procedures may not satisfy our standards of due process? His first wife and sons were there. His earlier and completely voluntary visits to them were uneventful, and he testified in his American trial that on one of those earlier visits the Soviets exonerated him of all war crimes. As a result, he actually chose to return to Ukraine. Under these circumstances, the United States can hardly be faulted for acceding to what was, on its face, a reasonable choice by Fedorenko. Apparently, the Soviets reopened the proceedings against him, perhaps on the basis of the evidence presented in the Fort Lauderdale trial, or other evidence such as Korotkey's statements or similar statements corroborating Korotkey. We do not know; nor do we know whether Fedorenko's guilty plea was voluntary or induced by false promises of leniency.

Should Fedorenko have been executed? The inescapable fundamental fact is that he played a part in a horrendous killing machine that probably murdered several hundred thousand persons on his watch. While his role might not have been central, it was essential, and while he performed that essential role, he knew exactly what the larger purpose of the operation was—the mass murder of Jews.

Should the fact that Fedorenko was not at Treblinka of his own free will legitimately mitigate his sentence, rendering the death penalty excessive? While Fedorenko was initially coerced into service for the Nazis at Treblinka, at some point, after enough leaves to the nearby town, it becomes safe to say that he returned voluntarily. While it is true that 20 percent of the Ukrainian guards who tried to escape were caught and killed, an 80 percent chance of survival gave Fedorenko vastly better odds on survival than he had when first drafted into the Soviet army. Also, by 1943, the German army was in retreat in the Soviet Union and the Germans had bigger problems than tracking down an escaped Ukrainian prison guard. Finally, the conduct government witnesses attributed to Fedorenko at Treblinka belies the notion that he did only the minimum in order to survive.

In considering the degree of Fedorenko's involvement, we assume that the essence of the testimony presented by survivors in his Florida trial was correct. Fedorenko's testimony distancing himself from the killing process, which even Judge Roettger disbelieved, strongly suggests that other exculpatory components of his testimony were not credible. The surviving witnesses painted a picture of an SS guard who murdered helpless prisoners—not the conduct of a reluctant and coerced individual. The Korotkey statement provided precisely the kind of corroboration to the survivor testimony that gave a ring of truth to the Fedorenko they described. The picture that emerges is that Fedorenko was a killer, *both* as an accomplice to the larger mass murders and as someone who murdered prisoners himself. If there is to be a death penalty, it does not offend a sense of justice to see it imposed on Fedorenko.

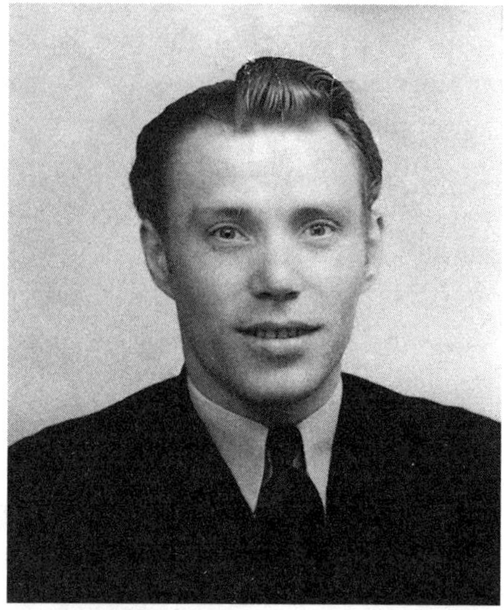

Anthony Sawoniuk in 1948. AP photo.

Anthony Sawoniuk during his trial on March 31, 1999.AP photo/Peter Jordan, PA.

10

The Trial of Anthony Sawoniuk at the Old Bailey

The Holocaust in the British Courtroom

The morning of February 8, 1999, was overcast, dreary, and cold, like any other winter day in London. Individuals navigating through the snow that fell overnight past the busy Central Criminal Courthouse in London, fondly known as the "Old Bailey," would hardly know that history was being made inside: the only criminal trial of the Holocaust to have occurred in Britain was about to begin.

The defendant on trial in Court 12 was being charged for multiple murders that had taken place fifty-seven years before, not in England but in German-occupied Europe. And the end result was that the defendant attained the dubious distinction of being the sole Nazi war criminal to be convicted by an English jury. The man, Anthony Sawoniuk, and his two-month trial in the Old Bailey—from February 8 to April 1, 1999—is the focus of this chapter.

Anthony Sawoniuk, the Nazi-Era Policeman

Anthony Sawoniuk was born on March 7, 1921, in Domachevo, a small town on the border between today's Belarus and Poland. The town lies about twenty miles south of Brest, the largest city in the area. During the interwar period, Domachevo, like Brest, was part of Poland. Following Poland's partition in September 1939 between Stalin's Soviet Union and Hitler's Germany it was incorporated into Belarussia (White Russia), where it became part of the Belarussian Soviet Socialist Republic. Today, it is part of the independent Republic of Belarus.

Domachevo's prewar population of approximately five thousand included Poles, Belarussians, ethnic Germans, and Jews. Like Brest, Domachevo had a substantial Jewish population, with two Jewish prayer houses. Because it was encircled by lush, large pine forests with beautiful scenery and healthy air, Domachevo became known as a spa resort, with Jews from throughout Poland vacationing there during the summer.

Andrusha (little Andrei), as he was known by all (even as an adult), experienced a difficult childhood. At the time of his birth, his mother, Pelagia, was a widow with one son, Nikolai. With Andrusha's birth, Nikolai gained a younger half-brother—and this relationship, as we shall see, had a small but significant role in Sawoniuk's arrest years later in Britain. Sawoniuk left school at the age of fourteen. His plight worsened when his mother died prior to the war. Between 1939 and 1941, when the region became part of the U.S.S.R., the brothers supported themselves by raising pigeons and doing odd jobs around town, often for the town's Jewish residents. In June 1941, within days of Germany's surprise attack on the Soviet Union, German troops entered Domachevo. Sawoniuk, now twenty years old, very quickly experienced a rise in status by joining the *Schutzmannschaft,* the local auxiliary police force set up by the German occupiers. Consisting of about thirty recruits, their task, in the words of the English Court of Appeal in 2000, was to "combat local crime, to provide protection against partisans (many of them Russian Communists who fled to the forests upon the German invasion) and to lend effect to the occupation policy of the German state."[1] "Lending effect" to the occupation policy meant, of course, killing Jews.

Andrusha's brother Nikolai also joined the *Schutzmannschaft* but, unlike Sawoniuk, left after a few weeks when he realized what was expected of him. Sawoniuk did not seem to mind the assignment.

A local census carried out in February 1942 by the German civil administration recorded 3,316 Jews living in Domachevo. By that time, the local Jews had been segregated into a ghetto, which the Germans set up three weeks after the invasion. The police station was at the entrance to the ghetto. The main function of this newly established force was to prevent Jews from escaping the ghetto and prevent food or provisions from being smuggled in.

The end of the Jews of Domachevo took place six months later in the fall of 1942, on the eve of the Jewish holiday of Yom Kippur. In the words of Israel Silber, one Jewish survivor:

> It was in the year 1942, on a Sunday before Yom Kippur, the Germans surrounded the ghetto, and took all the men, women, and children—a total of 2,700 souls to the Ossover hall opposite the German Church. Then began the most ghastly and terrible event. Everyone was forced to strip naked, taken aside in groups and shot dead.[2]

The German account of the September 1942 massacre, coming from a monthly report of the Gendarmerie County leader in Brest, records this mass murder operation:

> On September 19–20, 1942, an anti-Jewish *Aktion* was carried out in Domachevo and Tomashovka by a special commando of the SD together with the cavalry squadron of the Gendarmerie and the local police stationed in Domachevo, and in total some 2,900 Jews where shot. The action took place without any disturbance.[3]

In the aftermath of the *Aktion* (the German term for the mass arrest, deportation, and murder of Jews), local police were sent on their own "search and kill" operations for those Jews who may have escaped the initial eradication. The theory was that local police officers were more familiar with the forests of Domachevo, as well as other potential hiding places, which would allow them to hunt and kill any Jew who may have survived the massacre. The young Sawoniuk apparently conducted the "search and kill" operations and his other police tasks admirably. In November 1943, when the commander was killed by partisans, Sawoniuk took his position. That same month, his first wife Anna was also killed during a partisan attack. A short while later he married a second time to a local woman named Nina.

Sawoniuk served as a *Schutzmann* for about three years. As the Red Army began recapturing Soviet territory in July 1944, Sawoniuk fled with the Germans by joining the *Waffen-SS*. He achieved the rank of corporal. Introduced at trial by the prosecution as Exhibit 7 was a German SS document showing Sawoniuk's name, his correct date and place of birth, and even listing the correct name of his second wife "Nina S" (presumably "S" for Sawoniuk), who fled with him in 1944. It also noted his transfer from Warsaw to France, and his service in the *Waffen-SS* from July to November 1944.

Sawoniuk, however, was not a Nazi loyalist but an opportunist. When Germany's military successes began to falter, Sawoniuk defected. Exhibit 7 is a *Waffen-SS* AWOL document, referring to his going missing sometime in late November 1944. Using his Polish birth certificate, Sawoniuk enlisted in the Polish Free Army, which fought alongside the British and against the Germans. He served briefly in Egypt and Italy before sailing with his regiment to Glasgow, arriving on British soil on June 27, 1946.

Earlier that year the British government created the Polish Resettlement Corps (PRC), a holding unit for members of the Polish armed forces who had served with the British forces and did not wish to return to Communist Poland after the war. Run mainly by the British Army, the PRC was disbanded in 1949 after fulfilling its purpose of resettling the Polish soldiers who fought on the side of the Allies. It was reasonable to assume that anyone who fought for the Polish Free Army was not a supporter of the Nazi regime, and so Sawoniuk accordingly was allowed to stay in Britain.

Sawoniuk moved around Britain before finally taking up residence in London. He earlier abandoned Nina in France after she had followed him from Domachevo, and not long after arrival briefly married a third time. In 1958, he married a fourth time, and this marriage in 1961 produced a child, a son also named Anthony. The marriage dissolved when the son was only a few months old and the infant remained with his mother. Following his fourth marriage, Sawoniuk in 1958 became a naturalized British citizen. In 1961, he began working as a British Rail ticket inspector and continued at this job for twenty-five years until retirement in 1986.

Prelude to Prosecution: The War Crimes Act 1991

Retirement, however, did not bring on the good years for Sawoniuk. In 1986, the same year that he retired, the Los Angeles–based Simon Wiesenthal Center (SWC) submitted to Downing Street a list of seventeen suspected Nazi war criminals alleged to be living in the United Kingdom. The list was compiled by the SWC's Jerusalem-based Nazi hunter, Efraim Zuroff. At this point, the dragnet around Sawoniuk had not yet closed in, since he was not on Zuroff's list.

Claims that Britain became a haven for Nazis led Home Secretary Douglas Hurd in February 1988 to establish an official War Crimes Inquiry, to be headed by Sir Thomas Hetherington, a former director of public prosecutions, and William Chalmers, former head of the prosecutorial Crown Office in Scotland. The sixteen-month investigation studied more than three hundred potential suspects, and the ensuing Hetherington-Chalmers Report, issued in 1989, recommended that British law be broadened to allow prosecution of those who currently reside in Britain and committed murder, manslaughter, or genocide in German-occupied territories during the Second World War. According to the report:

> The crimes committed are so monstrous that they cannot be condoned: their prosecution could act as a deterrent to others in future wars. To take no action would taint the UK with the slur of being a haven for war criminals. . . . War criminals were not given an assurance that they would not be prosecuted here, and we see nothing in the policy or practice of successive British Governments that would prevent the present Government taking whatever action it considers suitable.[4]

There remained only one obstacle to prosecution: English law. At the time, English courts could not exercise jurisdiction even against the common law crime of individual murder committed abroad if the accused, found on British soil, was not a British citizen or resident at the time of the commission of the crime. Holocaust perpetrators living in Britain fell within this gap in the law, and so new legislation was necessary.[5]

It took two years after the issuance of the Hetherington-Chalmers Report for Parliament to pass the necessary legislation. And doing so was not an easy task. Lord Shawcross, Britain's lead prosecutor at Nuremberg, surprisingly led the opposition, and was joined by Lord Hailsham, a former lord chancellor. Hailsham accused the Thatcher government of "giving in to a special interest community"—plainly referring to Jews. After the House of Lords twice refused to accede to the legislation, the House of Commons, in a rarely used parliamentary procedure, overrode the will of the upper chamber and enacted the bill into law.

The War Crimes Act 1991 was "an Act to confer jurisdiction on United Kingdom courts in respect of certain grave violations of the laws and customs of war committed in German-held territory during the Second World War; and for connected purposes."[6] Section 1 of the War Crimes Act 1991 provides:

> (1) [P]roceedings for murder, manslaughter or culpable homicide may be brought against a person in the United Kingdom irrespective of his nationality at the time of the alleged offence if that offence—
>
> (a) was committed during the period beginning 1st September 1939 and ending with 5th June 1945 in a place which at the time was part of Germany or under German occupation; and
>
> (b) constituted a violation of the laws and customs of war.
>
> (2) No such proceedings shall . . . be brought against any person unless he was on 8th March 1990, or has subsequently become, a British citizen or resident in the United Kingdom, the Isle of Man or any of the Channel Islands.

The War Crimes Act 1991 was a remarkable piece of legislation in that it allowed proceedings for murder or another culpable homicide (i.e., not in self-defense) to be brought against a person irrespective of the nationality of the person. Moreover, it was the first time that Parliament allowed British courts to have jurisdiction over crimes committed outside its territory. The nexus to Britain was the suspect's tie to Britain either through citizenship or residency. Finally, the act directed British courts to look to international treaties dealing with laws and customs of war, specifically the Geneva and Hague Conventions in force during the Second World War, as the basis for determining whether the acts committed by the accused were in fact war crimes. In other words, the acts charged must not only constitute "murder, manslaughter or culpable homicide" under British domestic law; they must also be international war crimes.

To facilitate investigations, a War Crimes Unit was set up both within the police force, in the Metropolitan Police (New Scotland Yard), and the government-run criminal prosecution office, the Crown Prosecution Service. War Crimes Unit detectives, who began searching for evidence in Eastern Europe, Israel, Canada, the U.S., South Africa, and New Zealand, were skeptical at first but then came around to the importance of these prosecutions. Professor Anthony Glees, who served as academic adviser to the original Home Office War Crimes Inquiry, recalls: "At the beginning the police thought Mrs. Thatcher had just got a bee in her bonnet, but within a few months there was nobody who was not committed to prosecution. When you saw the files you realised these were people who had committed thousands of murders."[7]

Sawoniuk, though, was still safe, since he was not on the Hetherington-Chalmers list or the list submitted by the Simon Wiesenthal Center to the British government in 1986. He eventually came to the attention of the War Crimes Unit through fortuitous circumstances.

The Soviets began looking for Sawoniuk and other local collaborators soon after the end of the war when villagers identified Sawoniuk as a collaborator. As a result, the KGB opened a file on him, designated as "All Union Search File no. 1065." Over the years, the Soviets made repeated attempts to determine what had happened to the man serving as chief of the collaborator police force who left with the Germans on the heels of the Soviet liberation of Domachevo.

In 1951, the KGB received a break. Sawoniuk, already residing in the United Kingdom, wrote a letter to Nikolai, still living in Domachevo. At the time, it was common for all mail arriving from the West to be opened by the authorities. The Soviet security service now learned of Sawoniuk's whereabouts. However, because this was during the height of the Cold War, the KGB did not share their information with the British authorities. In the 1980s, as Mrs. Thatcher announced that the West could do business with Mikhail Gorbachev, relations between the two nations improved. As a result, the Soviets delivered for the first time to the British a list of Second World War criminals whom they suspected of having fled to the U.K. Sawoniuk, however, still went undetected because the transliteration the Soviets made into English had his name spelled as "Savanyuk." As a result, the computer search conducted by the War Crimes Unit of National Health Service and pensioner records did not pick up Sawoniuk's name. He was finally identified and located in 1996, living in the south London district of Bermondsey, when a historian working for the unit pointed out the alternative English-language spelling of his name.

Closing In and Indictment

It took nine years from the time the Soviets turned over their list of Nazi collaborators living in Britain for British officials to arrest Sawoniuk. On March 21, 1996, at 10:10 a.m., his past caught up with him when Scotland Yard detectives came knocking on his door. On April 1 and 3, 1996, detectives formally interviewed Sawoniuk at the police station in the presence of counsel. The interviews focused not on his army service under the Germans but on his activities in Domachevo during the German occupation.

Sawoniuk initially denied everything. He was never a policeman in Domachevo but rather was working as a forced laborer in Germany alongside other locals who had been forcibly shipped there after German occupation. Moreover, according to his account, Domachevo did not even have a local police force comprised of indigenous non-Germans. The only security function, he claimed, that the non-German locals performed was to keep watch for Russian partisans. These locals were unarmed and did not even wear uniforms. His claims became less credible when he stated that the Jewish population was not restricted in any way after the Nazi occupation and that there had not been a ghetto at Domachevo. Eventually, Sawoniuk admitted that he had served on the local police force and that at one point he was its senior officer. These admissions came after his indictment, but prior to his trial.

At this point, we note that Sawoniuk was not the first person prosecuted under the War Crimes Act. The Hetherington-Chalmers Report initially identified four hundred potential suspects, and the War Crimes Unit, after their investigation, whittled that list down to one hundred individuals. In 1996, five years after the act's passage, the War Crimes Unit prosecutors finally charged a suspect from that list: Syzmon Serafinowicz, another elderly Eastern European who served as a collaborationist police chief in another town in Belarussia. Coincidentally, Serafinowicz and Sawoniuk both served in the same *Waffen-SS* unit, though apparently they had not known each other. In another coincidence, alternative spellings of Serafinowicz's name also tripped up the investigators, even though Serafinowicz was listed in the telephone book and had lived in the same house in Banstead in Surrey since 1956.

The Serafinowicz case collapsed, however, on the eve of trial. In January 1997, the judge before whom Serafinowicz was to be tried issued a permanent stay of prosecution after a jury, hearing from medical experts, decided that the accused was unfit to stand trial because of dementia. The eighty-five-year-old Serafinowicz died eight months later. By this time, the War Crimes Unit had spent £2 million on the case.

British Holocaust historian David Cesarani blames the result on the conduct of the police investigators of the War Crimes Unit: "The Met unit squandered 18 months attempting to trace Szymon Serafinowicz . . . even though the correct version was in the phone book. They repeated the same mistake with Anton Sawoniuk."[8] Since Serafinowicz died later that year, Sawoniuk's conviction in 1999 consequently became the first and—to date—the sole successful prosecution of a Nazi war criminal in Britain.

In March 1997, the War Crimes Unit of the Crown Prosecution Service formally charged Sawoniuk, who was a decade younger than Serafinowicz and in better health, with five counts of murder. On May 29, 1998, magistrate Graham Parkinson of Bow Street Magistrates' Court committed Sawoniuk for trial but released him on bail pending the proceedings. Judge Parkinson, after hearing the proffered evidence from witnesses who came from Belarus and Israel, allowed four of the five charges to go forward. He dismissed the fifth charge because the necessary witness was unable to travel to London to testify at the pretrial hearings.

The charges against Sawoniuk were quite specific and concerned events covering a three-month period between the September 19–20, 1942, German *Aktion* against the Domachevo Jews and the end of that year. Each count charged Sawoniuk with the murder of one specific individual: two unidentified Jewish women and two identified Jewish men, all residents of Domachevo. All the murders were alleged to have been committed in the aftermath of the *Aktion*.

The witnesses the War Crimes Unit investigators located related the events in which Sawoniuk killed approximately twenty individuals during his time on the police force. Since English law requires only one allegation of murder for each count, the prosecution chose to charge Sawoniuk with just four murders, even in those instances where the witnesses could testify that he killed others at the same time.

Each of the four murder counts was supported by eyewitness testimony. Guilt or innocence would depend, therefore, on the credibility of the four eyewitnesses for each of the murders, as well as corroborating testimony of other witnesses from Domachevo and its environs who would testify about Sawoniuk's activities during German occupation. If Sawoniuk chose to take the stand to contradict the witnesses' testimony, his credibility would likewise be central to the case.

Unlike at Nuremberg, and to a great extent at the Eichmann trial, documentary evidence played a minor role in the Sawoniuk trial. No documents could be found showing that Sawoniuk was a policeman in the German-created local police force, or his involvement in the killing of anyone.

The *Waffen-SS* AWOL document located in the German archives, showing a Corporal Sawoniuk as having gone missing from his unit in November 1944 and introduced at trial (as noted above as Exhibit 7), ultimately was ruled inadmissible by the judge since it could not be properly authenticated according to English criminal procedure evidentiary rules.

Count 1 accused Sawoniuk of murdering an unknown Jewish woman sometime between September 19 and September 27, 1942. The formal charge stated that Sawoniuk, "a person resident in the United Kingdom on March 8, 1990, in Domachevo, Belorussia, a town under German occupation, murdered a Jewess in circumstances constituting a violation of the laws and customs of war."[9] The allegation was based entirely on eyewitness testimony of a local resident, Alexander Baglay, thirteen years old at the time.

According to the now sixty-nine-year-old Baglay, he and a sixteen-year-old companion who both resided in Borisy, a hamlet of thirty houses on the outskirts of Domachevo, went into the now-abandoned Domachevo ghetto in search of clothing. They were confronted by Sawoniuk and fellow officers, who took them back to the police station, located directly opposite the ghetto. They were given shovels, and taken back inside the ghetto. Baglay knew Sawoniuk, who had hired Baglay's father months earlier to disassemble and move the house from the ghetto that Sawoniuk was now living in.

In the ghetto, the group approached two other policemen who were guarding two older Jewish men and a younger Jewish woman, all standing next to a freshly dug hole. Sawoniuk ordered the three individuals to undress. The older men complied but the woman refused. It was not until Sawoniuk threatened her with a truncheon that she did so. The three undressed Jews were then lined up on their knees. Sawoniuk drew his pistol and shot each in the back of the head at point-blank range. Their lifeless bodies were then pushed into the hole that awaited their arrival. At that point, Sawoniuk ordered Baglay and his friend to grab the shovels and cover up the grave. Once the boys finished filling the hole with dirt, Sawoniuk offered the boys the victims' clothing, which both boys declined.

Baglay first told this story to the War Crimes Unit investigators in 1991. He had never previously related this incident to anyone. The friend died in 1986 and so could not corroborate his account. As noted above, even though Baglay claimed he witnessed Sawoniuk kill three people, two men and one woman, the prosecutors charged Sawoniuk only with the single count of murdering the woman.

Count 2 charged Sawoniuk with another single murder: of a Domachevo Jewish man named Schlemko sometime between September 19 and October 4, 1942. This count was also based entirely on an account given by another local witness, Ivan Stepaniuk, also a resident of Borisy. Stepaniuk claimed he witnessed Sawoniuk, along with two other policemen, beat and drag Schlemko into the woods a few days after the *Aktion*. When he lost sight of Sawoniuk and Schlemko, Stepaniuk heard the sound of gunfire echoing through the woods. Sawoniuk and the other policemen then returned with their carbines and shovels, with Schlemko being noticeably absent. Stepaniuk never actually saw Sawoniuk shoot Schlemko. He also did not know Sawoniuk's identify at the time of the shooting, and stated that he only learned Sawoniuk's name a few days later from Sawoniuk's brother.

Count 3 charged Sawoniuk with the murder of another unknown "Jewess in circumstances constituting a violation of the laws and customs of war."[10] This act was also said to have taken place between September 19 and October 4, 1942. The key witness for this count was Fedor Zan, another local from Borisy. Zan worked in Brest, and would take a train there from the Domachevo station. On his way home from work in September 1942, Zan got off the train early at the nearby village of Kobelka to visit his sister. From his sister's residence, he decided to cut across the woods to get home to Borisy. While walking home through the woods, he heard shouts and cries. He went towards the noise until he saw and heard Sawoniuk order a group of approximately fifteen Jewish women to undress. Not wanting to reveal his presence, Zan hid behind a tree, about 127–128 paces away. He heard Sawoniuk, who was the only policeman on the scene, instruct the women to place their clothing in a pile and then turn and face the pit. After they did so, Sawoniuk raised a machine gun and killed the women.

Count 4 charged Sawoniuk with the murder of another Domachevo Jewish man named Mir Barlas sometime between September 4 and December 31, 1942. This count was based on an account given by a former Jewish playmate of Sawoniuk, Ben Zion Blustein, who at age seventy-six came from Israel to testify against his childhood friend. According to Blustein:

> I had known [Sawoniuk] since I was nine or ten. He bred pigeons and as children we used to play. . . . [I]n the summer we used to wash in the stream near his house. I therefore used to meet him almost daily. . . . But [h]e became a man of power, a master, a lord, and I was a Jew. . . . He used to behave cruelly whenever he wanted and with whomsoever he wanted.[11]

Barlas, the victim in Count 4, was also a friend of Blustein. Blustein remembered how the Germans had detained and interrogated Barlas before handing him over to Sawoniuk and other police officers. A few days later, Sawoniuk told Blustein that "Barlas was very courageous"[12] and that they would soon meet again "in the next world."[13] Blustein never saw Barlas again. He did not actually see Barlas being killed or see Sawoniuk do the killing.

The Defense Moves to Stay the Proceedings

Hearing the case was Mr. Justice Francis Humphrey Potts. On the High Court since 1986, Potts was sixty-seven years old, and held a reputation for being strict in controlling the proceedings in his courtroom. Sawoniuk's defense team was headed by barrister William Clegg, QC. Queen's Counsel are senior barristers who have earned the designation of "QC." Because they wear silk robes in court, they are also known as "Silks." The title of Queen's Counsel is usually held by about 10 percent of the practicing bar, which included Clegg, who became a QC in 1991.

Clegg, then in his late forties, is a highly sought-out criminal defense barrister. He was likely chosen by Sawoniuk because of his success in getting a stay of prosecution for Serafinowicz. The prosecution team was headed by Sir John Nutting, QC, whose clients included the Queen, and who was ranked number 27 in a 2007 *Times* of London list of the "UK's most high profile lawyers." Nutting and Clegg had faced each other before as prosecution and defense barristers in the Serafinowicz case.

Clegg's first act on behalf of his client was to file a motion to stay the proceedings, seeking a result akin to that he achieved for Serafinowicz. In this case, however, unlike in *Regina v. Serafinowicz*, Clegg did not argue that Sawoniuk was not competent to stand trial. Rather, he contended that because the events in question took place so long ago it was impossible for Sawoniuk to get a fair trial under standards of English justice. Specifically, Clegg argued that Sawoniuk would be unable to find witnesses that could exculpate him, either because they had died since the events in question, or could not be located more than fifty years later. Lapse of time, Clegg also contended, likewise prevented Sawoniuk from obtaining documents that could exculpate him. In effect, Clegg was arguing that Nazi war criminals discovered today could not be prosecuted in England because such prosecution presents insurmountable challenges to the defense case, making it impossible for a defendant accused of Nazi-era crimes to receive a fair trial.

Mr. Justice Potts rejected Clegg's motion. As to unavailability of witnesses, he held that whether their absence was detriment or a bonus to the defense was entirely speculative. As to the witnesses presented by the prosecution, their reliability could be tested by the defense through a vigorous cross-examination. With regard to documentary evidence, he also held that the reliability of the documents could be tested within the trial process. The judge also noted that prosecution of Nazi war criminals for events taking place during the Second World War would invariably pose special challenges, and yet he was mandated by English law to conduct such a trial. Or to put it another way, as the appellate court later pointed out, it "must have been obvious to Parliament when passing the legislation that these types of evidentiary difficulties would arise."[14]

The Trial

When his trial began, Sawoniuk was "deaf in one ear and nearly blind in one eye. He [was] diabetic. He suffer[ed] from heart disease and high blood pressure. Some years ago . . . he underwent electroconvulsive therapy for a mental condition."[15] His appearance in court and demeanor, however, belied this description given by the Court of Appeal. Sociologist David Hirsh, who sat through the entire trial, describes Sawoniuk this way:

> [Sawoniuk] was, in many senses, an ordinary man. Physically, he was not tall. Aged 78 at the time of his trial, he had white hair, which was carefully barbered, and a round baby face with blue-grey eyes peering through his up-to-date glasses. He was always dressed smartly, in a

> blazer, creased trousers, and shiny shoes, like the old Polish soldier and British Rail ticket collector that he was. He limped, and used a stick, but did not seem particularly fragile. He seemed to be a man who knew how to look after himself. He sat in court next to his solicitors, not in the dock, since he was on bail. He followed the transcript of the proceedings as it appeared on the laptop computer in front of him. He occasionally whispered, rather loudly, perhaps because of his partial deafness, to his solicitors. They seemed friendly and called him Tony. Not once in the whole trial did Sawoniuk look to his right towards the press gallery, or to the public above it.[16]

The first step was to empanel a jury. Unlike in an American trial, attorneys in England do not have the right to conduct the process known as *voir dire,* whereby they question potential jurors regarding their background and have the right to exclude a certain number of jurors for no cause at all, and others for cause by convincing the judge that keeping a certain juror would be detrimental to their case. Considering the nature of the case, however, Mr. Justice Potts did announce that if they or their family had suffered from "German actions against Jewish or other races or religions" they should inform the court and would be excused. None of the eight men and four women responded, and so the trial went forward. As far as we are aware, none of the jurors were Jewish.

In his opening statement, Nutting made it clear to the jury that Sawoniuk was eager to join the local police force in Domachevo. He also informed the jury that Sawoniuk originally denied being a member of the police force, but later conceded this point prior to the start of trial. Nutting declared that the prosecution's case would be based on eyewitness testimony, and that the witnesses would testify as to crimes that had taken place more than a half-century ago. And though Nutting conceded it was entirely possible for witnesses in an ordinary criminal trial to have faulty memories after such an enormous time lapse, he argued that the lapse of time might work here in the prosecution's favor. Here, instead of time creating faulty memories, Nutting proposed that the witnesses could still remember actions committed by Sawoniuk because "they describe events which are literally unforgettable . . . which once witnessed would remain fixed in a man's memory for his life."[17]

In his defense opening address, Clegg proposed a far different scenario. He first rhetorically asked the jurors: "If an orphaned teenager was asked to join the local police, you may describe him as a willing volunteer, but can we just think what other employment the teenager may have open to him as a career under German occupation?"[18] The defense portrayed Sawoniuk as being painted into a corner; it was either work for the local police force and guard against partisans or run the risk of being deported into forced labor or living life on the run.

The Case for the Prosecution

The prosecution's first witness was the renowned American Holocaust scholar Christopher Browning. With Browning's help, Nutting set forth before the jurors the Nazi ideology that fueled the Holocaust and the Second World War. Nutting's approach and strategy was well organized. He would have Professor Browning, as his expert witness, set out a roadmap of the Nazis' Final Solution, and in particular the murder operations conducted by the Germans and local collaborators against the Jews in German-occupied Soviet Union. He would then follow with eyewitness accounts of how these murder measures were conducted in Domachevo and subsequently identify Sawoniuk as one these local murderers.

Fedor Zan, the next witness, would provide the first part of his testimony not in the London courtroom, but in Belarus. To inspect the crime scene, the proceedings were moved to Domachevo, eleven hundred miles away, where for four days the court entourage and reporters toured the various places where the alleged killings took place. The trip to Domachevo was a first in the history of English criminal procedure; the only other time that a British court convened outside the country was for the inquest in the death of Princess Diana in Paris. Sawoniuk, on the other hand, stayed in London, even though the trip to Domachevo was made at the request of the defense. Clegg argued that the extensive sets of maps and photos the prosecution would be introducing at trial would still not be sufficient to give jurors a feel for the place.

The group arrived to subzero temperatures which reached -14°F. One of the first stops was the site of the old police station and the former ghetto. There, Nutting pointed out the area where Baglay stated he stood fifty-seven years ago where, at age thirteen, he reportedly saw Sawoniuk shoot two Jewish men and one Jewish woman, constituting Count 1 of the indictment.

In another stop, Nutting pointed out to the jurors where Count 2 of the indictment had allegedly occurred: the woods where, according to witness Ivan Stepaniuk, Sawoniuk reportedly struck Schlemko with a shovel before marching him off into the forest and killing him.

The group also traveled to where Ben Zion Blustein would claim he witnessed the Germans hand over Mir Barlas, a local Jew, to Sawoniuk, relevant to Count 4. Other stops included interviewing on video witnesses who were too old and feeble to travel to England. The video testimony would be shown to the jurors back in court. Clegg recalls this trip as being a "surreal experience. [I can] remember quite literally walking through knee-high snow to a cottage in pitch dark, hammering on the door and going in with cameras and taking evidence from this old woman who was sitting in front of a fire with a cat on her lap, about things that had happened 60 years before."[19]

The trip concluded with viewing the crime scene for Count 3, with witness Zan leading the jury through the forest from his sister's place to where he saw Sawoniuk force fifteen Jewish women to undress before mowing them down with a machine gun into a pit. Mr. Justice Potts and the jury followed in single file line "trudging briskly through the thick layer of snow."[20]

Along the way Zan stopped on three separate occasions. The first stop was to show the jury where he was when he first heard the cries of women. The second was to demonstrate where he hid once he realized what was going on. The final stop was to show where Sawoniuk stood while this was going on. The critical issue was whether Zan was able to make an accurate identification of Sawoniuk from his place of hiding. From this demonstration, the prosecution and defense stipulated that Zan stood about 127–128 paces from the spot he supposedly saw Sawoniuk shooting the women, quite a distance.

Upon returning to the Old Bailey, the next witness was Ben Zion Blustein, the only Jewish witness to testify at trial. Blustein, seventy-six, was a year younger than Sawoniuk, his former childhood friend. At age nineteen, he was one of the few Jews from Domachevo to survive by hiding during the Yom Kippur massacre and then surreptitiously joining a group of Jews spared by the Germans to serve as forced laborers in the aftermath of the massacre. After the war, he immigrated to Israel and became a building contractor. He was now retired and living in Jerusalem.

Blustein was a difficult witness. Rather than just answering Nutting's questions on direct examination, he had a story to tell and insisted on telling it. Accordingly, the court had to repeatedly remind Blustein, who testified in Hebrew through an interpreter, to only answer questions that were asked of him and not go into narratives when there was not a question of legal significance pending. Hirsh observed that Blustein "claimed too much . . . he did not trust the court to assess his evidence."[21]

Blustein's testimony demonstrates the perils of having actual survivors of a genocide, whether the Holocaust or another mass atrocity, testify about the event, and especially many years after the events in question. Hirsh, in the chapter on the Sawoniuk trial in his *Cosmopolitan Trials* book, ably dissects the difficulties of transforming Holocaust memory into admissible testimony in courts of common law jurisdictions. Using Blustein's testimony as a typical example of such difficulties, he points out:

> Giving evidence in any criminal trial, especially for victims of the crime, must always be difficult. Holocaust survivors are accustomed to being in control of the presentation of their memoir and to being listened to by a supportive audience. For a survivor, the demand that the court makes, that it be allowed to take control of the presentation of memoir, to challenge it and to transform it into what it considers to be evidence, must be particularly difficult. [In this case,] Blustein resisted the court's mechanisms and tried to retain control over his own testimony.[22]

Blustein testified about how Sawoniuk joined the German-organized police force and the police's role in the persecution and eventual murder of the Domachevo Jews. But the bulk of his testimony was personal, focusing on his fate as well as the fate of his family and other Jews. Sawoniuk was at most a minor character in his account, and his name was not mentioned until Blustein had already been on the stand for hours, and even then only in passing. That, of course, was not what

Nutting wanted: his aim was to convict Sawoniuk and not to provide the jury the horrid details of the fate of the Domachevo Jews, or what happened to Blustein's family. It was only towards the end of Blustein's direct examination, after many hours of testimony, that Nutting was able to get him specifically to focus on the facts surrounding the allegations in Count 4: the murder of Mir Barlas.

Next came Clegg's cross-examination. For Blustein, the process of being grilled by an experienced criminal defense barrister aiming to discredit him must have seemed at times unbearable. Clegg first focused on the inconsistencies of Blustein's statements from testimony given in court as well as previous statements that dated back to 1944. He next focused on the fact that Blustein never mentioned Mir Barlas' death to British police when first questioned in 1995 in Israel. There is also no mention of Mir Barlas in Blustein's published memoir. He also never mentioned the murder of Barlas during his 1944 interrogation by the Soviets. Most critically, he conceded that he never actually saw Sawoniuk kill Mir Barlas.

The next critical witness was Alexander Baglay, whose testimony formed the basis for Count 1: the murder of an unknown Jewish woman and her compatriots that Baglay witnessed when he and his friend came to the ghetto after the massacre to scavenge for clothing. As Hirsh points out: "[O]f the four counts, [Count 1] was by far the strongest. [Alexander] Baglay had witnessed Sawoniuk kill three people; he had known Sawoniuk, and he had been close to him as the murder was committed."[23]

BAGLAY: [. . .]Andrusha ordered them to undress. The men were about 40. They undressed. The woman, about 28, was reluctant to take her pants off. Andrusha insisted. Andrusha threatened her with a beating. The Jews were emaciated and unshaven. Andrusha shot the Jews in the back of the head.

[Alexander Baglay explains that he and his friend were told to bury the bodies, and told that they could take the clothes.]

NUTTING: Who shot the Jews?

BAGLAY: Andrusha.

NUTTING: With what?

BAGLAY: With the pistol, in the back of the head.

NUTTING: Did they fall into the pit?
BAGLAY: Yes. One after the other.[24]

With Baglay standing only feet away, there were no identification issues. Rather, the sole issue the jury faced with his account was whether or not they found him to be a credible witness.

The next significant witness, Ivan Stepaniuk, gave testimony to prove Count 2, the murder of Schlemko a few days after the main massacre. As noted earlier, Stepaniuk recounted seeing Sawoniuk with other policemen leading Schlemko away towards the woods, with Sawoniuk beating him all the while and Schlemko constantly falling to the ground. After Stepaniuk lost sight of the group, he heard a gunshot. Sawoniuk and the other officers then emerged from the woods with rifles and shovels; Schlemko was noticeably absent. On cross-examination, Clegg was able to show that Stepaniuk did not in fact know who Sawoniuk was when he witnessed Schlemko being dragged away.

The next witness was the seventy-five-year-old Fedor Zan, the sole witness for Count 3. As noted earlier, Zan had been walking in the woods when he heard faint cries and screams in the distance. When he came closer, he testified, he saw Sawoniuk with a machine gun shouting orders at a group of fifteen women and then shooting all of them.

Clegg sought to discredit Zan's testimony by showing his bias against Sawoniuk. Zan conceded that his uncle and cousin had been partisans, and had been killed by the local police. Zan believed that Sawoniuk was one of the killers, but this murder allegation was not part of the criminal case against Sawoniuk.

During the prosecution's case, other locals testified about Sawoniuk's role as policeman and the brutal way that he conducted himself. One witness testified about an incident when Sawoniuk discovered a young Jewish woman trying to smuggle potatoes into the ghetto, and beat her savagely. Since assault was not a prosecutable offense under the War Crimes Act, Sawoniuk could not be charged for this incident.

The Defense Case

At the end of the case for the prosecution, Clegg motioned to dismiss Count 2 (murder of Barlas, as testified to by Blustein) and Count 4 (murder of Schlemko, as testified by Stepaniuk). Since the only evidence presented for these murders was the testimony of one witness for each murder, and since neither witness actually saw the killings, Mr. Justice Potts dismissed both counts.

At this point, odds appeared to favor Clegg being able to obtain a complete acquittal of his client. Both of the other two alleged murders dealt with victims whose names were unknown, and each was based entirely, like the dismissed counts, on testimony of just one witness, Alexander Baglay for Count 1 and Fedor Zan for Count 3. Each witness had testified about events that occurred over a half-century earlier and, just as critical, neither witness ever related these events prior to Sawoniuk's prosecution.

Everything pointed, therefore, to Sawoniuk not taking the stand by exercising his right to silence. It appears, however, that he insisted on testifying to rebut the charges against him. This proved to be a grave error.

On the stand, Sawoniuk admitted that he joined the local police force voluntarily and rose to a senior rank. This, however, was the extent of his admission. He denied that Jews were confined to the ghetto; he denied being present for the Yom Kippur massacre; he denied committing any acts of brutality or murder against Jews; he even denied knowing the eyewitnesses who testified they had known him. In his own words:

> I have done no crime whatsoever. My conscience is clear. I killed no-one. I would not dream of doing it. I am not a monster. . . . Everyone is telling lies. They have been told by the Russian KGB to say there was a ghetto. These devils came here with their lies against me. . . . I have nothing to hide. My conscience is clear and when I am dead, I am going to heaven.[25]

After Clegg's brief direct examination of Sawoniuk, Nutting proceeded to take apart his statements. It was not hard, since Sawoniuk continued to deny even historical facts, such as the existence of the Domachevo ghetto. He also denied being a German soldier.[26] When asked about the *Waffen-SS* document discovered in the German archives and providing detailed information about him, including his former wife's name, Sawoniuk claimed that it was a forgery, created either by the KGB or Scotland Yard. As the cross-examination progressed, Sawoniuk's lack of credibility must have become apparent to the jurors. When Nutting pressed the issue of whether or not an officer could leave the police force without fear of retaliation, he used Sawoniuk's brother as proof that there was indeed a choice. When pressed as to why his brother had left, Sawoniuk responded, "[Nikolai] didn't want to do things like hitting people or killing people." He then tried to mitigate the damage of his statement by testifying that his brother never told him why he left the police force but that his brother "didn't like the idea that the Jews didn't have their freedom."[27]

Closing arguments followed the defense case. Sawoniuk's testimony on the stand made Clegg's job more difficult. In his closing statement, he relied on a conspiracy theory to cast doubt on the prosecution witnesses. He reminded the jurors that none of the incidents which lead to the four counts were initially reported to the British War Crimes Unit. Instead, they slowly evolved after the witnesses knew who the suspect was; and as Clegg pointed out, all of the eyewitnesses, with the exception of Blustein, were from Borisy. Though the witnesses from Borisy were not Jewish, residents of the town at the time of German occupation were considered to be aligned with the partisans rather than with the German occupiers. Here before them was Sawoniuk, a self-proclaimed partisan hunter from the town where all but one of the eyewitnesses had lived. This was not mere coincidence, argued Clegg, but rather carefully planned revenge. Sawoniuk's trial in London finally gave the elderly former partisans from Borisy and their sympathizers an opportunity to hold someone accountable for the pain and tragedy they endured during the German occupation.

In his summing up, Mr. Justice Potts explained to the jury the heart of their upcoming deliberations:

> The stark issue in this case is one of fact. The Crown's case is that the defendant was a willing executioner of Nazi policy, that he shot the Jewesses referred to in count one and count [three]. The defendant's case is one of complete denial of either of these charges. He admits to being a policeman, but he says: "At all times I was a friend of the Jews." The witnesses, he says, who gave evidence against him are liars in league with the KGB and Scotland Yard. There is the issue, and it is for you to resolve it.[28]

The Verdict

During the prosecution's case, one of the female jurors fell ill and it was determined she would be out for at least a week. Ultimately, Mr. Justice Potts decided to proceed with eleven jurors considering they were already weeks into trial.

On April 1, 1999, exactly three years after Sawoniuk was first interviewed by the War Crimes Unit of Scotland Yard, the eleven-person jury returned to the wood-paneled courtroom with a verdict. After deliberating for fourteen hours over a period of three days, it found Sawoniuk guilty of both of the remaining counts.

To Count 1, the murder of two Jewish men and one Jewish woman, though the charge only made reference to a Jewish woman, the verdict was unanimous. To Count 3, the verdict was guilty by a majority of 10–1. The lack of unanimity was of no legal consequence; English law since 1967 has allowed criminal juries to return verdicts by a margin as low as 10 to 2, so long as the jury deliberates at least two hours.

One thing appears clear: Sawoniuk was convicted on the slimmest of evidence, consisting of uncorroborated testimony of just one witness for each of the murder counts. And though the acts occurred 56 years ago, neither witness had told their story prior to being interviewed by British investigators a half-century later. With the evidence they had, it would not have been surprising if the jury had acquitted Sawoniuk.

Why did the jury convict? We can only speculate, but it appears that when it finally came down to it, the jury believed Alexander Baglay and Fedor Zan and did not believe Anton Sawoniuk. One can only wonder whether this *Rashomon*-type clash of factual accounts would have been resolved differently by the jurors if Sawoniuk had not taken the stand or, upon doing so, had not denied all, including historical facts. Perhaps if he had been more forthcoming during his time on the stand, admitting additional facts beyond his admission on the eve of trial that he in fact served as a policeman, the jury might have found him more believable.

Former BBC correspondent Jon Silverman, who covered the trial, recalls a point during the cross-examination when Nutting asked Sawoniuk about his having served in the *Waffen-SS*. Sawoniuk not only denied doing so, he also lost his temper. Rage filled his face. To Silverman, the rage that Sawoniuk suddenly exhibited brought into the courtroom "Andrusha the policeman" who could have committed the mass killings testified to by Baglay and Zan, as well as the other killings and assaults that other witnesses had recounted before the jury.[29]

Sentencing

On April 1, 1999, Mr. Justice Potts sentenced Sawoniuk to life imprisonment. At age seventy-eight, Sawoniuk was one of the oldest persons to have been convicted of murder in Britain. At the hearing, the judge spoke directly to Sawoniuk:

> No word of mine can add anything of value to those already written and spoken about the events in which you played a part. I only say this, that though you held a lowly rank in the hierarchy of those involved in liquidating Jews in Eastern Europe, to the Jews of Domachevo it must have seemed otherwise. [One witness] said of you that when you became a policeman you became a man of power, a master and a lord. I am sure from the evidence that we have heard in this trial that he was right when he said that. You have been convicted of charges properly brought, you have had a fair trial, no jury could have given closer attention to the issues raised by this case than the one that has tried you. You have been convicted of 2 charges of murder on clear evidence in my judgment. I pass upon you the sentence fixed by law on each count, which is one of life imprisonment.[30]

The sentencing phase of *Regina v. Sawoniuk* did not pass without additional drama. In England, a life sentence for murder must be confirmed by the home secretary, who takes into account the requirements of retribution and general deterrence. Before doing so, however, the home secretary receives recommendations from the trial judge and the lord chief justice. The home secretary then sets a so-called "tariff"—the minimum amount of time a life-term defendant must spend in jail before being considered for parole. In this case, Mr. Justice Potts recommended that Sawoniuk should die in jail. In his report, he wrote: "Given the defendant's age and the nature of the offences, to release him before his death would, in my opinion, defeat the purpose of the War Crimes Act."[31] The lord chief justice, Lord Bingham, disagreed. He wrote:

> The judge's view is plainly a tenable, and perhaps preferable, approach to this unique case, and he has had the experience of living with these harrowing facts for weeks. An alternative approach, to which I myself incline, is that general deterrence has little part in this sentence and retribution must be moderated when delayed for nearly 60 years and visited on a man approaching the age of 80.[32]

Lord Bingham in turn recommended a tariff of five years. After the below-discussed appeals were exhausted, Jack Straw, the home secretary, ultimately agreed with Mr. Justice Potts and rejected Lord Bingham's recommendation. He decided that Sawoniuk should die in prison.

Appeals

Sawoniuk appealed to the Court of Appeal. In 2000, a three-judge appellate panel, headed by Lord Bingham, unanimously affirmed the conviction.[33] In its decision, the Court of Appeal did not grant leave for Sawoniuk to appeal to the Law Committee of the House of Lords, the predecessor body to the current Supreme Court of the United Kingdom. Consequently, Sawoniuk made his last challenge by going outside Britain and appealing to the European Court of Human Rights (ECtHR). Because the U.K. is a member of the Council of Europe and a party to the Council's European Convention of Human Rights (ECHR), a criminal defendant from a state party who has exhausted his domestic remedies can appeal to the ECtHR by arguing that the state party violated a provision of the ECHR in the course of prosecuting the defendant.

Before the ECtHR, Clegg argued that his client's right to a fair trial, guaranteed by Article 6 of the ECHR, was violated by British authorities. He also argued that Britain's imposition of a mandatory life sentence upon his elderly and frail client also violated Articles 3 and 5 of the Convention as being arbitrary and disproportional. In May 2001, a seven-judge panel of the ECtHR unanimously rejected these contentions.[34] The ECtHR found that the large gap of time between the crime and its prosecution does not necessarily make the trial unfair, especially since under international law no statute of limitations exists for war crimes. It concluded:

> This Court finds that no issue can arise under Article 6 insofar as the jury was left to decide for itself whether the evidence dating back to events in 1943 was credible and reliable. As the Court of Appeal pointed out, the key evidence in the case did not concern the purported identification, years after the event, of a suspected perpetrator of war crimes but the recollection by witnesses of shocking events, likely to have made a deep impact, which involved a person whom they already knew. . . . In conclusion, the Court finds, on examination of the complaints individually and taken together, that the applicant was not deprived of a fair trial within the meaning of Article 6 § 1. These complaints must therefore be rejected as being manifestly ill-founded. . . .[35]

On the morning of November 6, 2005, at age eighty-four, Anthony Sawoniuk died in Norwich prison of heart failure due to natural causes. He had been jailed for over six and a half years.

The Aftermath

As noted earlier, the War Crimes Act was a highly controversial piece of legislation, becoming law only by the House of Commons having to overrule the majority of the House of Lords. As a result, the law always seemed to be under strict scrutiny.

In the month following Sawoniuk's conviction, the commissioner of the Metropolitan Police announced that the War Crimes Unit was being disbanded for "operational" reasons. He added that the unit had become redundant because the police had "no more leads for the police to investigate."[36] Other units of the police could still investigate war crimes arising out of the Second World War, but only if information was brought to the police's attention. The latter statement was a mere formality. The death knell for further prosecutions sounded clear when the Met concurrently announced that it would begin to limit the War Crimes Act in its application. As noted by Cesarani in 2001:

> Although the War Crimes Act was intended to apply to anyone suspected of "grave violations of the laws and customs of war committed in German held territory during the second world war," in practice it was modified to restrict its scope dramatically. At a press conference

> in March 1999, following the conviction of Sawoniuk, a spokesman for the Met explained the criteria for the prosecution. In addition to safe identification and solid eye-witnesses, "proof that the defendant was in a position of command responsibility [was] also an important factor in deciding on the defendant's culpability." Sawoniuk met this standard, but others who were equally as guilty of mass murder did not. The exclusion of those who were not officers indicates that a decision was quietly made by law officers, presumably in concert with the Home Office, to ignore so-called "small fry" no matter how bloody their hands.[37]

Cost appears also to have been a major consideration. During its existence, it cost at least £1.5 million per year to run the unit. The total cost of trying Sawoniuk was £6.5 million.

Though the War Crimes Act 1991 remains technically on the books, the noble enterprise of prosecuting Nazi collaborators who "committed [war crimes] during the period beginning 1st September 1939 and ending with 5th June 1945 in a place which at the time was part of Germany or under German occupation" is over. Even if an aging Nazi war criminal was discovered today living in Britain, that person would be eighty-five or older. Unlike Germany, which is still willing to prosecute such geriatric Nazis or collaborators, or the United States, which is willing to denaturalize and deport them, the British appear uninterested in taking either course of action. The usual reason given is that these individuals are too feeble to assist in their defense and to undertake the rigors of a trial. It is an especially strange answer coming from Britain, where, as of 2010, forty-three peers over eighty-five years old serve in the House of Lords, helping to run the United Kingdom.

The "small fry" exclusion from prosecution that Cesarani criticized in 2001 continues a decade later. According to Cesarani, writing in 2010, "The collaborators in the U.K. who were identified in previous investigations are 'small fry' and the Government has not departed from its policy of only prosecuting those in command responsibility. Age and infirmity will always be an obstacle, more so if the alleged perpetrator was 'merely' taking orders."[38]

Here we must recall the words from the Hetherington-Chalmers Report that led to the passage of the War Crimes Act: "The crimes committed are so monstrous that they cannot be condoned: their prosecution could act as a deterrent to others in future wars. To take no action would taint the U.K. with the slur of being a haven for war criminals."[39] Britain's decision to prosecute only two individuals under the act—Sawoniuk and Serafanowicz—sadly turns that slur into a fact.

In June 2014 came a shocker when Stephen Ankier, a London-based, retired pharmacologist who researches Nazi crimes, discovered through a search of German, Polish, and British archives that an SS soldier who had helped murder thousands of Jews and ethnic Poles had lived undetected in London for sixty-six years. Ukrainian-born Serhij Woronyj served with an SS brigade involved in atrocities committed against Jews and Polish civilians, including putting down the Warsaw Uprising in 1944. Captured by the British in 1945, Woronyj entered Britain in 1947 as part of a group of eight thousand POWs who came as laborers and then were summarily freed by the authorities without conducting any serious search of their wartime activities. Woronyj married, had a daughter, and worked as a printer before dying of a heart attack in 2013.

What lessons can be learned? The Serafinowicz imbroglio illustrates that speedy prosecutions are essential for Holocaust-era war crime prosecutions, since any still-living culprits will be of advanced age. It also illustrates another important point: time is always to the advantage of a suspected war criminal. For example, such notorious post-Holocaust atrocities as the Rwandan genocide of 1994 and the mass murders and rapes in Bosnia in the early 1990s after the disintegration of Yugoslavia were committed two decades ago. This means that the perpetrators are now middle-aged and beyond, especially the elder leaders who instigated their younger compatriots to commit such crimes. If such perpetrators follow the route taken by the Nazi war criminals and find haven in Britain—as already has been done by perpetrators of the 1994 Rwandan genocide[40]—without being promptly prosecuted or deported, these modern-era perpetrators will also be able to rely on claims of ill health as a means of obtaining immunity. We may, therefore, find history repeating itself. Just like the hundreds of Nazi war criminals that found refuge in Britain without justice being meted out to them, perpetrators of modern-era atrocities likewise will be able to escape justice.

"Late but not too late." 2013 poster campaign in Germany seeking information on surviving Nazi war criminals. Simon Wiesenthal Center.

Conclusion

The ten Holocaust trials featured in this book span well over a half-century, from the Kharkov trial in 1943 to the Sawoniuk trial in 1999. Discussing them in one work illuminates at least a small portion of the wide-ranging legal enterprise that has taken place over the last several decades to deny impunity to the participants of the largest and most successful conspiracy of mass murder in history. Such efforts involved thousands of trials, but like the ten "forgotten trials" reviewed here, this enormous legal enterprise has largely been ignored.

This disregard is not only among the educated public. Historians of the Holocaust and other serious scholars have explored the most esoteric of subjects and events that took place in Europe during the Nazi era and thereafter, and yet, for the most part, have neglected the role of the law in confronting the horrors of Nazism. As legal historian David Fraser notes: "[W]ith few exceptions, the entire jurisprudential history of the prosecution of Nazi war criminals remains a matter of deep ignorance and neglect among Anglo-American scholars."[1]

This neglect is unfortunate since these trials illuminate much about the Holocaust. Most importantly, one crucial theme runs throughout them—no defendant denied the underlying facts. Since many of these defendants faced the death penalty and the rest faced lengthy terms of imprisonment up to life imprisonment, they had the greatest incentive to challenge the facts presented at the trials. Literally, these defendants' lives and their liberty were at stake. Notwithstanding this powerful incentive, one aspect all these trials have in common is the absence of such a challenge. Instead, the defenses were of a nature that acknowledged the prosecution's facts but claimed the defendants' ignorance, that the defendants were just following orders, that the defendants were coerced into their complicity in murder, that the victorious allies did the same thing, or, in rare cases, that the defendants were not present when the crimes were committed. Except for Blobel's aberrational claim in the *Einsatzgruppen* trial that only sixteen thousand Jews, not thirty-three thousand, were massacred at Babi Yar, there was never a serious challenge to the facts. Even Hermann Göring did not dispute that there was a policy to exterminate the Jews, he only claimed that he did not know its details.[2] Eichmann's defense was that he knew, but was only following orders.

This fact becomes especially significant as we drift into the era when prosecutions against those who took part in the massive conspiracy depicted in these trials begin to wane because of the age of the potential defendants. Those who survived the Holocaust and can provide direct and personal testimony as to its implementation are also diminishing in number. Revisionism in history is almost inevitable and the pernicious phenomenon of Holocaust denial will not disappear. On the contrary, with the absence of witnesses to the Holocaust and the ability to disseminate even the most improbable of falsehoods through the Internet, Holocaust denial of both the hardcore variety ("There were no gas chambers in Auschwitz" or "Six million Jews did not die") and its soft-core version ("There was no plan to annihilate the Jews" or "Jewish deaths were due to the nature of war itself") will persist, if not grow.[3] While much has been done to ensure that Holocaust denial will be met with hard facts, no facts are more compelling than those illuminated in the trials: the first Nuremberg trial, the Eichmann trial, and the many others, ten of which comprise this book. In each of these trials, the prosecution presented facts, which if true, would have had serious and often lethal consequences for the defendants. The defendants were given the means to challenge the facts and, invariably, they did not. This alone compels that these trials not be forgotten.

There is another theme that runs through these trials: the poison of anti-Semitism that fueled the mass murders. The mass killings in these cases were executed on a deeply personal level. Jews were shot, herded into gas chambers or into trucks to be gassed; they were placed into conditions of starvation and disease; beaten to death—almost invariably, the defendants had personal contact with their victims. (Pierre Laval is the only exception.) In all of these cases, the killings were justified on the ground that it was Jews who were being killed. This cannot have occurred in a vacuum; the history of anti-Semitism is measured in millennia and the Holocaust is its ultimate expression. One cannot review the brutal facts of these cases without a sense that those in past generations who kept this venomous hatred alive have some measure of moral culpability for the murder of millions.

Aside from the common thread of the murder of Jews, there are other themes that run through these trials. They reveal the dedication of the prosecutors,[4] lawyers who committed thousands of hours to reviewing documents, often in a language other than their own. In the case of later trials, they worked with old documents and aging witnesses, whose memories were burdened with the passage of time. The IMT lawyers operated under the chaotic conditions of a devastated Europe and had to deal with sometimes hostile Allies with their own agendas.

Putting these cases together was not easy, whether at Nuremberg in the summer and fall of 1945, or fifty-five years later at the Old Bailey, reconstructing homicides that had occurred in the then-Polish town of Domachevo, a town so small that it would appear only on the most detailed of maps. What each of these prosecutors had in common was an incredible commitment to the simple concept of justice. In this sense, we can draw a straight line from Kharkov to Sawoniuk, and find the same thing: hard work, diligence, and true dedication.

Trials take time, and usually much more time is needed for preparation than for the trial itself. In these trials, the emotional burden the witnesses endured to relive their most suppressed memories also overlay the proceedings. This presented a reality that both the prosecutor and witnesses had to deal with in an effort to emerge with a credible and viable case. To expect witnesses to testify to their experiences as survivor-victims without hate is asking for almost superhuman ability—but hate can cloud judgment as well as the memory of events. If the SS uniform embodied for them repeated and unimaginable torment, then could survivors be expected to remember accurately whether it was SS officer A or B who shot someone in the back of the head or herded someone off a train? Yet trials demand detail and precision, and it is up to prosecutors to work through anything that might cloud a witness's testimony, rendering the witness less than credible. Almost all prosecutions of Nazi-era crimes had such hurdles to overcome.

Likewise, the importance of defense lawyers should not be underplayed, since it is their passionate representation of their clients that often constitutes the best measure for determining the fairness of the proceedings. Ordinarily, one does not go to law school to defend mass murderers. But all of the defense counsel in these cases undertook their responsibilities seriously and skillfully, with perhaps the exception of Amon Göth's attorneys. Even with hindsight it is difficult to second-guess the strategies defense counsel chose and to say with any certainty that they erred. While trying to get concentration camp survivors to give precise dates and times for atrocities they witnessed may border on harassment (calendars and watches were not distributed at the death camps), defense counsel had the right to pursue such lines of examination to effectuate an alibi defense. The vigorous defense almost all of these lawyers provided is the absolute predicate for any larger assessment on the fairness of the proceedings.

While threads of uniformity run through the victim, perpetrator, and trial counsel components of these cases, that is *not* so with respect to the presiding judges. In this one aspect, the trials discussed in this book present a varied picture of the judicial actors who oversaw these efforts at post-Holocaust justice. We have seen the English court's deep commitment to law in the Sawoniuk case, the comparably deep commitment by the presiding American judge to get at pertinent facts in the *Einsatzgruppen* trial, and the sensitivity of Israeli judges to the extremely marginal nature of criminality in the *kapo* cases. At the other end of the spectrum, we have observed the narrow vision of the German court in the Auschwitz trial, the outright hostility of an American judge to the prosecution in the Fedorenko case, and the total indifference to process by the French judiciary in the trial of Laval.

An additional phenomenon covering the period of these ten trials, from 1943 to 1999, is the progressive formation of public memory of the Holocaust. During the war, there was no specific term used to describe the mass murders of the Jews. In the first Nazi war crimes trial in Kharkov in 1943, the word "Jew" is not even mentioned, though the victims of the perpetrators were mostly Jews. Despite all the evidence of a deliberate, state-sponsored agenda to annihilate the Jewish people that emerged at the trials beginning in 1945, only gradually did the worldwide public grasp the nature of the mass murders as more than a war crime or a crime against humanity, but as a genocide directed against a specific people—the Jews. While the word "holocaust" predates the war and was used in various contexts to describe some kind of tragedy, natural or manmade, the term "Holocaust" (with a capital H) only began to be used in public discourse as referring to the special tragedy of the Jews at the hands of the German and Austrian Nazis and their collaborators in the 1960s. Deborah Liptstadt traces the widespread adoption of "Holocaust" to the Eichmann trial: "It had already been used before the trial, including in the official translation of the Israeli Declaration of Independence. However, it was cemented into the lexicon of the non-Hebrew-speaking population when the court translators used it throughout the trial."[5]

The longevity of the process described in these trials should not be overlooked. The first trial (Kharkov) took place in 1943; the last, covered in this volume (Sawoniuk) in 1999. This fifty-six-year span of prosecutions and longer is as unprecedented as the underlying crime.

On March 2012, what is probably the last significant Nazi war crimes prosecution came to an end. In May 2011, John Demjanjuk was found guilty in a Munich courtroom for his role as an auxiliary guard at the Sobibor death camp,[6] where he was implicated in the murder of twenty-seven thousand persons, almost all Jews. According to the German court: "The guards knew exactly what would happen to the people arriving at the camp, from everyday abuse to gruesome murders. . . . [Duties rotated around the camp] so that every single guard would be involved in all parts of the process."[7] The court sentenced Demjanjuk to five years' imprisonment. Because the ninety-one-year-old defendant was not considered a flight risk, the court allowed him to remain free pending appeal. In March 2012, he died in a nursing home in Bavaria with his appeal still pending.

A case similar to Demjanjuk's ended in 2010, also with the death of the accused. In November 2010, eighty-nine-year-old Samuel Kunz, a former German concentration camp guard and one of the world's most-wanted Nazis, (he was number 3 on the Simon Wiesenthal Center's list of most-wanted Nazi war criminals) died in bed while under indictment.[8] Kunz was charged in Germany for murdering ten Jews in Belzec with his own hands and, more generally, for participating in the murders of over half a million Jews in the gas chambers there. His tasks as a German guard at Belzec in 1942–43 involved criminality archetypal of death camp guards: taking victims from trains, pushing them into gas chambers, and throwing victims' bodies into mass graves.[9]

The Demjanjuk conviction emboldened German prosecutors to search for other aging Nazis and collaborators for prosecution. Under the Demjanjuk precedent, it is now possible under German law to prosecute anyone who was involved in the operation of a Nazi death camp as an accessory to murder.[10] In May 2013, German state police arrested ninety-three-year-old Hans Lipschis, the first suspect to face charges as part of the drive launched after the Demjanjuk conviction to track down suspected Auschwitz guards who are believed to be still alive and living in Germany. Two months later, the Simon Wiesenthal Center brought its Nazi-hunting poster campaign, "Operation Last Chance," to Germany. Two thousand posters went up on July 23 in Berlin, Hamburg, and Cologne featuring the ubiquitous photo of the entrance to the Auschwitz-Birkenau death camp and the tagline "Late, But Not Too Late." The Center sought information from the German public about Nazis hiding in their midst, with a €25,000 ($33,000) reward as incentive. "Millions of innocents were murdered by Nazi war criminals. Some of the perpetrators are free and alive," the posters read. "Help us to bring them before a court." Rejecting the argument that passage of time and advanced age calls for some sympathy for the suspects, Efraim Zuroff, the chief Nazi hunter at the Simon Wiesenthal Center, explains: "Don't look at these people and see a frail old man or woman, think of someone who at the height of his physical strength devoted his energy to murdering innocent women and men. These are the last people on Earth deserving any sympathy because they had absolutely no sympathy for their victims."[11] Zuroff once ironically commented: "I sometimes say that I am the only Jew in the world who prays for the health of Nazi war criminals."[12] Shortly after Demjanjuk's death was announced, the *Jerusalem Post* published a lead editorial titled "Demjanjuk and Justice." Quoting Zuroff, the editorial speculated about the future of hunting Nazi war criminals and bringing them to trial:

> Demjanjuk died outside prison walls in a German retirement home while waiting for his appeal to be heard. Understandably, many—particularly

> Holocaust survivors—were disappointed by Demjanjuk's ability to avoid justice. . . . But even within the framework of justice all is not lost. The German court's conviction of Demjanjuk sets an important precedent, notes Efraim Zuroff. . . . In the past it was necessary to prove responsibility for a specific death to convict a Nazi war criminal. According to Germany's Demjanjuk decision, even serving as an accessory to murder is a punishable crime. Zuroff, who spoke to *The Jerusalem Post* from Prague, estimates that about . . . 80 [death camp prison guards] remain alive, about half of whom are still fit enough physically to stand trial. The Simon Wiesenthal Center is offering a 25,000 euro award for information leading to their capture. The hunt goes on, while adhering to the limitations of justice.[13]

It is not very likely that the "Hunt for the Fit Forty" will yield success. Assuming that there were forty such physically fit concentration camp guards alive in early 2012 when Demjanjuk died, this does not necessarily portend more trials. First, the forty must be found in Germany, since no other country today is making any serious efforts to put aging Nazis on trial for their crimes. (The denaturalization/deportation process, as Fedorenko shows, takes years.) Second, the extradited Nazi—or one found living in Germany—is not immediately put on trial. A magistrate must gather evidence and file a report, which is then parsed by the court. Once a case is started, it may take a few years before reaching the trial stage. The likelihood that a defendant at that point will not find a doctor to certify his inability to stand trial because of age and ill health is low. Thus, though the goal of more prosecutions (and the optimism of Nazi hunters like Zuroff) is laudable, it is not likely to be achieved. The legal journey that began in Kharkov most likely ended in Munich; Demjanjuk may well be the last Nazi-era war criminal to be charged with and actually tried for participating in the Holocaust.

Of course, this should not stop prosecutors from trying. In early 2014, German police raided the homes of nine elderly men suspected of serving as SS guards at Auschwitz. Three of the men, aged 88, 92, and 94, were arrested on allegations of having been accessories to murder and taken to a prison hospital. The fates of the other six, whose ages range from 88 to 92, remain uncertain since the raids did not yield sufficient evidence to warrant arrest.

What are we to make then of the efforts to prosecute Nazi war criminals and collaborators? Now that this legal enterprise is coming to an end, a legal reckoning is most apt. Historian Donald McKale in his 2012 study, *Nazis After Hitler: How Perpetrators of the Holocaust Cheated Justice and Truth*,[14] paints a most bleak picture of the project and its legacy.

> [T]he majority of Nazi perpetrators of the Holocaust survived without Hitler into the postwar era, a few briefly and most for many years. . . . Neither the perpetrators nor the world experienced an extensive, badly needed reckoning for what, between 1939 and 1945, nearly physically wiped out an entire people of Europe. Tragically, the post-Holocaust world had little sympathy for the victims and thus little will to punish the perpetrators.[15]

McKale is, of course, correct that of the hundreds of thousands of individuals that participated in the persecution of innocent civilians during the Second World War[16] only a minuscule number ever had to answer for their acts. But what makes the post-Holocaust period different from the aftermath of other earlier genocides in recent history is precisely the commitment over the last seventy years to bring perpetrators to justice. For example, no efforts were even contemplated to bring those responsible to justice after the genocide in 1904–7 in German South-West Africa of the Herero people by colonial Germans.[17] After the Armenian Genocide of 1915–23, several sets of criminal trials took place inside Turkey against the key architects of that genocide, but the defendants were able to avoid punishment by going into exile. Although the Allied leaders threatened to punish Ottoman officials for "crimes against humanity and civilization," lack of political will eventually dashed any hopes for justice.[18]

Legal scholar Mark Drumbl speaks of the "judicialization of World War II atrocities in Europe."[19] The fact that *some* prosecutors around the world had the will to bring aging Nazi perpetrators to justice, rather than allowing them to live out their lives peacefully, today serves as a model for preventing perpetrators of modern-day genocides and other mass atrocities from escaping prosecution. Ongoing prosecutions of the still-living perpetrators of the Khmer Rouge genocide in Cambodia of the 1970s may be an emerging example slightly akin to the post-Holocaust criminal prosecution cases. And, of course, the U.N.-created international tribunals for the former Yugoslavia and Rwanda and the prosecutions of the International Criminal Court in The Hague aim to end the culture of impunity.

In 2012, the prosecutors of the International Criminal Court secured their first conviction. After a three-year trial, fifty-one-year-old former Congolese warlord Thomas Lubanga was found guilty of crimes against humanity for recruiting and deploying child soldiers during a brutal five-year ethnic conflict in the Ituri region, the eastern part of the Democratic Republic of Congo, which ended in 2003 after an estimated sixty thousand people had been killed.

In 2008, Sudan's President Omar Hassan al-Bashir became the first head of state to be indicted by the ICC. In the press conference announcing the indictment, ICC prosecutor Luis Moreno-Ocampo explained why he was seeking to indict al-Bashir for genocide in the following terms: "These 2.5 million people are in camps [and] have no more water, no more food, no more cattle . . . [al-Bashir's forces] don't need gas chambers because the desert will kill them."[20] Moreno-Ocampo's gas chambers reference is an indication of the strong force that prosecutions of Holocaust-era perpetrators hold today in motivating prosecutors not to allow *genocidairies*—even if they are heads of state—to escape with impunity. And while, as of this writing, al-Bashir is still free and holding his seat of power in Sudan, the ICC indictment makes it unlikely that he will be allowed to die peacefully in his own bed. In this connection, these trials establish an important precedent: the passage of years and even decades will not cause the quest for justice to wane. Sowaniuk was prosecuted fifty-seven years after the underlying events. The passage of time is no defense to genocide.

The manifold proceedings in post-Holocaust criminal justice have also taken place in varied courtroom settings: before a full international criminal tribunal represented by the IMT at Nuremberg; quasi-international tribunals applying the international legal principles of Nuremberg and American procedural law in the twelve subsequent Nuremberg proceedings; domestic criminal courts and specially created tribunals staffed with local judges applying local penal statutes and procedures; and even quasi-judicial institutions such as the Jewish "honor courts" in Europe and the *beit din* in Manhattan. It is remarkable, however, that despite differences in both substantive law and procedural rules for each of these trials, their similarities override their differences. In each case, whether we are in a courtroom in Ukraine or Fort Lauderdale, or a displaced persons camp or former concentration camp in Germany, there is evidence of the victims: Jews, but also others, subjected to the imposition of a barbaric massive, organized, state-sponsored conspiracy to commit mass murder on a scale unprecedented in human history. Even though the venues may be different, the underlying story does not change much.

The trials in this book, starting with the Nuremberg ideal as portended in the Kharkov trial and then brought to life in the *Einsatzgruppen,* Dachau, and Ravensbrück trials, are not the end of a process. Current prosecutions for genocide, crimes against humanity, and war crimes, before both modern international criminal tribunals following the Nuremberg model and domestic courts using domestic law, continue to demonstrate that the sense of outrage and the commitment to justice that motivated the lawyers of the 1940s is alive and well. As aptly recognized by Louise Arbour, the former chief prosecutor for the Yugoslav and Rwandan war crimes tribunals, "Collectively, we're linked to Nuremberg. We mention its name every single day."[21]

It is tragic that triggers for prosecutions of genocide and other mass atrocities still exist, that the brutalization of civilian populations and massive theft, rape, and dismemberment of peoples is not just a historical vignette, but part of today's news. At the least, however, the ideas of the 1940s have evolved into a system of justice to deal with some of these crimes. Since the level of deterrence triggered by past prosecutions is virtually unquantifiable, we can only speculate on whether past prosecutions have had broader-reaching effects than just subjecting defendants to the criminal process. That alone, however, is an improvement over where we were seventy years ago, and perhaps that is the best we can hope for.

NOTES

NOTES TO THE INTRODUCTION

1. Michael J. Bazyler is the primary author of chapters 1, 4, 5, 7, and 10. Frank M. Tuerkheimer is the primary author of chapters 2, 3, 6, 8, and 9. Each is individually responsible for the ideas and conclusions drawn in his respective chapters.

2. Roderick Stackelberg and Sally A. Winkle, eds., *The Nazi Germany Sourcebook: An Anthology of Texts* (Routledge, 2002), 340.

3. Hilary Earl, *The Nuremberg Einsatzgruppen Trial, 1945–1958: Atrocity, Law and History* (Cambridge U. Press, 2009), 7. These numbers may have to be revised upward based on the heroic work done by Father Patrick Desbois, whose scouring of the backwaters of Ukraine has uncovered graves that suggest perhaps 1.5 million Jews were shot in Ukraine alone. See generally Patrick Desbois, *Holocaust by Bullets: A Priest's Journey to Uncover the Truth Behind the Murder of 1.5 Million Jews* (Palgrave Macmillan, 2009).

4. Two glaring errors were: the failure to insure that the IMT had jurisdiction over conspiracy to commit war crimes and crimes against humanity—only conspiracy to wage aggressive war was incorporated into the Nuremberg Charter; and the indictment of the senile Gustav Krupp instead of his son Alfried Krupp, who ran the Krupp empire beginning in 1942. The younger Krupp was prosecuted in one of the subsequent American military trials at Nuremberg. See Kevin Jon Heller, *The Nuremberg Military Tribunal and the Origins of International Criminal Law* (Oxford U. Press, 2011), 73.

5. Nevertheless, much of the historiography of the Holocaust began with the IMT trial, where evidence of the extermination of the Jews as a policy was first presented in the courtroom. It is also at the IMT where the estimate that six million Jews of Europe were killed between 1939 and 1945 was first introduced, a number that has withstood critical scrutiny over the years.

6. United Nations, *London Agreement*, Article 6(a).

7. Justice Robert H. Jackson, opening address at the Nuremberg Tribunal, reprinted in 1 U.S. Chief of Counsel for Prosecution of Axis Criminality, Nazi Conspiracy and Aggression 114 (U.S. Govt. Prtg. Off. 1946). Available at http://www.yale.edu/lawweb/avalon/imt/document/nca_vol1/chap_05.htm. For general discussion, see Jonathan A. Bush, "'The Supreme . . . Crime' and Its Origins: The Lost Legislative History of the Crime of Aggression," *Columbia L. Rev.* 102 (2002), 2324–424.

8. Telford Taylor, *Anatomy of the Nuremberg Trials: A Personal Memoir* (Little, Brown, 1992), xi. ("[L]ike so many others, I remained ignorant of the mass

extermination camps in Poland, and the full scope of the Holocaust did not dawn on me until several months later, at Nuremberg.")

9. The entire section (d) of the indictment reads:

> Implementing their "master race" policy, the [Nazi] conspirators joined in a program of relentless persecution of the Jews, designed to exterminate them. Annihilation of the Jews became an official State policy, carried out both by official action and by incitements to mob and individual violence. The conspirators openly avowed their purpose. For example, the defendant Rosenberg stated: "Anti-Semitism is the unifying element of the reconstruction of Germany." On another occasion he also stated: "Germany will regard the Jewish question as solved only after the very last Jew has left the greater German living space. . . . Europe will have its Jewish question solved only after the very last Jew has left the Continent." The defendant Ley declared: "We swear we are not going to abandon the struggle until the last Jew in Europe has been exterminated and is actually dead. It is not enough to isolate the Jewish enemy of mankind—the Jew has got to be exterminated." . . . The defendant Streicher declared: "The sun will not shine on the nations of the earth until the last Jew is dead." These avowals and incitements were typical of the declaration of the Nazi conspirators throughout the course of their conspiracy. The program of action against the Jews included disfranchisement, stigmatization, denial of civil rights, subjecting their persons and property to violence, deportation, enslavement, enforced labor, starvation, murder and mass extermination. The extent to which the conspirators succeeded in their purpose can only be estimated, but the annihilation was substantially complete in many localities of Europe. Of the 9,600,000 Jews who lived in the parts of Europe under Nazi domination, it is conservatively estimated that 5,700,000 have disappeared, most of them deliberately put to death by the Nazi conspirators. Only remnants of the Jewish population of Europe remain.

10. Shawcross's summation can be viewed on the United States Holocaust Memorial Museum website.

11. David Fraser, "Shadows of Law, Shadows of the Shoah: Towards a Legal History of the Nazi Killing Machine," *Oxford J. Legal Studies* 31, no. 4 (2011), 19. In this article Fraser reviews Heller's *Nuremberg Military Tribunal*, the first book about the "other Nuremberg trials": the twelve subsequent trials undertaken by the American military in their occupied zone of Germany in the same Nuremberg courthouse where the IMT trial took place. These trials sought to bring to justice lesser-ranking Nazis than those on the dock at the IMT, and remain, as Fraser points, in "relative obscurity." Ibid., 4. In chapter 6, we cover one of these obscure Nuremberg trials: the prosecution of the German commanders of the *Einsatzgruppen* squads who murdered Jews and other civilians in Soviet territory captured by the German army.

12. One of us, Michael Bazyler, has authored a book that used the term "justice" alongside the word "Holocaust" (Michael J. Bazyler, *Holocaust Justice: The Battle for Restitution in America's Courts* [NYU Press, 2004]), but even there Bazyler speaks

only of "some measure of justice" or some form of "rough justice" or "imperfect justice." See also Michael Marrus, *Some Measure of Justice: The Holocaust Restitution Campaign of the 1990s* (U. Wisconsin Press, 2009); Stuart E. Eizenstat, *Imperfect Justice: Looted Assets, Slave Labor, and the Unfinished Business of World War II* (PublicAffairs, 2003).

13. Henry Weinstein, "Obituary: Simon Wiesenthal," *L.A. Times*, September 20, 2005. (Quoting Michael Berenbaum: "And yet the need for the illusion of justice is so essential to the rebuilding that we need to go forward on it.")

NOTES TO CHAPTER 1

1. Martin Gilbert, *The Second World War: A Complete History* (Holt, rev. ed., 2004), 160. Historian Timothy Snyder rightly labels Nazi Germany's invasion of the Soviet Union "the bloodiest occupation in the history of the world." Timothy Snyder, "Hitler vs. Stalin: Who Killed More?", *New York. Review of Books*, March 10, 2011.

2. David M. Glantz, *Kharkov 1942: Anatomy of a Military Disaster through Soviet Eyes* (Ian Allan, 2010), xi.

3. Yitzhak Arad, "The Destruction of the Jews in German-Occupied Territories of the Soviet Union," in *The Unknown Black Book: The Holocaust in the German-Occupied Soviet Territories*, ed. Joshua Rubenstein and Ilya Altman (Indiana U. Press, 2008), xvi.

4. *The Unknown Black Book*, 99–103 (testimonies of surviving Nazi victims from Kharkov).

5. An Operational Situation Report U.S.S.R. mentioning the execution in Drobitsky Yar has never been located.

6. Hermann Feuer, trans., "Operational Situation Report U.S.S.R. No. 164." http://www.holocaustresearchproject.org/einsatz/situationreport164.html (accessed March 5, 2014).

7. Joshua Rubenstein, "The War and the Final Solution on the Russian Front," in *The Unknown Black Book*, 23. The victims included Grossman's mother, murdered in Grossman's Ukrainian hometown of Berdichev.

8. Arad, "The Destruction of the Jews," xvii.

9. Greg Dawson, *Judgment before Nuremberg: The Holocaust in the Ukraine and the First Nazi War Crimes Trial* (Pegasus Books, 2012).

10. Edmund Stevens, *Russia Is No Riddle* (Greenberg, 1945). For a biography of Stevens, see Cheryl Heckler, *An Accidental Journalist: The Adventures of Edmund Stevens 1934–1945* (U. Missouri Press, 2007).

11. Literally translated from French as "placing on stage." The expression is used to describe the design aspects of a theatre or film production, which essentially means "telling a story."

12. Stevens, *Russia Is No Riddle*, ix.

13. Ibid., 111, 116.

14. Ibid., 112.

15. Ibid., 113.

16. *The People's Verdict: A Full Report of the Proceedings at the Krasnodar and Kharkov German Atrocity Trials* (Hutchinson, 1944), 56.

17. The April 19, 1943, decree reads, in pertinent part:

> 1. To mandate that German, Italian, Romanian, Hungarian and Finnish fascist villains implicated in the killing and torture of the civilian population and captive Red Army soldiers, as well as spies and traitors to the Motherland from among Soviet citizens, be punished by hanging.
>
> 2. Accomplices from among the local population, implicated in assisting the villains and engaging in reprisals and violence against the civilian population and captive Red Army soldiers are punished by hanging or by banishment to penal servitude for terms of 15 to 20 years.
>
> 3. The hearing of cases . . . is assigned to field courts-martial attached to divisions of the regular army and consisting of the chairman of the military tribunal of the division (chairman of the court), the chief of the special department of the division and the deputy commander of the division for political affairs (members of the court), with the participation of the procurator of the division.
>
> 4. The sentences pronounced by the field courts-martial attached to divisions are approved by the commander of the division and put into effect immediately.
>
> 5. Execution of the sentences pronounced by the field courts-martial attached to divisions—hanging for those sentenced to death—is carried out publicly, before a popular audience, and the bodies of those hanged are to be left on the scaffold for several days so that everyone will know what punishment and retribution awaits all those who commit violence and reprisals against the civilian population and betray their Motherland.

18. Alexander Prusin, "Fascist Criminals to the Gallows!: The Holocaust and War Crimes Trials December 1945–February 1946," *Holocaust and Genocide Studies* 17, no. 1 (Spring 2003), 3–4.

19. Ibid. Sovietologist Harold Berman explains that "[d]uring the war, death by hanging was introduced for highly malicious treason." Harold J. Berman, "Principles of Soviet Criminal Law," *Yale L. J.* 56, no. 5 (1947), 823 n.17.

20. The indictment included a description of the atrocities that had been committed, summaries of testimony from the pretrial interrogations of the defendants, statements of witnesses, and findings of the medico-legal experts. The subsequent trial testimony, for the most part, was based on the text of the indictment.

21. Stevens, *Russia Is No Riddle*, 112.

22. George Ginsburgs, "Laws of War and War Crimes on the Russian Front during World War II: The Soviet View," *Soviet Studies* 11, no. 3 (1960), 253, 267.

23. *The People's Verdict*, 64 (testimony of Wilhelm Langheld).

24. Ibid., 65–66.

25. Ibid., 62–63.

26. Stevens, *Russia is No Riddle*, 113.

27. *The People's Verdict*, 68 (testimony of Hans Ritz).

28. Ibid., 71–72.

29. Ibid.

30. Ibid., 77.

31. Ibid., 84–85 (testimony of Mikhail Bulanov).

32. Ibid., 85.

33. Ibid., 88–106.

34. Ibid., 110–11.

35. Ibid., 45 (testimony of Langheld).

36. Ibid., 82 (testimony of Reinhard Retzlaff).

37. At the end of the First World War, the Allies agreed to permit the Germans to prosecute those alleged to have committed war crimes under German criminal law. The subsequent trials were held in the German city of Leipzig and are known as the Leipzig trials. As explained in chapter 6, the failure of German authorities to effectively prosecute, convict, and punish under German law made clear that a similar alternative was out of the question at the end of the Second World War.

38. *The People's Verdict*, 114 (N. K. Dunayev closing statement).

39. Ibid., 116–17

40. Ibid., 117 (N. V. Kommodov closing statement).

41. Ibid., 116.

42. Ibid.

43. Ibid. 117.

44. Ibid., 117–18.

45. Ibid., 118.

46. Ibid., 120.

47. Ibid.

48. Ibid., 118–19.

49. Ibid.

50. Ibid., 120, 123–24.

51. Stevens, *Russia Is No Riddle*, 115.

52. Ibid., 115–16.

53. Arieh J. Kochavi, *Prelude to Nuremberg: Allied War Crimes Policy and the Question of Punishment* (U. North Carolina Press, 1998), 67.

54. Ibid., 67–68.

55. Arieh J. Kochavi, "The Moscow Declaration, the Kharkov Trial, and the Question of a Policy on Major War Criminals in the Second World War," *History* 76, no. 248 (1991), 404–5 (quoting letter from Averell W. Harriman, the American ambassador to the Soviet Union, to Cordell Hull, the American secretary of state, December 23, 1943)).

56. Ibid. (quoting *Pravda*).

57. Ibid., iii, 850–51 (quoting Harriman to Hull).

58. "Kharkov Trials," *Washington Post*, December 20, 1943, p. 5.

59. Kochavi, "The Moscow Declaration," 404–5 (quoting Harriman to Hull).

60. Barnet Nover, "The Guilty Must Die: Meaning of the Kharkov Trial," *Washington Post*, December 22, 1943, p. 13.

61. *The People's Verdict*, 112 (italics added).

62. Ibid., 122.

63. *The Unknown Black Book*, 29–30 (quoting Ehrenburg's dispatches for *Krasnaya Zvezda* [Red Star] newspaper).

64. Robert Chandler, "Translator's Introduction," in Vasily Grossman, *Life and Fate*, trans. Robert Chandler (N.Y. Review Books, 1985), xiii–xiv. Chandler's reference to "[a]dmitting that Jews constituted the overwhelming majority of the dead" must refer to the fact that of all the different groups that were murdered, the Jews constituted the largest group.

65. William Chase, "Stalin as Producer: The Moscow Show Trials and the Construction of Mortal Threats," in *Stalin: A New History*, ed. Sarah R. Davies and James R. Harris (Cambridge U. Press, 2005), 228.

66. Robert Gellately, *Lenin, Stalin and Hitler: The Age of Social Catastrophe* (Vintage, 2009), 270.

67. Susan K. Arnold, "Book Note" [review of *Stay the Hand of Vengeance: The Politics of War Crimes Tribunals*, by Gary Jonathan Bass], 172 *Mil. L. Rev.* 195–96 (June 2002).

68. David Luban, "A Theory of Crimes Against Humanity," 29 *Yale. J. Int'l L.* 85, 144 (2004).

69. Lawrence Douglas, *The Memory of Judgment: Making Law and History in the Trials of the Holocaust* (Yale U. Press, 2001), 2.

70. Asli Ü. Bâli, "Justice Under Occupation: Rule of Law and the Ethics of Nation-Building in Iraq," 30 *Yale J. Int'l. L.* 431, 459 (2005).

71. Jeremy Peterson, "Unpacking Show Trials: Situating the Trial of Saddam Hussein," 48 *Harvard Int'l L. J.* 257, 268 (2007).

72. Kochavi, *Prelude to Nuremberg*, 68.

73. Dawson, *Judgment before Nuremberg*, 289. Dawson tells the story of his mother's survival of the Holocaust in Kharkov and postwar emigration to the United States in Greg Dawson, *Hiding in the Spotlight: A Musical Prodigy's Story of Survival 1941–1946* (Pegasus Books, 2009).

74. Kochavi, *Prelude to Nuremberg*, 69 (quoting A. N. Trainin).

75. I. G. Ehrenburg, "War April 1943–March 1944," *Memoirs* (1944) (quoted in Larisa Volovik, *Progovor okochatelnyii i obzalovaniu nie podlezhit: pervii v istorii process nad naziskami prestupnikami*, Kharkov, Dekabr' 1943 [The sentence is final and not appealable: The first court proceedings in history against Nazi criminals, Kharkov, December 1943] (2007)), accessed March 5, 2014, http://berkovich-zametki.com/2007/Zametki/Nomer19/Volovik1.htm (translation by authors).

76. Prusin, "Fascist Criminals," 7.

77. The figures are estimates, and based on the research of the German scholar Andreas Hilger. See Andreas Hilger, "Die Gerechtigkeit nehme ihren Lauf!: die Reden des sowjetischen Hauptanklägers im Nürnberger Prozess der deutschen Hauptkriegsverbrecher," in *Transnationale Vergangenheitspolitik* ["Justice takes its

course: the speeches of the Soviet chief prosecutor at the Nuremberg trials of German major war criminals," *Transnational Politics of the Past*], 193. A comprehensive study has yet to be published of the postwar trials of Germans and Austrians in the Soviet Union. According to an unpublished fact sheet compiled by the United States Holocaust Memorial Museum, "Post War Adjudication of War Crimes Fact Sheet," twenty-one trials of Nazi war criminals took place in the Soviet Union between 1961 and 1965.

78. Richard Bessel, *Germany 1945: From War to Peace* (HarperCollins, 2009), 202–3, 251.

79. Zvi Gitelman, "Politics and the Historiography of the Holocaust in the Soviet Union," in *Bitter Legacy: Confronting the Holocaust in the USSR*, ed. Zvi Gitelman (Indiana U. Press, 1997), 18–19.

80. Ibid.

81. Ibid., 15.

82. Dawson, *Judgment before Nuremberg*, 7.

83. Ibid.

84. Gitelman, "Politics and the Historiography of the Holocaust in the Soviet Union," 19.

85. Ibid. (quoting G. Alexandrov, the head of the Party Secretariat's Agitprop Department in the U.S.S.R., in 1947).

86. Mordechai Altshuler, "Jewish Holocaust Commemoration Activity in the USSR under Stalin" (trans. Naftali Greenwood), 11. Shoah Resource Center, International School for Holocaust Studies. Available at http://www.yadvashem.org/odot_pdf/Microsoft%20Word%20-%205422.pdf. Originally published in *Yad Vashem Studies* 30 (2002).

87. Ibid., 21.

88. "Across the Former Soviet Union—Gas, Bathroom and Shoah Memorial: Proposed Construction Causes Uproar," *JTA*, January 22, 2004. Available at http://www.jta.org/2004/01/22/archive/across-the-former-soviet-union-gas-bathroom-and-shoah-memorial-proposed-construction-causes-uproar.

89. Dawson, *Judgment before Nuremberg*, 45–46. Kiev, the capital of Ukraine and a much larger city than Kharkov, has yet to have a museum dedicated to the history of the mass murder of Jews in the Ukraine during the Nazi occupation.

NOTES TO CHAPTER 2

1. The German invasion of France began on May 10, 1940. On June 14, German forces entered an undefended Paris. On June 22, an armistice was signed between the German conqueror and the vanquished French.

2. Marlise Simons, "Chirac Affirms France's Guilt In Fate of Jews," *N.Y. Times*, July 17, 1995.

3. For works on the subject of French collaboration with Nazi Germany, see Julian Jackson, *France: The Dark Years 1940–1944* (Oxford U. Press, 2001); Alan Riding, *And the Show Went On: Cultural Life in Nazi-Occupied Paris* (Knopf, 2010).

4. The information in this section is drawn from Geoffrey Warner, *Pierre Laval and the Eclipse of France* (Eyre & Spottiswoode, 1968), 1–148. See also René de Chambrun, *Pierre Laval: Traitor or Patriot?* (Charles Scribner's Sons, 1948).

5. While in the United States, Laval received a ticker-tape parade along lower Broadway. According to custom, because Laval was a visiting dignitary, a plaque bearing his name was placed at the southern end of Broadway, where it still can be seen.

6. Warner writes that in 1938 Laval suggested he go to Italy to resolve open issues between France and Italy. Mussolini indicated he did not want Laval to come and the French authorities taped a phone conversation between the Italian foreign minister, Galeazzo Ciano, and its chargé d'affaires, in which Ciano made clear the Italians did not want a politician to visit, "particularly M. Laval." Mussolini specifically instructed Ciano to reject the mission on the ground that its only value would be as a "great publicity device for Laval." This was not disclosed to Laval at the time, but was made public later when Laval criticized the existing French government for not utilizing him to deal with Italy. Warner, *Laval,* 146.

7. The Dutch government had opted to carry on in exile, an example urged by proponents of this alternative. Ibid., 172.

8. Ibid., 182–83.

9. Ibid., 172–79.

10. Ibid., 185–86.

11. Ibid., 189.

12. Ibid., 191.

13. Ibid., 193–211. Whatever "democratic" or pro-British sentiment there might have been in France, it was undermined by events near Oran in Algeria where the French fleet, one of the biggest in the world, was anchored. Winston Churchill, fearing it might be seized or turned over to the Germans, ordered the Royal Navy to attack the fleet, sinking several ships and causing the deaths of thirteen hundred French sailors. Ibid., 195.

14. Ibid., 227–41.

15. Ibid., 235, 246.

16. Ibid., 246–47.

17. Ibid.

18. Ibid.

19. Ibid.

20. Ibid., 247–60.

21. This discussion of Laval's return to power is based on ibid., 284–90.

22. Ibid., 285.

23. Ibid., 287.

24. Ibid., 289-90.

25. Ibid., 292.

26. See the subsequent discussion in this chapter detailing the evidence at Laval's trial.

27. Warner, *Laval,* 299–300.

28. Even though there was an armistice between Germany and France, there was no peace treaty. Consequently, the Germans were in no hurry to release the French POWs. Their continued captivity provided Germany with leverage and bargaining power. Laval repeatedly tried to initiate discussions for a peace treaty with Germany, but his efforts were rebuffed with the bottom-line position that a peace treaty would have to wait for the end of all hostilities.

29. Ultimately, over seven hundred thousand men were sent from France to work in Germany.

30. Warner, *Laval*, 301, citing a contemporary newspaper.

31. At his own trial, Marshal Pétain tried to disassociate himself from the statement, claiming he was horrified by it. The credible evidence at the hearing seems to have supported Laval, who insisted that Pétain knew about the statement ahead of time and did not react negatively to it. Ibid., 301–2.

32. Göring directed Heydrich to implement the Final Solution to the Jewish question, discussed in further detail in chapter 6.

33. Michael Marrus and Robert Paxton, *Vichy France and the Jews* (Schocken Books, 1983), 3.

34. Ibid., 4.

35. Marrus and Paxton, *Vichy France*, 18; Warner, *Laval*, 47.

36. Warner, *Laval*, 305.

37. Marrus and Paxton state: "For the first time in the history of the Final Solution in France [August, 1943] Laval said 'No'" (*Vichy France*, 325). See also Warner, *Laval*, 375.

38. Marrus and Paxton, *Vichy France*, 343.

39. Did Laval know the fate of those deported eastward? Of course he denied knowing, as many did. However, Laval probably knew that seventy-five thousand Jews had been deported and that virtually nothing was heard from them once they left France. It is extremely unlikely that relatives of those deported did not at some point express concern to the French government over the silence that followed their loved ones' deportations.

40. Laval's son-in-law, René de Chambrun, provided this quote from a private meeting. Warner, *Laval*, 306.

41. Ibid., 403–4.

42. Ibid., 404–5. It is astounding to think that Laval, at this stage, truly thought he had a political future in France.

43. Ibid., 406–8.

44. Laval tried unsuccessfully to obtain assistance through his son-in-law's father, General de Chambrun, who was married to a relative of Nicholas Longworth, one-time speaker of the House of Representatives and husband to Alice Roosevelt Longworth, President Theodore Roosevelt's daughter. Laval's son-in-law, René de Chambrun, and Laval's daughter, Josée, devoted a major part of their lives to rehabilitating Laval's image. See Chambrun, *Laval: Traitor or Patriot?*; Josée Laval, *Diary of Pierre Laval* (Charles Scribner's Sons, 1948).

45. See Alice Kaplan, *The Collaborator: The Trial and Execution of Robert Brasillach* (U. Chicago Press, 2000), xvi, 308; Megan Koreman, *The Expectation of Justice: France, 1944–1946* (Duke U. Press, 1999), xv, 340.

46. Ibid.

47. Ibid. In this respect, the experience in France does not differ significantly from what happened in Germany. See chapters 3 and 6.

48. These provisions are no longer in effect and have been replaced by a new penal code.

49. "Philippe Pétain (1856–1951)," *BBC History*, http://www.bbc.co.uk/history/historic_figures/petain_philippe.shtml, accessed March 5, 2014.

50. The later discussion of the prosecution of administrators of Auschwitz in the Frankfurt Auschwitz trial, chapter 8, entails essentially the same system.

51. Warner, *Laval*, 409. In the case of the Frankfurt Auschwitz trial, this stage took five years. See chapter 8.

52. The October 21, 1945, election included a referendum on whether there should be a new constitution for France, favored by the de Gaulle coalition. Presumably, the trial was rushed partially to discredit the old regime through Laval's conviction.

53. Warner, *Laval*, 408–9.

54. *Le Procès Laval* (Albin Michel, 1948), 31. This volume contains a transcript of the entire trial and will be relied on extensively in this section. References to it will simply be "P," followed by the page number(s).

55. The main Nuremberg trial presided over by the International Military Tribunal was to begin just a few weeks later, on November 20, 1945.

56. P 7: "*Nous craignons que la hâte apportée à ouvrir les débats soit inspirée, non par des préoccupations judiciaries, mais motivée par des raison politiques.*" ["We fear that the haste which opens these proceedings is based not on judicial parameters but is motivated by political reasons."]

57. P 48.

58. P 71.

59. P 96.

60. P 97.

61. Ibid.

62. Ibid. "*Il mérite, comme Laval, douze balles dans la peau.*" Warner indicates that the pro-Laval spectator was the son of Pierre Cathala, a friend of Laval and former ministerial colleague. Warner, *Laval*, 411 n.2.

63. P 97.

64. Given the volatility of the juror reactions, in an American courtroom such expressions of prejudgment would most likely lead to a mistrial. But of course that was impossible given the requirement that the entire process end before the October 21 election, only two weeks away.

65. P 100–15.

66. P 117.

67. P 117, 121.

68. P 130.

69. P 131–32.

70. P 140.

71. Warner, *Laval*, 410–11, citing pertinent pages of transcript and a book written by defense attorney Naud.

72. P 193–97.

73. P 200. The court did not address whether contempt is a serious sanction when the penalty for the underlying charge is death.

74. P 205.

75. P 205–6. "*Monsieur le Président, vous formulez à la mệme fois la question et la réponse.*"

76. P 206.

77. Ibid.

78. P 206–7.

79. He used the French term "*formidable.*" P 206.

80. P 207. "*On vous a déjà jugé, et la France vous a jugé aussi.*"

81. Ibid.

82. P 208. "*Monsieur le President, la façon injurieuse dont vous m'avez posé les questions tout à l'heure et les manifestions auxquelles se sont livrés certains jurés me montrent que je peux ệtre la victime d'un crime judiciare. Je m'en veux pas ệtre le complice. J'aime mieux me taire.*"

83. Ibid.

84. P 211.

85. P 213.

86. P 217. "*Si vous voulez.*"

87. P 227. Doyen also testified in the trial against Pétain, stating that he told Pétain that Laval was doing everything he could to assist Germany. Doyen noted that after Laval was removed from his position (in December 1940), he received a note saying that Laval's dismissal did not mean a change in the policy of collaboration. *Canberra Times*, July 30, 1945, p. 1, col. 5.

88. P 302–5.

89. P 231.

90. P 231–32.

91. P 232.

92. P 233–38.

93. P 238.

94. P 244.

95. P 244–45.

96. P 245.

97. Ibid.

98. P 246.

99. P 246–47.

100. "*Je souhaite la victoire d l'Allemagne.*" He also added that without such a victory, communism would take over everywhere. See Marrus and Paxton, *Vichy France*, 231.

101. P 247.

102. P 247–48.

103. "*Je veux la victoire del'Allemagne.*"

104. P 248.

105. Ibid.

106. P 251.

107. Ibid.

108. P 249.

109. P 253–54.

110. P 257–58. Since Noel refused to testify, his testimony in the Pétain case was placed into evidence. The prosecutor did not allude to it in his closing argument, and so it is doubtful that it played any significant role in the ultimate determination by the court. However, such use of testimony in an American court would be considered inadmissible and unreliable hearsay. Laval did not have the opportunity to cross-examine Noel at the Pétain trial and Pétain's motive in questioning him might well have been to shift blame from himself to Laval.

111. P 362.

112. P 305–9. Historically, the Anglo-American criminal justice system has also permitted the confiscation of the property of a person convicted of treason. A. O. Wright, *An Exposition of the Constitution of the United States* (Midland, 1888), 224.

113. Warner, *Laval*, 415.

114. This is discussed in slightly greater detail in ibid., 414–15.

115. Ibid., 415–16.

116. "The Execution of Pierre Laval," *Guardian*, October 16, 1946.

117. Warner, *Laval*, 74.

118. The *Relève* program was designed to liberate prisoners of *war.*The million-plus French soldiers in Germany custody were never referred to as anything other than prisoners of war.

119. Marrus and Paxton, *Vichy France*, 219.

120. Chambrun, *Laval: Traitor or Patriot?*, 106; Marrus and Paxton, *Vichy France*, 219.

121. Warner, *Laval*, 300.

122. Taylor, *Anatomy*, 599. While Sauckel was convicted under principles of international criminal law, Laval was convicted under French criminal law.

123. Warner, *Laval*, 373.

124. Ibid., 373–75.

125. For example, the October 3, 1940, *Statut des juifs* excluded Jews from much of public life in France, with narrow exceptions for those who had served in the military during the First World War. Marrus and Paxton, *Vichy France*, 3–4.

126. Warner, *Laval*, 305.

127. Ibid, 301.

128. See, e.g., Warner, *Laval*, 147; Marrus and Paxton, *Vichy France*, 18, 346. Since Jews had fled central Europe to France in the last half of the 1930s, there was a considerable "foreign" Jewish population in France—mainly refugees. In a somewhat brutal comment to the U.S. chargé d'affaires to the Vichy government, Laval said they would give the place a bad name and he would get rid of them. Marrus and Paxton, *Vichy France*, 18.

129. Marrus and Paxton, *Vichy France*, 220.

130. Warner, *Laval*, 305.

131. Marrus and Paxton, *Vichy France*, 248–49.

132. Ibid., 244, 245.

133. Ibid., 248

134. Ibid., 252.

135. Ibid., 266–67.

136. Ibid., 269. While imprisoned and awaiting trial, Laval wrote that he tried to find out, by questioning German officials, what happened to the Jews sent to Poland. He knew, he said, that they were working there under terrible conditions, most often likely to suffer and die. Ibid., 346, quoting Laval's notes. While it is not clear when Laval reached this realization, the outside world did know by the end of 1942 about the fate of Jews sent "to the East." On December 17, 1942, the British foreign secretary, Anthony Eden, stated to the House of Commons that the German authorities were "now carrying into effect Hitler's oft-repeated intention to exterminate the Jewish people of Europe." "Britain Condemns Massacre of Jews," *BBC*, December 17, 1942. Available at http://news.bbc.co.uk/onthisday/hi/dates/stories/december/17/newsid_3547000/3547151.stm.

137. Violations of treaties underlay the prosecutions in Nuremberg. In Laval's case, the French Penal Code was the basis for prosecution.

138. Lesser figures who committed crimes during the Second World War were tried later in France. Three memorable trials are those of Klaus Barbie, Paul Touvier, and Maurice Papon.

In 1987, Klaus Barbie, known as the Butcher of Lyons, was tried for war crimes and murder. He was found guilty and sentenced to life imprisonment. He died four years later, in prison. Barbie, as the head of the Gestapo in Lyons, was responsible for the deportation of many Jews, but perhaps most notoriously for the torture methods that led to his capture of Jean Moulin, head of the French Resistance, whom he also tortured and killed.

Paul Touvier was a lower-ranked Vichy official who, at Barbie's direction, was involved in the killing of seven Jewish hostages. Arrested in 1989, he was not tried until 1994, when he was found guilty and sentenced to life imprisonment. He died in prison two years later. Interestingly, his defense at the trial was similar to Laval's: just as Laval claimed that he saved French Jews by arranging for the deportation of non-French Jews, Touvier claimed, without success, that Barbie wanted him to execute thirty hostages and he bargained him down to seven. "Paul Touvier," Centre d'Histoire de la Résistance et de la Déportation. Available at http://www.chrd.lyon.fr/chrd/sections/fr/pages_fantomes/biographies/paul_touvier/.

The case of Maurice Papon is perhaps the most searing because it demonstrated to France, almost fifty years after the war, the degree of French involvement in German criminality, and the extent to which such involvement was overlooked in the ensuing decades. Papon was a senior official of the Vichy regime operating in the Bordeaux area and responsible, over a two-year period, for sending several trains with 1,600 Jews, including about 130 children from the Bordeaux region, to internment camps, ending in the murder of almost all the deportees at Auschwitz. He eluded the status of collaborator and became a high-ranking official in the de Gaulle government and the French budget minister in the late 1970s and early 1980s.

Evidence of his responsibility in the Holocaust emerged in 1981. A string of legal battles then began. An investigation started in 1983 ended three years later because of a mistake by the investigating magistrate. New charges were filed the following year and the trial, which began in 1997, ended in 1999. Papon claimed the trial was unfair and compared himself to Alfred Dreyfus. Nevertheless, he was convicted of complicity in sending numerous trainloads of Jews to their deaths and sentenced to ten years' imprisonment. He fled to Switzerland during his appeal, was caught, and began serving his sentence in 1999. Papon continued to litigate his conviction, while asking at the same time to be released because of poor health. Ultimately, Papon succeeded on the latter ground and was released in 2002, serving only three years of his sentence. He died five years later at the age of ninety-six. For a volume discussing all three trials and their relationship to law, history, and memory, see *Barbie, Touvier, Papon: Des procès pour la mémoire*, ed. Denis Salas and Jean-Paul Jean (Autrement, 2002).

NOTES TO CHAPTER 3

1. The entire proceedings relating to the Dachau trial can be found on microfilm housed in the National Archives in Bethesda, Maryland, and at the library at the Baylor Law School in Waco, Texas. The authors are indebted to both institutions for their cooperation and assistance in making the microfilm available. Once the trial begins, pages are Bate stamped numerically; those pages will be cited in this chapter with the prefix "R." Summaries of the proceedings appear there, including background before the beginning of the trial. The numbers cited in the text appear in one of those summaries entitled "The Dachau Concentration Camp Case," beginning on page 5.

2. R 413–16.

3. R 545–54.

4. "Dachau Concentration Camp Case" (hereafter "Camp"), 5.

5. R 1266–69.

6. "Timeline of Dachau," *Jewish Virtual Library*. Available at http://www.org/wlc/en/article.pho?Moduled=10005214.

7. The exact location of the concentration camp, as well as its satellite camps, was not known with precision at the time of liberation. Consequently, the American

forces of the 42nd and 45th divisions of the Seventh Army arrived at different ends of the camp almost simultaneously and were not sure, until they actually got there, that they were liberating a concentration camp.

8. "[W]e had seen men in battle blown apart, burnt to death, and die many different ways, but we were never prepared for this. Several of the dead lay there with their eyes open, a picture I will never get out of my mind. It seems they were looking at us and saying, 'What took you so long?'" Private John Lee, 45th Division soldier, who was one of the first men on the scene. Noted at http://www.scrapbookpages.com/DachauScrapbook/DachauLiberation/DeathTrain.html.

9. Flint Whitlock, *The Rock of Anzio: From Sicily to Dachau, A History of the 45th Infantry Division* (Westview Press, 1998), 356–58.

10. Ibid., 364.

11. David L. Israel, *The Day the Thunderbird Died* (Emek Press, 2005).

12. Howard A. Buechner, *Dachau, the Hour of the Avenger: An Eyewitness Account* (Thunderbird Press, 1986).

13. See John Linden, *Surrender of the Dachau Concentration Camp 29 Apr 45—The True Account* (Sycamore Press, 1997), 9–10.

14. Buechner, *Dachau* .

15. Ibid.

16. Ibid..

17. These events on the liberation of Dachau were to emerge at the trials the military conducted at Dachau related to the Malmedy massacre, the killing of 86 of 120 American soldiers who had surrendered to the Germans in the Battle of the Bulge. Charged with these killings, the defense attempted unsuccessfully to place into evidence the killing of the SS men at Dachau.

18. The United States Supreme Court recently alluded to these principles in *Hamdan v. United States,* 548 U.S. 557, 590–91 (2006), a case relating to the authority of the American military to use military commissions to try detainees held at the Guantánamo Bay camp.

19. Not all Dachau camps were included in the charge. The charge did embrace the main Dachau camp and six of the Kaufering subcamps.

20. As recent charges have shown—allegations against the president of the Sudan and charges relating to the atrocities committed in the former Yugoslavia and Rwanda in the 1990s—international criminal law has evolved since Nuremberg. Today, crimes against civilians may be committed against the same nationals as the defendant and also without the need for a state of war.

21. For an account of the prosecution, based on Denson's papers discovered in his basement after his death in 1998, containing thirty thousand pages of trial transcripts, microfilm records and other documentation, see Joshua Greene, *Justice at Dachau: The Trials of An American Prosecutor* (Broadway Books, 2003). See also Fern Overley Hilton, *The Dachau Defendants: Life Stories from Testimony and Documents of the War Crimes Prosecutions* (McFarland, 2004); Lisa Yavnai, "U.S. Army War Crimes Trials in Germany 1945–1947," in *Atrocities on Trial: Historical Perspectives*

on the Politics of Prosecuting War Crimes, ed. Patricia Heberer and Jürgen Matthäus (U. Nebraska Press, 2008). For an account of the trials by one of the court reporters there, who later came to claim that major injustices were committed at the trials, see Joseph Halow, *Innocent at Dachau* (Legion for the Survival of Freedom, 1993).

22. The terms "defendant" and "accused" are used interchangeably in this chapter. Technically, there only were accused, as the charging sheet makes no reference to defendants.

23. The possibly ubiquitous status of the *Waffen-SS* surfaced in 1985 when President Ronald Reagan placed a wreath at a monument to SS men at the cemetery in Bitburg, Germany. Responding to the outrage that an American president would participate in any event ostensibly honoring members of the SS, the president said, much as the defendants, that the *Waffen-SS* was essentially a military group, fighting soldiers and not perpetrators of Nazi horrors. See Bernard Weinraub, "Reagan Joins Kohl in Brief Memorial at Bitburg Graves," *N.Y. Times*, May 6, 1985, p. 1, col. 8. Evidence produced at the Dachau and other trials reveals the *Waffen-SS* to have been active participants in atrocities.

24. R 48.

25. R 80.

26. Ibid.

27. R 82, 83.

28. R 90–91.

29. R 92.

30. The number of people murdered at Dachau accelerated enormously as the war drew to a close. In the four months of 1945 prior to liberation, there were 13,158 deaths, a number roughly equal to the total deaths in the entire 1940–44 period. Reel 4, prosecution exhibit 35.

31. R 1395.

32. For example testimony of Dr. Norbert Fried, a Kaufering subcamp prisoner from mid-1944 to liberation, see R 587–614.

33. "Camp," 55. R 345.

34. "Camp," 52.

35. Ibid., 53.

36. R 98–169.

37. R 150.

38. R 445–51.

39. R 98–169.

40. R 519–27.

41. R 169–209.

42. Statement of Wilhom Visintainer.

43. To add to the perversity of the experiment, men pulled out from the water were laid naked next to two naked women to see how quickly their body temperature would rise, if at all.

44. R 98–169.

45. R 858–87.

46. R1829.

47. A letter to that effect from the Rockefeller Foundation, reflecting a $3,500 grant, was placed into evidence.

48. Priests were subjected to lesser work details than the general inmate population. Consequently, they were ideal targets for malaria tests since any deterioration in their condition could be attributed to the disease, rather than strenuous labor coupled with malnutrition. The testimony of Father Theodore Koch, R. 350–62, is typical of how priests were subjected to these experiments.

49. R 98–169.

50. In Schilling's pretrial statement he said that he inoculated between nine hundred and one thousand prisoners, a number much closer to Blaha's testimony. Reel 4, prosecution exhibit 122A.

51. These are standard efforts in a U.S. criminal case on behalf of a defendant in an effort to raise a reasonable doubt as to the charge. It is a sign of the great degree of effort defense counsel made on behalf of their clients.

52. R 1528.

53. R 1540.

54. R 539. Testimony of Father Frederick Hoffman that Jarolin regularly beat prisoners. R 368–76.

55. R 1205–11.

56. Jarolin's lengthy and detailed statement was prosecution exhibit 124A.

57. Exhibit 124A.

58. R 419–27.

59. R 1442–50.

60. The accused Betz, who testified just before Mahl, said he attended two executions in 1941 and after that the only harm he inflicted on inmates was slapping. R 1436–48.

61. R 1442–50.

62. R 1826–27.

63. R 1829.

64. R 1836.

65. R 1840–41.

66. A similar provision can be found in Article 8 of the Charter of the International Military Tribunal.

67. R 1848.

68. R 1890.

69. R 1897.

70. R 1898.

71. R 1918–20.

72. R 1920–22.

73. In a rebuttal closing, Lieutenant Colonel Denson said that Schilling was a common murderer, injecting inmates with substances he knew could kill them and

that it was a disgrace to the memory of Walter Reed and Louis Pasteur to mention them in the same breath as Schilling. R 1949.

74. R 1964.

75. R 1965.

76. R 1970–71.

77. R 1967.

78. R 1974.

79. R 1980–88.

80. Reel 1, p.age 10, of introductory statement.

81. R 698–704.

82. R 1980–81.

83. See, for example, R 1409–10, 1662–63, 1672.

84. Preparing for the cross-examination of prosecution witnesses, itself a laborious process, precludes the use of substantial time during the prosecution's case for the preparation of a client's testimony.

85. R 651–59.

86. Where a *kapo* appears to relish the torture he inflicts on others or seems to go out of his way to inflict pain needlessly or gratuitously, such conduct may be evidence of a state of mind more consistent with that of SS camp administrators. This did not seem to be Mahl's case.

87. Michael A. Musmanno, *The Eichmann Kommandos* (Macrae Smith, 1961), 76.

NOTES TO CHAPTER 4

1. David M. Crowe, *Oskar Schindler: The Untold Account of His Life, Wartime Activities, and the True Story Behind The List* (Westview Press, 2004), 217. English-language translations of portions of the Göth trial proceedings are reproduced in the United Nations War Crimes Reports, v. VII (1948) (hereafter "UNWCC.") Selected English-language transcript portions are also available at the website of the Holocaust Education & Archive Research Team (H.E.A.R.T.), headed by Chris Webb, at www.holocaustresearchproject.org, and all testimony herein comes from the H.E.A.R.T. website materials.

2. As historian Jan Gross notes: "Poland suffered proportionally the greatest material and population losses of all belligerents in the Second World War." Jan T. Gross, "Themes for a Social History of War Experience and Collaboration," in *The Politics of Retribution in Europe: World War II and Its Aftermath*, ed. István Deák, Jan T. Gross, and Tony Judt (Princeton U. Press 2000), 17. For general discussion of Polish losses during the Second World War, see Richard C. Lukas, *Forgotten Holocaust: The Poles Under German Occupation 1939–1944* (Hippocrene Books, 2d rev. ed., 2001), and Mateusz Gniazdowski, "Losses Inflicted on Poland by Germany during World War II: Assessments and Estimates—an Outline," *Polish Quarterly of International Affairs* 1 (2007), 94. Estimates of Polish losses are still open to debate. As Gniazdowski puts it: "After almost 60 years from the end of the war that brought about changes of borders and subsequent migrations, the possibility of conducting a reliable verification and correction of previous estimates may be questioned." Ibid., 126.

3. Quoted in Robert Forczyk, *Warsaw 1944: Poland's Bid for Freedom* (Osprey Publishing, 2009), 90.

4. As we show, while the indictment describes the victims in generic terms—"*inmates* murdered" at Płaszów and "*people* perished" in the ghettos—the general became specific as soon as the trial got underway. The crimes were described specifically and repeatedly as crimes directed against the "Jewish nation" and against individuals because they were Jews.

5. For a recent biography, see Johannes Sachslehner, *Der Tod ist ein Meister aus Wien: Leben und Taten des Amon Leopold Göth* [Death is a Master from Vienna: The Life and Deeds of Amon Leopold Göth] (Styria Premium, 2008).

6. Crowe, *Schindler*, 237.

7. Trial of Amon Göth, testimony of Dr. Alexander Biberstein, quoted in Michael Wildt, "The Invented and the Real: Historiographical Notes on Schindler's List," *History Workshop Journal* 41 (Spring 1996), 245.

8. Interview with Helen Sternlicht Jonas, United States Holocaust Memorial Museum, *Voices of Anti-Semitism*, February 2009.

9. Crowe, *Schindler*, 354. The conundrum created by the perversity of German SS law that legally allowed for genocide but punished unsanctioned mistreatment of Jewish prisoners and private theft is aptly noted by Holocaust historian Saul Friedländer: "[SS head] Heinrich Himmler was of course confronted with an ongoing and intractable issue, how to stem wanton murder in an organization set up for mass murder, how to stem widespread corruption in an organization set up for large-scale looting." Saul Friedländer, *Nazi Germany and the Jews 1939–1945: The Years of Extermination* (HarperCollins 2007), 544.

10. Mietek Pemper, *The Road to Rescue: The Untold Story of Schindler's List* (Other Press, 2005), 174.

11. *Commandant of Auschwitz: The Autobiography of Rudolf Höss*, trans. Costantine FitzGibbon (Phoenix Press, 2000), 175.

12. The original House of Commons proceeding at which Eden read the statement is available at http://hansard.millbanksystems.com/commons/1942/dec/17/united-nations-declaration.

13. The IMT proceedings were themselves dogged at the time by criticisms of victor's justice, *ex post facto* justice, and other deficiencies in legal process, such as the unavailability of a judicial appeal. Nevertheless, because the IMT tribunal was an international tribunal and established by the victorious Allies, it was also seen as the model for how to judicially prosecute Nazi criminality. The Polish judicial authorities, therefore, consciously modeled themselves on the IMT and referred to it during the NTN trials. See, e.g., Guénaël Mettraux, ed., *Perspectives on the Nuremberg Trial* (Oxford U. Press, 2008).

14. Alexander V. Prusin, "Poland's Nuremberg: The Seven Court Cases of the Supreme National Tribunal, 1946–1948," *Holocaust and Genocide Studies* 24, no. 1 (Spring 2010), 5.

15. Shlomo Avineri, "The Return to History and Its Consequences for the Jewish Communities in Eastern Europe," in *The Dangers of Anti-Semitism in Central and*

Eastern Europe in the Wake of 1989–90, ed. Yehuda Bauer (Hebrew U. Jerusalem, 1991), 98, and quoted in Larry V. Thompson, ed. *Lessons and Legacies IV: Reflections on Religion, Justice, Sexuality, and Genocide*, (Northwestern U. Press, 2003), 145.

16. The seven trials of the NTN were as follows: (1) trial of Arhur Greiser, who carried out a brutal policy of Germanization in the so-called Reichsgau Watherland, a portion of western Poland annexed to the Reich where he was *Gauleiter* (Nazi Party leader) and governor (June–July 1946) (death penalty carried out); (2) trial of Amon Göth (August–September 1946)) (death penalty carried out); (3) trial of four high-ranking Nazi officials in Warsaw: Ludwig Fischer, Ludwig Leist, Josef Meisinger, Max Daume (death penalty carried out for Fischer, Meisinger, and Daume; Leist received eight years); (4) trial of Rudolf Höss, commandant of Auschwitz (March 1947) (death penalty carried out); (5) trial of forty-one staff members of Auschwitz, including commandant Arthur Liebehenschel (November–December 1947) (twenty-three death sentences carried out, sixteen imprisonments of various terms, and one acquittal); (6) trial of Albert Forster, governor of Reichsgau Danzig-West Prussia (April 1948) (death penalty carried out); and (7) trial of Josef Bühler, state secretary and deputy governor to the General Government (June 1948) (death penalty carried out).

17. Excerpts from the verdict in connection with the accused Hans Münch, http://www.jewishvirtuallibrary.org/jsource/Holocaust/Munchtrial.html.

18. Prusin, "Poland's Nuremberg," 1–25.

19. Prusin, "Poland's Nuremberg," 25 (citing Polish scholar Elzbieta Kobierska-Motas).

20. It is still in force today, forming the basis by which the Polish Institute of National Remembrance investigated in 2002 the "killing of Polish citizens of Jewish origin in the town of Jedwabne, on 10 July 1941" after publication of Jan Gross's *Neighbors*. See Jan T. Gross, *Neighbors: The Destruction of the Jewish Community in Jedwabnie, Poland* (Princeton U. Press, 2001).

21. *Dekret PKWN "o wymiarze kary dla faszystowsko-hitlerowskich zbrodniarzy winnych zabójstw i znęcania się nad ludnością cywilną i jeńcami oraz dla zdrajców Narodu Polskiego,"* August 31, 1944, *Dziennik Ustaw*, no. 4, poz. (item) 16.

22. Quoted in Andrzej Rzeplinsky, "Prosecution of Nazi Crimes in Poland in 1939–2004" paper presented before the First International Expert Meeting on War Crimes, Genocide and Crimes Against Humanity, INTERPOL, March 23–25, 2004.

23. UNWCC, 7 (English-translated text of decree).

24. Prusin, "Poland's Nuremberg," 3.

25. The Central Commission, its successor, still exists and now has jurisdiction to investigate and initiate prosecution of crimes from the Communist-era in Poland.

26. Prusin, "Poland's Nuremberg," 3.

27. Marek J. Chodakiewicz, "The Dialectics of Pain: The Interrogation Methods of the Communist Secret Police in Poland," paper presented at the 61st annual meeting of the Polish Institute of Arts and Sciences of America, McGill University, June 6–7, 2003, p. 108.

28. One of those tried was Dr. Leon Gross, a Jewish prisoner-physician, who assisted Göth in selections at Płaszów. Found guilty, he was executed by the Poles in 1946. See Chapter 7.

29. UNWCC, 7.

30. Cyprian and his fellow NTN prosecutor Jerzy Sawicki (who also was a member of the Polish delegation to the IMT), later co-authored the first study (not yet translated into English) of the NTN. See Tadeusz Cyprian and Jerzy Sawicki, *Siedem procesów przed Najwyższym Trybunałem Narodowym*, [Seven Trials before the Supreme National Tribunal] (Institut Zachodni, 1962).

31. UNWCC, 5. (The corresponding Polish Penal Code section were Articles 225, 235, 236, 246, 248, 257, and 262, respectively.)

32. The first defendant to be tried before the NTN, Arthur Greiser, who carried out a brutal campaign of Germanization of western Poland annexed to the Reich in the territory where he was the Nazi governor, was also accused of "physical and spiritual genocide," akin to Göth. Göth's trial, therefore, was the second time that genocide was charged in Poland, not as a crime itself, but as a descriptive term of the crimes committed by the defendants. See Catherine Epstein, *Model Nazi: Arthur Greier and the Occupation of Western Poland* (Oxford U. Press, 2012).

33. Raphael Lemkin, *Axis Rule in Occupied Europe: Laws of Occupation; Analysis of Government; Proposals for Redress* (Carnegie Endowment for International Peace, 1944), 79; reprinted in Raphael Lemkin, *Axis Rule in Occupied Europe: Laws of Occupation, Analysis of Government, Proposals for Redress*, introduction by Samantha Power (Lawbook Exchange, 2005).

34. Lemkin, *Axis Rule*, chap. IX.

35. Ibid.

36. This is equivalent to the formulation made by Lemkin in coining "genocide" in English: Greek *genos* (people) and Latin *caedere* (to kill). *Axis Rule*, 79.

37. UNWCC, 9.

38. Ibid.

39. "The wrongs which we seek to condemn and punish have been so calculated, so malignant, and so devastating, that civilization cannot tolerate their being ignored, because it cannot survive their being repeated." Opening address of Justice Robert H. Jackson before the IMT.

40. UNWCC, 8.

41. Janina Wierzbowska, "Amon Göth przed sądem w Krakowie" [Amon Göth before the court in Kcraków], *Glos Ludu* 242 (September 4, 1946), quoted in Edyta Gawron, "Amon Göth's Trial in Cracow: Its Impact on Holocaust Awareness in Poland," in *Holocaust and Justice: Representation and Historiography of the Holocaust in Post-War Trials*, ed. David Bankier and Dan Michman (Berghahn, 2010), 281.

42. H.E.A.R.T., part I.

43. UNWCC, 8.

44. Pemper, *The Road to Rescue*, 180.

45. Ibid., 177.

46. Ibid.

47. Ibid., 178.

48. Ibid., 178–79.

49. Ibid., 79.

50. UNWCC, 4.

51. *Proces Ludobójcy Amona Götha przed Najwyższym Trybunałem Narodowym* [Trial of the mass murderer Amon Göth before the Supreme National Tribunal] (1947).

52. "Krakow-Plaszow Camp Remembered," by Meir Eldar, accessed March 5, 2014, http://www1.yadvashem.org/download/education/conf/Eldar.pdf.

53. As aptly summarized by Prusin: "Höss . . . stunned the court audience with his mild manners, quiet voice, and most important, his admission of guilt. Having realized, apparently, that his fate was sealed—he had already testified in Nuremberg—Höss corroborated the charges of genocide against himself and against other Auschwitz functionaries." Prusin, "Poland's Nuremberg," 11–12.

54. *Proces Ludóbojcy*, 215–16, quoted in Prusin, "Poland's Nuremberg," 11.

55. Crowe, *Schindler*, 215.

56. UNWCC, 37.

57. Article 3, paragraph 1, of the 1932 Penal Code specifically stated that "Polish criminal law is applicable to all persons who committed a crime on the territory of the Polish State."

58. Ibid., 1.

59. Ibid., 9.

60. In the Greiser verdict, the NTN used genocide as a descriptive term, as part of the crime of waging aggressive war, each time putting the word in parentheses. ("[Greiser was] one of the first, most active, and most trusted colleagues of Adolf Hitler in the realization of German power in east central Europe by means of warlike and biological aggression, *including the cultural extermination (genocide) of neighboring peoples*, especially the Polish people so hated by Germans.") Quoted in Epstein, *Model* Nazi, 326. In a later portion of its judgment, it used the word again, once more in parenthesis, but this time as a descriptive term for what it called "new crimes against the interests of humanity"—what the IMT court in Nuremberg would call simply "crimes against humanity ("in the form of murdering peoples *(according to the latest Anglo-Saxon terminology: genocide)*"). Ibid., 327.

61. Quoted in Michael Mann, *The Dark Side of Democracy: Explaining Ethnic Cleansing* (Cambridge U. Press, 2005), 253. In 1983, Kalder Göth committed suicide, one day after giving an interview for a documentary on Oskar Schindler.

NOTES TO CHAPTER 5

1. For a general discussion of British war crimes trials in occupied Germany, see Donald Bloxham, "British War Crimes Trial Policy in Germany, 1945–1957: Implementation and Collapse," *J. British Studies* 42, no. 1 (January 2003), 91–118; Lorie Charlesworth, "Forgotten Justice: Forgetting Law's History and Victim's Justice in

British 'Minor' War Crime Trials in Germany 1945–8," *Amicus Curiae* 74 (Summer 2008), 2; Anthony Glees, "The Making of British Policy on War Crimes: History as Politics in the UK," *Contemporary European History* 1, no. 2 (July 1992), 171; A. P. V. Rogers, "War Crimes Trials under the Royal Warrant: British Practice 1945–1949," *Int'l & Comp. L. Q.* 39 (1990), 780.

2. See Steve Fielding, *Pierrepoint: A Family of Executioners: The Story of Britain's Infamous Hangmen* (John Blake, 2008).

3. No treatise has yet been published focusing strictly on the Ravensbrück Hamburg trials. For an article in German, see Hanna Elling and Ursula Krause-Schmitt, "Die Ravensbrück–Prozesse vor dem britischen Militärgericht," *Informationen* 35 (October 1992), 13–37.

4. Daniel Patrick Brown, *The Camp Women: The Female Auxiliaries Who Assisted the SS in Running the Nazi Concentration Camp System* (Schiffer, 2002), 8.

5. Claudia Taake, *Angeklagt: SS-Frauen von Gericht* (Universitat Oldenburg, 2000), 11 (quoted and cited in Brown, *The Camp Women,* 12 n.14).

6. Brown's book, *The Camp Women* (11 n.3 and 240), has other ranks listed for the female guards, *Erste Aufseherin* and *Erstaufseherin,* but these apparently are not correct. Email from Ursula Krause-Schmitt to Michael Bazyler, December, 17, 2010.

7. See Ulf Schmidt, "The Scars of Ravensbrück: Medical Experiments and British War Crimes Policy, 1945–1950," in *Atrocities on Trial,* ed. Heberer and Matthäus, 124.

8. Bradley F. Smith, *The Road to Nuremberg* (Basic Books, 1981), 205.

9. Donald Bloxham, *Genocide on Trial: War Crimes Trials and the Formation of Holocaust History and Memory* (Oxford U. Press, 2001), 97.

10. Ibid., 82.

11. Rogers, "War Crimes Trials," 786.

12. Ibid. (quoting United Nations War Crimes Commission, *Law Reports of Trials War Criminals* (1947), I:105, XV:28).

13. Ibid., 781.

14. In addition to the memoirs of Ravensbrück survivors cited in other notes, general discussions can be found in Bernhard Strebel, *Das KZ Ravensbrück. Geschichte eines Lagerkomplexes* (Schöningh, 2003); Carol Adams, ed., *Women of Ravensbrück: Portraits of Courage* (U. Central Florida Press, 1997); Ericka Buchmann, *Die Frauen von Ravensbrück* (Kongress-Verlag,1959); Sigrid Jacobeit. *Ravensbruckerinnen*, (Stiftung Brandenburgische, 1995); Jack Gaylord Morrison, *Ravensbruck: Everyday Life in a Women's Concentration Camp, 1939–45* (Markus Wiener, 2000). Two books have focused exclusively on the Jewish population of Ravensbrück: Rochelle G. Saidel, *The Jewish Women of Ravensbrück Concentration Camp* (U. Wisconsin Press, 2004), and Judith Buber Agassi, *Jewish Women Prisoners of Ravensbrück: Who Were They?* (OneWorld, 2007).

15. From April 1941 until the liberation there was also a male camp on the site with close to twenty thousand prisoners, about 10 percent of them Jews. The crimes committed in the male camp were not part of the trial process at Hamburg.

16. Agassi, *Jewish Women Prisoners*, 9.

17. Germaine Tillion, *Ravensbrück*, trans. Gerald Satterwaite (Doubleday, 1975), 69–70.

18. Brown, *The Camp Women*, 8.

19. Saidel, *Jewish Women of Ravensbrück*, 3.

20. Ibid., 19–20.

21. Gemma LaGuardia Gluck, *My Story*, ed. S. L. Shneiderman (David McKay, 1961), 61.

22. Several former female prisoners who worked in the *Kommandantur* (commandant's office) until the end stated that the camp records were all burned in the crematoria ovens.

23. Schmidt, "Scars of Ravensbrück," 142.

24. Ibid.

25. Da Cunha served as tank commander with the British forces and was wounded in France a few weeks after D-Day. While still recuperating, he was summoned to join JAG as a war crimes investigator by JAG Brigadier Henry Shapcott. "Obituary—His Honour John da Cunha," *Telegraph* (London), July 19, 2006.

26. Schmidt, "Scars of Ravensbrück," 142.

27. Schwarzhuber came to Ravensbrück from Auschwitz just before its liberation. At Auschwitz, he had supervised gassing operations and so was familiar with organizing that system at Ravensbrück.

28. Quoted in Lord Russell of Liverpool, *The Scourge of the Swastika: A Short History of Nazi War Crimes* (Cassell, 1954), 198.

29. Ramdohr deposition, PIZ Collection.

30. Russell, *Scourge*, 205.

31. Ibid., 206.

32. Ibid., 207.

33. Public Record Office, London (hereafter "PRO"), file WO 0235, 0319_00005.

34. Susan Benedict, "The Nadir of Nursing: The Nurse Perpetrators of Ravensbrück Concentration Camp," *Nursing History Review* 11 (2003), 129–46: 135, 136 (quoting PRO, file WO 309/692/81961).

35. Russell, *Scourge*, 208.

36. Ibid., 209.

37. Ibid. (quoting testimony of Violette le Coq).

38. Ibid., 201.

39. Benedict, "Nadir of Nursing," 137 (citing Stiftung Gedenkstaten, Mahn-und Gedenkstaffe Ravensbrück, File: vol. 2, area 1243, testimony of Vera Salvequart).

40. Ibid., 138 (quoting Public Record Office, London. File WO 309/690/81961, testimony of Lotte Sontag).

41. Russell, *Scourge*, 214.

42. Quoted in http://yourarchives.nationalarchives.gov.uk/index.php?title=WO_235/308. Accessed March 5, 2014.

43. Brigadier R. C. Halse, deputy judge advocate-general, review of evidence report, BAOR/15418/881–884/JAG (June 24, 1948) ("Ravensbrück IV Review Report"), para. 6–7.

44. Ibid., para. 12.

45. Ibid.

46. Ibid.

47. Ibid.

48. Ibid.

49. Ibid.

50. Ibid.

51. Ibid.

52. Ibid.

53. Ibid., para. 11.

54. Ibid., para. 15.

55. Benedict, "Nadir of Nursing," 132 (quoting PRO, file WO 309/692, testimony of Martha Pauline Haake).

56. Halse, "Ravensbrück IV Review Report," para. 14.

57. Ibid.

58. Ibid.

59. Brigadier R.C. Halse, deputy judge advocate-general, review of evidence report, BAOR/15418/724/JAG (December 30, 1947) ("Ravensbrück II Review Report"), 1–2.

60. Halse, "Ravensbrück II Review Report," 1.

61. Ibid., 2.

62. Ibid., 1.

63. PRO, file WO 0235, 0534_00043.

64. Letter of defense counsel Dr. A. Meyer-Labastille, enclosure to petition for Dr. Benno Orendi (June 17, 1948), PRO, file WO 0235, 0769_00922.

65. Brown, *The Camp Women*, 12 n.19.

66. Schmidt, "Scars of Ravensbrück," 149 (quoting Geneviève de Gaulle Anthonioz, *The Dawn of Hope: A Memoir of Ravensbrück* [Arcade, 1999]).

67. Donald Bloxham, "Punishing German Soldiers during the Cold War: The Case of Erich von Manstein," *Patterns of Prejudice* 33 (1999), 42.

68. Ibid., 26.

69. Quoted in David Cesarani, *Justice Delayed: How Britain Became A Refuge For Nazi War Criminals* (Phoenix Press, 2001 [1992]), 174.

70. Ibid., 175.

71. Gary Bass, *Stay the Hand of Vengeance: The Politics of War Crimes Tribunals* (Princeton U. Press, 2001), 185–86.

72. Lenience was not shown in all cases. For example, *Aufseherin* Gertrud Rabestein was tried in East Germany in the 1950s and sentenced to life imprisonment. She died in jail forty years later.

73. Insa Eschebach, "Interpreting Female Perpetrators: Ravensbrück Guards in the Courts of East Germany, 1946–1955," in *Lessons and Legacies V: The Holocaust and Justice,* ed. Ronald Smelser (Northwestern U. Press, 2002), 256.

74. Ibid., 257.

75. Ibid., 261.

76. *In re the Extradition of Ryan*, 360 F. Supp. 270 (E.D.N.Y. 1973).

77. Douglas Martin, "A Nazi Past, a Queens Home Life, an Overlooked Death," *N.Y. Times*, December 2, 2005.

78. Oliver Harvey, "A 'Kind, Sweet' Granny Hiding an Evil Secret," *Sun* (London), February 21, 2009.

79. Ibid.

80. Ibid.

81. Ibid.

82. Ibid.

NOTES TO CHAPTER 6

1. In a speech before the German Reichstag (parliament) on January 30, 1939, on the sixth anniversary of his rise to power, Hitler stated:

> Today I want to be a prophet again. If international Jewry within Europe and abroad should succeed once more in plunging the peoples into a world war, then the consequence will be not the Bolshevization of the world and therewith a victory of Jewry, but the annihilation of the Jewish race in Europe.

The speech was filmed and can be viewed on YouTube.

2. Telford Taylor, *The Anatomy of the Nuremberg Trial: A Personal Memoir* (Little, Brown, 1992), 16.

3. It is a barometer of how little was known about crimes against humanity that Justice Jackson, in his opening statement as chief American prosecutor at the IMT trial in November 1945, made no reference to Auschwitz, an omission undoubtedly the product of unawareness, not design.

4. As drafted, the Nuremberg Charter gave the IMT jurisdiction only over conspiracy to wage aggressive war, not conspiracy to commit war crimes and crimes against humanity. Taylor, *Anatomy*, 75–76.

5. Article 10 of the Nuremberg Charter.

6. See Bloxham, *Genocide on Trial*, 49–52.

7. Benjamin B. Ferencz, "Nuremberg Trials and Tribulations," 25. Available at http://www.benferencz.org/stories/4.html. For a biography of Ferencz, see Tom Hofmann, *Benjamin Ferencz, Nuremberg Prosecutor and Peace Advocate* (McFarland, 2013).

8. Ferencz, "Nuremberg," 31.

9. Ibid.

10. There had been significant opposition even to the first Nuremberg trial on the theory that such prosecutions were based on laws not in existence at the time of the events prosecuted. One of the more prominent opponents of the trials was Senator Robert Taft of Ohio, a serious contender for the Republican presidential nomination in 1952. Taylor, *Anatomy*, 634.

11. SS Commander Emil Haussman.

12. SS Brigadier General Otto Rasch.

13. For an excellent analysis of the *Einsatzgruppen* trial, which includes a chapter detailing the defendants, see Hillary Earl, *The Nuremberg SS-Einsatzgruppen Trial, 1945–1958: Atrocity, Law and History* (Cambridge U. Press, 2009), 96–134.

14. Ferencz, "Nuremberg," 32.

15. Earl, *Nuremberg SS-Einsatzgruppen*, 223–52.

16. Ferencz made this statement in a conversation with one of the authors.

17. National Archives Microfilm Publications, *Record of the United States Nuremberg War Crimes Trials, United States v. Ohlendorf et al.*, Case IX, September 15, 1947–April 10, 1948.

18. Earl, *Nuremberg SS-Einsatzgruppen*, 46–95.

19. *Trial of War Criminals before the Nuernberg Military Tribunals, Volume IV* (U.S. Government Printing Office, 1949), 30. Available at http://www.loc.gov/rr/frd/Military_Law/pdf/NT_war-criminals_Vol-IV.pdf. (hereafter "Tribunals"), Ferencz's opening statement is available on YouTube, as well as on his website: www.benferencz.org.

20. Ferencz, "Nuremberg," 34.

21. Ferencz's words at the beginning of his opening: "We shall show that these deeds of men in uniform were the methodical execution of long-range plans to destroy ethnic, national, political, and religious groups which stood condemned in the Nazi mind. Genocide, the extermination of whole categories of human beings, was a foremost instrument of the Nazi doctrine." Tribunals, 30. For a description of the Ferenecz/Lemkin meeting, see Ferencz, "Nuremberg," 34.

22. Ferencz, "Nuremberg," 33.

23. Tribunals, 154, 160, 161, 166.

24. Ferencz, "Nuremberg," 33.

25. Musmanno's book, *The Eichmann Kommandos*, mentions that at one point in the trial, during the description of the shooting process, the court reporter, even though undoubtedly desensitized to the violence she was noting, was nevertheless unable to retain her last meal, requiring a brief adjournment. Musmanno, *Eichmann Kommandos*, 159.

26. Ferencz, "Nuremberg," 34.

27. Musmanno, *Eichmann Kommandos*, 214.

28. Defendant Schubert's affidavit of February 24, 1947. Tribunals, 207–8.

29. As an SS officer who placed obedience to orders above all else, Ohlendorf nevertheless claimed he refused to utilize gas vans as a method of murder.

30. Ferencz, "Nuremberg," 34.

31. Ibid.

32. Tribunals, 198–99.

33. Under the Federal Rules of Evidence, proof that a document is found in a place consistent with its content is a factor in authenticating the document. FRE 901(b)(8). Although not in existence at the time of the *Einsatzgruppen* trial, the rule embodies a common law principle then in effect.

34. Ferencz explains that if a defendant claimed a document was inaccurate or mistranslated, he was shown the original and that ended any issues of authenticity. Ferencz, "Nuremberg," 32, 33.

35. Tribunals, 271.

36. Ferencz, "Nuremberg," 35.

37. Musmanno, *Eichmann Kommandos,* 253.

38. A somewhat similar analysis can be made of the cross-examination of Göring at the first Nuremberg trial. Much has been made of Justice Jackson's lack of success in cross-examining Göring because the court permitted him to answer questions in a manner that went beyond the question. Taylor, *Anatomy*, 335–48. This made the cross-examination difficult, and Jackson floundered as a result. The evidence against Göring, especially on the key charge of conspiring to wage aggressive war, however, was overwhelming. The latitude he was given while being cross-examined was an unmistakable sign that he was to be found guilty and that the court wanted to ensure that he was seen to have gotten a fair shake. Concerns over Jackson's ego were not a part of the court's calculus.

39. Tribunals, 457–62.

40. Tribunals, 394.

41. Ibid., 355.

42. Ibid., 357. The defendant Gustav Noßke was even more personal, pointing out that his wife was shot and killed by a well-aimed shot from an anti-tank gun as she emerged from a shelter. Tribunals, 404.

43. As they underlay the Nuremberg prosecutions, the laws of war were predicated on the Hague Conventions of 1899 and 1907, a period well before the organized use of airpower in war.

44. Tribunals, 381.

45. Ibid., 466.

46. Ibid., 467.

47. See Earl, *Nuremberg SS-Einsatzgruppen*, 104–13, for an extended discussion on the ages and backgrounds of the defendants.

48. "*Die Juden sind unser Unglück.*"

49. Tribunals, 356.

50. Stalin said: "One cannot regard the war against Fascist Germany as an ordinary war. It is not only a war between two armies. It is at the same time the great war of the entire Soviet people against the Fascist German troops." Ibid., 465–66. The pertinent extract of Stalin's speech appears at ibid., 365.

51. Ibid., 382.

52. Tribunals, 249.

53. See Article 8 of the Nuremberg Charter.

54. Tribunals, 310.

55. Ibid., 472–73.

56. Musmanno, *Eichmann Kommandos*, 234–35.

57. Ibid.

58. Tribunals, 251–52.

59. It is a safe assumption that if someone as prominent as Thomas was not a defendant it was because he was not alive.

60. Musmanno, *Eichmann Kommandos*, 227.

61. Earl refers to a similar type of evidence with respect to the defendant Braune, who repeatedly disobeyed Reich orders without suffering consequences when later transferred to Nazi-occupied Norway. Earl, *Nuremberg SS-Einsatzgruppen*, 244–45.

62. Tribunals, 585.

63. Ibid., 587. Taylor, in his closing argument, urged that Graf be convicted on all charges, mentioning him twice, but not referring in any detail to the evidence relating to Graf. Ibid., 373.

64. Ibid., 249.

65. For example, see Dr. Hans Gawlik on behalf of defendant Naumann. Ibid., 329, 336–37.

66. Ibid., 376.

67. Ibid., 377.

68. Ibid., 378.69. Ibid., 249.

70. Ibid., 482, 485.

71. Ibid., 484, 485.

72. Ferencz, "Nuremberg," 32.

73. Ferencz notes that Musmanno seemed fascinated by Ohlendorf. Ferencz, "Nuremberg," 34. From the questioning, it appears almost that Musmanno viewed Ohlendorf as an intellectual foil. Musmanno appeared convinced, whether by what he perceived as the logic of his position or because he was the judge, that he would prevail in any entanglement with Ohlendorf. See also Earl, *Nuremberg SS-Einsatzgruppen*, 262.

74. Musmanno, *Eichmann*, 256–58.

75. Ruehl was found guilty only of membership in a criminal organization. Evidence of his further involvement was presented largely by affidavit and the court declined to find additional criminality on the basis of this hearsay evidence. Further, Ruehl's low rank made it unlikely that he was instrumental in any executions and his limited service with the *Einsatzgruppe*—three months—also was considered pertinent. However, his background made his membership in a criminal organization more inculpatory than Graf's refusal to participate.

76. Earl, *Nuremberg SS-Einsatzgruppen*, 263.

77. Ibid., 267.

78. Earl discusses this in far more detail in pages 265–95 of her book.

79. Ferencz, "Nuremberg," 36.

80. See generally, Earl, *Nuremberg SS-Einsatzgruppen*, 265–95.

81. Ferencz viewed Ohlendorf as an intelligent and relatively honest man and so visited him just prior to the execution and asked, in German, whether there was some message Ferencz could convey to Ohlendrof's family or something similar. Ohlendorf's response was that "the Jews in America would suffer for what

[Ferenecz] had done." Ferenecz got up, said "Goodbye, Mr. Ohlendorf" in English, and left. Ferencz, "Nuremberg," 36.

82. Tribunals, 544–45.

83. Ibid., 560–61.

84. Bloxham, *Genocide on Trial*, 162–63.

NOTES TO CHAPTER 7

1. Walter Laqueur, ed., *The Holocaust Encyclopedia* (Yale U. Press, 2001), 379.

2. Lisa Yavnai, "Vengeance or Justice? Trials of Kapos," panel presentation at the International Institute for Holocaust Research at Yad Vashem, Holocaust and Justice: Post-War Trials and the Holocaust: Representation, Awareness and Historiography (2006). A slightly different version of this presentation is offered as a podcast by Yad Vashem, http://www1.yadvashem.org/yv/en/holocaust/insights/podcast/nuremberg_yavnai.asp (accessed March 5, 2014).

3. Primo Levi, *The Drowned and the Saved* (Vintage, 1989), 42. Levi's "gray zone" is discussed and analyzed in Adam Brown, *Judging "Privileged" Jews: Holocaust Ethics, Representation, and the "Grey Zone"* (Berghahn, 2013).

4. Lawrence L. Langer, *Versions of Survival: The Holocaust and the Human Spirit* (SUNY Press, 1982), 72.

5. See Orna Ben-Naftali and Yogev Tuval, "Punishing International Crimes Committed by the Persecuted: The Kapo Trials in Israel," *J. Int'l. Crim. Justice* (2006), 128–78; Idith Zertal, *Israel's Holocaust and the Politics of Nationhood*, trans. Chaya Galai (Cambridge U. Press, 2005), 58–79; Hanna Yablonka, "The Development of Holocaust Consciousness in Israel: The Nuremberg, Kapos, Kastner and Eichmann Trials," *Israel Studies* 8, no. 3 (2003), 1–24; Tom Segev, *The Seventh Million: Israel and the Holocaust*, trans. Haim Watzman (Owl Books, 2000), 225–75. Sir Hersch Lauterpacht, the brilliant Anglo-Jewish international law scholar, summarized some of the early trials in his capacity as editor of the British International Law Reports. See 18 I.L.R. 538–43 (1951).

6. Ben-Naftali and Tuval, "Punishing International Crimes," 129 n.4.

7. Ibid., 151.

8. Christopher Browning, *Remembering Survival: Inside a Nazi Slave-Labor Camp* (Norton, 2010), 119 (italics in original).

9. Levi, *The Drowned and the Saved*, 43.

10. We do have a study of trials of Jewish collaborators in Poland; see Gabriel N. Finder and Alexander V. Prusin, "Jewish Collaborators on Trial in Poland 1944–1946," *Polin* 20 (2008), 122–48.

11. Hans Safrian, *Eichmann's Men*, trans. Ute Stargardt (Cambridge U. Press, 2010), 218.

12. Ibid.

13. Finder and Prusin, "Jewish Collaborators," 135.

14. No high member of the *Judenrat* was ever charged in these courts.

15. Isaiah Trunk, *Judenrat: The Jewish Councils in Eastern Europe Under Nazi Occupation* (Macmillan, 1972), 51–52.

16. Beth B. Cohen, *Case Closed: Holocaust Survivors in Postwar America* (Rutgers U. Press, 2007), 1.

17. "The Nation," *L.A. Times*, February 5, 1988.

18. Jonathan M. Wenig, "Enforcing the Lessons of History: Israel Judges the Holocaust," in *The Law of War Crimes*, ed. Timothy L. H. McCormack and Gerry J. Simpson (Springer 1997), 105 (citing *Honigman v. Att'y Gen. of the State of Israel*, 7 *Piskei Din* [Law Reports] 296, 303 [1951]).

19. Segev, *Seventh Million*, 259–60.

20. Ibid., 260 (citing "Proposed Law Against Jewish War Criminals," *Haaretz*, November 10, 1949, p. 4.

21. Zertal, *Israel's Holocaust*, 62.

22. Ben-Naftali and Tuval, "Punishing International Crimes," 143 (quoting and translating 20 PR mtg no. 131 [first vote], March 27, 1950, 1147).

23. Ibid.

24. Zertal, *Israel's Holocaust*, 60 (quoting Rosen, Session 131) (italics added).

25. Ibid., 65–66.

26. Agassi, *Jewish Women Prisoners*, 13.

27. Ibid., 13–14.

28. Ayala H. Emmett, *Our Sisters' Promised Land: Women, Politics, and Israeli-Palestinian Coexistence* (U. Michigan Press, 2003), 147.

29. Ben-Naftali and Tuval, "Punishing International Crimes," 148–49 (quoting Member of the Knesset [MK] Eliezer Perminger).

30. Hannah Arendt, *Eichmann in Jerusalem* (Penguin, 1994 [1963]), 10.

31. "Statement of MK Eliezer Preminger," meeting of the Constitution, Law and Justice Committee of the Knesset, March 29, 1950 (quoted in Ben-Naftali and Tuval, "Punishing International Crimes," 148 n.75).

32. Ben-Naftali and Tuval, "Punishing International Crimes," 148.

33. Nazis and Nazi Collaborators (Punishment) Law 5710/1950 (hereafter "NNCL"), promulgated in *Sefer Hakhukim* 57, August 9, 1950, p. 281. The Knesset passed the bill eight days earlier, on August 1, 1950.

34. Lawrence Douglas, *The Memory of Judgment: Making Law and History in the Trials of the Holocaust* (Yale U. Press, 2001), 117.

35. NNCL, arts. 1(a) and (b).

36. "'[T]he period of the Nazi regime' means the period which began on . . . [January 30, 1933] and ended on . . . [May 8, 1945]." NNCL, art. 16.

37. NNCL, art. 1. Acts (6) and (7) are criminal acts not specifically set out in the Genocide Convention. Act (6) criminalizes cultural genocide, excluded from the Genocide Convention. Act (7) is found in the Genocide Convention as a separate crime of incitement to genocide.

38. Ben-Naftali and Tuval, "Punishing International Crimes," 160 n.125.

39. Zertal, *Israel's Holocaust*, 67 (italics in original).

40. No Jew was charged under the NNCL with crimes against the Jewish people, the primary charge against Adolf Eichmann in his trial in 1961.

41. Zertal, *Israel's Holocaust*, 87.

42. Segev, *Seventh Million*, 262.

43. Ibid.

44. Segev, *Seventh Million*, 262 n.21 (see 557, quoting *SCO* 1959, XIII:1056).

45. Ibid., 67 (citing Verdicts E (District Courts), S. C. [Severe Criminal (Files)], 2/52, 142–52).

46. Ibid.

47. Ben-Naftali and Tuval, "Punishing International Crimes," 170 (quoting *Tarnek*).

48. Zertal, *Israel's Holocaust*, 69.

49. *Attorney General of the State of Israel v. Yehezkel Ben Alish Enigster*, 18 ILR 540 (Tel Aviv Dist. Ct. 1952).

50. Ben-Naftali and Tuval, "Punishing International Crimes," 167 (quoting *Enigster*, 18 ILR 540).

51. Zertal, *Israel's Holocaust*, 72 (quoting Verdicts E (District Courts), S. C., 9/51, pp. 152–80).

52. Ibid., 71 (quoting Verdicts E (District Courts), S.C., 9/51, 152–80).

53. Ben-Naftali and Tuval, "Punishing International Crimes," 168 (quoting *Enigster*, 18 ILR 540).

54. Ibid.

55. Zertal, *Israel's Holocaust*, 75 (citing Verdicts E (District Courts), S. C., 9/51, pp. 178–80).

56. Ibid.

57. Ibid., 76 (citing *Hirsch Berenblatt v. Attorney General*, Criminal Appeal No. 77/64, Legal Verdicts, vol. 18, 1964, 70–108).

58. Ibid., 77. For a recent article unearthing the Berenblatt trial, see Avihu Ronen, Hadas Agmon, and Asaf Danziger, "Collaborator or Would-Be-Rescuer? The Barenblat Trial and the Image of a Judenrat Member in 1960s Israel," *Yad Vashem Studies* 3, no. 1 (2011). The authors note that *Time* magazine reported on the trial. See "Jew against Jew," *Time*, March 23, 1963.

59. Ben-Naftali and Tuval, "Punishing International Crimes," 170 (quoting Berenblatt appeal at 101).

60. Ibid., 174 (quoting Berenblatt appeal at 95–96).

61. Primo Levi, *Survival in Auschwitz: The Nazi Assault on Humanity*, trans. Stuart Woolf (Simon & Schuster, 1996), 96.

62. Ibid., 42.

63. Ibid., 40.

64. Ibid., 91.

65. Levi, *The Drowned and the Saved*, 44 (italics added).

66. Letter to Trudy, Somewhere in Germany, April 29, 1945, Benjamin Ferencz Papers, United States Holocaust Memorial Museum, RG 12.001.03*01. We are grateful to Lisa Yavnai for finding this letter and quoting it in her paper, which she kindly shared with one of the authors. See Yavnai, "Vengeance or Justice?", 5–6.

67. Giorgio Agamben, *Remnants of Auschwitz: The Witness and the Archive*, trans. Daniel Heller-Roazen (Zone Books, 2002), 170.

68. Loudon S. Wainwright, "You Are the Man Who Killed My Brother," *Life*, December 11, 1950. Google Books makes available a scanned copy of the article. The American Jewish Congress also published a summary of the proceedings. See "In the matter of Benjamin Krieger v. Majer Mittelman, Decision," *Congress Weekly* 17, no. 33 (December 11, 1950). For a recent article focusing on a different aspect of the case, *see* "*Krieger v. Mittelman* and Jewish Perceptions of the Refugee in the Early Cold War," *Judaism* (Spring–Summer 2006), 40–54.

69. Wainright, "You Are the Man," 132.

70. Ibid., 135.

71. Ibid.

72. Ibid.

73. Ibid.

74. Ibid.

75. Ibid.

76. Ibid., 144.

77. Ibid.

78. Ibid.

79. Ibid.

80. Ibid.

81. Rebecca Kaplan Boroson, *Jewish Week* (N.Y.), May 22, 1987, p. 17 (quoting Elie Wiesel). Claude Lanzmann's 2013 documentary *The Last of the Unjust* offers a similar theme through the words of its subject, Benjamin Murmelstein. Murmelstein was a prominent Viennese rabbi appointed by the Germans to serve as the last Jewish elder of the Theresienstadt ghetto in occupied Czechoslovakia, where some thirty-three thousand Jews died, many from disease and malnutrition. He became a hated figure after the war among many in the survivor community for his perceived collaboration; German-born Israeli philosopher Gershom Scholem even calling for his hanging. The film ends with Murmelstein telling Lanzmann in German: "An elder of the Jews can be condemned . . . but he cannot be judged" [*Ein Judenaeltester kann verurteilt werden . . . aber nicht beurteilt*].

NOTES TO CHAPTER 8

1. A death camp can be described as a concentration camp where new arrivals were murdered en masse on arrival, as opposed to a concentration camp where large numbers of inmates were murdered mainly through overwork, starvation, and disease. Even in death camps, in a small number of cases, prisoners assigned to assist in the killing process averted death, but only temporarily. A small number of these individuals managed to survive and often became victim witnesses in later trials.

2. See Alan Heath, *The Nazi Death Camp at Chełmno and Ner*, http://youtube.com/watch?v=eOrSv8iN5GU; Dick de Mildt, *In the Name of the People: Perpetrators*

of Genocide in the Reflection of their Post-War Prosecution in West Germany (Martinus Nijhoff, 1996).

3. De Mildt, *Perpetrators*, 243.

4. See H.E.A.R.T.'s Chelmno death camp staff list, available at http://www.holocaustresearchproject.org/othercamps/chelmnoSSstafflist.html. The sentences were, understandably, condemned as astoundingly light.

5. At one of the Sobibor trials, testimony by a survivor as to the relative decency of an SS guard resulted in the guard's acquittal. De Mildt, *Perpetrators*, 293.

6. A detailed description of these trials can be found in De Mildt, *Perpetrators*, 248–301.

7. *The Statutory Criminal Law of Germany*, section 211 (Library of Congress, 1947); *The American Series of Foreign Penal Codes: Germany*, section 211 (Fred Rothman, 1961).

8. De Mildt, *Perpetrators*, 254–55.

9. The DVD is divided into several parts and a time-bar indicates at what point in the part the testimony is presented. References to the DVD will follow that format. For example, testimony noted twenty minutes into part 2 will be cited as FATr 2-20:00. The DVD can be overrelied on. While it obviously provides an accurate source for the testimony given at the trial, it does so without regard to the weight of the evidence. For example, the producers of the DVD included the chilling testimony of Josef Kral who described how the defendant Boger forced him to eat five bowls of over-salted herring and then had him hung backwards and whipped, thus creating a three-pronged torture: unimaginable thirst, excruciating shoulder pain, and flogging. FATr 2-6:12. The court, however, rejected Kral's testimony. Devin Pendas, *The Frankfurt Auschwitz Trial, 1963–1965: Genocide, History and the Limits of Law* (Cambridge U. Press, 2006) 239.

10. See, e.g., FATr 1-15:41 (Kugler on Mengele); FATr 1-18:57 (Bauer on Eichmann).

11. International Auschwitz Committee, http://www.auschwitz.info/e/history.html.

12. FATr 1-18:57, 1-19:52. The lead prosecutor in the Frankfurt Auschwitz trial, Joachim Kugler, discusses an earlier effort to capture Josef Mengele, the infamous doctor at Auschwitz who supervised brutal medical experiments on inmates. Kugler says the German government followed conventional extradition methods on learning that Mengele was in Zurich. Mengele then fled to Brazil. Kugler is convinced that the Swiss feared that Mengele would claim political refugee status, the Swiss courts would uphold his claim, and Switzerland would then face adverse international repercussions. Mengele was never caught and is believed to have drowned while swimming off the coast of Brazil. FATr 1-15:40.

13. Rebecca Whitman, *Beyond Justice: The Auschwitz Trial* (Harvard U. Press, 2005), 63.

14. Pendas, *Frankfurt*, 91–93.

15. Ibid., 80–87.

16. The film taken of Höss's testimony at the first Nuremberg trial has become infamous. It is replayed at the Frankfurt Auschwitz trial at FATr 2-30:12. The numbers Höss gives are too high.

17. FATr 2-42:00.

18. FATr 1-48:30.

19. Of course, the plunder did not begin at the death camps. From what he had seen in his home town in Czechoslovakia prior to his arrest and deportation, Vrba recalled that after Jews were arrested and removed from the town, their homes and land were sold at a pittance, usually to those who did not say "good morning" at the beginning of the day but rather to those who said "Heil Hitler." FATr 2-44:00.

20. FATr 1-54:15.

21. FATr 1-50:00.

22. FATr 3-18:09.

23. FATr 2-20:08.

24. Langbein observed that it was traumatic for many witnesses who came to Frankfurt to testify. Germans had been their torturers and the German language had been the medium implementing their misery. Langbein noted that many Frankfurt residents, mainly women, made conscientious efforts to greet such witnesses at the airport, assisted them in getting around, and in general, made their reintroduction to Germany as smooth as possible. He noted that lifelong friendships evolved out of some of these interactions. FATr 2-19:45.

25. FATr 2-4:25.

26. Pendas, *Frankfurt*, 157. Lingens's testimony also showed, to some extent, the limitations of conventional courtroom identification. Lingens testified that defendants Capesius and a Dr. Klein looked alike. Using normal parameters for facial similarity, this was not true and would tend to cause her credibility to be questioned. Lingens explained, however, that what each of these two men shared was a facial expression that was half-intelligent combined with a cold brutality hidden behind the mask of a petit bourgeois. These distinct features counted for far more in the identification process than the relationship between nose, eyes, mouth, etc. Ibid., 167.

27. Under the German system, civil plaintiffs—*Nebenkläger*—may participate in a criminal trial with their own counsel. In this case, there were two groups of such "side-plaintiffs": a group from East Germany and a group of individuals from many countries, represented, respectively, by two prominent attorneys, Friedrich Kaul and Henry Ormond. Kaul, a citizen of the German Democratic Republic, tended to see events through the eyes of an East German and he clashed frequently with Dr. Hans Laternser, the principal defense attorney. Laternser practiced law during the Third Reich although he periodically had difficulties with the authorities. Laternser represented many Germans charged with Nazi crimes. Ibid., 90–97.

28. Wittmann, *Beyond Justice*, 233–35. 29. FATr 2-52:30.

30. Pendas, *Frankfurt*, 236.

31. FATr 2-54:10. "*Ich habe mit Vergasung nichts zu tun.*"

32. FATr 2-54:42. "*Ich bekommt keine Kenntnis davon und so habe ich nichts davon [Vergasung] gewusst . . . .*" At a different time, in response to questions from the court, Mulka had been a little less assertive in his claim of ignorance, stating that while he had heard about the gas chambers, he had never seen them. Pendas, *Frankfurt*, 134–35.

33. FATr 2-55:27.

34. Pendas, *Frankfurt*, 236.

35. Ibid., 237.

36. Wittmann, *Beyond Justice*, 135.

37. Pendas, *Frankfurt*, 44.

38. Ibid., 117–18.

39. Ibid., 164.

40. Ibid., 163–64.

41. Ibid., 240–41.

42. FATr 2-10:10.

43. Pendas, *Frankfurt*, 42–45.

44. FATr 3-7:36.

45. FATr 3-9:15 to 14:19 (includes posttrial interview).

46. Pendas, *Frankfurt*, 290.

47. FATr 3-34:40.

48. FATr 3-42:53.49. FATr 2-26:10.

50. Gonczi explained that the floor was moistened so the bodies could be dragged across it since neither he nor others assigned to this task had the strength to carry the bodies. FATr 2-26:10.

51. FATr 2-49:30.

52. FATr 3-41:35.

53. Pendas, *Frankfurt*, 221.

54. Wittmann, *Beyond Justice*, 140.

55. FATr 2-16:04.

56. Pendas *Frankfurt*, 163.

57. Wittmann, *Beyond Justice*, 61. The death sentence imposed by the Soviets was for membership in a criminal organization, the SS. The sentence was later commuted to twenty-five years in prison, and Kaduk was released after serving eleven years. Much later, Kaduk confirmed the accuracy of the testimony at the trial. See http://www.holocaustrreseachproject.org/othercamps/kaduk.html.

58. Once credibility assessments were made, it was concluded that the evidence against these three defendants was insufficient to warrant a finding of guilty.

59. Pendas, *Frankfurt*, 233.

60. Wittmann, *Beyond Justice*, 211.

61. Section 49 of the German Penal Code.

62. Wittmann, *Beyond Justice*, 246–74.

63. The prosecutors, it appears, were of a younger generation and teenagers towards the end of the Third Reich.

64. Pendas, *Frankfurt*, 101.

NOTES TO CHAPTER 9

1. "Office of Special Investigations," United States Holocaust Memorial Museum.

2. The United States Department of Justice, Human Rights and Special Prosecutions Section, http://www.justice.gov/criminal/hrsp.

3. Criminal charges against Holocaust perpetrators are doubly barred. First, there was no United States statute at the time which applied; second, any statute which might be passed could not be applied retroactively since the U.S. Constitution specifically bars Congress from enacting laws that apply to conduct occurring prior to the laws' passage (*ex post facto* legislation). Article I, Section 9(3).

4. *Schneiderman v. United States*, 320 U.S. 118, 158 (1946).

5. Section 1451 of Title 8, United States Code.

6. Section 2 of the Displaced Persons Act, 62 Stat. 1009. See *Fedorenko v. United States*, 449 U.S. 490 (1981) for the application of this statute to Fedorenko, discussed later in the text.

7. A much larger number of Treblinka survivors testified at the Treblinka trial held in Düsseldorf in 1965. De Mildt, *Perpetrators*, 258.

8. For a detailed description of Treblinka and its history, see Witold Christowski, *Extermination Camp Treblinka* (Valentine Mitchell, 2004).

9. Approximately 310,000 Jews were sent from Warsaw to Treblinka.

10. "*Lazarett*," term used for military or concentration camp infirmary. Eric Joseph Epstein and Phillip Rosen, *Dictionary of the Holocaust: Biography, Geography and Terminology* (Greenwood Press, 1972), 172.

11. Christowski, *Extermination*, 85–97, provides details on the escape, the number actually breaking out (about two hundred) and the number ultimately successful in the escape (about eighty-five).

12. See Susan J. Linz, *The Impact of WWII on the Soviet Union* (Rowman & Littlefield, 1985), 130. For a comprehensive work on German treatment of Soviet POWs, see Christian Streit, *Keine Kameraden: Die Wehrmacht und die sowjetschen Kriegsgefangenen 1941–1945* (J. H. W. Dietz Nacht, 1991).

13. Transcript of the Fedorenko trial, No. 77-2668-Civ-NCR (S.D. Fla. 1978): 1254–1309 (hereafter "T").

14. *United States v. Fedorenko*, 455 F. Supp. 893, 895 (S.D. Fla. 1978).

15. T 1370–76.

16. Section 1451 of Title 8, United States Code.

17. T 133–61.

18. T 151–61.

19. Ibid.

20. T 177.

21. T 253–58.

22. T 412–33.

23. T 480-81.

24. T 617–77.

25. T 666–67. It is interesting to see corroboration of this witness in the literature on the Holocaust. See De Mildt, *Perpetrators*, 206, where he explains that the SS guard who saved a Jew, Boraks, received a lighter sentence as a result.

26. T 892.

27. T 708–69.

28. T 1091.

29. Rule 403 of the Federal Rules of Evidence permits the exclusion of evidence if its cumulative nature substantially outweighs its probative value.

30. T 961–97.

31. T 1043–86. An illustration of the individualized brutality that accompanied the mechanized killing: an SS guard killed one of Epstein's brothers by smashing his skull when the brother wandered out of line. Ibid.

32. T 1178–99.

33. At this point Judge Roettger indicated it might be years before he decided the case, since there was an issue as to whether former Ukrainian guards then living in the Soviet Union, which was not cooperating with the government to make them available, had evidence favorable to Fedorenko. This issue permeated the trial but, in the end, did not cause a delay. T 1085–86.

34. Vol. 14, 104–228.

35. All of these character witnesses had been deposed in Connecticut where they lived, saving Fedorenko the expense of bringing them to Florida. Their depositions were read into evidence.

36. Vol. 14, 60–77.

37. T 1298–1324.

38. T 1324–43.

39. T 1530–34.

40. T 1440–71, 1489–1534.

41. T 1535–51.

42. T 1598–1679.

43. *United States v. Fedorenko*, 455 F. Supp. 893 (S.D. Fla. 1978).

44. Judge Roettger also noted the comparably irrelevant fact in his decision that the trial was the focus of demonstrations and protests on behalf of refugee groups against Fedorenko. The Jewish Defense League organized some of the protests and a commonly heard protester chant was: "Who do we want? Fedorenko. How do we want him? Dead."

45. *United States v. Fedorenko*, 455 F. Supp. 893, p. 913.

46. Of course, none of those persons made false statements on their entry applications, placing them in an entirely different category than Fedorenko, who lied on his application.

47. *United States v. Fedorenko*, 597 F.2d 946 (5th Cir. 1979).

48. *Fedorenko v. United* States, 449 U.S. 490 (1981). Normally the solicitor general appears for the United States before the Supreme Court. Historically, the attorney general choses one case to appear in place of the solicitor. Attorney General Benjamin Civiletti chose Fedorenko as the case.

49. Five justices affirmed on the basis of the Displaced Persons Act in an opinion written by Justice Thurgood Marshall; Chief Justice Warren Burger concurred. Two justices voted to have the lower court reconsider the case on the materiality question, and Justice John Paul Stevens dissented outright.

50. The majority concluded that the lower courts may have used the wrong materiality test since the one used came from a case involving the denial of citizenship based on a false statement, rather than denial of entry to the United States.

51. *Federenko v. United States*, 449 U.S. 490 at 514, n .34.

52. Barringer, "Soviet Reports," *N.Y. Times*, July 28, 1987, p. A3, col. 1.

53. The translation of Korotkey can be found in Volume 14. The page numbers, unfortunately, are undecipherable.

NOTES TO CHAPTER 10

1. *Regina v. Sawoniuk*, (2000) 2 Crim. App. 220.

2. Israel Silber, "The End of the Jews in Domachevo," JewishGen, http://www.jewishgen.org/yizkor/Brest/bre087.html (accessed October 20, 2010).

3. Ray Brandon and Wendy Lower, eds., *The Shoah in Ukraine: History, Testimony, Memory* (Indiana U. Press, 2008), 258–59.

4. Report of the War Crimes Inquiry, Cm 744 (1989), quoted in 188 Parl. Deb., H.C. (6th ser.) (1991) 23–92.

5. The suspects, of course, could be extradited. However, the suspected Holocaust perpetrators were all collaborators hailing from territories then controlled either by the Soviet Union or one of its Eastern European client states. Even if an extradition request was received from these states, the British were reluctant to send suspects behind the Iron Curtain.

6. War Crimes Act, 1991, c. 13 (U.K.).

7. Anthony Glees, quoted in Tim Luckhurst, "Why Won't Britain Jail This War Criminal," *Guardian*, September 2, 2001.

8. David Cesarani, "Getting Away with Murder," *Guardian*, April 25, 2001.

9. *Sawoniuk*, 2 Crim. App. at 222.

10. Ibid.

11. Ben Zion Blustein, quoted in Jill Serjeant, "Elderly Jew Tells War Crimes Trial of Ghetto Horror," *Reuters*, February 23, 1999.

12. David Hirsh, *Law against Genocide: Cosmopolitan Trials* (GlassHouse Press, 2003), 108.

13. Ibid., quoting Blustein's trial testimony.

14. *Regina v. Sawoniuk*, Crim. L.R. 2000, June, 506–9.

15. *Sawoniuk*, 2 Crim. App. at 224.

16. Hirsh, *Law against Genocide*, 96–97.

17. Sir John Nutting, QC, quoted in Andrew Buncombe, "Enthusiastic Nazi Who Took Pleasure in Slaughter of Jews," *Independent* (London), February 10, 1999.

18. William Clegg, QC, quoted in Matt Wells, "Nazis' Offer to Accused 'Could Not be Refused," *Scotsman* (Edinburgh), February 13, 1999.

19. Roger Hermiston, "The Master Defender," *Suffolk Magazine* (May 2009), 24.

20. Ibid.

21. Hirsh, *Law against Genocide*, 110.

22. David Hirsh, "The Trial of Andrei Sawoniuk: Holocaust Testimony under Cross-Examination," *Social & Legal Studies* 10, no. 4 (2001), 530 (paragraphs rearranged).

23. Ibid., 119.

24. Direct examination of Alexander Baglay, quoted in Hirsh, *Law against Genocide,* 120.

25. Sawoniuk, quoted in Alun Thorne, "The Monster Who Almost Got Away," *Birmingham Post*, November 8, 2005.

26. Cross-examination of Sawoniuk, quoted in "Sawoniuk Threatens to Storm Out," *BBC*, March 23, 1999. Available at http://news.bbc.co.uk/2/hi/uk_news/302032.stm (accessed March 5, 2014).

27. Hirsh, *Law against Genocide,* 124.

28. Mr. Justice Potts, quoted in *Sawoniuk*, 2 Crim. App. at 223.

29. Interview with Jon Silverman, September 15, 2010.

30. Ian Bryan and Peter Rowe, "The Role of Evidence in War Crimes Trials: The Common Land and the Yugoslav Tribunal," *Yearbook Int'l Hum. L.* 2 (1999), 317.

31. Mr. Justice Potts, quoted in Francis Gibb, "Hope of Release For War Criminal," *Times* (London), June 25, 1999.

32. Lord Bingham, quoted in ibid.

33. *R. v. Sawoniuk*, (2000) 2 Crim. App. 220.

34. Sawoniuk v. United Kingdom, 63716/00 ECHR (29 May 2001) 1–10.

35. Ibid.

36. Ibid.

37. Cesarani, "Getting Away with Murder."

38. Email from David Cesarani to Michael Bazyler, October 8, 2010.

39. Report of the War Crimes Inquiry, Cm 744 (1989), quoted in Parl. Deb., H.L. (5th ser.) (1989).

40. See Jon Swain, "Britain Is Now a Haven for Rwandan Genocide Suspects," *Times* (London), April 12, 2009.

NOTES TO THE CONCLUSION

1. David Fraser, "Shadows of Law, Shadows of the Shoah: Towards a Legal History of Nazi Killing Machine," *Oxford J. Legal Studies* 32, no.2 (2012), 1–19. A number of excellent studies of postwar trials have come from a new generation of scholars, who only recently have begun examining the subject. See, for example, Kevin Jon Heller, *The Nuremberg Military Tribunals and the Origins of International Criminal Law* (Oxford U. Press, 2011); Hilary Earl, *The Nuremberg SS-Einsatzgruppen Trial, 1945–1958: Atrocity, Law, and History* (Cambridge U. Press, 2010); David O. Pendas, *The Frankfurt Auschwitz Trial, 1963–1965: Genocide, History and the Limits of the Law* (Cambridge U. Press, 2010); Rebecca Wittmann, *Beyond Justice: The Auschwitz Trial* (Harvard U. Press, 2010); Tomaz

Jardim, *The Mauthausen Trial: American Military Justice in Germany* (Harvard U. Press, 2012); Valerie Geneviève Hébert, *Hitler's Generals on Trial: The Last War Crimes Tribunal at Nuremberg* (U. Press of Kansas, 2010); David Fraser, *Daviborsch's Cart: Narrating the Holocaust in Australian War Crimes Trials* (U. Nebraska Press, 2010).

2. Sir David Maxwell-Fyfe (British prosecutor): "Will you please answer my question? Do you still say neither Hitler nor you knew of the policy to exterminate the Jews?" Göring: "As far as Hitler was concerned, I have said I do not think so. As far as I am concerned, I have said that I did not know, even approximately, to what extent these things were taking place." (IMT Proceeding, Day 87, March 21, 1946.)

3. Historian Deborah Lipstadt is usually credited with coining the term "soft-core" Holocaust denial. See "Demjanjuk and Justice," *Jerusalem Post*, March 18, 2012. See also Manfred Gertsenfeld, "Holocaust Trivialization," *Jewish Center for Public Affairs*, April 9, 2008, available at jcpa.org/article/holocaust-trvialization/, and Clemens Heni, "Secondary Anti-Semitism," *Jewish Center for Public Affairs*, November 2, 2008, available at jcpa.org/article/secondary-anti-semitism-from-hard-core-to-soft-core-denial-of-the-shoah.

4. We say this even though we may disagree with the decision to indict or seek the level of punishment made by some of these prosecutors. See, for example, our discussions of the trials of the *kapos* in the chapters on the Dachau, Ravensbrück, and Jewish *kapo* trials.

5. See Jon Petrie, "The Secular Word HOLOCAUST: Scholarly Myths, History, and 20th Century Meanings," *Journal of Genocide Research* 2, no. 1 (2000), 31–63, available at http://www.armenews.com/IMG/pdf/petrie_the_secular_word_holocaust.pdf; Deborah Lipstadt, *The Eichmann Trial* (Schocken Books, 2011), 188.

6. Roman Lehberger, "Demanjuk War Crimes Conviction Caps 30-Year Battle," *CNN*, May 12, 2011, available at http://www.cnn.com/2011/WORLD/europe/05/12/germany.demjanjuk.trial. For discussion of the Demjanjuk trial in Germany, see Heinrich Wefing, *Der Fall Demjanjuk: Der letzte große NS-Prozess* (Beck, 2011), and Lawrence Douglas, "Ivan the Recumbent, or Demjanjuk in Munich: Enduring the 'Last Great Nazi Trial,'" *Harper's*, (March 2009), 45. Demjanjuk's legal saga, which ended with his death in Germany in 2012, spans thirty-five years and three continents. Ivan (he changed it in America to "John") Demjanjuk arrived in the United States as a refugee in 1952, eventually settling in Cleveland, Ohio. In 1977, he was accused by the U.S. Department of Justice's Office of Special Investigations of being a Nazi SS camp guard during the war (like his fellow Ukrainian Fedor Fedorenko discussed in chapter 9). In 1986, following denaturalization proceedings, the United States extradited Demjanjuk to face trial in Israel for being the notorious Ukrainian guard "Ivan the Terrible" of the Treblinka death camp. An Israeli court convicted and sentenced him to death; however, in 1993 the Supreme Court of Israel overturned his conviction when new evidence indicating that he was likely not the notorious Ivan of Treblinka came to light. The United States restored his citizenship and allowed him to return. Then in 2002, the Department of Justice once again initiated a new round of legal proceedings that stripped Demjanjuk's citizenship a second time. In 2009,

the United States extradited him to Germany to stand trial for being a guard at the Sobibor death camp.

7. Lehberger, "Demjanjuk War Crimes."

8. "It's incredibly frustrating [that Kunz died before trial]. . . . But it was important that he was indicted. At least a small measure of justice was achieved." Alexandra Topping, "Suspected Nazi Death Camp Guard Samuel Kunz Dies before Trial," *Guardian*, November 22, 2010 (quoting Efraim Zuroff).

9. In 2009, accused ninety-five-year-old former Nazi Erich Steidtmann died while awaiting trial. The former police captain was suspected of taking part in mass shootings of Jews in the Warsaw ghetto uprising in 1943, sixty-six years earlier. Interestingly, Steidtmann's past was not revealed until 2007, when he inadvertently exposed himself through a libel case brought against a woman who claimed to have been his lover during the war in her autobiography. Before the full facts could be established, however, he died peacefully at home.

10. Serge Klarsfeld, France's best-known Nazi hunter, stated that these efforts to prosecute under the Demjanjuk precedent left him with a "bitter aftertaste." He explained: "A principle is being applied that is more Soviet than democratic: you were at a camp thus you are guilty. It's up to you to prove your innocence." Klarsfeld blamed Germany for not acting earlier, and now trying to make up for its dereliction. "At the time when it was possible to try the criminals, when there was evidence, Germany failed to do its work." "Nazi Hunters Launch German Poster Campaign," *Agence France-Presse*, July 23, 2013.

11. Ibid.

12. Topping, "Suspected Nazi" (quoting Efraim Zuroff).

13. " Demjanjuk and Justice," *Jerusalem Post*, March 18, 2012.

14. Donald M. McKale, *Nazis after Hitler: How Perpetrators of the Holocaust Cheated Justice and Truth* (Rowman & Littlefield, 2012). For another recent study with a similar theme, see Gerard Steinacher, *Nazis on the Run: How Hitler's Henchmen Fled Justice* (Oxford U. Press, 2012).

15. McKale, *Nazis after Hitler*, 345.

16. Alan S. Rosenbaum, *Prosecuting Nazi War Criminals* (Westview Press, 1993), 8 (quoting Efraim Zuroff).

17. For discussion of the Herero genocide, see Jeremy Sarkin-Hughes, *Germany's Genocide of the Herero: Kaiser Wilhelm II, His General, His Settlers, His Soldiers* (James Currey Books, 2011).

18. Vahakn N. Dadrian and Taner Akçam, *Judgment At Istanbul: The Armenian Genocide Trials* (Berghahn, 2011).

19. Mark A. Drumbl, *Atrocity, Punishment and International Law* (Cambridge U. Press, 2007), 48. And as we show in this volume, such judicialization did not begin in Nuremberg in 1945, but almost two years earlier in Kharkov in December 1943.

20. "Darfur Genocide Charges for Sudanese President Omar al-Bashir," *Guardian*, July 14, 2008.

21. John Hagan, *Justice in the Balkans: Prosecuting War Crimes in The Hague Tribunal* (U. Chicago Press, 2003), 18 (quoting Louise Arbour).

BIBLIOGRAPHY

Arendt, Hannah. *Eichmann in Jerusalem: A Report on the Banality of Evil.* Penguin, 1994 [1963].

Bankier, David, and Dan Michman, *Holocaust and Justice: Representation and Historiography of the Holocaust in Post-War Trials.* Berghahn Books, 2010.

Bass, Gary. *Stay the Hand of Vengeance: The Politics of War Crimes Tribunals.* University of Princeton Press, 2000.

Bauer, Yehuda. *The Dangers of Anti-Semitism in Central and Eastern Europe in the Wake of 1989-1990.* Hebrew University of Jerusalem, 1991.

Bazyler, Michael J. *Holocaust Justice: The Battle for Restitution in America's Courts.* New York University Press, 2004.

Ben-Naftali, Orna, and Yogev Tuval, "Punishing International Crimes Committed by the Persecuted: The Kapo Trials in Israel." *Journal of International Criminal Justice* 4, no. 1 (2006): 128.

Bieńczyk-Missala, Agnieszka, and Sławomir Dębski, eds. *Rafał Lemkin: A Hero of Humankind.* Polish Institute of National Affairs, 2010.

Bloxham, Donald. *Genocide on Trial: War Crimes Trials and the Formation of Holocaust History and Memory.* Oxford University Press, 2001.

Brandon, Ray, and Wendy Lower. *The Shoah in Ukraine: History, Testimony, Memorialization.* Indiana University Press, 2008.

Brode, Patrick. *Casual Slaughters and Accidental Judgments: Canadian War Crimes Prosecutions 1944–1948.* University of Toronto Press, 1997.

Brown, Adam. *Judging "Privileged" Jews: Holocaust Ethics, Representation, and the "Grey Zone."* Berghahn, 2013.

Brown, Daniel Patrick. *The Camp Women: The Female Auxiliaries Who Assisted the SS in Running the Nazi Concentration Camp System.* Schiffer, 2002.

Browning, Christopher. *Remembering Survival: Inside a Nazi Slave-Labor Camp.* Norton, 2010.

Buber Agassi, Judith. *The Jewish Women Prisoners of Ravensbrück: Who Were They?* Oneworld, 2007.

Buchmann, Erika. *Die Frauen von Ravensbrück.* Kongress-Verlag, 1959.

Buechner, Howard A. *Dachau, the Hour of the Avenger: An Eyewitness Account.* Thunderbird Press, 1986.

Cesarani, David. *Justice Delayed: How Britain Became a Refuge for Nazi War Criminals.* Heinemann, 1992.

Chambrun, Rene de. *Pierre Laval: Traitor or Patriot?* Scribner, 1948.

Chrostowski, Witold. *Extermination Camp Treblinka*. Valentine Mitchell, 2004.

Crowe, David M. *Oskar Schindler: The Untold Account of His Life, Wartime Activities, and the True Story behind The List*. Westview Press, 2004.

Cyprian, Tadeusz, and Jerzy Sawicki. *Siedem procesów przed Najwyższym Trybunałem Narodowym*, [*Seven Trials before the Supreme National Tribunal*]. Institut Zachodni, 1962.

Dawson, Greg. *Judgment before Nuremberg: The Holocaust in the Ukraine and the First Nazi War Crimes Trial*. Pegasus Books, 2012.

Desbois, Patrick. *The Holocaust by Bullets: A Priest's Journey to Uncover the Truth behind the Murder of 1.5 Million Jews*. Palgrave Macmillan, 2009.

Douglas, Lawrence. *The Memory of Judgment: Making Law and History in the Trials of the Holocaust*. Yale University Press, 2001.

Drumbl, Mark A. *Atrocity, Punishment and International Law*. Cambridge University Press, 2007.

Earl, Hillary. *The Nuremberg SS-Einsatzgruppen Trial, 1945–1958: Atrocity, Law and History*. Cambridge University Press, 2009.

Epstein, Catherine. *Model Nazi: Arthur Greiser and the Occupation of Western Poland*. Oxford University Press, 2012.

Evans, Richard I. *Lying About Hitler: History, Holocaust, and the David Irving Trial*. Basic Books, 2001.

Finder, Gabriel N., and Alexander V. Prusin. "Jewish Collaborators on Trial in Poland 1944–1946." *Polin* 20 (2008): 122.

Finkielkraut, Alain. *Remembering in Vain: The Klaus Barbie Trial and Crimes against Humanity*. Columbia University Press, 1992.

Forczyk, Robert, and Peter Dennis. *Warsaw 1944: Poland's Bid for Freedom*. Osprey Publishing, 2009.

Fraser, David. *Daviborsch's Cart: Narrating the Holocaust in Australian War Crimes Trials*. University of Nebraska Press, 2010.

———. "Shadows of Law, Shadows of the Shoah: Towards a Legal History of the Nazi Killing Machine." *Oxford Journal of Legal Studies* 31, no. 4 (2011): 401.

Gaulle-Anthonioz, Geneviéve. *The Dawn of Hope: A Memoir of Ravensbrück*. Arcade, 1999.

Gershenson, Olga. *The Phantom Holocaust: Soviet Cinema and Jewish Catastrophe*. Rutgers University Press, 2013.

Ginsburgs, George. "Laws of War and War Crimes on the Russian Front during World War II: The Soviet View." *Soviet Studies* 11, no. 3 (1960): 253.

Glantz, David M. *Kharkov 1942: Anatomy of a Military Disaster Through Soviet Eyes*. Ian Allan, 2010.

Gluck, Gemma LaGuardia. *My Story*, ed. S. L. Shneiderman. D. McKay, 1961.

Greene, Joshua. *Justice at Dachau: The Trials of An American Prosecutor*. Broadway Books, 2003.

Gross, Jan. *Neighbors: The Destruction of the Jewish Community in Jedwabne, Poland*. Princeton University Press, 2001.

Guttenplan, D. D. *The Holocaust on Trial.* Norton, 2001.

Halow, Joseph. *Innocent at Dachau.* Legion for the Survival of Freedom, 1993.

Hausner, Gideon. *Justice in Jerusalem.* Nelson, 1967.

Heberer, Patricia, and Jürgen Matthäus. *Atrocities on Trial: Historical Perspectives on the Politics of Prosecuting War Crimes.* University of Nebraska Press, 2008.

Hébert, Valerie Geneviève. *Hitler's Generals on Trial: The Last War Crimes Tribunal at Nuremberg.* University Press of Kansas, 2010.

Heckler, Cheryl. *An Accidental Journalist: The Adventures of Edmund Stevens, 1934–1945.* University of Missouri Press, 2007.

Heller, Kevin Jon. *The Nuremberg Military Tribunal and the Origins of International Criminal Law.* Oxford University Press, 2011.

Hilton, Fern Overley. *The Dachau Defendants: Life Stories from Testimony and Documents of the War Crimes Prosecutions.* McFarland, 2004.

Hirsh, David. *Law against Genocide: Cosmopolitan Trials.* GlassHouse Press, 2003.

———. "The Trial of Andrei Sawoniuk: Holocaust Testimony under Cross-Examination." *Social & Legal Studies* 10, no. 4 (2001): 530.

Hofmann, Tom. *Benjamin Ferencz, Nuremberg Prosecutor and Peace Advocate.* McFarland, 2013.

Höss, Rudolf. *Commandant of Auschwitz: The Autobiography of Rudolf Höss,* trans. Costantine FitzGibbon. Phoenix Press, 2000.

Israel, David L. *The Day the Thunderbird Cried.* Emek Press, 2005.

Jackson, Julian. *France: The Dark Years 1940–1944.* Oxford University Press, 2001.

Jacobeit, Sigrid, and Elisabeth Brümann-Güdter. *Ravensbrückerinnen.* Hentrich, 1995.

Jardim, Tomaz. *The Mauthausen Trial: American Military Justice in Germany.* Harvard University Press, 2012.

Kessler, Matthias. "*Ich muß doch meinen Vater lieben, oder?*" ["But I must love my father, mustn't I?"]. Eichborn, 2002.

Kladov, Ignatz Fedorovich. *The People's Verdict: A Full Report of the Proceedings at the Krasnodar and Kharkov German Atrocity Trials.* Hutchinson, 1944.

Kochavi, Arieh J. "The Moscow Declaration, the Kharkov Trial, and the Question of a Policy on Major War Criminals in the Second World War." *History* 76, no. 248 (1991): 404.

———. *Prelude to Nuremberg: Allied War Crimes Policy and the Question of Punishment.* University of North Carolina Press, 1998.

Kretzer, Anette. *NS-Täterschaft und Geschlect: Der erste Britische Ravensbrück-Prozess 1946–1947 in Hamburg.* Metropol, 2009.

Laval, Pierre. *Diary of Pierre Laval.* Scribner, 1948.

Le Procès Laval. Albin Michel Edition, 1948.

Lemkin, Raphael. *Axis Rule in Occupied Europe: Laws of Occupation, Analysis of Government Proposasl for Redress.* Carnegie Endowment for International Peace, 1944.

Levi, Primo. *The Drowned and the Saved.* Vintage, 1989.

———. *Survival in Auschwitz: The Nazi Assault on Humanity,* trans. S. J. Woolf. Simon & Schuster, 1996.

Linden, John. *Surrender of the Dachau Concentration Camp, 29 Apr 45: The True Account*. Sycamore Press, 1997.

Linz, Susan J. *The Impact of WWII on the Soviet Union*. Rowman & Littlefield, 1985.

Lipstadt, Deborah. *The Eichmann Trial*. Nextbooks/Schocken Books, 2011.

Lukas, Richard C. *Forgotten Holocaust: The Poles under German Occupation 1939–1944*, rev. ed. Hippocrene Books, 2001.

Marrus, Michael, and Robert Paxton. *Vichy France and the Jews*. Schocken Books, 1983.

McKale, Donald M. *Nazis after Hitler: How Perpetrators of the Holocaust Cheated Justice and Truth*. Rowman & Littlefield, 2012.

Mettraux, Guénaël. *Perspectives on the Nuremberg Trial*. Oxford University Press, 2008.

Mildt, Dick de. *In the Name of the People. Perpetrators of Genocide in the Reflection of Their Post-War Prosecution in West Germany: The Euthanasia and Aktion Reinhard Trial Cases*. Martinus Nijhoff, 1996.

Morrison, Jack G. *Ravensbrück: Everyday Life in a Women's Concentration Camp, 1939–1945*. Wiener, 2000.

Musmanno, Michael A. *The Eichmann Kommandos*. Macrae Smith, 1961.

Pendas, Devin. *The Frankfurt Auschwitz Trial, 1963–1965*. Cambridge University Press, 2006.

Pemper, Mieczyslaw, Viktoria Hertling, and David Dollenmayer. *The Road to Rescue: The Untold Story of Schindler's List*. Other Press, 2005.

Proces Ludobójcy Amona Götha przed Najwyższym Trybunałem Narodowym [Trial of the Mass Murderer Amon Göth before the Supreme National Tribunal]. Centralna Zydowska Komisja Historyczna w Polsce, 1947.

Prusin, Alexander. "Fascist Criminals to the Gallows! The Holocaust and War Crimes Trials December 1945–February 1946," *Holocaust and Genocide Studies* 17, no. 1 (Spring 2003): 3.

———. "Poland's Nuremberg: The Seven Court Cases of the Supreme National Tribunal, 1946–1948." *Holocaust and Genocide Studies* 24, no. 1 (Spring 2010): 5.

Riding, Alan. *And the Show Went On: Cultural Life in Nazi-Occupied Paris*. Knopf, 2010.

Ronen, Avihu, Hadas Agmon, and Asaf Danziger, "Collaborator or Would-Be-Rescuer? The Barenblat Trial and the Image of a Judenrat Member in 1960s Israel." *Yad Vashem Studies* 39, no. 1 (2011): 117.

Rosenbaum, Alan S. *Prosecuting Nazi War Criminals*. Westview Press, 1993.

Rubenstein, Joshua, and Ilya Altman. *The Unknown Black Book: The Holocaust in the German-Occupied Soviet Territories*. Indiana University Press, 2008.

Russell, Edward F. L. *The Scourge of the Swastika: A Short History of Nazi War Crimes*. Cassell, 1954.

Sachslehner, Johannes. *Der Tod ist ein Meister aus Wien: Leben und Taten des Amon Leopold Göth*. Styria, 2008.

Safrian, Hans. *Eichmann's Men, trans. Ute Stargardt*. Cambridge University Press, 2010.

Saidel, Rochelle G. *The Jewish Women of Ravensbrück Concentration Camp*. University of Wisconsin Press, 2004.

Salas, Denis, and Jean-Paul Jean, eds. *Barbie, Touvier, Papon: Des procès pour la mémoire.* Autrement, 2002.

Segev, Tom. *The Seventh Million: The Israelis and the Holocaust*, trans. Haim Watzman. Henry Holtz, 2000.

Smelser, Ronald M. *Lessons and Legacies V: The Holocaust and Justice.* Northwestern University Press, 2002.

Smith, Bradley F. *The Road to Nuremberg.* Basic Books, 1981.

Steinacher, Gerard. *Nazis on the Run: How Hitler's Henchmen Fled Justice.* Oxford University Press, 2012.

Stevens, Edmund. *Russia Is No Riddle.* Greenberg, 1945.

Strebel, Bernhard. *Das KZ Ravensbrück: Geschichte eines Langerkomplexes.* F. Schöningh, 2003.

Streit, Christian. *Keine Kameraden: Die Wehrmacht und die sowjetschen Kriegsgefangenen 1941–1945.* J. H. W. Dietz Nacht, 1991.

Stuart, Heikelina Verrijn, and Marlene Simons, *The Prosecutor and the Judge: Benjamin Ferencz and Antonio Cassese.* Amsterdam University Press, 2009.

Taake, Claudia. *Angeklagt: SS-Frauen von Gericht.* BIS, Bibliotheks-und Informations system der Universitat Oldenburg, 1988.

Taylor, Telford. *The Anatomy of the Nuremberg Trials: A Personal Memoir.* Little, Brown and Company, 1993.

Terwilliger, Julia A., and Carole Elizabeth Adams. *Women of Ravensbrück: Portraits of Courage.* University of Central Florida Press, 1997.

Tillion, Germaine. *Ravensbrück: An Eyewitness Account of a Women's Concentration Camp,* trans. Gerald Satterwaite. Anchor Press/Doubleday, 1975.

Trials of War Criminals before the Nuernberg Military Tribunals under Control Council Law No. 10, vol. IV, Nuernberg October 1946–April 1949. U.S. Government Printing Office, 1949.

Trunk, Isaiah. *Judenrat: The Jewish Councils in Eastern Europe under Nazi Occupation.* Macmillan, 1972.

Warner, Geoffrey. *Pierre Laval and the Eclipse of France.* Eyre & Spottiswoode, 1968.

Wefing, Heinrich. *Der Fall Demjanjuk: Der letzte große NS-Prozess.* Beck, 2011.

Whitlock, Flint. *The Rock of Anzio: From Sicily to Dachau, A History of the 45th Infantry Division.* Westview Press, 1998.

Wittmann, Rebecca. *Beyond Justice.* Harvard University Press, 2005.

Yablonka, Hanna. "The Development of Holocaust Consciousness in Israel: The Nuremberg, Kapos, Kastner and Eichmann Trials." *Israel Studies* 8, no. 3 (2003): 1.

Zertal, Idith. *Israel's Holocaust and the Politics of Nationhood,* trans. Chaya Galai. Cambridge University Press, 2005.

INDEX

Page numbers in italics refer to illustrations

ABOUT THE AUTHORS

MICHAEL J. BAZYLER is Professor of Law and The "1939" Society Law Scholar in Holocaust and Human Rights Studies at the Dale E. Fowler School of Law, Chapman University in Orange, California. He is the holder of previous fellowships at the United States Holocaust Memorial Museum in Washington, D.C., the Yad Vashem Holocaust Center in Israel, and Harvard Law School.

FRANK TUERKHEIMER is both a trial lawyer and law professor. He is Professor of Law Emeritus at the University of Wisconsin and has been a federal prosecutor in New York and Madison, Wisconsin, and an Associate Special Watergate Prosecutor. He has taught litigation-focused courses at the University of Wisconsin since 1970 and since 1997 has taught "Trials of the Holocaust" in the United States and Germany.